Criminal Behaviour:
A Psychological Analysis

Criminal Behaviour:
A Psychological Analysis

M. Philip Feldman

*Psychology Department,
University of Birmingham*

JOHN WILEY & SONS
Chichester · New York · Brisbane · Toronto

Library of Congress Cataloging in Publication Data:

Feldman, Maurice Philip.
    Criminal behaviour: a psychological analysis.

    1. Crime and criminals. 2. Criminal
psychology. I. Title.
HV6025.F39   364.3   76–13229

ISBN 0 471 99401 4

Photosetting by Thomson Press (India) Limited, New Delhi
and printed in Great Britain at The Pitman Press Ltd., Bath

To

Stella

Preface

In recent years the extensive and well-supported findings of the experimental psychology of learning have been applied to a number of areas of applied psychology, most notably to those behaviours labelled abnormal. This book is in part an attempt to extend such an analysis to criminal behaviour by reviewing, inevitably incompletely, the recent upsurge of research activity in both laboratory and field settings relevant to the explanation and control of criminal behaviour. Two other approaches to crime are represented: one largely psychological in origin, namely, the importance of predisposing individual differences, and one largely sociological, the contribution of social labelling as a reaction to criminal behaviour. A non-specialist like myself can hope to give only the flavour of this important development in sociology. Scientific findings both influence social action and are made within a social context. An attempt has been made to discuss some of the ethical and other implications of psychological research into the causes and control of criminal behaviour.

I have not included any discussion of the psychodynamic explanation of criminal behaviour; it should be presented by someone who is both more sympathetic to it and much more knowledgeable than myself. However, I have included a substantial section on the psychotherapeutic treatment of offenders because this can be considered as it stands, in terms of the criteria of efficacy and efficiency in achieving given objectives, without a need to go into underlying principles.

If this book has a central theme, it is the behaviourist message as applied to criminal behaviour: the division of the world into the criminal and the law-abiding is largely a comforting delusion; predisposing individual differences are relevant, but environmental control of the acquisition, performance and maintenance of criminal behaviour is powerful and pervasive. However, just as environmental variables are crucial to learning to offend, so they may be equally important sources for social policies intended to ensure an effective defence against crime.

Chapter 1 lays the foundation for the rest of the book. It sets out definitions and descriptive features of criminal behaviour concerning both offences and offenders which require explanation and, it is widely agreed, some form of social defence. Emphasis is placed on offences against property and persons; the more controversial 'victimless offences' are outside the scope of this book.

In addition, we discuss problems concerning strategies of research into explanation and control. The evidence that those officially labelled criminal are an incomplete and biased sample of the total population of offenders makes it particularly appropriate to draw on experimental laboratory and field studies.

The next chapter concerns learning not to offend. It includes the two major approaches, the cognitive–developmental view, which emphasizes maturation rather than experience, and the learning view, which asserts and details the importance of social experiences and social training, particularly in childhood. The theory of childhood deprivation is also reviewed.

Chapter 3 applies learning principles to the acquisition, performance and maintenance of the two broad classes of criminal behaviour, crimes against property and against the person, the experimental analogues of which are aggression and transgression. The 'internal' cognitive control of behaviour, as well as 'external' control, is given some weight throughout the chapters on learning. The possibility for limiting crimes by help given to the victim or to the police is considered in Chapter 4, which concerns pro-social behaviour. It consists of a learning analysis of helping behaviour and includes also a statement of equity theory, a recent social psychological development of criminological relevance.

The next three chapters all deal with some aspect of individual differences. Chapter 5 considers the genetic inheritance of criminal behaviour by means of data on sex differences, family, twin and adoption studies, chromosomal abnormalities and body-build, and also discusses analogies drawn from ethological studies. The next chapter overviews personality and crime in the context of the current controversy between the consistency and specificity approaches to individual differences in behaviour. A detailed account and critique is given of the Eysenckian approach to crime and an attempt is made to integrate the competing approaches.

Chapter 7 describes the legal approach to the 'mentally disordered' offender, sex offences and psychopathy, and critically assesses explanatory studies of psychopathic behaviour. This section of the chapter argues for the relative similarity of the explanations proposed for both psychopathic and criminal behaviour.

An attempt is made in Chapter 8 to set out briefly a number of sociological approaches to crime. It is argued that some of these are over-concerned with working-class crime to the exclusion of crime in general; others are readily reinterpretable in terms of well-established learning principles. Emphasis is placed on the considerable importance of labelling theory in complementing, rather than competing with, the learning and individual difference approaches to explanation.

Chapters 9 and 10 consider the nature and effectiveness of the methods which have been used to control criminal behaviour. Chapter 9 covers the current penal system and the negative consequences said to accompany imprisonment. Chapter 10 reviews the relatively more recent psychological approach to control, reviewing both psychotherapeutic and behavioural methods. Finally, Chapter 11 considers the social context of control. It contrasts the legal and determinist approaches to behaviour, reviews legal and civil rights objections to determinist-based methods of control and discusses the ethical dilemma of the behavioural scientist in the study and control of crime.

A very brief final chapter makes a summary statement of the major conclusions and attempts to integrate the learning, individual difference and labelling approaches to explanation and control.

I hope that this book will be useful to all those interested in crime, particularly undergraduate and postgraduate psychology students, researchers and practitioners in forensic studies, social scientists, social workers and psychiatrists with an interest in a key social issue, as well as members of the legal and law enforcement professions, particularly those who welcome a fresh attempt to contribute to a perennial problem.

I began this book in the warmth of Honolulu during a year's visiting appointment at the University of Hawaii, and completed it in the very different climate of Birmingham. I am grateful to the University of Birmingham for allowing me leave of absence, and to the University of Hawaii for welcoming me and being generous with my teaching duties. Many postgraduate students in both universities have contributed valuable comments and I must mention particularly John Allsopp, Liz Kuipers, David Crawford, Colin Reynolds and Julian Fuller. Peter Moodie of the Birmingham University Faculty of Law has been a most valuable guide to criminal law and to sociological approaches to crime. My colleagues in the Department of Psychology, Derek Blackman and Ray Cochrane, have been helpful and patient in discussions of learning and of deviancy. None of those named can be held in any way responsible for the inevitable errors of fact and of judgment which I have made. I am particularly grateful to several secretaries who have struggled with my equally difficult tapes and handwriting, particularly Chris Benkwitz, Chris Thomas, Barbara Hudson and Eileen Brookes.

Finally, my thanks to my literary agent, Frances Kelly, and my publishers, who have the necessary combination of perception, patience and firmness.

M. Philip Feldman
1976

Contents

4 Learning to Limit Criminal Acts: Pro-social Behaviour

5 Biological Factors

Chapter 1

Description : Offences and Offenders

Offences: Definitions and Figures

Definitions

Before defining terms, it should be noted that 'crime' and 'offence', 'criminal' and 'offender', tend to be used interchangeably and bear the same respective meanings. In the USA the terms 'delinquent' and 'deliquency' are also used. They are also used in Britain, particularly in the context of juvenile crime. They tend to be synonymous with 'offender' and 'criminality', respectively. In this book we shall frequently use the terms 'crime' and 'criminal behaviour'. The latters refers to all the behavioural events associated with the commission of a behaviour legally defined as a crime.

In Britain, while there is no statutory definition of the term 'crime', the following statement by the distinguished jurist Glanville Williams is likely to be widely acceptable: 'A crime is an act that is capable of being followed by criminal proceedings, having one of the types of outcome (punishment, etc.) known to follow these proceedings' (1955, p. 21).

In the USA the situation is even more difficult, because of the distinction between 'Federal rights' and 'States rights'. However, the Model Legal Code which is now in preparation seems unlikely to differ very greatly from the above in principle, although it is likely to spell out in more detail the defining attributes of the term 'crime', as well as stating the purposes of the criminal law.

The decision as to whether or not an observed behavioural event is to be regarded as *a* crime, and hence prosecuted or not, is largely a matter for the police, both in Britain and in the USA (with the exception, in Britain, of murder). Moreover, the police decide on the *particular* crime which the behaviour represents—and may thus 'downgrade' it or 'upgrade' it. The 'police' in this context means sometimes a constable (officer) on the beat, sometimes the station sergeant (desk sergeant). Thus the police have very considerable powers of discretion, with obvious consequences for the official statistics of crime, as we shall see.

If a charge is made, the person charged appears in court. In British law, in most cases (the exceptions include offences of strict liability, such as parking offences) certain conditions must be fulfilled. There must have occurred either an event or a state of affairs which is proscribed by criminal law and must have been caused by the defendants conduct, which must have taken place in specified circumstances. Traditionally, the above requirements have been labelled the *actus reus*. Thus far we are in the area of readily observable descriptive events. But we next move into the more hypothetical explanatory and contentious area of 'mental events'. The defendant's conduct must have been accompanied by a specified state of mind *(mens rea)*. Finally, these requirements must be proved by the prosecution beyond reasonable doubt. The difficulty is the requirement of *mens rea*. The *'actus'* does not become *'reus'* unless the *'mens'* is *'rea'* to a requisite degree. The 'states of mind' which would lead to criminal liability are those of 'intention' and 'recklessness', whereas those of 'negligence' and 'blameless inadvertence' would not. The above represents the situation in Britain. American law appears somewhat similar in respect of the 'mental element'. It should be noted that the *'mens'* is considered *'rea'* in the greater majority of prosecuted offences (this can be inferred because 'state of mind' reports are requested only in a minority of cases). Manifestly, terms like 'mind' and 'intention' play little part in contemporary psychology. We shall return to the problem in Chapter 6 when we discuss the mentally abnormal offender, a topic of great and increasing practical importance.

The Social Context

Two apparently disparate fields, abnormal behaviour and criminal behaviour, have several important features in common. In both, the numbers of individuals displaying deviant behaviours represented in official statistics vastly under-state the true numbers. In both, because of the convenience for research purposes of populations of persons housed in special institutions—prisons and mental hospitals—research has tended to be carried out on such populations. There is a further similarity also, namely, that in both fields it has been asserted, particularly by labelling theorists (see Chapter 8), that no act is intrinsically deviant; the extent to which the behaviour is abnormal depends upon the view of the behaviour held by socially sanctioned experts—judges, psychiatrists and other professionals. The corollary of this assertion is that what is deemed psychologically abnormal varies between cultures. In the field of crime, the labelling view has as its basic assumption that the behaviours legally proscribed as criminal similarly vary from culture, the label 'crime' being applied by the powerful to control the less powerful in order to further their own economic and political ends. In Chapter 8 we shall examine the labelling theory explanation of crime in the context of an overview of sociological approaches. For the present we shall concentrate on the assertion of cultural relativism (and the related assertion, that of temporal relativism). In fact, according to Lemert (1972), practically all societies disapprove of certain behaviours, prominent among which are murder, rape and theft. A similar conclusion followed from a review of criminal law by Hoebel (1954). Welford (1975) divides criminal acts into those about which there is cross-cultural and temporal consistency and those which excite both dissension and attempts at removal from the list of proscribed behaviours (termed decriminalization). It is the former group which is, according to Welford, 'true criminal law' and the desirable focus of study by criminology. It consists of 'violations of property and persons by others'. This book will similarly be concerned with such offences, in which one person, or persons, damages another person or persons. The offender and the victim are *different* individuals. We must first, however, consider the latter of Welford's two groups.

Victimless Offences

In addition to protecting property, persons and the general well-being of society as a whole (the 'victim' is often remote and even potential rather than actual, as in the case of many motoring and tax offences), the criminal law has also been used to direct the behaviour of private individuals in those situations usually termed 'moral'—which have to do with drink, drugs, sex and gambling. To a large extent the 'offender' in such situations is also the 'victim', although it may be argued that society as a whole might suffer from drug abuse (because of a possible reduction of fitness for work) and the immediate family of a gambler might suffer from his activities—at least if he continually lost.

There are two distinct points of view in this area. The first considers, in the words of Lord Justice Devlin: 'Society cannot ignore the morality of the individual any more than it can its loyality; it flourishes on both and without either it dies' (Devlin, 1959). The alternative view was put vigorously by the Wolfenden Committee Report (1957), which led to the reform of the British law on homosexual behaviour: 'It is not, in our view, the function of the law to intererfere in the private lives of citizens, or to seek to enforce any particular pattern of behaviour, further than it is necessary to carry out the purposes we have outlined.' The report continued: 'Unless a deliberate attempt is to be made by society, acting through the agency of the law, to equate the sphere of crime with that of sin, there must remain a realm of private morality and immorality, which is in brief and crude terms, not the law's business.' Several of the Wolfenden Committee's recommendations were eventually accepted, and homosexual behaviour between consenting adults over the age of 21 is no longer a criminal offence in Britain. In fact, the number of persons convicted of such an offence was no more than 250 a year, but the number of *potential offenders* was in the hundreds of thousands and the number of offending acts in the millions. At a stroke, for a substantial minority of the population there was one less behaviour for which they were liable to criminal prosecution (the behaviour concerned was never a problem for the heterosexual majority—unlike, for example, theft, which is a relevant temptation for all).

A similar debate is going on throughout the Western world over the possession and use of cannabis, commonly known as pot. The number of arrests is obviously minute in comparison with the total number of offences (Schofield, 1971). Yet in Britain in 1969 there were 4683 convictions for cannabis use, and 4094 for possession. A quarter of all those convicted of cannabis offences in 1967 were sent to prison, the majority without *any* previous criminal record, despite the relative lack of damage caused by cannabis to those using it as compared to both alcohol and tobacco (Schofield, 1971). Schofield considers the cannabis law as an example of 'overcriminalization' (labelling as an offence a private behaviour, where there is no victim) and speculates about the real harm attentdant on a spell in prison—a topic we shall return to in Chapter 9. The consequences of overcriminalization for general attitudes to the criminal law, and hence for criminal behaviour, have been argued by Kadish (1967) to be as follows.

1. The rarity of enforcement leads to it being selective and arbitrary.

2. The difficulty of detection might lead to undesirable police practices.

3. It creates a deviant subculture.

4. The knowledge that the law is being violated creates a disrespect for the law.

5. No real harm has been shown to result from the deviant conduct.

6. It allows extortion and police corruption, for example the blackmailing of homosexuals.

7. It is at variance with the consensus of the community.

A great many fascinating research questions are raised by the above assertions, for example the effect on attitudes and behaviours concerning 'property' and 'person' offences of attempts at enforcement of the criminal law concerning 'morals' offences. In conclusion, our consideration of the description, explanation and control of criminal behaviour will be concerned with two major classes of offences, against property and against persons.

How Many Offences: The Official Statistics

Wolfgang (1971) has listed the following reasons in answer to the question: why official statistics?

1. To measure the total volume of crime and plan counteraction.

2. To map the statistical distribution of criminal acts in the population in general and by such indices as age, sex, class and race.

3. To classify criminal acts by their seriousness.

4. To establish basic data for theory-building and hypothesis-testing.

5. To measure the enforceability of legal norms.

6. To measure the efficiency of preventive measures and the effectiveness of treatment of different types of offenders.

7. To measure the impact on crime of other social variables, such as television.

8. To measure the changes in crime rates in ethnic subgroups. (It is assumed that falling rates would indicate the general social and economic progress of the subgroups.)

9. To measure the extent of impairment of the freedom of citizens. ('High' crime rates might simply indicate an oppressively large number of behaviours

defined as crimes as well as effective enforcement of the legal system.)

10. To compute the total current costs of law enforcement and plan future budgets.

11. To assess the efficacy of the penal system for different types of offenders.

12. To provide data for making rational disposal decisions.

The above is a list of objectives. All are admirable, provided that the statistics collected give an accurate picture of the true facts of criminal behaviour. Serious omissions or biases can lead to serious distortions, both of research efforts and findings and of social policy.

Detailed listings of official statistics can be found in the Uniform Crime Reports collected annually, in the USA by the FBI and in Britain by the Home Office, under the heading of 'Criminal Statistics'. Excellent appraisals of the meaning of official statistics are provided by Walker (1965; 1971). The Uniform Crime Reports divide offences into two parts. Part I offences are the more serious, for example larceny of $50 or over. The less serious, for example larceny of under $50, which are less likely to be reported to the police, are included in Part II. In Britain the broad distinction is between indictable and non-indicatable (also termed summary) offences. The former are the more serious, including the great bulk of offences against property and the person, the latter are deemed less serious and consist, in the main, of motoring offences.

In any one year in Britain persons found guilty before the courts are likely to be divisible somewhat as follows: traffic offences, about 60–65 per cent; property offences, about 12–15 per cent; offences against the person, about 2–4 per cent. The remainder include large numbers of cases of drunkenness, revenue evasion, railway offences and breaches of local bylaws and similar regulations (Walker, 1971). The relative proportions of property and persons offences appear rather similar in the USA. The official statistics of both countries suggest a rapid and continued rise in offences 'known to the police'. For example, in 1974 the British figure for indictable offences reached two million for the first time and represented an 84 per cent increase in 10 years. International comparisons are difficult for a variety of reasons, including lack of complete consensus as to what constitutes a crime, lack of uniformity in methods of reporting and recording and differential law enforcement across racial and class groups in different countries. However, some comparisons are possible, particularly between some of the advanced industrial countries (USA, England, Japan and Western Germany) in which definition and reporting are relatively similar. The combined populations of the three latter countries amount to about the same as that of the USA alone, yet reported gun murders in the USA were 48 times as frequent during the 1960's as in the other three countries combined. Moreover, whereas the gun murder rate (the number per 100,000 of the population) in the USA was increasing in the years surveyed, the rate in the other three countries showed little change. Large differences in the same direction were also found for forcible rape, robbery (theft including violence) and aggravated assault (which includes the more serious categories of personal injury). However, for burglary (breaking and entering a dwelling for purposes of theft) the rates in the four countries surveyed were much more similar, that in the USA being only slightly in excess of the other three. Providing that the reported/not reported ratio is roughly equal, it can be concluded that one of the major differences in the crime field between the USA and the other three industrial countries is the use of violence against the person.

There are considerable difficulties with the official statistics, both of offences and of offenders, as we note below under a number of heads, which largely concern some aspect of underestimation or of bias. There is a specific difficulty which relates to crimes resulting in death—an event which is likely to be reported and recorded in the great majority of instances. The murder rate, in contrast with most crimes, seems largely unchanged, despite the removal (in Britain) of the death penalty. Apart from the definitional problem—when is a violent death to be prosecuted as murder and when is it manslaughter—there is another problem. This is that improvements in medical knowledge enable victims to be kept alive who would previously have died. Even if they eventually die but have survived for a year and a day, the charge cannot be of murder. A behavioural act which even 20 years ago would have led to death and possibly an addition to the murder statistics today may result in the lesser charge of some form of assault.

How Many Offences: The 'Dark Figure'

The problem of the 'dark figure'—the unrecorded percentage of the events under study—is common to all social sciences (Walker, 1971). It is widely agreed by criminologists that the 'dark figure' for unrecorded crime is considerably larger than the figure for recorded crime, and larger for some crimes than for others.

Crimes go *unreported* for a variety of reasons. First, the persons involved, whether as participants or witnesses, may simply not realize that they, or others, are breaking the law; large numbers of schoolboy fights and motoring offences fall into this group. Second, those concerned may be aware that an offence has been committed, but are willing 'victims'. Examples are abortion and homosexual behaviours between consenting persons, in countries in which these behaviours are illegal. The latter case is particularly striking; only a very tiny proportion of private homosexual acts lead to prosecution (Feldman, 1973). Third, although the offender may be aware of his wrongdoing, the victim may not be. For example, goods pilfered by an employee may not be noticed by an employer unless strict stock-control procedures are used. Fourth, and possibly the largest category of all, there may be no immediate 'victim', for example litter dropped in a public place, or a tax return incorrectly and knowingly misrepresented. Finally, even when there is an aware and unwilling victim, he may not report the offence, because of fear of retaliation by the offender, doubts that the police action will be effective, or because doing so might reveal his own guilt (the money stolen from the victim might have been undisclosed for tax purposes). Employers are frequently unwilling to bring in the police, possibly because of the general atmosphere of suspicion created in the firm. Robin (1970) reported that only 17 per cent of department-store employee offences in an American survey which came to the attention of the employer were prosecuted. A similar study in England (Martin, 1962) found the figure varied according to the size of the firm, the police being more likely to be contacted in the case of larger organizations.

The great majority of shoplifting by customers is not noticed, even when store detectives are employed. An American field study, carried out by Saul Astor (*New York Times*, 1970), is particularly striking. Over 1500 shoppers in four stores in three large US cities were carefully observed. One out of every 15 proved to be a shoplifter; only one in 100 of those who stole was caught. It was not stated whether the shops noted the missing goods or reported them to the police. Dorothy McArdle, writing in the *Washington Post* (1972), noted the large-scale loss of 'momentoes' following official White House parties and cited as an example a party given for 4000 Daughters of the American Revolution, not an organization usually noted for its lawlessness, and their menfolk, in the spring of 1969. 'At the end of the party, every single ashtray had vanished.' Similar losses were noted of cutlery and soap (oddly enough, only from the ladies', not from the men's rooms). This is a nice example of the importance of the situation in determining criminal behaviour—the greater the 'reward' and the lower the 'cost' (presumably it would be too mutually embarrassing to search White House guests) the greater the level of offending.

Changes over time in the likelihood of an offence being reported may suggest trends in the true frequency of occurrence of the offence which are nevertheless misleading. For example, McClintock et al. (1963) have suggested that the then recent increase in reports of violence in London may indicate only an increasing belief that violent behaviour is reprehensible and should be reported. It could even have been that, far from increasing, violence was, in fact, decreasing. In any event, there is no simple correspondence between occurrence and reporting.

Unrecorded Offences

As might be expected, the more serious the loss suffered by the victim of a theft, the more likely is it to be reported to the police. Nevertheless, in a study of the police statistics of Washington for 1965, cited by Hood and Sparks 1970, p. 34), about one-third of the most serious crimes (e.g. aggravated assault and lareceny of $50) which victims claimed to have reported were unrecorded by the police. Thus, even if an offence is reported it is not necessarily recorded as such by the police, who have considerable discretion, even over offences actually observed by the police themselves. Almost every motorist has had the experience of being let off 'with a warning' of a quite unofficial kind (as compared with an official 'caution'). Offences reported and found to be carried out by children under the age of criminal liability used not to be required to be recorded. The police are overworked; it is reasonable to suppose that they will select for recording and action offences which are judged both more serious and more detectable. This is an example of the reward–cost view of human behaviour (human beings tend to act so as to maximize their rewards and minimize their costs), a view which is applicable equally to the behaviour of offenders and of the guardians of the law. A different source of recording variation occurs when a particular police district decides to pay more attention to a particular offence. For example, from time to time a chief of police has decided on a 'drive' against homosexual behaviour in public lavatories. The result is a sudden 'increase' in the rate of homosexual offences, from which it would be quite incorrect to conclude an increase in homosexual activity.

How Many Offences: Filling in the 'Dark Figure'

The unsatisfactory nature of the official statistics as reliable indicants of the total volume of crime, due both to under-reporting and under-recording, has prompted two other approaches, the reports of victims and the reports of offenders.

Reports by Victims. A good example is a survey of a probability sample of 10,000 households carried out in the USA in the summer of 1966 (Ennis, 1967). Adult members of the households were interviewed to identify all household members who had been a victim of a crime in the preceding 12 months. The victims themselves were then interviewed. Legal experts evaluated the actual criminal nature of the incidents reported. Instances of non-reporting were examined to establish the reasons for failure to report. Considerable under-reporting was revealed (by comparison with the Uniform Crime Reports rates), except for murder. For example, the police were not notified in a third of the cases of robbery and aggravated assault nor in two-fifths of burglaries. Possible defects of sampling and interview technique caution against placing too much weight on the exact figures for under-reporting, but it is clear that under-reporting is widespread, particularly for the less serious offences. The most important single reason for failure to report crimes against property was that the police were considered ineffective or unconcerned. Conversely, for crimes against persons, the most important reason was that the offence was a private matter. Other reasons surveyed were much less important for both groups of offences. These included not wanting to take up one's own time, confusion or ignorance of how to report and fear of reprisals.

Reports by Offenders. Hood and Sparks (1970) list three important purposes of self-report studies: first, an assessment of how many people have offended, and how frequently; second, they abolish the notion of a typology of 'offenders' and 'non-offenders', replacing it by a dimension; and third, they enable a comparison of 'official' offences, labelled as such by courts, with those who have not been so labelled. The majority of explanatory studies of offending have been carried out on convicted individuals, with all the attendant problems discussed so far. The controlled use of the self-report method will enable us to study offending, its antecedents and correlates, in the population at large. Before looking at data obtained by the self-report method, we need to consider a number of methodological problems connected with it.

When a respondent has admitted an offence, is his answer a true one (did he actually carry out the behaviour, or is he seeking to create an effect)? If he did indeed carry it out, was he aware that it was a crime, or did he assume, even actually believe, it to be legal? If he denies any offence, is he doing the opposite (concealing a behaviour he did carry out, and knew to be a crime)? Are certain social groups more likely to exaggerate systematically then others; are some groups more likely to deny? Do exaggeration or denial depend on the perceived connection with the legal authorities of the person administering the questionnaire or interview? To answer most of the above problems we require some method of comparing the 'true' occurrence of offences with those the individual concerned reports, or denies, having carried out, in short some method of validating the self-report technique. The only completely satisfactory method is to observe the population concerned in the situation of interest, as was done in the American shoplifting study referred to above. We should then not need to ask the population concerned about their behaviour—it has already been noted by an unbiased and accurate observer—in order, for example, to compare individuals characterized by different levels of offending behaviour. A less satisfactory method, used by Gold (1966), is to question other informants who had also been concerned in the behaviour reported, or denied, by the respondent. If both informants concur, and do so independently, the likelihood of the report being correct is increased, though it is still possible that both may be exaggerating or denying. However, if they differ in their accounts, there is no way of knowing which one is accurate. Gold found little systematic difference in disparity between respondents and informants according to either race or sex, a finding which supports the applicability of the self-report technique across sex and social class boundaries.

Does anonymity of report make a difference? Kulik *et al.* (1968) administered a check-list of offences to high-school boys who filled it in both anonymously and non-anonymously. The respondents admitted more offences in the former condition, but only for theft and not for such offences as the use of drugs and violence. Even in the case of the difference found for theft, while it was statistically significant, little substantive difference would result for research purposes from using the responses given in one condition rather than the other; for example, the rank orders of the boys (number of offences admitted) were almost the same for the two methods.

Is it possible to detect aware deception by objective means? Clark and Tifft (1966) used the so-called 'lie-detector' (actually a polygraph, which records simultaneously several physiological response measures, such as pulse-rate and sweating) to assess the validity of replies to a self-report measure. They found that simply taking the lie-detector test increased the amount of deviant behaviour admitted as compared with an earlier self-report administration without the lie-detector. Using the lie-detector as a goad to honesty of reporting seems likely to improve honesty of response, because of the respondent's brief in the infallibility of the lie-detector method. In fact, its actual validity is rather low (Martin, 1973). However, using the lie-detector for this purpose requires an initial check on the scientific sophistication of the subject taking the test. The incorporation of lie scales into personality questionnaires (e.g. the Eysenck Personality Inventory, see Chapter 7) may also be used to identify possible deniers (a high score would be grounds for doubt) but would not indicate the true state of affairs. Finally, lie-detector methods are quite inappropriate when a respondent intends complete accuracy of reportage, but is simply unable to recall accurately events which may have occurred much earlier. (Self-report studies sometimes extend several years retrospectively.)

Any study which seeks to generalize from a sample of respondents to the population at large must demonstrate representativeness of the sample. Self-report studies have usually been carried out without regard to the requirements of satisfactory sampling procedures. The majority of studies have been carried out on schoolchildren, in the school setting, thus omitting those who had either dropped out of school by the age studied or were playing truant at the time. Both omissions would probably result in an underestimation of the total level of offending. An excellent example of a carefully constructed sample, from which generalizations can safely be made, is provided by Schofield (1965a), who studied the sexual behaviour of British adolescents. In the criminal field, a British self-report study of offending by adolescent boys (Belson, 1975) appears much the best from the sampling point of view.

A final problem which should be mentioned concerns the comparability of studies. This requires not only similarity of the sample used, but similarity of questionnaire items. Unfortunately, there is little standardization of item content, even by the same researcher (Box, 1971). Standardization may be assisted by the identification of similar groups of offending behaviours using factor-analytic techniques (Gibson, 1967), which will assist in the reduction of the hundreds of possible items to a manageable number. Another method of achieving comparability is to establish the judged *seriousness* of a behaviour, using judges' ratings (Sellin and Wolfgang, 1964). Each offence then receives a score, for example, forcible entry = 2, murder = 26 (so that one murder would then equal 13 forcible entries!). One use of a seriousness scale would be in studying the antecedent circumstances for committing a particular offence by a particular group of persons. For whatever purpose they were used, judgements of seriousness should be obtained from a sample representative of the population under study. The Sellin–Wolfgang index was developed from samples of policemen, judges and undergraduates, all of them minorities in the population at large.

Having looked at some of the problems associated with the self-report technique, what of the findings? Several reviews are available (Hood and Sparks, 1970; West, 1967; Box, 1971) and only brief mention will be made of the results obtained. Our principal interest is in the potential value of the method for testing research hypotheses on offenders in the general population, rather than using officially designated samples of offenders. It is striking that self-report studies have largely ignored adults, with one exception, a study by Wallerstein and Wyle (1947) carried out over 25 years ago, yet law-breaking, rarely officially indexed, is widely found in older age groups, as we shall see when we consider 'white-collar' and other occupational crimes.

Wallerstein and Wyle (1947) sent a mail questionnaire of 49 offences to 1800 New York men and women. (It should be noted that the sample of respondents was almost certainly non-random, so that generalizability is doubtful. Nevertheless, the results are at the very least suggestive, and strongly support the desirability of adequately designed self-report studies of adults.)

The relative *lack* of difference between the sexes is of interest, the average overall being 18 for the males and 11 for the females. Wallerstein and Wyle recorded that even ministers of religion admitted an average of 8·2 of the 49 offences covered. (In passing, it is worth noting that females admitted more offences than male ministers of religion.) Two-thirds of the males and 29 per cent of the females admitted at least one felony (the more serious offences). This study indicates the wide occurrence of offending, and the artificial nature of the division into offenders and others.

According to Hood and Sparks (1970), 'Both in the United States and England it has been suggested that by the age of eighteen somewhere between 10 and 20 per cent of the male population will have been convicted by a court of a criminal offence. ... Self-report studies indicate that they represent on average only a quarter of those who have actually committed these offences' (p. 47). Examples of American self-report studies of adolescents, which support Hood and Sparks' conclusion, are those by Short and Nye (1958), Porterfield (1946) and Empey and Erickson (1966). Scandinavian studies (Elmhorn, 1965; Christie, 1965) reveal a similar picture. Belson's British study (1975) was based on extensive interviews of 1445 London boys, almost all aged 13–16, who were drawn on the random principle from a universe of newly 60,000 London homes. They were brought to the Survey Research Centre by car and were paid for their participation. Eighty-six per cent of the 'target sample' was intervied. The age and class attributes of the remainder suggested that their inclusion would have made little difference to the results. The questions were constructed and administered with great care but were restricted to the offence of theft—44 types in all—and varied from 'I have kept something I have found' (admitted by almost all respondents) to 'I have taken a car or van' (5 per cent). Seventy per cent had stolen from a shop, 35 per cent from family or relatives, 25 per cent from work, and from a car, lorry or van, and 17 per cent had 'got in a place and stolen'. Clearly, the majority of the boys had carried out at least one offence which, had it been detected, reported and prosecuted, could have led to an appearance in the official statistics. Hood and Sparks' conclusion (see above) is well justified.

The Dark Figure: Differential Reporting?

Both victim reports and self-reports support the view that the official statistics sharply under-represent the true figures for most offences, homicide being an exception. Is the rate of reporting likely to differ according to the broad class of 'victim'—private individual or organization? According to Box (1971), what he terms the more 'respectable' crimes of embezzlement, fraud, forgery, tax evasion, corporation crime and shoplifting, typically carried out against organizations, are less likely to be reported than are those of larceny, robbery, assault, breaking and entering and car theft. Because of the opportunity provided by the work situation, the former group are 'middle-class' offences. The latter group, according to official statistics of convicted offenders, are largely working-class offences. They are also more likely to be reported. Hence, different rates of reporting of 'middle' and 'lower-class' crimes may supply a major source of the apparent association between crime and lower social status which we shall discuss shortly.

Very few studies have compared the occurrence of a crime against an organization with crimes against individuals for the extent of reporting to the police, as did the American victim survey of households discussed earlier, and none which employed acceptable sampling procedures. However, the available evidence suggests that for shoplifting, the only offence subjected to detailed investigation thus far, organization victims of this type of theft are less likely to report to the police than are private persons who have suffered thefts (Martin, 1962). In order to be reported a crime has to be known to a potential complainant. Private persons are likely to be aware that possessions are missing and thieves entering a house are likely to leave signs of entry. In contrast, many business organizations lack accurate control of inventories and many of those carrying out offences against organizations are themselves employees with easy access. Thus, differential awareness of 'middle-class' offences, as against 'working-class' offences, may be as important as differential reporting by victims, if not more so.

Offenders: From Offence to Sentence

We have seen that many offences are not reported, and have noted the possibility that this is more true of the so-called 'middle-class' offences than of 'working-class' offences. Once an offence has been reported, police action may follow. Only a proportion of crimes 'notified to the police' are 'cleared up'—that is, attributed to a *particular* offender, either by the offender admitting guilt to the court or the court returning a guilty verdict. The proportion of reported murders cleared up in Britain is in excess of 80 per cent; by contrast, the population of reported larcenies from unattended vehicles which is cleared up is little more than 20 per cent (Walker, 1971). Once again there is a disparity: many offenders are never punished. Is there a disparity according to social class; that is, are working-class offenders more likely to enter the official statistics of offenders? Similar questions concern the other groups represented in the official statistics much more heavily than the proportion they comprise of the general population: young persons, males and (in the USA) blacks.

According to Chambliss (1969), this is indeed the case. He has asserted that the 'lower-class' person is (i) more likely to be scrutinized and therefore to be observed in any violation of the law, (ii) more likely to be arrested if discovered under suspicious circumstances, (iii) more likely to spend the time between arrest and trial in jail, (iv) more likely to come to trial, (v) more likely to be found guilty and (vi) if found guilty more likely to receive harsh punishment than his middle-or upper-class counterpart.

Offenders: Official Statistics and Self-reports of Offending

Chambliss is asserting that if there is an over-representation of various social groups it is not because they are *in fact* more likely to offend, but because of the response of official agencies; thus the official statistics represent not an accurate picture of reality but a biased *construction*.

We look first at the official statistics of offenders and the picture they reveal concerning the race and social class characteristics of those who figure in the statistics. Much the most ambitious study to date is that of Wolfgang *et al.* (1972), who studied the Philadelphia police records of all boys born in 1945 who lived in Philadelphia at least between their tenth and eighteenth birthdays. They were able to trace the great majority of the cohort, 9945 in all, of whom 35 per cent (termed offenders) had been involved with the police at least once, so that an official recording of the act resulted. They used police, rather than court records as the basic source of data because they considered them to be the procedurally earliest sources of information. In addition to all such acts being listed, each received a quantitative seriousness score based on the Sellin–Wolfgang index (Sellin and Wolfgang, 1964). The authors admit the possibility of a recorded police contact and a resulting charge of which the accused eventually was found innocent, but suggest (and produce some supporting evidence) that this factor is relatively unimportant. They accept the desirability of indexing self-reported offending, but did not do so. Self-reports would have made a valuable comparison; given the massive investment of time and money in this very large project, the absence of self-report data is most regrettable. Even the very carefully maintained police records of Philadelphia can be no better than the data entered into them.

The division of offenders into white and non-white was straightforward, that by socio-economic status (SES) much less so. The authors settled for a division into upper and lower SES by median income of the area in which the subject resided. Other divisions are possible, for example by parental occupation, and the Wolfgang *et al.* study is open to criticism on this point.

The major findings were as follows:

1. The 35 per cent who were recorded as offenders were distributed unevenly by class and race; 26 per cent of the total white upper SES group; 36 per cent of both the white lower SES and non-white upper SES groups; and 52 per cent of the non-white lower SES group.

2. Dividing the offenders into one-time offenders, recidivists (2–4 offenders) and chronic offenders (more than four offences) produced even more striking results. The proportions of the four categories of offenders who were one-time offenders decreased sharply from higher SES whites (two-thirds) to lower SES non-whites (one-third), the other two groups both comprising about a half one-time offenders. Moreover, whereas only one higher SES white boy in 50 was a chronic offender, this was true of one non-white lower SES boy in seven.

3. The racial disparity is even more clear when the quantitative measure of seriousness is studied. For example, all 14 homicides, which attract the highest seriousness score, were attributed to non-whites, as were 38 out of the 44 rapes (a rate per thousand cohort subjects of 13·1 for the non-whites as against 0·9 for the whites for the offence of rape). Racial disparities were much greater for offences against the person than against property (except for robbery, which combines elements of both).

4. White boys tended to 'specialize' more in property offences; non-whites in assaults. Nevertheless, white boys committed fewer thefts, but did steal more per offence.

This study thus shows clearly that as far as police *records* in Philadelphia are concerned, lower SES and non-white boys offend more and more seriously than do their white and higher SES counterparts, boys who are both non-white and lower SES being most strongly over-represented.

A British study by Wadsworth (1975) also suggest a considerable over-representation of working-class boys in the official statistics of offenders. He was able to follow up 88 per cent of all males born in England and Wales in one week of March 1946 and who had reached the age of 20 by the time of the survey. Data were available on their law-breaking including both cautions and findings of guilt. The relative contributions of the upper middle, lower middle, upper working and lower working-class boys were in the ratios 1:3:3:6, respectively. When only boys with more than one court appearance were considered, the disparity was even greater. Moreover, the working-class boys made their first appearance earlier than did middle-class boys.

However, a glaring omission in both the Philadelphia study and Wadsworth's British study was the total absence of self-report data, so that we have to turn to other studies to ask the question whether those who figure in official statistics (whether police or court records) are a representative or a biased sample of those who offend.

One of the most careful American studies is that by Gold (1966). A random sample of 552 13–16-year-old school children in Flint, Michigan, were interviewed by persons of the same race and sex as themselves. This enabled the exclusion of behavious deemed illegal by the respondents, but in fact not officially illegal. The offences noted were those carried out in the previous three years. An attempt at validation was made by using other informants, as noted earlier. As a result, 72 per cent of the respondents were rated as 'truth-tellers', 11 per cent as 'questionables' and 17 per cent as 'concealers'. There were no statistically significant differences between race or sex in any of these three categories. The possibility of systamatic personality differences in truth-telling was not investingated, nor was it possible to check the self-reports of solitary delinquents. The more serious offences were more frequently concealed. 'Seriousness' (S, an approximation to the Sellin and Wolfgang scale, 1964) and 'frequency' (F) were used to quantify offences.

While social status was inversely related to self-reported offences, the size of the relationship was considerably less than the official statistics would suggest. Over the full range of the scales both the S and the F indices revealed a lower to higher social status ratio of only 1·5 : 1 as opposed to the 4·5 : 1 indicated by the court records in the same town. However, at the highest of the four levels into which S and F scores were arbitrarily divided, the ratio of lower to higher status was 3·5 to 1. Using the two higher levels the ratio was 1·75 : 1. As both S and F scores increased so did the likelihood of detection. Even so, only 28 per cent of those who comprised the highest level of the S index had ever been apprehended. The comparable figure for the highest level of the F index was 19 per cent. Gold concluded that for the boys in his study there were more potent determiners of offending behaviour than social status, although this was a factor which cannot be ignored. For the females surveyed, self-reported delinquency was both low and unrelated to social status.

Gold's study suggests that official reaction (right from zeal of surveillance to outcome of court appearance) to those low in social status is much more severs than to those of higher social status, particularly for the less serious offences. This is supported by a study by Erickson (1971) of the impression conveyed by official statistics of the group nature of juvenile delinquency. (The group nature of delinquency is related to the social status issue because gang membership is more typical of lower than higher status boys.) Erickson reported that a significantly lower proportion of self-reported offences was carried out in groups than court records would suggest. Nevertheless, it remained true that the most serious offences tended to be carried out in groups. Erickson concluded that official reactions to offences committed in groups are more severe than they are to solitary offences and cites this as an example of the many self-confirming prophecies to be found in the judicial and penal systems.

The same researcher (Erickson, 1972) reported results which support the *opposite* view from Gold's study of self-report and official statistics—namely, that the latter distort the true facts of offending. Erickson correlated self-reported delinquent behaviour in 282 high-school boys in the Utah town of Provo with their own estimates of future violations, and the number of their arrests and appearances in court, both in the past and in the following three years. Guttman scaling techniques were used to develop an eight-item scale related to past delinquency and a 12 item scale of future delinquency. Unfortunately, not all the items included were obviously illegal—for example, defying the authority of teachers, and using tobacco. It may have been that a high frequency of response to such officially non-illegal items inflated the total self-reported scores.

The correlations found between the various measures were rather high: that between self-reported delinquency and *all* court appearances (both past and future) being 0·95 or 0·78, depending on the type of correlational statistic employed (the lower one being more satisfactory, as it corrected for tied ranks). The next highest correlations obtained were past and future court appearances (0·85 or 0·46), and self-reported and past court appearances (0·71 or 0·58). Thus the study suggest that official response reflects real-life behaviour: the more criminal behaviour, the more court appearances. It would be important to repeat this study in a large urban community (Provo has a population of 53,000), with non-illegal items eliminated from the self-report scales and control exercised for the possibility of more zealous surveillance by the legal authorities of those with existing court records.

Belson's British self-report study is in agreement with Gold's American findings, that while the official statistics exaggerate the difference, some class differences do remain—at least at the self-report level. Whether they would hold true for directly observed criminal behaviour is not known (it is possible that either middle-class boys under-report or working-class boys over-report, or that both distortions operate). Belson divided his respondents into six groups by paternal occupations, from A (professional, semi-professional and executive) to F (unskilled). There was little difference between the groups for the statement 'I have kept something I have found', but the percentage admitting 'I have stolen from a shop' rose somewhat across the groups—from 37 per cent (A) to 65 per cent (E) (semi-skilled)—before falling again to 55 per cent (F). Much greater disparities were found for 'stealing from work' and for 'getting into a place and stealing'. For the former the rise from A to E was from 9 per cent to 38 per cent and for the latter from 6 per cent to 23 per cent: group F showed a small drop and a small increase over E for the two questions, respectively. The social class picture was rather different for the statements concerning theft from family or relatives and theft from someone at school. The former tended to *decline* from group A to group F, the latter showed no clear trend. Moreover, stealing from work is an opportunity for those already at work—a higher proportion of working-class boys than middle-class boys are likely to have been working by age 16 at the time of the study. Nevertheless, the average incidences reported for all types of theft steadily increase from group A to group E—from 22 per cent to 36 per cent with a slight decline to 33 per cent for group E. In addition, those working-class boys who stole at all were more likely to report high amounts of theft than were middle-class boys who stole. It can be concluded once again that a social class disparity for self-reported theft by one group of London boys does indeed exist, but that the disparity is less than the official statistics would suggest. A review and statistical analysis of a number of studies of juvenile offending (Bytheway, 1975) supports the conclusion that self-report data show a small but statistically significant tendency for more offending by working-class than by middle-class boys.

The problem of the representativeness of the official statistics of offences appears again when we study the variables of age and sex. An analysis of the data on offenders convicted of indictable offences in the UK suggests that crime is largely a pursuit of youth; the rate per thousand of the population rises to a peak in the mid-teens and thereafter steadily declines. Moreover, it appears to be young *males* who are heavily over-represented. At all ages, in all countries in which statistics have been kept, the disparity between the sexes is considerable, being about five times greater for males for all offences combined and 35 times as great for housebreaking (Wootton, 1959). It is only in shoplifting that women are convicted more frequently than men, and then only slightly so. This has been explained on the grounds that women shop very much more frequently than men, so that it is asserted that an analysis in terms of the proportion of the sexes 'at risk' would show that men shoppers steal more frequently than women shoppers. However, Astor's American field study of shoppers, cited earlier, fails to support this view. Of the women observed, 7·4 per cent stole something; for men, the figure was 5 per cent. Nor did youth come out much more badly. People over 35 stole only marginally less than those under 35. Clearly, if we use the official data on sex differences in crime as reliable descriptive evidence, for which explanations must be sought, we may be asking the wrong questions, at least in part. Lady Wootton's dramatic statement (1959): '. . . if men behaved like women, the Courts would be idle and the prisons empty' may be true so far as *convicted offenders* are concerned; it may be much less true that the rate of *offences* would diminish markedly, particularly those in which physical strength is relatively unimportant. If this is indeed correct, the key research question would then become: why do a majority cease offending when they become adults and a minority continue to do so? However, it is also possible that while the majority of young adults cease carrying out the *type* of offences they admit as adolescents, when they enter the world of work new opportunities open up for adding to their legitimate income by various illegal practices. This has been studied mainly in the more middle-class occupations, under the heading of 'while-collar crime', but 'occupational offenders' (a more inclusive term, Clinard, 1968) are likely to be found on the factory floor as well as in the executive suite. The point is that a combination of easily available financial rewards and a low probability of detection almost inevitably increases the likelihood of offending. Such conditions seem likely to operate widely throughout industry and the professions. Financial or property gain by illegal means at low risk is probably *less possible* for the schoolboy than for his parent, who spends his entire working day in the situation in which illegal gain is possible. Schools may be poorer sources of opportunity than factories and offices. Clinard (1968) includes under the heading of occupational offenders large and small businessmen, politicians, government employees, doctors, pharmacists and others. Investigations, particularly in the USA have shown widespread violation of the criminal law by businesses, up to the largest size and in all areas of industry and commerce. The illegal activities included acts in restraint of trade, such as monopoly practices, patent infringement, financial manipulations and (in wartime) black marketeering. Convictions of American public and elected officials occur with some frequency. *Time* (1972) noted in an article headed 'Busting Public Servants' that in New Jersey alone 67 officials had been indicted and 35 convicted over the past three years, including mayors, legislators, judges, highway officials, postmasters and a congressman. Other examples listed were from Miami, Philadelphia, New Orleans, Baltimore, New York City and Albany, N.Y. Criminal proceedings against British public servants and politicians seem more rare, but this apparent national difference may reflect only the notably greater zeal of the American press—perhaps due to less restrictive libel laws—and the tradition whereby American attorneys achieve public prominence by exposing the misdeeds of incumbent office-holders. Trade union officials (again the evidence is largely American) have engaged in such criminal activities as misappropriation of union funds and the use of fraudulent means to maintain control of their unions.

Illegal activities by doctors include fee-splitting (illegal in the USA, and against the self-policed code of medical ethics in Britain). This entails the doctor giving the treatment sharing a fee with the referring doctor. It is illegal because referrals may be based on the size of the fee rather than the proficiency of the practitioner. Clinard quotes Dr. Paul R. Hawley, director of the American College of Surgeons, as stating 'The American people would be shocked at ... the amount of unnecessary surgery performed on patients through the country' (Clinard, 1968, p. 271). Illegal practices are similarly rather widespread among lawyers. They include the misappropriation of funds entrusted to them, and securing perjured testimony. Nor should we forget adult taxpayers in general, particularly those whose tax is not deducted directly at source. How many self-employed persons can claim never to have evaded tax illegally? According to Sutherland (1941), 'The financial loss to society from white collar crime is probably greater than the financial loss from burglaries, robberies and larcenies'. Writing of white-collar crime in Britain, Box (1971) states 'All of those (i.e. occupational and tax offences) are only dimly reflected in the official records ... because ... they are almost never subject to police interference'. Perhaps the most obvious of all adult crimes concerns motoring offences, only a tiny proportion of which reach the stage of a court appearance (Willett, 1964).

Wallerstein and Wyle (1947) documented criminal behaviour by the clergy (see above). Even the police are not immune. Indeed, this is most unlikely *a priori*; they are peculiarly exposed to criminal opportunities. A study carried out in New York for the Patrolman's Benevolent Association (*Sunday Times*, 1974) used hidden cameras to compare the behaviour of ordinary citizens finding a 'dropped' wallet with that of policemen previously given 'integrity tests' by the Police Department. Whereas 84 per cent of the public kept the wallet, only 30 per cent of the policemen did so when handed a wallet by an undercover agent posing as a member of the public. This result may be taken either as reassuring evidence that the police are more law-abiding than their fellow-citizens or as a disquieting indication that many are all too human.

All of this is not to argue that the average adult spends his entire working life in the pursuit of illegal self-advantage; simply that such activities are not totally confined to the 'criminal classes', but are found in varying degrees of frequency, in different forms according to the nature of the occupation, throughout the majority of the population, and a true sample of all offenders, both those apprehended and those not, would be less heavily weighted in the direction of working-class young black males than the official statistics suggest.

Offenders: Who is Caught

Belson's British study (1975) provides some very striking evidence on the key question of class and other disparities between those self-reported thieves who are caught by the police and those who are not. He divided the boys into four groups according to the number of self-reported thefts. An analysis of the quarter, which divided the boys by paternal occupation into four groups (A, B + C, D + E, and F), indicated that the percentage caught was disproportionately *high* for boys with unskilled fathers and disproportionately *low* for boys with professional and executive fathers. Thus, of those who steal, the better off are markedly less likely to be caught. Unfortunately, Belson did not report data relating this to *type* of theft. The possible disparity between 'public' thefts (shops, houses, etc.) and 'private' thefts (home, friends, etc.) is of relevance to the question of official bias. However, the great majority of the 44 types of theft were from 'public' places rather than 'private' ones, so that the reported disparities in being caught are unlikely to be accountable to more than a small extent by the middle-class boys choosing to steal from targets less likely to report a discovered theft, although this possibility should not be ignored. Belson also found that the better-educated boys were less likely to be caught by the police. It seems then that working-class origin boys are rather more likely than middle-class boys to be caught. Why should this be so? There are at least two explanations: increased police surveillance of boys of 'working-class appearance' when a crime has been committed or suspected together with a greater likelihood of arresting and charging working-class boys, and a greater skill in committing the non-family type of theft by the (on average) more intelligent middle-class boy. There are no findings on the latter possibility, but some which are relevant to the former. We consider them in the next section.

Offenders: Who is Prosecuted

There are some additional findings which support the possibility of bias against particular groups during the sequence from offence to court appearance. A systematic group bias in both the surveillance of shoppers and the prosecution of apprehended shoplifters is shown by a study by Cameron (1964). Store detectives were not only more likely to observe and follow adolescents and blacks, rather than white adults, particularly those perceived as middle-class, but were also selective in prosecuting those arrested. Whereas only 6·5 per cent of all adults arrested were blacks, they made up 24 per cent of those prosecuted, the bias extending to both male and female blacks.

A similar selective bias emerged from a study by Robin (1970) of a private detective agency employed by several American firms. Charges were brought by the employing firms against only one-third of the executives apprehended in illegal conduct, but against two-thirds of the cleaners similarly caught. The bias was related only slightly to the value of the property involved and to the length of service of the employee, much more strongly to the person's employment status. Black and Reiss (1970) found that after an arrest had been made complainants were more in favour of pressing charges when the suspect was black or poor than when he was white or middle-class.

Nor are the police certain to be immune from bias. (This bears on the Philadelphia cohort study, see above.) There are rather wide powers of police discretion within which bias might operate. The police may decide not to proceed against an arrested person. They then inform him of their decision either by direct interview or by letter. Both in the USA and in Britain, the younger the suspect, the more likely he is to be cautioned rather than prosecuted (Hood and Sparks, 1970). At all ages females are more likely than males to receive cautions (Walker, 1965). Gold (1966) reported that cautioning was more likely for middle-class than for working-class boys. Finally, Wilson (1968) found that white juveniles were more likely to be let off with a caution than were black youngsters. The behaviour of the police, in cautioning or arresting, appears to relate to their prediction of the likelihood of agencies other than the courts effectively controlling the future behaviour of the offender (Hood and Sparks, 1970). It may well be that the older adolescent who is black, working-class and male is indeed more likely to reoffend than his younger, white, middle-class and female counterpart, but there is a rather strong element here of the self-fulfilling prophecy.

Age, sex and skin colour are immediately obvious characteristics. Another perceived feature which appears to influence the attitude of the police is the general appearance of the suspect: both his expressive features, such as gesture and stance, and his static attributes, such as length of hair. Vernon (1964) reviews evidence which shows that both of the above types of physical data are used frequently by interviewers to predict personality and future behaviour; the actual relationship between expressive and static attributes and future behaviours is, however, minimal. According to Hood and Sparks (1970), the major factors taken into account by the police (in prosecuting rather than cautioning) are: seriousness of the offence, previous convictions, quality of parental control, style of dress and, most important, the attitude of the offender when confronted by the police. Piliavin and Briar (1964) reported that the most important cue used by the police is the way the suspect responds; for example, a quick confession as opposed to a denial increased the chances of an informal response by the police. They also found that youths classified as 'uncooperative' were significantly more likely to be arrested than those classified as 'cooperative'. Very similar results have been reported by Werner et al. (1975), the key behaviours being politeness, cooperation, presenting prompt evidence of identity and answering questions. Box (1971) suggests, although he cites no actual data, that middle-class persons are better than their working-class counterparts at creating the desired impression on the police.

Offenders in Court

The final stage of the 'social construction of official statistics', as Box (1971) terms the process, occurs when the charged person appears in court.

The Philadelphia cohort study (Wolfgang *et al.*, 1972) provided interesting data on the disposal of juvenile offenders, from the moment of apprehension to the receipt of a sentence by the court. A designated officer handles the disposition according to a number of criteria, including previous police contact, current offence, offender's family situation and attitude towards the police and his anticipation of juvenile court action in the event of an arrest. Analysis of dispositions was by the previously described variables of race and SES and type of disposition—a 'remedial' outcome (unofficial action by the police) or arrest, usually leading to a court appearance. The authors comment, 'However we split and splice the material at hand, non-whites received more severe dispositions' (p. 220), and further, 'Differential dispositions based on race may be the result of discrimination, prejudice, bias' (p. 221). Whereas only 13 per cent of white one-time offenders were arrested, the figure for non-whites was 30 per cent. A similar disparity was found between white and non-white recidivists. The disparity appeared largely to be accounted for by the more serious offences, for which there was the familiar progression from lower SES non-whites to higher SES whites, the former being twice as likely as the latter to be arrested. Moreover, the disparity was largely due to race and not to SES, there being only small differences between upper and lower SES whites and between upper and lower SES non-whites. The authors then carried out an analysis to trace the impact of disposition for a particular offence on the probability of subsequent offences. This showed a greater probability of a second offence if the first offence had led to an arrest than if it had led to a remedial disposition. The same was true of subsequent offences. In sum, 'two factors—seriousness of the offence and severe disposition are associated with a substantial proportion of recidivism' (p. 237). Thus, the suggestion is that the heavy-representation of non-white lower SES boys in the recidivist and chronic categories noted earlier may have been partially due to the severity of police action—arrest rather than remedial disposition. The implication follows that if, for example, white higher SES boys carrying out the same initial offence as non-whites had been dealt with as severely as the latter, they would have been more strongly represented in the recidivist and chronic groups than actually was the case. A fuller discussion of this possibility, which is at the core of the labelling explanation of crime, will be postponed until Chapter 8. Suffice it for the present to conclude that the heavy over-representation of lower SES non-whites in those appearing in court, and thus potentially liable to receive a sentence which would include them in the official statistics of offenders, may not reflect solely the greater criminal behaviour of that group. Belson (1975) reported the same for Britain: the sons of the less skilled are more likely to be sent to court.

A guilty verdict is not, of course, the only one possible; many defendants are acquitted, providing a potential basis for differential rates of acquittal— between the social classes, the sexes, and so on. Unfortunately, rather little empirical work has been carried out on the relationship between group member-ship and acquittal.

From data on 3500 jury trials, Kalven and Zeisel (1966) found 27 which were of men for the murder of their wives and 17 of women for the murder of their husbands. Whereas the acquittal rate of the former was only 7 per cent, that of the latter was 41 per cent. In discussing this finding, Walker (1971) notes the ways in which the two groups studied might have differed in addition to their sex, for example in age and in skin colour, hence affecting the observed outcome. He might also have pointed to the possibility of a systematically more able defence (or at any rate more ably presented pleas in mitigation) put up by the lawyers of the females than those of the males. Juries and judges might be less severe on female than on male murders. A guilty plea, or verdict, does not lead to a uniform sentence; defence lawyers, jurors and sentencing agents may all influence the outcome.

Defence Lawyers. The calibre of the defence lawyer is related to the likelihood of plea bargaining (an agreement between the accused and the police to plead guilty to a lesser charge, allowing a swift passage of the case). This is rewarding to all concerned: the crime, or crimes, joins the number of those 'cleared up by the police'; the machinery of the court, always overloaded, proceeds swiftly; and the accused receives a lesser penalty than he might have done otherwise. Newman (1956) found that 27 per cent of those legally represented managed to plead guilty to a lesser charge, compared with 12 per cent of those without a lawyer, and 57 per cent of the former, compared with 32 per cent of the latter, were promised that the prosecution would press for a lighter sentence. Plea bargaining might also be concerned in any change in the officially listed offence between indictment and court appearance. Garfinkel (1949) found that whereas 70 per cent of blacks initially indicted for first-degree murder were finally charged with that offence, the comparable figure for whites was 40 per cent. Another way of obtaining a concession from the judiciary is to get the case dismissed at a preliminary hearing, or in a lower court. The quality of the lawyer employed might be expected to make a difference: this is the case. Oaks and Lehman (1970) found that dismissals of felony cases in Cook County, Illinois, were obtained by 29 per cent of those employing private counsel as compared with 8 per cent of those represented by a public defender (the rough equivalent of the British legal aid system). It is a not unreasonable inference that the more able lawyers, able to command very high fees, do not need the fees provided by the legal aid system, and hence are less likely to act as public defenders.

(The contrary assumption would be that lawyers as a group are on average more altruistic than other humans.) While being legally represented *at all* helps, having financial access to the most able lawyers helps still more. The middle classes are not only more likely to be able to afford good lawyers; they may also have a greater incentive to 'clear their name', having more to lose by failing to do so. The granting of bail, enabling a greater length of time for the preparation of the defence—and hence a more successful defence—is related to the economic level of the person seeking bail (Nagel, 1970). The result of all the above factors is that a further potential contribution is made to the social construction of official statistics. (The above remarks apply to the American public defender system; the British legal aid system provides for the costs of up to very expensive counsel.)

Decisions as to guilt are made either by lay jurymen or by magistrates, judges or other official sentencing agents.

Juror Behaviour. A comprehensive review by Mitchell and Byrne (1973a) concluded that three major classes of variables influenced juror decisions.

1. The personal characteristics of the defendant, including his physical appearance, race, sex and age, family status and income, as well as descriptions of his behaviour by others.

2. The procedural characteristics of the trial, such as the order of presentation of the arguments and their novelty, the evidence and behaviour of witnesses, and the jurors' knowledge of possible punishments.

3. The personal characteristics of the jurors, such as their degree of authoritarianism (those high on authoritarianism measures are deferential to supervisors and antagonistic to subordinates, social inferiors and minority group members), their attitudes to punishment, particularly corporal punishment, and their social status, education and sex.

The third of the above conclusions was anticipated by Winnick (1961): 'It is logical to expect that Juror X will perceive the world very much as he did when he was Mr. X and will not overnight become a judicious evaluator of evidence merely because he is sworn in' (p. 107). It is also reasonable to expect that the experimental findings concerning group influence (McGuire, 1969) will apply to jury discussions, for example the greater influence on the outcome of a discussion of those higher in social status and hence in the ability to confer relevant rewards such as social approval. It seems not unlikely that middle-class jurors are more likely to favour middle-class than working-class defendants (and *vice versa*), and in general the degree of similarity between jurors and accused is likely to be an important variable in juror behaviour. The matter has been studied experimentally by Mitchell and Byrne (1973b) using a questionnaire presentation to undergraduates of a case concerning stolen examination papers. Details of the defendant's views on certain topics were also made available, and the perceived similarities of the defendant to the 'juror' (high or low on an authoritarianism scale, Byrne and Lamberth, 1971,) were also manipulated. They were asked to decide on guilt and to recommend punishment. It was found that highly authoritarian jurors were both more biased in favour of a similar defendant, and more biased against a dissimilar one, than were egalitarian jurors (low on authoritarianism) as regards both guilt and punishment. Mitchell and Byrne (1973b), using a simulated trial situation, found that while low authoritarians were responsive to a judicial instruction to disregard testimony about the defendant's characteristics, whether positive or negative in nature, in recommending punishment, high authoritarians still responded to the defendant's characteristics. The authors' recommendations will be thought somewhat revolutionary by lawyers, and to infringe the civil rights of potential jurors by libertarians. They suggest screening out high authoritarians from jury membership and excluding all irrelevant and biasing information from jurors, even to the extent of recording the trial on videotape and editing it before transmission. Berg and Vidmar (1975) have confirmed that while high authoritarians recall more about evidence relating to defendant character, low authoritarians recall more about situational evidence. Once again their study was of a simulated jury situation, but it is reasonable to expect real-life jury members to behave similarly—according to level of authoritarianism.

Finally, we have to consider the stage at which a sentence is actually pronounced. To do so we turn to a relatively recent area of research, that of sentencing practice. Variations in the sentence given for the same offence are of interest to criminologists for several reasons: first, they may influence the attitude to the law, both of those sentenced and the public at large, and hence the future offending behaviour of both; second, they imply the varying nature of the punishment side of the decision matrix, concerning whether or not to commit a particular offence; third, variations in the learning experience consequent on punishment may affect future offending behaviour (the experience of prison is likely to be different from that of probation). The wide variations encountered in pactice suggest the importance of the personal features of the sentencing agents and of their interaction with those of the person sentenced, exactly as is found in other interpersonal perception situations.

Sentencing Practices and Sentencing Agents. Ample evidence of crude differences in sentencing practices between courts in the same country and even in the same area of the country is cited by Hood and Sparks: 'In the United States Federal Courts in 1962 the average sentence of imprisonment for all cases ranged from 12·1 months in the northern circuit of New York (65 cases) to 57·6 months in the southern district of Iowa (41 cases)' (Hood and Sparks, 1970, p. 142). Similar variations were found for specific offences, imprisonment for forgery varying from 7·2 months to 54 months. The same kind of findings have been obtained in England. In the courts of two neighbouring northern towns, Rotherham and Halifax, the proportions of young persons put on probation in the early 1950's were 12 per cent and 79 per cent respectively (Grünhut, 1956). Several years later (1962–3) in Barnsley, another town in northern

England, 73 per cent of boys under 14 and 65 per cent of those between 14 and 17 were find. The corresponding national figures were 17 per cent and 28 per cent, respectively (Patchett and McClean, 1956).

Hood and Sparks (1970, p. 146) consider a study by Green (1961) to be 'the most sophisticated sentencing enquiry completed" (at the time of the Hood and Sparks book, cf. Hogarth, below). Green studied 1437 cases dealt with by 18 judges in the Philadelphia Court of Quarter Session. He found a reasonable degree of consistency between the judges both for the cases of greater seriousness and greater mildness, but 'as cases moved from the extremes of gravity or mildness towards intermediacy, judicial standards tend to become less stable and sentencing increasingly reflects the individuality of the judge' (Green, 1961, cited by Hood and Sparks, 1970, p. 147). Other studies reviewed by Hood and Sparks also emphasize the 'individuality of the judge' without spelling out what this means. It seems to imply both the personality of the judges and their attitudes towards offenders and the purposes of the sentencing process.

An ambitious attempt to delineate the attitudinal variables affecting the decisions of sentencing agents was made in a Canadian study by Hogarth (1971). Almost all the full-time magistrates in the province of Ontario (71 out of 78) participated. Detailed written descriptions were prepared of 150 cases covering seven indictable offences, both 'property' and 'person' in type, including data on both the offence and the offender. The magistrates were asked to give each a 'sentence' and were also interviewed in detail concerning their general attitudes to the law and to offenders. The following were among the results obtained.

1. The *selection* of institutional sentence was associated with the previous criminal record of the offender and his current culpability.

2. The *length* of sentence imposed was significantly correlated with the length of record and the seriousness of the crime (Sellin–Wolfgang index) and not with the occupation, marital status, age and sex of the offender, the nature of the plea or the attributes of the victim. However, all of the above 'objective' facts *combined* accounted for only 7 per cent of the total variance in sentencing behaviour.

In contrast, the general attitudes of the judges in three areas accounted for 50 per cent of the variance: their 'concern for justice'; their 'tolerance of social deviance'; and their 'belief in the efficacy of punishment'. For example, those magistrates who relied heavily on fines did not feel that 'punishment corrects', those who sent offenders to institutions did do so.

What this study suggests is that individual magistrates operate according to their general beliefs concerning, for example, the efficacy of different kinds of punishment. These personal guideliness help them to resolve the doubts and uncertainties set up by each individual case. Once a personal sentencing style has been established, it is likely both to continue and to serve as a model for new members of the court, through the principles of observational learning. However, the Hogarth study is not entirely generalizable to the real situation of the court room: the participants did not *see* the accused person, and so could not be influenced by his appearance, behaviour and overall 'demeanour' throughout the trial. (It will be recalled that the way a suspected person behaves towards a police officer is a major determinant of the officer's decision to arrest, caution, etc.)

There is some recent evidence concerning this omission. Dion *et al.* (1972) have shown that compared to unattractive people, better-looking people were viewed as likely to possess a variety of socially desirable attributes and as more likely to be successful. Several studies (see Berscheid and Walster, 1969) have shown that attractiveness increases liking, and Landy and Aronson (1969) that liking for a defendant increases leniency. Using a simulated jury task, Efran (1974) reported that subjects assigned less punishment to good-looking than to unattractive transgressors. A similar finding was reported by Dion (1972), who also found that the unattractive were considered more likely to reoffend—possibly because of their more limited personal resources, which also gave them less opportunity for non-criminally achieved rewards. Thus, the generalization seems reasonable: sentencing agents will be more lenient towards the more attractive; if middle-class persons are more skilled at presenting themselves as attractive than are the working-class, we have a further source of bias against the latter. A limitation has been shown by Sigall and Ostrove (1975): in a simulated situation somewhat harsher 'sentences' were given to an attractive than to an unattractive swindler—swindling being considered an 'attractiveness related crime. The attractive–leniency relationship held strongly for burglary, an unattractive burglar being given a much more severe 'sentence' than an attractive one. It should be noted that real life juries do not give sentences, but it is not unreasonable to expect sentencing agents to be influenced by attractiveness.

To what extent, in fact, as opposed to potentially, does the bias of sentencing agents operate systematically for or against certain social groups? A study by Hood (1962) of sentencing in magistrates' courts in Britain concluded: 'There is some evidence in favour of the hypothesis that middle-class magistrates dealing with working-class offenders, in relatively small and stable middle-class communities, are likely to be relatively severe'. American evidence of sentencing bias is rather more clear but mostly concerns bias between the races. For example, a study of shoplifting by Cameron (1964) found that while 22 per cent of black women found guilty were sent to jail, only 4 per cent of white women found guilty were so sentenced. Further, only 10 per cent of the white women sentenced to imprisonment were sent to jail for more than 30 days, as compared to 26 per cent of the black women.

Hood and Sparks (1970, pp. 168–9) have produced a detailed model of the many variables which enter into the sentencing decision and suggest that for any particular court it should be possible to predict the sentence in a given case. They point out that the common constraints on all judges—for example, the conventions and rules laid down by courts of appeal—tend to reduce variation. The seminars on sentencing practice, held periodically for all types of sentencing agents and now a common feature of the British penal system, are designed to exert a similar effect. It shall remains possible that *both* appeal court judges and sentencing seminars may be influenced by, and propagate, certain beliefs concerning offenders in particular and human behaviour in general which they may communicate to those sitting in the lower courts. Similarity of sentencing practice may indicate no more than that the sentencing agents have all been exposed to the same systematic training; it does not tell us whether the training freed them from, or reinforced, stereotypic modes of thinking.

It can be concluded that at the stage of sentencing a further process of selection may occur; some persons will go forward to join the ranks of those in custodial institutions, others will receive a punishment which will retain them outside institutions, with consequent exposure to different learning settings and hence potentially different future behaviours. The possibility is that the middle-class, whites and female are more likely than the working-class, blacks and male to take the latter route than the former, when the offence concerned has been relatively similar.

Conclusions and Implications

Conclusions on Offences and Offenders

It can be seen that at each stage following the *same initial offending behaviour*—complaint, search, arrest, trial, conviction and type of sentence—there is a greater possibility that certain social groups of the population will proceed to the next stage than will other groups. Moreover, certain offences are more likely to lead offenders into custody than others. The final composition of those in custody will be a fuction *both* of the facts of offending and of being detected *and* of the systematic bias in selection which occurs at each stage of the process. A conservative appraisal of the data would suggest that there are initial disparities in the frequency and seriousness of offending between working-and middle-class persons, males and females and (in the USA) blacks and whites. However, the sequence of official responses significantly amplifies the various disparities, so that the appearance of reality provided by the official statistics is *partially* a construction. An analogy is provided by the psychology of sex differences (see Chapter 5). It seems likely that *on average* males and females potentially differ at birth, due to biological inheritance, in certain important areas of behaviour. However, social training experiences increase and exaggerate the differentiation. Behavioural differences between adult males and females are thus due to an amalgam of biological and social influences, the *direction* of effect being the same.

So far as explanatory studies of offending behaviour are concerned, the implication of this general approach is quite clear: studies carried out solely on custodial pupulations may tell us about the behaviour of the gents of the law enforcement and penal systems and the effects of institutions on the behaviours of offenders, as well as about the causes of criminal behaviour.

Moreover, the several sources of the data obtained by such studies will be extremely difficult to untangle.

Perhaps the most important selection process of all is that those to be found in institutions are not only more likely to be drawn from certain social groups; they are a special group also in that *they have been caught*. The probability of apprehension not only relates to victim complaint, police surveillance and police efficiency, but also to the skill of the offender in selecting an offence with a low probability of detection, in carrying out the offence efficiently and in covering his tracks. If we were to study businessmen, we would hardly confine our attention to those who go bankrupt, struggle along for a low profit, or are otherwise at the unsuccessful end of the dimension of business competence. It is similarly one-sided to study only unsuccessful offenders—for this is how those who are encountered in custodial institutions may be described.

Implications for Research into the Explanation of Criminal Behaviour

Studies of crime and criminals rest, like studies of human behaviour in general, on certain assumptions (which then become research strategies) concerning the desirable population for study and on certain models of individual differences in human behaviour. The assumptions made and the model selected inevitably guide the activities of research workers at the descriptive stage, and thus markedly affect the choice of theories to be tested at the explanatory stage as well as the methods adopted for social response and control. It is thus of crucial importance to set out both the strategies which research workers in this field have adopted and the models of human behaviour which inform their conduct at all three stages of the research enterprise. Strategies and models overlap somewhat, but it is convenient for purposes of exposition to consider them separately.

Research Strategies. In all areas of human behaviour research workers face the problem of *how* to ask the questions in which they are interested. In practice, this means selecting the groups of individuals deemed to display the behaviour concerned. In the context of criminal behaviour it might appear obvious, and rightly so, to study convicted offenders. Within the group of those convicted it is often more convenient to study those sentenced to prison—they are literally a captive population. However, both decisions imply major assumptions which may or may not be correct. The price if they are incorrect is a very high one—explanatory studies which seek to account for the descriptive 'facts' may well be devoted to a distorted and incomplete picture of reality and thus fail to give a complete explanation. Thus, research workers have tended to start with the picture of crime and criminals as revealed by the official statistics. As we have seen, the statistics somewhat distort the reality. Not only do they include only a sample of the total population of crimes and criminals (many offenders are not caught) but that sample appears to be a biased one, being the result of a lengthy sequence through surveillance, arrest, prosecution and sentence.

The impression given by the official statistics is that the 'typical' criminal is young, male, working-class and, in the United States, black. This has led to a rather heavy concentration of explanatory studies of crime (see Chapter 8) and of attempts to control crime on the criminal activity of a designated group of individuals and not on that of the remainder of the population—those persons of both sexes who are older and/or middle-class. An obvious source of additional bias is that those officially criminal are those who have been caught. If it is true that the official statistics are biased, it follows that research activities based upon them inevitably will lead to incomplete explanations and less than optimally effective methods of control.

An alternative strategy to achieve representativeness of research samples is to study self-reported offenders. This raises certain problems as we have seen— some respondents may under-report, particularly concerning the more serious offences, others may over-report. However, carefully carried out, self-report studies are likely to yield samples of individuals less subject to bias than are those culled from the official statistics.

Those convicted of crimes may be sentenced either to imprisonment, or some other form of detention, or to a punishment of a non-custodial kind. Many studies of offenders have been concerned with the former group. Here the research strategy makes the important additional assumption that not only are the prisoners representative of offenders in general, they are also unchanged by their stay in the institution concerned. This assumption is particularly important for studies which compare personality measures of prisoners and non-offenders. It may be that prisoners remain conveniently frozen in the personality features they displayed on entry, but it is more likely that personality measures taken of prisoners are affected by the special experiences provided by the prison environment. Thus personality scores are an amalgam of the influences experienced *prior* to the offence which led to a prison sentence and the effects of prison. This makes it quite unsatisfactory to test on a prison population a theory which predicts personality differences between offenders and non-offenders due to different genetic inheritance or different pre-offence experiences or both. A preferable strategy is to study non-imprisoned convicted offenders, or possibility better still, non-convicted, self-reported offenders.

Models of Individual Difference in Behaviour. Essentially, psychologists and others concerned with explaining human behaviour have operated within three models of individual differences. The first, the typological model, assumes that people can be divided into separate groups without overlap for the behaviour in question. A simple example is the division into 'extraverts' instead of into degrees of extraversion (see below). The typological model implies that the differences are both permanent and apply in all situations. Thus the 'psychopath' is a 'psychopath' at all times and in all places, irrespective of instigating circumstances. By definition, although this is rarely spelled out, the 'non-psychopath' or 'normal' is never psychopathic at any time or in any place. The notion of typology has been applied also to the production of typologies of offenders. Gibbons (1975), who has spent many years in this endeavour, has concluded recently that he is increasingly 'sceptical' about the prospects for uncovering a relatively parsimonious set of criminal role 'careers' (p. 153). He considers that valid, classificatory, schemes leading, hopefully, to significant aetiological discoveries may be very difficult, if not impossible, to construct. Moreover, it may not be necessary to do so in order to intervene effectively. Instead, he asserts the need to search for contingent events for criminal behaviour—in other words, for situational determinants.

A second approach to individual differences is embodied in the dimensional view; this suggests that 'criminality', like other personality variables, varies along a continuous quantitative dimension, with each position shading into the next. This approach is well represented by Eysenck, whose work is discussed in detail in Chapter 6. The dimensional approach developed historically from the notion of types, but now definitely eschews such a simplistic approach. Its proponents acknowledge the importance of current situation and learning experiences but tend to lay much the heaviest emphasis on biological predispositions to a particular level of potential 'criminality'.

Both the typological and the dimensional views stress what persons bring with them into situations in which they then behave illegally, rather than the effect on individuals of the opportunities and constraints concerning illegal behaviours provided in the situation. This is the emphasis of the third model of individual differences—which we can term loosely the behaviourist model. It suggests that behaviour, including criminal behaviour, in a particular situation is a function both of the features of the current situation and the outcomes of previous experiences in that and relatively similar situations. The 'behaviourist' view is thus apparently solely environmental, and indeed its proponents have tended to underplay biological influences on behaviour. But this is by no means an inevitable picture and indeed may represent a misconception of the behaviourist position, which is essentially a way of looking at behaviour, not a statement about its causes. During the course of this book we shall suggest that both biological and environmental determinants combine to produce individual differences in criminal behaviour. An important implication of the behaviourist approach, and to some extent of the dimensional one also, particularly as expounded by Eysenck, is that the methods and findings of experimental psychology, originally laboratory-based and centred on 'normal' behaviour, are equally applicable to real-life, 'abnormal' behaviours. Thus the principles which account for the acquisition, maintenance and performance of behaviours in general will apply also to particular 'deviant' behaviours. From the point of view of research strategy, because the typological and dimensional approaches tend to emphasize persons, rather than their behaviour, they focus research on comparisons of criminals and non-criminals *per se*. They are thus heavily dependent on the representativeness and lack of bias of the official statistics of offences and offenders. The behaviourist approach is less focused; it points us to criminal *behaviour*, whether exemplified by officially designated or self-reporting persons, and the prior experiences which maintain and the current situations which evoke such behaviour. Thus, it is argued, the relative neutrality of the behaviourist approach is best suited to the descriptive stage of our enquiry into criminal behaviour. It *may* be the case that some *persons* will emerge as consistently criminal, possibly due to strong biological predispositions, or to consistent environmental experiences, or the two acting together, but this is the *conclusion* of an enquiry. At the outset it is preferable to be as open-minded as possible—and therefore to study both convicted and unconvicted offenders, and those who have not yet offended, as well as to use both experimental arrangements and field situations. In other words, a desirable research strategy, in the field of crime, would follow that of experimental psychology in general: study the criminal behaviour, actual and potential, of people in general, and not only that of special, designated groups.

As a standard practice, research workers should compare the relative advantages and disadvantages of custodial *versus* non-custodial populations prior to desiging research studies into criminal behaviour. The three main approaches to the explanation of crime emphasize, respectively, specific learning experiences (see Chapters 2–4), predisposition to individual differences (see Chapters 5–7) and socio-economic–political factors (see Chapter 8). The strategy of research into criminal behaviour, including a selection of populations for study, should be such as to allow all three explanations to be given a complete, searching and unbiased a test as possible. It is probably true that the prospective type of study is the most satisfactory way of carrying out explanatory research into real-life human behaviours of all types. Thus, it would be desirable to follow from birth a random sample of the population, noting along the way the genetic inheritance, early childhood behaviours, parental training methods, peer group, school and work influences, actual criminal behaviours, the social response to those behaviours and the effects of such responses on the individual concerned, and so on. All three broad approaches to explanation could then be tested adequately. The constraints of time mean that in practice the choice is between a contemporary or a retrospective study, to be carried out either on a custodial or a non-custodial population. All three approaches to explanation are likely to be tested best on groups as unbiased in composition as possible. This means that research studies should at least include non-custodial populations. Indeed, it could be argued that the combined effects of biased selection and of custodial life might so distort the results of studies of prisoners as to lead research workers to a positive preference for studies of non-custodial groups. However, concentrating solely on persons not in custody would omit many offenders who have carried out the most serious crimes, such as murder. Conversely, studies designed to trace the acquisition of criminal behaviours by those who have not yet offended must be carried out on such individuals and not on existing offenders, whether in custody or not.

Clearly, the nature of the research question will dictate the research strategy adopted. In all cases, research will be most useful and most generalizable when sampling bias is kept to a minimum. The data reviewed in this chapter have made it clear that samples of offenders in custody suffer from rather severe selection bias. It is essential for research workers to be aware of this problem, and to design explanatory studies of criminal behaviour so as to reduce the effects of bias to the smallest degree possible. It follows that research workers should make considerable use of the self-report method of selecting people for study and that refinements in the standardization, reliability and validity of the method are urgent priorities.

Chapter 2

Learning Not to Offend: Childhood Experience and Training

Introduction

In accounting for criminal behaviour, psychologists have tended to fall into two camps. The first, which we shall deal with in this chapter, has emphasized failures in the acquisition of attitudes and behaviours opposed to criminal acts. The second, which we shall consider in the next chapter, emphasizes the positive acquisition of criminal attitudes and behaviours—learning to offend rather than failure to learn not to offend.

There are two emphases in work on the failure to acquire socially acceptable behaviours. One is rather sparse on detail of the socialization process, emphasizing instead that providing the right broad conditions are available moral development will occur almost inevitably. Thus Piaget and Kohlberg have spelled out the sequence of development; Bowlby has insisted on the biological mother–child bond as both a necessary, even sufficient, condition for effective socialization. Other workers have concentrated on what parents actually do in training their children and have related parental rearing practices to criminal or non-criminal outcomes. A detailed account of the process of social training has been given by Aronfreed. Both of the above emphases agree on the crucial importance of parent–child interactions. A few workers have drawn attention to the total resources available to the family, particularly economic resources. Finally, there is an increasing tendency to regard the direction of effect between parents and children as two-way, rather than inevitably from parents to children. All workers in the 'socialization camp' have concentrated on relatively young children learning social rules from their parents; other social settings have received little or no attention—except for that form of the adolescent peer group termed the gang which we mention in Chapter 8. The present chapter is concerned with failures to learn social rules by children in general. In the next section of the book, Chapters 5, 6 and 7 take up the question of individual differences in responsiveness to social training.

Moral Development

There are two major descriptive systems of moral development, those of Piaget and Kohlberg, both of which explicitly assume the unfolding of a sequence of changes roughly correlated with age as the individual matures, changes which are largely independent of specific learning experiences but arise from the inherent structure of human cognitive functioning. It has been asserted that such systems of moral development have a biological basis: 'A large number of biological mechanisms undoubtedly conspire to provide the precondition for moral conduct' (Hogan, 1973, p. 218). Hogan provides no empirical evidence for his assertion.

The Piagetian View

Piaget (1932) developed a theory of moral development within the context of his monumental researches, which have extended over the past half-century, into cognitive development in general. He argues that the capacity to act adaptively is bound up with the attainment of a knowledge of the world. There are three principal stages in cognitive development. During the first, from age 2 to age 7 and termed the pre-operational stage, actions are internalized as thoughts, and tend to precede thought. Events are perceived in absolute, not relative terms. This is preeminently the stage of *ego-centrism*, during which others are perceived to revolve around the self. The second, from 7 to adolescence, is termed the stage of *concrete operations*. During this stage the child is capable of operational thinking (making comparisons between events and relating them to each other). In the third stage, which begins with adolescence, the child is able to carry out formal *cognitive operations*, such as comparing possible future relationships and events.

Relating this general structure to moral development, Piaget characterizes the first stage as the one in which rules are given by powerful others, the second in which children perceive that they can invent and modify rules, and the third in which they perceive the primacy of abstract rules over the particular situation. There will tend to be a time lag, according to his general approach, 'practical morality' (the behavioural component) preceding 'theoretical morality' (the attitudinal component).

Kohlberg's Theory

This theory (Kohlberg, 1964) is more complex and more detailed than Piaget's, and consists of six stages, in three blocks of two stages each. Like Piaget's theory, each is age-related, although Kohlberg tends not to specify the age concerned, simply emphasizing the sequential ordering of the stages.
A. The pre-moral period
Stage 1. Moral behaviour is largely predicated on the basis of avoiding punishment.
Stage 2. The hedonistic stage. Each person seeks the maximum return to himself largely irrespective of the return to the other.
B. The period of conventional conformity to rules
Stage 3. Persons conform and adjust to others.

Stage 4. There is respect for and a duty to authority, such as social and religious authority, and an avoidance of censure by authority.

C. The morality of self-accepted principles. The period of autonomy

Stage 5. The primacy of contracts, individual rights, democratically derived and self-accepted principles and laws.

Stage 6. The full development of a morality of individual and universal principles which may transcend those of the existing legal systems (e.g. the concept of an 'illegal military order', such as to shoot women and children).

An Overview of Systems of Moral Development

Aronfreed (1968) has listed the features which the systems of Piaget and Kohlberg have in common.

1. Both systems employ the same research method. They elicit from children their rationale for their judgments of specific acts, frequently using as test stimuli hypothetical situations.

2. There is a sequence of age-correlated changes, summarized as follows.

(a) The judged severity of a transgression is first related to the amount of visible damage and later shifts to the intention of the transgressor.

(b) The younger child has a concept of immanent (given) justice. The older child relates the severity of a transgression to its consequences for others. For the younger child the scale of punishment is a function of the severity of the offence, whereas the older one takes into account attempts at restitution.

(c) Finally, there is a transition from a concept of the rules as fixed and immutable to one whereby they are seen as relative to persons and situations and mutually alterable.

In general, the younger child only takes into account what is good or bad for the actor. The older child makes a gradual shift from social conformity, through the need to take the welfare of others into account, to the highest stage of intrinsic concepts of right and wrong.

Rest *et al.* (1969) successfully replicated a study by Turiel (1966) which demonstrated that while children could be moved rather easily from a particular stage of moral development to one stage higher by suitable training experiences, it was much more difficult to move them in the reverse direction. Attempts to move them more than one stage higher were largely successful. These studies imply that there is both a certain *directionality* in movement as well as some restraint on the rate of development. However, a number of studies indicate considerable doubt about the similarity of the level reached within different social groups, as well as the *inevitability* of progress irrespective of specific learning experiences, as the following results indicate.

Although the general finding is one of a shift from an external to an internal orientation, this is slower in working-class than in middle-class children (Gold, 1958; Kohlberg, 1969) even after intellience-test scores have been controlled. Aronfreed (1968) suggests that the social class difference relates to the different child-rearing techniques used by working- and middle-class parents, the latter more frequently training post-transgression self-criticism (Aronfreed, 1961, see below), thought to be a major source of internalization. Among adults, McCord and Clemes (1964) found differences in moral judgments between groups of adults differing in their degree of commitment to religious and political institutions. Klinger *et al.* (1964) reported that children of both sexes were more lenient in judging dishonest behaviour when the offender was of the same sex as themselves than when he or she was of the opposite sex. College students attributed more responsibility to the offender for a severe accident when they lacked information as to intention than when more of the circumstances were known (Walster, 1966). Walster (1967) failed to replicate her earlier finding concerning the factors controlling the attribution of responsibility for an accident, as did Shaver (1970a, b). Nevertheless, the overall tenor of all the above studies strongly supports the importance of specific situational variables as affecting moral judgments.

Apparent support was found for the similarity of moral development across groups subject to different social influences in an Israeli study by Kugelmass and Breznitz (1967). They compared large numbers of children who had grown up in cities with those who were *kibbutz* (collective settlement) reared, the latter thought to be exposed much more strongly to peer group influences and less to the influences of parents. They found no difference in the use of the concept of intention in moral evaluations. However, there are other major differences between city and *kibbutz* settings which could complicate the comparison; the latter is a rural, not an urban, community, and its general ethos centres around collective rather than individual norms. A more satisfactory study would be one carried out on children from one type of social setting, subjected to the same parental training method, but exposed to different levels of peer influence.

Particularly damaging to the view that moral development is independent of the specifics of the situation is a study by Boehm and Nass (1962) which found that the stage of development reached by children aged 6 to 12, as indicated by Piaget's method of estimation, varied with the *particular* hypothetical situation used, suggesting the importance of the specific prior learning experiences peculiar to each of the situations.

There is considerable evidence that far from being stable and dependent only on the stage of development attained, moral judgments are readily modifiable using standard techniques and situations. Values have been shown to change under stress experiences (Lifton, 1961) and in response to social influence techniques (Brock and Buss, 1964). Bandura and McDonald (1963) showed that observational learning changed moral judgments. Lefurgy and Walshin (1969) found that in group situations, planned so that the rest of the group were at one stage above or one stage below the level of moral development of the remaining member, the latter adjusted up or down, to fit the majority. The effects of the conformity experience were detectable up to 100 days later. By contrast, Keasey (1973) found that exposing children to conflict resulted in little movement beyond the moral level previously reached. Exposure to a model resulted in more movement, but this had little long-term effect (over a period of several weeks). It is likely that a number of exposures would have produced more movement than only one presentation. Both acquisition and retention tend to be greater for several repetitions of a given stimulus. Apparent support for the developmental approach is provided by two studies which are relevant both to the stages versus learning controversy as well as to explanatory theories of crime. In a study by Kohlberg (1969), judges who rated prisoners' statement about the morality of offending behaviour agreed that they fell at levels 1 and 2 of Kohlberg's sequence (see above). However, as no comparison group of other adults was used, this finding is of little value. Fodor (1972) compared the mean moral development level of 40 official delinquents and 40 non-delinquents matched for age, ethnic group, IQ and mother's educational level, using Kohlberg's standard procedure. The qualitative moral level of the delinquents was significantly lower, although the mean scores of both groups placed them in stage 3, indicating that the difference was statistical, not substantive. There appear to be no studies of the relationship between self-reported offending and moral development level.

We can draw a number of major conclusions from the research on stages of moral development. First, the stages may be successive, but they are acquired through learning, and the direction of development may also be reversed by appropriate learning experiences. Second, both the rate of change and the occurrence of change are not inevitable, but are dependent on specific experiences. Third, both major approaches fail to specify the process by which the hypothesized successive structures of conscience are acquired—beyond Kohlberg's assumption that the child spontaneously integrates the structures from social situations. Any satisfactory theory of socialization must make it clear how social training experience alter attitudes and behaviours and what are the different consequences of different kinds of experiences.

Maternal Deprivation

As Morgan (1975) points out, the maternal deprivation theory has had a considerable and far-reaching influence both on social policy and on the training and professional practice of social workers and other agents of social policy. 'However intolerable the child's home conditions, complete separateness is thought to have effects even more intolerable' (Morgan, 1975 p. 15). The originator of the theory and its continuing major influence is John Bowlby.

Bowlby's Contribution: Assertions and Studies

Bowlby's views are set out trenchantly in the following assertions. The first states the child's need for maternal affection, the second relates deprivation of affection to the development of criminal or psychopathic behaviours.

1. 'Essential for mental health is that a child should experience a warm, intimate, and continuous relationship with his mother (or permanent mother substitute) in which both find satisfaction and enjoyment.' Maternal deprivation

is defined as 'a state of affairs in which a child does not have this relationship'. (Both quotations from Bowlby and Salter-Ainsworth, 1965, pp. 13–4.)

2. 'Maternal separateness and parental rejection are believed together to account for a majority of the more intractable cases (of delinquency) including the "constitutional psychopaths" and the "moral defectives"' (Bowlby, 1949, p. 37).

The link between deprivation and crime is provided by the assertion that deprivation powerfully damages the ability to form affectionate relationships with others—who may then be damaged without remorse. The deprived child becomes the affectionless thief. Bowlby has further asserted (Bowlby and Salter-Ainsworth, 1965, p. 54) that the affectionless character can arise from lack of opportunities to form a stable attachment to a mother figure in the first three or four years of life, limited (three to six months) periods of deprivation in the first three or four years, or changes from one mother figure to another in the same period. The distinction between total and partial deprivation of the same mother and changes from one to another is often lost in the studies carried out to test the basic hypothesis, but *all three* types of experience are asserted as causal, separately or in combination.

Bowlby has himself contributed two empirical studies. The first was published in 1946. Bowlby collected a group of children he had seen at a child guidance clinic, who had been reported as stealing, and compared them with a control group equal in number and similarly referred to the clinic but not for stealing. He reported two major findings: there were 14 'affectionless characters' among the thieves, none among the controls; 17 of the thieves (12 in the 'affectionless' group) had suffered complete and prolonged separation from their mothers *versus* only two of the controls. Thus, there was an apparent strong association between separation, affectionlessness and thieving. However, the study was methodologically deficient in a number of ways.

1. The children were referred for stealing by a variety of sources, but mainly by parents and not the courts. They were not a random sample of children who appear in the juvenile courts.

2. Neither thieves nor controls were typical of the general child population—a third showed exceptionally high intelligence.

3. Combining 1 and 2, the majority of both groups were parent-referred, in the days in which parental referrals tended to be almost entirely from middle-class settings.

4. No check of stealing was made in the control group.

5. The control group was a control only in the sense that their ages and levels of intelligence fell within the upper and lower limits of those of the delinquent group. There was no attempt at either random selection of the control group or proper yoked matching.

6. The designation of personality—affectionless, etc.—was based entirely on Bowlby's unstructured clinical interviews, which were not carried out blind (without knowledge of whether the child was a thief or not).

7. The appellation 'affectionless' was supposed to indicate lack of normal

affection to anyone. Nevertheless, as Morgan (1975) points out, Bowlby's detailed description of several of the affectionless group makes clear that they had affection for grandparents, siblings, friends, etc. The common factor, which seem to have earned the appellation, is a lack of affection for the *mother* — or, more precisely, the mother's *belief* that this was the case. Morgan (1975) comments, 'Grandfathers, babies, sisters, other children, appear to be disqualified as objects of normal affection' (p. 45).

Some time later, Bowlby *et al.* (1956) carried out a further study to test the link between deprivation and affectionless delinquency. They compared 60 children who had entered a sanatorium for tuberculous patients before the age of four with a sample of school classmates of like age and sex. The length of separation ranged from six to 21 months and the ages at follow-up from six years and 10 months to 13 years and seven months. Comparisons at follow-up were made of IQ scores, behaviour in the IQ test situation and teachers' answers to a two-part questionnaire concerning the child's school behaviour. The first part concerned the child's relationship with the teacher and other children; the second allowed the teacher to note symptoms observed and to comment on the child and his family. The results were rather disappointing from the viewpoint of the maternal deprivation theory—none of the differences between the sanatorium children and the controls reached statistical significance, with the exception of behaviour in the IQ-testing situations. However, the IQ scores actually attained did not appear markedly affected. The most important comparison, that based on teachers' reports, showed no difference between the groups. Bowlby and his colleagues were doubtful of the reliability of some of the reports and subjected them to scrutiny, unreliable ones being discarded. A reanalysis of the reports judged reliable indicated that 11 of the 28 items showed as more maladjusted for the sanatorium group. However, only five of these 11 comparison items achieved statistical significance—to do with daydreaming, being rough and not being competitive. These results are hardly, as Morgan (1975) points out, evidence for great personality damage. Moreover, the lack of controls exercised—the teachers knew which children had been to the sanatorium—and the secondary selection by the researchers render this study of doubtful scientific value.

Several other studies have attempted to test the maternal deprivation theory. The results of some support the theory. Wardle (1961) studied children attending a child guidance clinic, and found that those who were stealing, or otherwise behaving badly, came significantly more often than non-delinquents from broken homes, had a higher incidence of separation from mother of more than six months' duration, and more frequently had parents who themselves came from broken homes. Koller (1971) found a greater frequency of parental loss in training schools, again in Britain, than in a comparison group. Chilton and Markle (1972) compared the home backgrounds of over 5000 children who figured in the juvenile court records of the United States and who had attracted a charge classed as serious with those of the general US juvenile population. There was a significantly increased tendency for the delinquent group to come from families which were incomplete (only one parent present) or disrupted (by death or divorce). By contrast, using groups less open to selection bias, Naess (1959) found no greater incidence of separation among offenders than non-offenders. Rutter (1971) found no raised incidence of anti-social conduct among children separated from one parent. Little (1965) tested whether, among youths in Borstal, those with a history of loss of parents or separation from parents had a greater likelihood of reconvictions. His conclusions were almost completely negative. Although an unexpectedly high incidence of separations was noted (over four-fifths had experienced separation from one or both parents in childhood) no significant connections were found between the presence, timing or severity of the parental deprivations and the likelihood of reconviction and the nature of the offences committed.

Unfortunately, all the above studies, both those supporting the theory and those contradicting it, used official convictions as the basis for membership of their group of offenders, and frequently the additional attribute of incarceration in a correctional institution. Homes described as 'deprived' may make less vigorous attempts to maintain their children at home following conviction. The police may be more inclined to prosecute a child from a 'bad' environment. Coming from a 'bad' home may in itself markedly raise the likelihood of receiving an institutional type of sentence. The great frequency of separation experiences is shown by a study by Douglas and Bromfield (1958) using the British National Sample of 5380 children born in one week in March, 1946. One in three had been separated from their mothers for at least a week before the age of four and a half.

It can be concluded that scientific support for the maternal deprivation theory is very much less impressive than the major influence of the theory on social policy would lead one to expect. There is probably nothing unique about the biological mother, simply that she is liely to be the most familiar adutlt figure, the one most frequently and reliably associated with comfort and relief from anxiety (Rutter, 1972). In operant language, deprivation from the familiar is equivalent to the withdrawal of positive reinforcers, and is experienced as subjectively distressing. The more regular the previous schedule, the more distressing will be a *sudden* and *total* withdrawal.

However, before leaving this topic we might note a number of carefully conducted animal studies, the best known of which are the work of Harlow and his associates (e.g. Harlow, 1965; Seay *et al.*, 1964). They have shown very clearly that monkeys reared apart both from their natural mothers and from other monkey peers made extremely ineffectual mothers who were, in fact, overtly aggressive to their own offspring. Harlow showed that the harmful effects of being reared apart from the mother were largely mitigated by being reared with other infant monkeys and, moreover, that the motherless monkey mothers who were inadequate with their first offspring were much more adequate with their second offspring.

In a series of studies, Miller and his colleagues (see Miller, 1967, for an overview) showed that monkeys previously trained in individual avoidance conditioning could then serve as a stimulus for a second monkey in a co-operative avoidance conditioning study. The facial distress of the first monkey was communicated over closed-circuit television to the second monkey, who performed an avoidance response which enabled the stimulus animal to avoid an impending shock. Next, Miller *et al.* (1967) showed that monkeys reared apart from their mothers from birth were much inferior to normally reared monkeys in the cooperative avoidance situation, both as stimulus and as response subjects. Their inferiority was particularly marked when they served as the response animal. It is of interest that the reared-apart animals were not inferior to the normally reared animals in prior individual avoidance learning. This general area of research is important enough to require a considerably higher quality of work than it has attracted hitherto. It is to be hoped that human studies will be carried out with the combination of vigour and imagination which characterizes the animal studies discussad above.

Finally, the maternal deprivation theory asserts that the mother–child bond is not only a necessary condition for the acquisition of personal behaviour, it is also a sufficient one. While there is a strong suggestion (Feldman, 1976a) that the efficacy of the training methods of the behaviour therapies is enhanced by a good 'relationship' between therapist and patient, it is highly unlikely that the effects of these therapies can be accounted for entirely, even largely, in such terms. A good relationship may or may not be a necessary condition for effective therapy; it is certainly not a sufficient one. The effective social training of children may also be found to be enhanced by a good relationship, but it is unlikely that love will be all that is needed. The maternal deprivation theory omits any consideration of the process of social training or the methods of training. Our review of the work on moral development made clear the importance of specific learning experiences. We next turn our attention to the questions of process and of method.

Childhood Socialization

The most detailed and carefully worked out learning-based approach to socialization is that of Aronfreed (1968). The socialization approach concentrates on the social response to the individual who has broken a rule. Aronfreed's account is more a prescription for what would constitute effective social training, if systematically carried out, than a description of what parents and other trainers actually do.

It is important to remind ourselves that Aronfreed, in common with everyone else in the field, concentrates solely on the pre-adult stage of life, and most particularly on the pre-adolescent stage, as being crucial for the development of social behaviours which then (by implication) remain unchanged for the rest of the life-span. This is to the exclusion of the later influence of friendship groups, the work situation and the wider culture.

We begin with a discussion of the general concept of internalization before proceeding to the major mechanisms of (child) socialization.

The Concept of Internalization

Aronfreed (1968) argues that large areas of social behaviour can be brought under internalized control even without the involvement of evaluative cognitions—that is, without awareness that one is functioning independently of external cues. However, evaluative cognitions increase the likelihood of internalization as well as its strength. Behavioural suppression may be maintained for long periods, even under circumstances in which suppression is no longer appropriate and may even have aversive consequences, for example the self-punitive behaviour conventionally termed masochism (Sandler, 1964). However, in many situations suppression may be assisted by minimal levels of warning cues, or by their representation in fractional form, for example a sign representing a pedestrian crossing, as opposed to a physically present policeman. The development of internalization is assisted both by attaching anxiety to forbidden behaviour and by positive reinforcements for acceptable behaviours. Other persons tend to be sources of such reinforcements, hence the importance of the level of predisposition to repond to social reinforcement (see the discussion of Eysenck's theory in Chapter 6). The availability of social reinforcement is also important. Such reinforcement is conveyed by a very wide range of cues which transmit approval or disapproval. Even the absence of an overt reaction by a control agent may convey approval or disapproval—by contrast with his preceding reaction (Offenbach, 1966). Children are still affected by such cues even when they may not be able to verbalize them. Moreover, socially transmitted warning signals act as reinforcing safety signals for alternative responses to a punishable transgression (Aronfreed, 1964). They signal that the alternatives adopted are acceptable. The whole sequence of behaviour comes under internal control.

Behaviours acquired under partial or delayed reinforcement are more resistant to extinction than those acquired under continuous or immediate reinforcement, and so are more likely to be internalized. Well-established avoidance behaviours are maintained by infrequent and possibly unpredictable 'booster' trials—external cues do not suddenly disappear once internal control has been established. Thus the maintenance of internal control is assisted by the occasional pairing with punishment, by a social agent, or such social stimuli as the facial indication of irritability. The suppression of unacceptable behaviours may facilitate the development of suitable alternative responses, particularly if these are modelled and subsequently directly reinforced, or if they are already in the individual's repertoire. It should be noted that Aronfreed appears to use the term punishment to include both negative reinforcement (the withdrawal of positive reinforcers) and the application of an aversive stimulus. Many learning theorists reserve 'punishment' for the latter situation. Aronfreed uses reward as an equivalent term to 'positive reinforcer'.

Essentially, 'internalization' refers to a progressively reduced dependence on external surveillance. The process is assisted by the ability to represent symbolically the relationship between an act and its outcome and the connections between verbal and emotional signals (for example, 'He has suggested that we steal, I feel frightened at the thought'). Verbal labelling, which is partially related to intelligence and to age, enhances the development of emotional responses.

The control of overt behaviours (including avoiding a forbidden stimulus) is enhanced by verbalizing the probable outcomes. Whereas delaying a reward is assisted by avoiding signals related to the pleasurable consequences to come, avoiding punishable behaviours is enhanced by the opposite—exposing oneself to signals about the unpleasant consequences of transgression and the future punishment (Walters, 1964). Attending to such signals may be enhanced either by prior instruction (Fagan and Witryol, 1966) or by increasing the attention-gaining quality of punishment-related stimuli during the delay period (Brackbill, 1964.)

Once it is well established, skill in the use of language enables internalized control to be built on the earlier acquired external control, particularly by bridging the long delays which sometimes occur between behaviours and their consequences. There is a continuing interaction between internal and external cues to behaviour. External cues provide reminders of responses the control of which has become internalized, an example being the receipt of occasional exhortations to apologize for misdemeanours. Conversely, the avoidance of external cues due to overriding internal control may maintain a behaviour which is no longer appropriate, for example an irrational fear of a neutral situation such as heights or open spaces, or the maintenance of sexual taboos despite changing social *mores*. Internal control is broadened by generalization to cues on the same stimulus dimension and strengthened by cognitive (i.e. 'internal') rehearsal. Feldman and McCulloch (1971) argued that the differences they found between clients in response to the aversion therapy of sexual deviations could be accounted for in part by learned or innate individual differences in the cognitive rehearsal, outside the treatment situation, of the events which occurred in treatment. Another difference between successful and unsuccessful clients was that within the sessions of treatment the former learned avoidance responses to formerly attractive stimuli both more rapidly and more consistently. A study by Bandura and Jeffery (1973) indicates that both effective learning and rehearsal improve the retention of responses more than either alone. In general, more anxious and obsessional (and probably more introverted) persons, as in the Feldman and McCulloch series, may rehearse more frequently and intensely. Meichenbaum and Goodman (1971) found that training children to 'talk to themselves' assisted in the development of self-control in avoiding transgression. The effectiveness of covert cognitive rehearsal in enhancing overt behaviour rehearsal has also been shown by McFall and Lillesand (1971). Greenwald (1967) reported that the persisting effects of a verbal message are partially accounted for by an individual rehearsing his own cognitive reactions to the communication. Finally, it seems likely that there are individual differences in the content of what is rehearsed, based on individual differences in attention to the content of incoming information. Some persons tend to be inattentive to pleasant information, others to unpleasant information (Merbaum and Kazaoka, 1967). Training offenders not only in general habits of cognitive rehearsal but in attending to and rehearsing unpleasant events will be relevant to the control of criminal behaviour, particularly if the punishing consequences of transgressions are presented together with rewarded socially sanctioned alternatives.

Internal and external modes of control should be seen as lying on the same dimension rather than as quite separate modes. There may be a link between the typical mode of social control involved for the particular individual and his position on the locus of control dimension (the generalized expectancies held for the relationship between one's own behaviours and their outcomes, Rotter, 1966). Perceived control over outcomes may compensate, for example, for a delay in the receipt of a reward, perhaps even for the occurrence of an aversive outcome. There may be a reciprocal balance between internal and external control, in that when one is deficient the presence of the other will compensate for it. Those particularly responsive to social reinforcement may be more likely to violate rules when direct external constraints are absent and the receipt of social reinforcement is contingent on rule-breaking (Lesser and Abelson, 1959; Retting and Sinha, 1966). Finally, such external reactions to transgression as confession or apology (see below) seem more under the actual or anticipated control of social agents than under internal control.

Mechanisms of Socialization

Again we follow largely the account given by Aronfreed (1968). He sees the two crucial bases for socialization as being the changes in affective tone which are associated with the learning process central to socialization and an exposure to a social environment. In other words, the presence of a social context within which learning may occur and the actual occurrence of learning experiences, particularly those of the classical conditioning type, which are appropriate both in form and content. Internalization then depends upon the transfer of changes in 'affectivity' (affective tone) from external to internal reactions. The sequence is: (a) cues are produced in the course of the child's own performance; (b) symbolic, cognitive cues develop which gradually become independent of (a). The child encounters environmental stimuli which are either positive or aversive in content and arouse either positive or aversive states in the child. Some stimuli may correlate with unlearned predispositions, for example those associated with the presence or absence of a nurturant person (mother, nursemaid, etc., Maccoby, 1966). Next, the outcomes of specific overt behaviour may be either reinforcing or suppressing. Such outcomes relate both to the child's own behaviour (behaviour-contingent learning) and to that of others (observational learning). In both cases the outcomes may be reproduced cognitively by the child when the appropriate external cues next appear. Hence, internal control takes over from external control.

The same act, particularly in real life, may have either positive or aversive outcomes—or both together, for example in adult life, a theft which yields a good financial return but also a prison sentence. Which outcome becomes most strongly part of the individual's repertoire, hence influencing more strongly his future behaviour, depends partly on the time relationships between the two outcomes; a punishment which follows an earlier positive outcome will be less aversive than the total absence of a positive outcome. Prior experiences in delay of reward situations (Mischel, 1968) will also play a part. If delays in the past have been followed reliably by rewards, they will be less aversive both in the present and in the future than if the individual has previously experienced the unreliability of an eventual reward. In fact, the delay of well-established rewards enhances the resistance to extinction of the rewarded behaviours, provided that the delay response has already been acquired. Behaviour suppression is also assisted by time-out from an established schedule of reward. Responses associated with infrequent and inconsistent initial punishment —allowing frequent reward opportunities—are rather resistant to suppression. Such a schedule of social training may contribute to the development of psychopathic types of behaviour (see Chapter 7).

While a combination of punishments to suppress undesired behaviours and positive reinforcers to strengthen desired ones results in the most effective socialization, studies with children suggest that punishment alone, for bad behaviour, may be more effective than the sole use of positive reinforcement for good behaviour (Penney, 1967). However, such findings may depend on the relative levels of intensity of the rewards and punishments used. For example, low levels of punishment may suppress behaviours less effectively than high levels of reward positively reinforce them, and *vice versa*. The balance of the rewards and costs, encountered both in previous learning experiences and in the current situation, is crucial. Whereas delayed reward enhances the resistance to extinction of reliably rewarded responses, delayed punishment is less effective in suppressing behaviour than immediate punishment, although the development of language and the provision of cues signalling eventual punishment helps to bridge the gap. The efficacy of later punishment is reduced by prior experiences of lower levels of punishment which proved ineffective in suppressing the behaviour concerned. This is analogous to the concept of immunization against persuasion (McGuire, 1969 and see Chapter 3). A subjectively experienced, and to some degree objectively measurable, state of discomfort and distress termed anxiety frequently becomes attached to the receipt of punishment, depending on a number of factors considered below, most of which relate to the temporal relationship between the occurrence of punishment and the experience of anxiety (Aronfreed, 1968). In the listing which follows, the term transgression refers to behaviour which is punishable, such punishment being unpleasant enough to produce a perceptible degree of anxiety. When subsequent transgressions are contemplated they evoke anxiety, which is attached to anticipatory thoughts and other precursors of the previously punished act, as well as to its overt performance. Central to this discussion is the two-process theory of learning (Mowrer, 1960) according to which the first stage in the learning of avoidance is the classical conditioning of anxiety to external or internal cues for behaviour, as a result of punishment. The second stage is that those behaviours which are effective in the reduction of anxiety are reinforced, because anxiety reduction is pleasurable. Examples of such acts include not carrying out the punished response, as well as carrying it out but avoiding external punishment.

Aronfreed makes a number of key points.

1. The closer its occurrence to the beginning of a transgression, the greater is the increment of anxiety. This means that punishment received very early during the commission of a forbidden act evokes more anxiety than punishment received later in the response sequence, or after it has been completed.

2. A corollary of 1. The more punishment is delayed, the less anxiety is evoked (shown in animals by Azrin, 1956 and in children by Aronfreed and Reber, 1965). Delay of punishment also reduces the extent of internalization. The probability of turning to an alternative behaviour, such as preferring a previously unattractive object to an attractive one which has been associated with punishment, is also inversely related to the delay of punishment; the longer the delay, the less likely is the punished person to turn to the previously unattractive alternative. Finally, suppression is enhanced by the provision of cues (advance warning signals) which indicate that punishment may be avoided by performing alternative responses. Thus, for the most effective outcome of punishment, not only provide alternatives, but make sure the person knows that they are at hand.

3. However, if a social agent interferes so early that the undesired behaviour is not performed at all, suppression is less effective (Burton et al., 1961). The experience of an association between punishment and the undesired behaviour is required for effective suppression, particularly for suppression to generalize to associated undesired behaviours. Once punishment has been experienced and escaped by performing a rewarded alternative response, anticipatory warning signals enabling punishment to be avoided may be introduced.

4. In some contradistinction to the above points, the cognitive representation of punishment by language tends to reduce the crucial importance of the exact timing of punishment. Aronfreed (1966) showed in children that a delayed punishment, made during the delay between transgression and punishment, resulted in greater suppression than no delay, but no verbal statement. To resolve the apparent contradiction, it is possible that the most effective suppression of all would be achieved by a condition Aronfreed did not use—immediate punishment accompanied by a relevant verbal statement which would then give the punishment a verbal 'label' and assist the transfer of training to other situations (Kendler, 1968). A discussion of the role of negative reinforcement in promoting behaviour change is given in Chapter 10 in the context of psychological approaches to the control of criminal behaviour.

Cognitive and Emotional Reactions to Transgression

Aronfreed (1968) largely restricted his account to the reactions of children to their completed transgressions, but we shall extend the discussion to include the reactions which are typically encountered in adults, as well as dealing with anticipatory reactions to future transgressions.

The development of reactions to transgression depends on training by socializing agents. They do not develop in a social vacuum. Eventually such reactions become internalized, are represented cognitively and are relatively independent of external surveillance. Both in dogs (Solomon *et al.*, 1968) and in children (Aronfreed and Reber, 1965) anxiety is greater when punishment occurs later than when it occurs early in the course of a transgression, so that reactions to transgression, the purpose of which is anxiety reduction, are more likely in the former case. The future avoidance of a transgression is more likely if the punishment occurs early, as opposed to later, in the course of a transgression. The cognitive settings in which they are learned help to determine the effectiveness of reactions to transgression in reducing post-transgression anxiety. Finally, as with behaviours in general, both behaviour-contingent and observational learning experiences are relevant to the development of reactions to transgression.

1. *Self-criticism.* According to Aronfreed (1968), this is the most common reaction to transgression by children. The child may come to prefer the component of punishment represented by self-criticism to the experience of anxiety generated by the anticipation of punishment by an adult; hence it is the verbal component of punishment which the child reproduces. Aronfreed (1964) showed that attaching a verbal label to a punished behaviour (in effect an operational definition of self-criticism) increases the use of the label by children in response to the transgressions they commit. Aronfreed *et al.* (1963) showed that the explicit provision of relevant verbal labels during punishment facilitated self-criticism after future transgressions. The use of labels is highly resistant to extinction (Aronfreed, 1964). Hence, self-criticism is acquired through the child's experience of the association between the verbal element of a punishment and the termination of its anticipatory anxiety through the use of the label. Other things being equal, a nurturant relationship results in a greater association of anxiety with punishment for transgression—hence a greater anxiety reduction by self-criticism. Thus, a nurturant relationship indirectly fosters the development of self-critical reactions.

2. *Reparation.* This reaction has a corrective nature. It relates to the perception of the effect of a transgression on others and is most clearly evident when material restitution is actually involved. However, the prototype of reparation is affection or concern for the victim. Whether the recipient shares the conviction of the donor that restitution is adequate is, of course, quite another matter, a point taken up in Chapter 4 under the heading of equity theory. Reparation sometimes takes the form of behaviours largely irrelevant to the transgression

itself, such as volunteering for an unpleasant task (Wallace and Sadalla, 1966). With the increasing acquisition of cognitive resources (related both to age and intelligence), reparation becomes increasingly accurate. Aronfreed (1963) showed that reparation is sensitive to punishment during training, and that it is likely to respond to modelling, particularly by parents, who demonstrate the various means of 'making up' for what has been done.

In a series of experiments, Freedman *et al.* (1967) induced subjects to lie or to cause others unnecessary trouble, and found them more ready afterwards to do people favours. However, if these required being with the people they had harmed, they were less ready to help. These studies suggest that some transgressors (perhaps the less habitual ones) both attempt to balance the offence with a good deed and to avoid contact with the person harmed. If compensation was possible, derogation of the victim was less likely than if it was not possible; moreover, reparation was much more likely to be given if that available exactly matched the damage done than if it exceeded it, or fell short.

3. *Confession.* This refers to a verbal report to another person of one's wrongdoing. In some instances, for example, when someone turns Queen's (States') evidence, confession is highly rewarded by immunity from prosecution, but such a person runs the risk of heavy punishment by those he has incriminated.

The child's use of confession, according to Aronfreed (1968), is dependent on selective reinforcement by parents for such a response and on its effectiveness in avoiding or reducing punishment. Thus: 'I won't punish you if you own up'. But does confession increase the avoidance of future transgression? Perhaps a nurturant relationship, a statement of intent not to repeat the act and the provision of alternative responses, as well as positive reinforcements for adopting such alternatives, are all necessary conditions for a confession to reduce future transgression. Confession may either produce punishment or avoid it, depending on the response of the person to whom confession has been made. If confession is followed only by externally delivered punishment, then it seems less likely to be used in the future—except if the punishment consequent on confession is less severe than the eventual punishment following the discovery of an unconfessed transgression. Clearly, the estimate of such probabilities plays a part in the choice of the reaction to transgression adopted in any current situation.

Reactions to Transgression Related to External Punishment. Such reactions fall into two groups, one related to punishment-seeking the other to punishment-avoiding, the first being less obvious and probably much more rare. According to Aronfreed (1968), punishment-seeking occurs when social experience reinforces a dependence on external punishment and a poor discrimination of cues which distinguish between punished and non-punished behaviour.

The individual first carries out the act, then appreciates that he has done wrong, and lacking such internalized reactions as self-criticism or reparation (or perhaps the means to make restitution) seeks an external source of punishment. Persons who are chronically highly anxious and/or low in intelligence, both features hindering discrimination learning, would be particularly likely to resort to punishment-seeking, as would those who had been provided with particularly poor opportunities for discrimination training. In addition, as noted earlier when we discussed the reaction of confession, some situations may encourage punishment-seeking in order to avoid an even greater punishment. In this case, punishment-seeking is really a form of punishment-avoiding. There is also the situation is which apparent punishment-seeking—the 'I will confess all' type of behaviour—may be highly reinforced by the praise given for 'facing up to the worst'.

In general, punishment avoidance seems a more likely reaction to transgression, particularly when the risk of detection, except through the self-incrimination which results from confession, is perceived as rather low. Punishment avoidance includes hiding the evidence of the transgression and being vigilant to cues of possible punishment, as well as attempting to make impotent the official agents of punishment by threats or bribery.

The various reactions to transgression we have discussed are intended to reduce the anxiety associated with transgression, whether the anxiety stems stems from 'letting down' a person in a nurturant relationship, or simply the fear of punishment. The longer the habitual delay of a punishment, which however is perceived as certain in the long run (based on past experiences that 'you get found out eventually') and the greater the employment of verbal representations of punishment, the less effective in reducing anxiety are the various reactions to transgression. For example, if the transgressor believes it to be true that the Mounties (or the FBI, Scotland Yard, etc.) 'always get their man', he will continue to be plagued by anxiety long past the time of the offence, despite the employment of all the reactions designed to reduce anxiety without increasing the likelihood of detection.

The Role of 'Nurturance'

Children's responses to their own transgressions tend to be those modelled by their parents. Aronfreed considers this to be part of a generalized disposition to reproduce the role of a nurturant model. This rather general view does not account for such specifics of internalized control as exactly which reactions to transgressions are learned. In a very indulgent society there are few constraints. There is thus little opportunity for awareness of transgression and hence internalization relates to the very occasional and temporary withdrawal of existing nurturance. In any kind of society, if there is little nuturance there is no affection to withdraw, so that there is no basis for the deprivation of affection to exert a controlling influence on behaviour. There is some evidence that, providing some minimal level of nurturance exists, the withdrawal of affection is a component of most, if not all, forms of punishment of children by parents. Sears et al. (1957) found the frequency of the use of affection withdrawal as a control technique to be correlated with internalization, but only in the cases of children whose parents were generally nurturant towards them. Hence, an early childhood grossly marked by rejection and aversive experiences in general reduces the effectiveness of the latter use of affection withdrawal either as a threat or as an actual punishment. The converse is also true. Early social attachments to nurturant social agents facilitate the occurrence of empathic and vicarious experiences. In turn, such experiences help the individual to learn not to cause distress to others, as well as to extend help to others in distress. Early training experiences in social cues which indicate the responses of others (such as signals of distress) tend not to acquire empathic value if they are emitted by a non-nurturant mother. In other words, a precondition for learning to care about other people is being cared for oneself, witnessing the caring person in distress and learning how to respond to that distress and so ease it, for example by confessing, providing restitution or by helping in some other way.

It follows that there is a threshold of social nurturance for the establishment of internal control, below which the development of internal control is much less likely, above which such development, while more possible, is not inevitable. Thus we can combine the valuable element of the maternal deprivation approach with the details of the learning experiences necessary for effective socialization. However, both nurturance and rejection (which we considered above under the overall heading of deprivation) are vague terms and require much more detailed, operational definition than they have received to date. Such definitions would place emphasis on social trainers—fathers, peers, etc., as well as mothers—being effective to the extent that they are both evaluated positively by those they train and may either give or withhold valued reinforcers.

Families: Child-training Practices

Techniques of Training

Hoffman and Saltzstein (1967) distinguish three broad techniques.

1. Power assertion. The use of physical punishment and/or the deprivation of material objects or privileges, or the threat of punishment or deprivation.

2. Love withdrawal. The parent more or less openly withdraws affection, for example by ignoring the child, or threatens to withdraw affection.

3. Induction. The parent develops empathic and sympathetic responses by referring to the consequences of the child's action for the parent ('You've upset me', etc.).

The first method is associated with the development of an external orientation, based on the fear of external detection and punishment. The latter two methods are associated with the development of an internal orientation characterized by guilt and an independence of external sanctions (Aronfreed, 1968). There are consistent research findings in support of the greater effectiveness of the love-oriented techniques (methods 2 and 3) in producing an internal orientation (Aronfreed, 1961; Burton et al., 1961; Hoffman and Saltzstein, 1967).

The-last named study is one of the most ambitious and complex published to date and illustrates the difficulties and the shortcomings of this area of research. The level of moral development of children differing in sex and social class was assessed by questionnaire and compared with the discipline technique typically used by their parents as discovered by interview. The highest level of moral development within the middle-class sample was associated with the use of the induction technique, the next with love withdrawal and the lowest with power assertion. In the working-class group, the use of induction was reported rather infrequently and the relationships between technique and moral development were less clear in general, possibly indicating a greater contribution than in middle-class children of such extra-familial influences as the peer group. It should be emphasized that both sets of measures were indirect. Direct observation, both of parent–child interaction and of children's behaviour in a wide variety of temptation situations, would be preferable.

Insofar as the results obtained to date by indirect methods may be confirmed by the more direct research methods advocated above, the possible explanations which have been put forward are of interest, both in accounting for the current data and in organizing more adequate studies in the future. Hoffman and Saltzstein's (1967) listing of these explanations is set out below in summary form. All of them focus on a different aspect of the behaviour of parents in producing differences in level of moral development between children exposed to different methods of training (the highest level being produced by induction, the lowest by power assertion); they may be partially complementary rather than mutually exclusive.

1. The difference in model presented by the parent during the disciplinary encounter. The parent either openly expresses anger or controls anger. The former parent models overt aggressiveness towards others, the latter models the control of aggression. Hence, the use of the overt punishment technique increases the reliance of the child on external control.

2. The duration of punishment. The use of physical punishment or material deprivation rapidly dissipates the parent's anger and relieves the child of guilt rather quickly. By contrast, the love-oriented techniques, being more verbal, extend their effects over longer time-periods; anxiety is less quickly dissipated, so that internal control is more likely to be established.

3. The timing of punishment. In the love-withdrawal method, punishment (more precisely the withdrawal of a reinforcer) terminates when the child engages in a corrective act (confession, reparation, etc.), whereas physical punishment is more likely to start and finish prior to any corrective act.

4. Punishing the child by withholding love has the effect of intensifying the child's effort to retain love by behaving in ways of which the parent approves.

5. The two love-oriented techniques, particularly the one termed induction by Hoffman and Saltzstein (1967), provide the cognitive and emotional resources for examining transgressive actions and correcting them.

The last of the above list is the view held by Hoffman and Saltzstein themselves and by Aronfreed. These workers emphasize very strongly the importance of empathy as an emotional resource, which adds to the aroused need for love the pain which the child experiences vicariously for having harmed another, thus intensifying the motivation to learn rules and control his behaviour. The reason for the greater internalization of control by the love-oriented techniques is thus seen as the lesser dependence of the anxiety they elicit on the physical presence of the socializing agent and on the external contingencies of reinforcement. Those trained by the power-oriented (overt punishment) technique are controlled only by the external risk of punishment. To be continuously effective, this must be both prolonged, intense from the beginning (people readily habituate to very gradually increasing levels of punishment) and certain. 'Internal' punishers are much more likely to be always 'on duty', because we 'carry them around with us', than are external punishers. Finally, the love-oriented techniques focus attention less on punishment than on the behaviours necessary to restore parental affection or reduce parental distress, behaviours which must be carried out by the child himself. The physical punishment version of the power technique does not withdraw something of value, rather it inflicts something disliked, and emphasizes what must *not* be done rather than what *should* be done. The love-oriented techniques, because they emphasize positive responses, more effectively replace transgressions with socially acceptable alternative responses. Persons trained by them are more likely to take responsibility both for redressing transgressions and for avoiding them in the future.

Child-training Techniques and Subsequent Criminal Attitudes and Behaviour

A number of studies have sought to correlate the child-rearing techniques used by parents with later official arrest records.

1. Glueck and Glueck (1950). The home backgrounds of 500 delinquents and 500 matched non-delinquents were studied by interviewing parents and other relatives. The discipline given to offenders was predominantly lax and erratic on the part of the father. Both parents used a great deal of physical punishment and little reasoning and praise. The parents of non-offenders, on the other hand, were described as firm, kindly and consistent, reasoned much more, and much less frequently used physical punishment.

2. McCord et al. (1959). In this study the home backgrounds of 253 boys aged 10, all of whom were expected to become offenders, were investigated. A follow-up of the boys made it possible to compare the homes of those who subsequently offended with the homes of those who did not. Again, lax and erratic discipline, which also involved extreme punitiveness and inconsistent demands, was strongly associated with criminal behaviour.

3. Bandura and Walters (1959). They studied 26 boys with histories of anti-social aggression, most in the care of probation officers, with a matched control group of boys who were neither particularly aggressive nor particularly withdrawn. The mothers of the aggressive boys were less effective at socializing their children and their sons were more attached to them than to their fathers.

Both parents, but especially the father, tended to encourage aggression outside the home but to suppress it with punishment at home. They also made greater use of physical punishments and such verbal assaults as ridicule and nagging, and they reasoned less with their sons.

4. Maleska and Muszynski (1970). Children who admitted stealing were more likely than controls to have parents who used physical punishemt, were intolerant of their needs and uninterested in them.

5. Brigham *et al.* (1967). Fifty-seven out of a total of 350 inmates of a federal correctional institution were selected because they were white literate and not in a work-release programme, and divided by self-report into predominantly solitary and predominantly group offenders. Questionnaires administered to the parents indicated that the mothers of the solitary offenders as compared to those of group offenders were more likely to use the love-withdrawal techniques (although less likely to be loving and more likely to be rejecting). The only difference between the fathers was that those of solitary offenders were more likely to be neglecting. The authors conclude that the mother–son relationship of the (predominantly) middle-class solitary offender is more disturbed than that of the (predominantly) working-class group offenders. However, they do refer to a possible selection bias—middle-class boys are institutionalized only when they are both more criminal in behaviour than working-class offenders and come from more severely rejecting homes.

Four general comments may be made about the above studies. First, all except study 2 relied on retrospective reports. Second, the direction of effect was not controlled for. Punishment techniques may have been resorted to because the child proved not to respond to love-oriented techniques. We return towards the end of this chapter to the major importance of viewing parents and children as reciprocally influencing each other, rather than the direction of effect being one-way. It is necessary, therefore, for research studies of socialization to begin as soon after birth as possible, as well as to use direct observational rather than interview techniques. Third, although the mother may still be the major socializing agent, the father's role may be very much more important than was thought in the past. It follows that observational studies should include that period of the day when father is at home. Fourth, and of particular importance, the fact that parents reported their use of a particular method does not mean that they in fact did so, either exclusively or even mainly, nor that, whatever method was used, it was carried out in the most effective way and, as we have seen, 'effectiveness' subsumes a complex technology of behavioural management.

Several studies have focused on the general cohesiveness of the family unit and the quality of care provided for the children as being more important than the specific training technique used.

Douglas and Ross (1968) examined the relationship between official offending and the home backgrounds as part of the longitudinal study of those born in Britain in the first week of March, 1946. In all, 288 boys (15 per cent of the total) and 35 girls (4 per cent) had been officially cautioned or had been sentenced. The boys were further divided into a 'trival' group (sentenced for non-indictable offences), a 'serious' group (one indictable offence) and a group of 'repeaters' (more than one sentence for an indictable offence). As rated by health visitors, the parents of offenders gave less care to their children than did those of non-offenders, made less use of available medical and social services, lived in worse housing conditions and showed little interest in their sons' educational progress, the disparities between offenders and non-offenders being greater for the serious and repeater groups than for the trivial group. The school behaviour of the former two groups was also worse, as were their school attainments. Both areas of behaviour remained worse throughout their school careers, there being no progressive deterioration, suggesting that the differences had existed at least from the age of 5. While they might have been maintained by teachers, there is no indication that labelling by teachers (see Chapter 8) increased them.

Offending was not associated with having an unemployed father, a mother working, a dead father, or with being separated from parents provided that the boy remained in the same environment with relatives or friends. However, there was a tendency for an increase in the incidence of offending in the children of those separated or divorced if these events occurred before the child was six.

Nye (1958) reported that the family setting of a group of self-reported offenders was one of parental quarrelling and mutual rejection by children and parents. The offender group tended to have differing religious and moral values from their parents. A contrasting picture was found for a comparison group of self-reported non-offenders. Nye argues that this indicates the greater importance of the cohesiveness of the total family setting over specific rearing techniques, but agrees that modelling plays a major role in enabling a cohesive family unit to transmit the desired social values.

The detailed London study of self-reported offending by adolescent boys (Belson, 1975) also enquired into the home background of those interviewed. While a broken home, as usually defined, was not related significantly to offending, there was a strong link with what Belson terms a 'miserable home', rather supporting Nye's conclusion. Parental control (during the boy's first 10 years) over his spare-time activities and associations did not emerge as important. Belson points out that over and above parental control of spare-time activities, all boys go to school, where they may be exposed to social models of stealing. Reinforcing this point is Belson's finding that training in 'not stealing' significantly reduced the level of theft only when such training was received at a relatively intense level from all three of the following sources: home, school and church.

A large-scale prospective study by West and his colleagues has been under way for some years. The first report (West, 1969) outlined the sample of 411 boys aged eight to nine recruited in 1960 from six junior schools in the same area of London, described as 'a typically English working class neighbourhood in the process of slow physical and cultural change'. By the time the boys had reached the age of 14, 7·3 per cent had been convicted by the juvenile court at least once and a rather high proportion were 'known' by the police or teachers to be offenders. Children identified by teachers as 'bad in conduct' at the age of eight (termed the 'acting-out' group) were also low in peer popularity and high on rating scales of neuroticism and extraversion (see Chapter 7). This group (nearly one-fifth of the total sample) were significantly more likely than the rest to be convicted (12·9 per cent *versus* 5·9 per cent). Moreover, one-third of them were described by psychiatric social workers visiting their homes at the age of 14 as displaying 'behaviour problems' as compared to only 4·6 per cent of the remainder. The acting-out group included a higher proportion than the remainder of the sample who were heavily built (see Chapter 5 for the relationship between body-build and offending) dull in intelligence, members of large families, of low socio-economic standard, badly housed and had parents who were 'lax' in discipline, an unstable mother and a father with more than one criminal conviction. West states: 'Socially deprived, unloving, erratic, inconsistent, and careless parents tend to produce badly behaved boys' (p. 197). He emphasizes that the most important single factor discriminating poorly behaved boys and ineffectual parents from peers and neighbours, respectively, was the family social level—a constellation of poor income, poor housing and a large number of children which may precede and hinder effective socialization, a possibility referred to above in the discussion on deprivation and offending. West also points to the possible long-term importance of early labelling in unfavourable terms by teachers and schoolmates.

The objection that their earlier study focused only on officially defined offending is partially avoided in a report by Farrington and West (1971) which used the same sample. They compared the school behaviours at age nine of a group of 51 boys found guilty in juvenile courts between the ages of 10 and 15 and of 32 boys self-reported as 'aggressive' with those of the rest of the sample. Both deviant groups were over-represented in the worst-behaved and under-represented in the best-behaved segment of the total sample as rated by teachers, and both were poorer in educational attainment. Whereas the mothers of the offender sample were rated by social workers as more cruel and neglecting and more involved in marital conflict than those of the sample in general, no such differences were found for the mothers of the aggressive group. However, the home discipline of the two deviant groups, particularly that of the aggressive group, was reported to be more lax than that of the remainder. The authors conclude that official offending is equivalent to self-described aggression, and that both have their origin in social deprivation. Thus it seems that social deprivation increases the difficulty of social training. However, the Farrington and West study did not use self-reported offending (typically stealing) as a dependent measure. West's latest report (Knight and West, 1975) describes the 83 'most delinquent' of the sample when they had reached the ages of 18 to 20, divided into two groups, one termed 'temporary delinquent' who had apparently ceased offending, the other 'continued delinquent' who were still doing so. What distinguished the two groups up to the age of 18? Whereas the continued group had offended for money, usually alone, the temporary group had done so for enjoyment and in groups. The former were of lower socio-economic background and had more family criminality than the latter. No differences were found in questionnaire-measured intelligence or aggression.

The authors conclude that persistent offending results not from personality problems but from poverty and exposure to social influences favourable to offending—the latter was given less emphasis in this group's earlier studies. One promising line of enquiry, only partly followed up, relates to the reward–cost view of offending to be discussed in Chapter 3. Briefly, this suggests that the persistence of criminal behaviour relates to the balance of rewards and costs, both previously experienced and present in the current situation. For example, a lucrative offence, not detected, or attracting only a light sentence, is more likely to be repeated than an offence bringing a poor financial return and a heavy sentence. The 'temporaries' reported the deterrent effect of previously experienced convictions and punishments, but no comparative data are presented for the relative financial returns, the proportion of offences detected and type and severity of punishment received.

The term 'resources' needs to be spelled out. It will include the presence of two parents rather than one, the amount of time parents have readily available for child-training and a knowledge of effective methods of training. A home in which there is only one parent will have fewer resources than an intact one to fight through the legal process, outlined in Chapter 1, at each stage of which there may be a selection bias against the poor and those generally less adequate in coping with the social system. In addition, the remaining parent in a one-parent family has to carry out all the chores usually shared with the spouse; there is simply less time for social training. As a result, the child is not only less under parental surveillance but may spend more time outside the home exposed to peer group influences which may be favourable to criminal behaviour. Hence, the 'fault' is not in parental deficit, but in positive learning experiences outside the home. The same argument applies to families in which there is marital strain. Parents distracted by their own problems have less time to train children consistently and may even welcome the relief from the company of the child afforded by the friends with whom the child can then spend more time. In all families under strain the temptation will be to use those techniques of training which are the least time-consuming but also the least effective—the power- rather than the love-oriented ones.

We next take up the possibility that over and above differences in the resources available for social training and in the method of training used, some children are harder to socialize than others, right from birth.

The Direction of Effects in Socialization

In an important review, Bell (1968) discusses the long-held assumption that the parent is the agent of the overall culture, with the child as the recipient of socialization, a *tabula rasa* ready for the imprint of social training. In fact, many reports indicate the lack of similarity of parental behaviour towards children in the same family, suggesting the contribution of stimulus differences between the children. There is much animal evidence for the selective effects of offspring in influencing parental behaviour. If this is true for animals, whose behaviour is fairly rigid compared to that of humans, even greater effects would be expected in the latter. There is widespread evidence of stimulus control over behaviour in general, and this should be expected to be true in particular instances. Among the features modifying parental behaviour will be several present in children at birth. Bell places most emphasis on congenital differences in person orientation and in assertiveness. For example, those high on the variable of person orientation will attend to parents and thus reinforce social responses emanating from them, so that they will induce relatively high levels of nurturance and will be responsive to the love-oriented types of socialization techniques. The opposite of all of these responses and consequences will be true for those congenitally low on person orientation. Over the course of time, initial differences in person orientation will be enhanced by the reciprocally produced differences in social reinforcement. The control repertoire employed by parents is thus responsive both to cultural demands and to the stimuli and reinforcements provided by the child.

Bell goes on to argue that there are two types of parental control repertoire, both of which relate to culturally transmitted norms: upper-limit control behaviour reduces and redirects behaviour which exceeds parental standards; lower-limit behaviour stimulates the behaviour of children which falls below parental standards. It follows that parents cannot be termed 'permissive' or 'demanding' without a knowledge both of the stimulation provided by the offspring and their own upper and lower control limits. On the basis of these arguments, Bell reinterprets some of the socialization data and theory described earlier. Bandura and Walters' (1959) emphasis on the parental modelling of aggression is replaced by the assumption that the children concerned were congenitally highly assertive and activated upper-level control repertoires which quickly escalated into the use of physical punishment. Next, Aronfreed's (1968) conclusion that an internalized moral orientation is fostered by love-oriented techniques is challenged by the possibility that 'externally controlled' children are congenitally low on person orientation. Hence, the reduced effectiveness of withdrawing social reinforcement (attention or affection) or of an emphasis on socially transmitted distress, the central elements of the love-oriented techniques.

Finally, Bell cites evidence of significant genetic contributions' which cut across age, sex, social class and cultural differences, both to person orientation (Scarr, 1965) and to general vigour and dominance (Vandenberg, 1966). The reduction in behavioural differences between the sexes as social training opportunities are equalized (see Chapter 5) does not in itself invalidate the importance for people in general, irrespective of sex, of predisposing biological contributions to broad areas of behaviour. Ball has established the case for systematic research into the contribution to the socialization process of such predispositions, particularly that relating to person orientation. Research should not only describe parental control behaviours but also the characteristics of the child to which these are applied, as well as the nature of the parent–child interaction, all from a very early age, in fact even before birth. For example, parents hoping for a girl, but obtaining a boy, may treat a male offspring rather differently from parents who initially wanted a boy.

Clearly, the individual characteristics of the child may be very important. Some children may both evoke affection and respond to it more than others. Both 'less lovable' children and children who behave badly because parents spend less time on training them or use relatively ineffective techniques will attract successively less and less parental affection. Hence even if the love-oriented techniques are occasionally used, they will be less effective for the reasons outlined earlier. Thus an unfavourable cycle is set up. What is needed, therefore, is a self-report study on a random sample of the population, which will relate actual offending to indices of the home setting which are based on child–parent interaction observed over a long period of time and described in objective, rather than in blanket, terms such as 'unsatisfactory'. Moreover, the observers should be entirely ignorant of the offending behviour of the children. Such observations should, if possible, antedate the offending career of the child. If the child has been designated, officially, as an offender, and has been found to come from a home which is 'unsatisfactory' in some respect, it may have been the criminal behaviour which disrupted the home life, not the disruption of the home which produced the criminal behaviour. Once again, it is crucial to be aware that the direction of effect may be either way.

The criticisms which have been levelled should not be taken to imply that childhood learning experiences in the home are without importance for future development. Aronfreed's carefully researched and argued account of the socialization process leaves no doubt on that score. However, such experiences in childhood are not of *exclusive* importance; their effects are modifiable both by post-childhood learning as well as by other childhood influences, particularly those of peers.

Social Learning Throughout the Lifespan

The vast majority of socialization research has concentrated on young children learning not to perform forbidden behaviours, the implicit assumptions being that the positive reinforcement of transgression is of less importance than negative reinforcement, that the early years of life are crucial for all types of learning, and that such learning experiences take place in the family setting rather than anywhere else, so that later experiences are of limited consequence. Yet many of the behaviours which people learn arise out of situations which are encountered outside the family, often much later in life, such as the work situation, mixing socially with other adults, and so on. The probable importance of such extra-familial settings in the criminological field is clear from a review by Wootton (1959) of studies concerning the age of the first offence of adult prisoners. A considerable proportion of such prisoners had no record of offending before the age of 21. Unless the members of this group were systematically better at escaping detection than their fellows, the conclusion must be that just as socially acceptable behaviours are learned *throughout* life, so are illegal behaviours. On this note of emphasis on the probable importance of post-childhood social learning experiences we conclude our review of childhood experience and training.

Chapter 3

Learning to Offend : Property and Persons

Introduction

The experimental psychology of learning is readily applicable to the task of explaining the acquisition, performance and maintenance of offences against persons and against property. We shall discuss the processes relevant to the acquisition of these criminal behaviours, drawing on material concerning both observational and response-contingent learning. Next, we shall review the situational variables which influence the performance of criminal behaviours, when we shall emphasize the crucial importance of experienced consequences of the behaviours and the schedules of reinforcement. Learning to offend relates to social settings as well as to specific experiences, and we shall consider some of the scattered material concerning settings. We have divided the relevant material on learning to offend into the two broad categories of offences, but this is largely for the sake of convenience of exposition, or because a particular process or antecedent event has attracted more attention in the one context than in the other. Much of the material to be covered is drawn from laboratory research which provides an analogue for real-life criminal behviours. Some of the data are drawn from studies in field settings, but rather little concerns actual criminal behaviour, reflecting the relative lack of research on real-life crime which has been informed by the methods and findings of experimental psychology. The account which follows may form a useful framework for future research. The laboratory and field studies which are analogous to property offences and person offences have typically been termed *transgression* and *aggression*, respectively. Transgression research relates to the offences described as theft, larceny, housebreaking, forgery and receiving. Although the offence of robbery involves an element of force, it nevertheless is more suitably classed as a property offence for our present purpose because the physical violence used is a means to the acquisition of money or goods. Aggression research relates to such offences as homicide, assault and rape.

Before proceeding to the broad categories of property and persons, it will be useful to overview three areas of basic psychological research of particular relevance to both categories, namely, observational learning, attitude formation and change and two-person and group social situations. All three areas of research relate to the influence of other people on a potential offender.

Social Influence: Research and Relevance

Observational Learning

People may acquire responses either by their own direct experiences (behaviour-contingent learning) or by observing the experiences of others. Thus observational learning is concerned with responses which are acquired without any direct reinforcement to the learner. Instead, he observes the behaviour of another person, termed a *model*.

Bandura (1973) points out a number of reasons for the major importance of observational learning, including avoiding costly mistakes, of obvious relevance to criminal behaviour, and speeding up the rate of learning. The effects of observational learning include the acquisition of new patterns of behaviour, the strengthening or weakening of previously learned inhibitions and the facilitation (in performance) of previously learned responses. In addition, observational learning facilitates the suppression of behaviours previously displayed by the observer (Walters *et al.*, 1965, in children; Lefcourt *et al.*, 1966 in adults).

Observational learning is governed by a number of subsystems. *Attentional processes* require exposure to a model, the selection of relevant behaviours and their accurate perception. A key factor here is the individual's existing associational preference (the 'company he keeps'). For example, compare the differences in the opportunities for the observational learning of criminal behaviours of a boy moving into an area of a city in which most boys are actively criminal and one moving to a Quaker boarding-school in which hardly any of the boys ever offend. Given a range of available models, which of them will attract most attention depends on the results the actions of the various models typically produce for himself and others, those externally evident symbols of status which indicate the greatest degree of competence and success and the interpersonal attraction each model evokes. Exposure to several competing models will reflect the final outcome of the above attributes. In general, selective attention is given to those features of a model's behaviour which are the most positively reinforced by his environment and hence will be perceived as most potentially reinforcing for the observer. Finally, and of great though neglected importance, observational learning is not confined to any one period of time, for example childhood (an impression which might be gained from the concentration of experimental research on modelling in children), but is a continual and ongoing process throughout the whole of a person's life.

The products of observational learning need to be *retained*. Effective retention requires that the memory of modelled behaviour be transformed into verbal and visual symbols. These may be rehearsed by the individual away from the presence of the model. Indeed, the apparent speed of observational learning makes it almost inevitable that rehearsal occurs. With increasing practice, both observation and copying become more accurate. The accuracy of copying is assisted both by practice and by external positive reinforcement of correct, and negative reinforcement of incorrect, imitation.

Modelled responses may or may not reproduced by the observer. To do so he must possess the requisite skills and physical capabilities, as well as opportunity. The lack of any of these, as well as other restraining factors, will sharply reduce the likelihood of audiences repeating the robberies depicted in detail in countless films. Once a modelled response is reproduced by the observer it is subject to direct reinforcement influences—both enhancement and diminution—on single occasions and on many occasions, by single reinforcements and by schedules of reinforcement.

Observational learning enables the acquisition not only of overt responses but of covert *emotional* responses. The fidelity of the cognitive response to an observed outcome is enhanced by the observer consciously verbalizing 'to himself' what he sees or hears. Aronfreed (1968) points out that modelling must be distinguished from the generally facilitating effect of the mere presence of others (Zajonce, 1968). In addition, the performance of one instance of a broad domain of behaviour such as aggression may be facilitated by the observation of a different example of aggression. Modelling effects are increased by raising the level of physiological arousal of the observer up to an optimal level of arousal beyond which the efficiency of learning declines, a phenomenon common to learning of all types. The level of arousal seems more important than its source.

The great majority of research into observational learning has been on young children being modelled by other children, or, more usually, by adults, and not on adolescents or adults being modelled by their peers. Moreover, field studies, as opposed to laboratory research, are rare. Insufficient attention has been paid to the modelling influence of the peers of older children and of adults outside the family, of small social groups and of crowds (Bandura, 1960; Milgram and Toch, 1969). Yet such influences are likely both to be of major importance and to exert their effects throughout the life-span of the individual. For example, many political commentators have pointed to the importance of the model for appropriate political behaviour provided by President Nixon's earlier career for his subordinates in their conduct of the 1972 presidential campaign.

In discussing the importance of extra-familial models, Bandura (1960) concentrates on the role of the immediate peers of school-age children. He points out that because of the age difference between themselves and their children parents may provide only rather general guidance rather than specific models for behaviour. Peer and parental modelling may conflict; peers may both supplement and supplant parents. The extent to which parents influence their children's choice of friends, and hence the models to which they are exposed, will vary greatly, depending partially on the general cultural emphasis on obedience to parental wishes. With increasing age, peers are more heavily drawn on as models, particularly in times of rapid cultural and technological change. Parents will be less adequate as models when upward social mobility is possible and is sought, both when the desired behaviours are 'respectable', when teachers or middle-class peers may serve as models, and when they are not, when affluent local-level offenders may do so. Literature, long a potential source of modelling influences, has been joined in this century by films, and since World War II by television. Later in this chapter we shall look briefly at the research linking aggression and televised violence.

Attitude Formation and Change: Persuasive Communications

The study of attitudes has been a major part of social psychology for the past half-century. A great many attempts at definition of the term attitude have been made, perhaps the most widely accepted emphasizing its *evaluative* component. Attitudes are thus favourable or unfavourable beliefs about an act or event, object or person. They represent both potential responses and the evaluation of previously made responses.

Attitudes may be changed in a planned and systematic manner both by persuasive communications and by formal learning methods. In laboratory settings the latter achieve more powerful effects, but laboratory findings may understate the effectiveness of persuasive communications in real-life settings, particularly if prior communications are regarded as *enhancing* the efficacy of overt behavioural experiences rather than replacing them. A preliminary verbal communication may increase the probability of a person performing a particular act; once performed and positively reinforced, it will be repeated, a likelihood strengthened by the verbal representation of the act and its covert rehearsal. In the present context the sequence of changes would run as follows: an existing attitude relatively unfavourable for example to shoplifting is confronted by a persuasive message to the effect that (a) detection is unlikely, (b) most people shoplift. Depending on several characteristics of the message, including its source, its channel and so on (see below), the previous attitude may change to one favourable to shoplifting. Given a suitable opportunity, and the required skills, the shoplifting act will be performed, probably successfully in view of the low rate of detection of shoplifting, reflected upon and probably repeated. Viewed in this fashion, attitudes are seen to *interact* with behaviours.

The amount of change of a currently held attitude in the direction of a spoken or written communication is dependent on a great many variables which have been thoroughly reviewed by McGuire (1969). The following resumé will be seen to be relevant both to the acquisition of attitudes favourable to offending and to attempts to modify such attitudes in a socially acceptable direction. Applications and illustrations of criminological relevance will be interspersed thoughout the summary of McGuire's review which follows. McGuire divides the matrix of communication into five components: the source, the message, the channel, the receiver and the destination.

Source Factors. The major components of variation in the source (the deliverer of a message) are competence (status and intelligence), attractiveness (like-ability) and the power to administer positive and negative sanctions, together with a concern about compliance with the message and the ability to scrutinize compliance. Communications in favour of criminal activity delivered by a successful offender are likely to be effective when the offender is likeable, socially powerful and can administer or withhold reinforcements valued by the individual receiving the message, and when the offender and the receiver are in frequent contact with each other.

Message Factors. Persuasive appeals may be emotional (against authority, etc.) fear-related or rational. For all three forms positive reinforcement during the message increases compliance (for example, 'talking about it over a drink'). With respect to order of presentation, it is generally more effective to give the agreeable information initially. The degree of discrepancy of the message from the receiver's initial position is important. When the source is of low credibility, the greater the discrepancy, the less the belief engendered. However, for a highly credible source the results are *opposite* (Bergin, 1962). This is the technique of the 'big lie'. The explanation may be found in cognitive dissonance theory. 'I can either change my evaluation of X' (the highly credible source) 'or I can believe what he says, odd though it sounds. It's easier to do the latter.' The alternative, derogating the source, may involve a much greater readjustment of large areas of currently held attitudes.

Channel Factors. They concern the mode of presentation of the message. Heard speech is more persuasive than read speech, as is a message delivered face-to-face compared to one delivered through an artificial channel (a tape-recorder, or closed-circuit television).

Receiver Factors. These are largely concerned with differences between the persons to whom the message is addressed, the relevant one in the present context being persuasability. In chapter 7 we shall discuss the controversy over the very existence of stable individual differences in behaviour over and above the specifics of previous learning experiences and the current situation. For the present we shall note that persuasability is largely unrelated to mental age, and is greater in females than in males, possibly due to their greater (on average) verbal ability and hence more effective message reception. Persons chronically low in self-esteem tend to be slightly more persuasible; persons situationally manipulated by failure experiences to be temporarily low in self-esteem are highly responsive to persuasion. Hence, persons with initially high expectations for academic or occupational success but who fail, or seem about to do so, may be particularly susceptible to the induction of attitudes favourable to offending behaviours, particularly when delivered by a source which is highly credible, likeable, etc. (See Chapter 8 for a more detailed discussion.)

Destination Factors. As well as the decrements over the course of time in the recall of a message used in laboratory studies which memory research would lead us to expect, there have been also reports of increments in recall. These would be expected on the basis of the cognitive rehearsal of messages, particularly of those of major importance in the life of the receiver. Such crucial messages are likely to be more frequent in real life, than in laboratory studies, in which the content of the messages used is typically trivial. Moreover, care is usually taken in the laboratory to avoid interfering with the induced attitude change by post-change practice of the associated behaviour. In addition to covert rehearsal, attitude changes in real-life situations may well be strengthened by the influenced person actually carrying out the behaviour concerned. If this has a positively reinforced outcome, another increment is added to the previously induced attitude change. In turn, the further strengthened change of attitude increases the probability of the overt response being repeated, and so on in a sequence of action and reaction between attitude and behaviour in both directions.

Immunization against Persuasion. McGuire means by 'immunization' preparatory treatments which make the receiver less prone to change his attitudes when subsequently exposed to a persuasive communication than if he had not been so prepared. The analogy is with the injection of a low level of a toxic agent which immunizes the recipient against the harmful effects of much higher subsequent doses. In the criminological context, an example would be a parent or fellow worker preparing a child or colleague for the attempts of others to persuade them of the merits of criminal behaviours by listing the arguments expected to be used, together with counterarguments. The resistance of an attitude against a subsequent persuasive communication designed to change it is enhanced more by the receipt of weak counterarguments, together with their refutation, than by the presentation of additional arguments in support of the currently held attitude. A public commitment to an attitude confers more resistance than a commitment made in private; the effect is still greater if the individual carries out overt behaviours on the basis of the attitude, particularly if he does so for small, rather than large, rewards. Finally, resistance is enhanced by inducing anxiety prior to immunization only in those low in chronic anxiety; the effect is opposite for those high in chronic anxiety.

Attitude Formation and Change: The Learning Approach

Conventional learning techniques tend to use rather brief and simple stimuli, in contrast to the sometimes long and complex messages of the verbal communication approach reviewed above. An example is the assocation of the picture of a presidential candidate with an already favourably evaluated stimulus (Mr Nixon stroking a lovable dog; the converse is a picture of Mr Johnson holding his dog by the ears). Staats and his colleagues (Staats and Staats, 1958; Staats, 1966) have *classically conditioned* a wide variety of attitudinal responses and have demonstrated stimulus generalization (Das and Nanda, 1963). Attitudes have been regarded as suitable for *operant conditioning* and can be shaped, like any other behaviours, by the appropriate variation of reinforcement contingencies, the effects of which generalize to other attitudes and tasks. The effectiveness of reinforcement is partially related to the influenced person's evaluation of the person providing the reinforcement (Krasner, 1965). *Observational learning* has been shown to be of importance in the acquisition and modification of attitudes, both in laboratory and therapeutic settings (Bandura, 1969).

A most important source of attitude change is the performance of an overt response *discrepant* from an existing attitude, for example a person who regards himself as honest, but when tempted steals. Attitude change tends to *follow* behaviour change rather reliably. As Bandura (1969) points out, it may be easier to influence specific overt actions than covert attitudes, because the controlling contingencies are clear. In addition, it is difficult for a person to deny that he has carried out an overt act. Finally, overt behaviours are likely to be powerfully reinforced by their immediate external consequences, increasing the probability of repetition and of further attitude change in the same direction. In the criminological context, the foregoing means that inducing someone actually to carry out an offence is likely to have a more powerful effect both on attitudes and subsequent behaviours than restricting treatment to persuasive messages in favour of the offence. In practice, a combination of methods is probably most effective. This means manipulating attitudes by initial persuasive communications, and subsequently inducing overt actions by appropriate stimulus conditions.

Social Situations

Two-person Situations. We shall assume for convenience that the direction of influence is from person A to person B, and not reciprocal as is sometimes more likely in real life. We have already seen that person A may serve as a model for A acquire new responses and inhibit or enhance existing ones, as well as reinforcing positively or negatively the responses emitted by B himself. In addition, we have seen that certain attributes of the source of a message increase the likelihood of the message being accepted. The effectiveness of A as a dispenser of social reinforcement is related to his effectiveness as a source of positive or negative reinforcers for B, and in turn this is largely related to the degree or interpersonal attraction he has for B (Berscheid and Walster, 1969). Attraction includes both the capacity to reward and the relative rarity of reward. Thibaut and Kelley (1959) considered attraction between two persons involved in a situation to be a function of the extent to which each participant receives a reward–cost outcome in excess of some minimum level termed the comparison level (CL). This is the average value of all the outcomes known to the person, both actually experienced and vicarious, past and current. In the situation of a person exposed to learning influences favourable to offending behaviours, the CL notion would operate as follows. Influencing agent A, a current offender, is trying to communicate to B, who is currently law-abiding, attitudes favourable to offending. B has few friends, admires A greatly and seeks his friendship.

If giving B his friendship is made contingent by A on a changed attitude by B, his influence attempt is likely to be successful, first in changing the attitudes expressed verbally by B and eventually in a change in B's overt behaviour. Conversely, if B has many friends, and/or does not admire A, value his friendship highly or seek his support in some other way, the influence attempt is likely to be unsuccessful. Rewardingness is also contributed to by status, by credibility and by power over objective resources such as money and occupational advancement as well as over less tangible assets such as friendship.

Group Influences on Behaviour. Membership of groups provides ready possibilities both for observational learning from social models and for developing awareness in group members of the rewardingness of models and hence the extent to which it will be advantageous to emulate them. In addition, persons who contribute to the cohesiveness of a group by conforming to the standards of the majority will be positively reinforced, those who do not will be punished, for example by exclusion from the group. One of those standards may be to behave illegally, such as joining in price-fixing by a group of dealers, or stealing from the work situation. The 'odd man out' will be unpopular in both instances. Groups exact a price for the social support and friendship they provide. As well as coercive power, a group also exerts referent power, supplying discriminative stimuli of approved *versus* disapproved behaviours ('people like us, do/do not do, this sort of thing'). New members quickly become aware of what is sanctioned and what is not. Both coercive and referent effects are at their greatest when there are no exceptions among group members to the behaviour concerned.

There are general pressures towards conformity which will influence new members of, for example, a professional association in which illegal practices are common. In addition, such practices will be modelled more effectively by leading members than by less senior persons because of their greater social visibility. Validation by group leaders markedly increases the legitimacy of even apparently deviant behaviours; the greater the power of the leader, the greater the effect ('if it's alright for the chairman/president it must be alright for me'). A review of laboratory research on group structure and influence is provided by Collins and Raven (1969).

A great many studies, also reviewed by Collins and Raven, have been concerned with decision-making by groups as compared with by individuals, an area of particular relevance being that of risk-taking. The general finding has been that groups accept levels of risk higher than those accepted by the individual members prior to discussion by the group. One possible reason is the diffusion of responsibility between several persons; another is the reduction in anxiety consequent on group affiliation (Schachter, 1959). Whatever its explanation, the 'risky shift' phenomenon is of considerable criminological relevance. For example, an individual is more likely to decide on a criminal act in the context of a group discussion. If the act is rewarded, he is likely to repeat it on his own. A rather important source of an increase in risk-taking by groups is that there is a mutual reinforcement of any tendency to avoid information which is likely to increase anxiety, such as the consequences of an offence being detected.

Research on crowds and broad social movements, including their importance as sources of influence, is reviewed by Milgram and Toch (1969). Their definition of a crowd is: 'Group behaviour which originates spontaneously, is relatively unorganized, fairly unpredictable and planless in its course of development, and which depends upon interstimulation among participants' (p. 50). Being a member of a crowd may instigate a person to perform behaviours such as lynching which he would otherwise avoid. Membership of social movements may model behaviours such as aeroplane hijacking, which have been variously described as heroic or dastardly, depending upon whether one is a supporter or an opponent of the particular social movement concerned.

Transgression: Acquisition

Attitude Change

Initially unfavourable attitudes to transgression may be modified in a number of ways prior to the occurrence of a transgression—persuasive communications, classical conditioning and operant conditioning—as well as post-transgression as a consequence of a successfully carried out and positively reinforced act. The more favourable the attitude, the more likely an overt transgression. If this is positively reinforced, the future probability of a similar behaviour is increased.

The more successful the consequences of transgression (for example in terms of size of return compared to amount of effort) and the less the risk, the more rapidly will there be a switch from a previous habit of avoidance of transgression, acquired through early socialization, to a set of attitudes favourable to transgression. Of course, in real life there will be a constant flow of vicarious and actual experiences relating both to the avoidance of transgression and yielding to it, resulting in the development of a range of attitudes and behaviours each specific to a particular situation. These will vary from situations in which the individual would virtually never transgress to those in which he would virtually always do so. There may also be a degree of consistency across situations—some people may be much more likely than others to respond to temptation in any given combination of circumstances. We shall look in Chapter 7 at the evidence on the consistency of criminal behaviour in general.

Observational Learning

The greater the opportunity for the observational learning of transgression, the more likely is it that such behaviours will be learned. 'The depredator who has escaped punishment due to his offence is constantly present; an encouraging example of success to all his class' (Chadwick, 1829). A contemporary, anecdotal, example of modelling is provided by a recent news item (*Guardian*,

1975). A French Army deserter who had taken five hostages finally surrendered to the police after the authorities had paid him a ransom of £600,000. He stated that his technique was modelled on that used the previous week by men who took hostages in a Paris bank. There are a number of laboratory studies on the modelling of transgression in children. For example, Porro (1968) reported that children who viewed a filmed model exhibit self-approving responses to her own transgressions were significantly more likely to handle a toy they had been forbidden to touch than were children who observed the same model criticize herself for transgression. Non-punishment of a model for transgression has much the same effect on children as the receipt by the model of positive reinforcement (Walters *et al.*, 1965). All the observational learning effects noted in other areas of behaviour, such as the acquisition of behaviours and the disinhibition of old restrictions, have been demonstrated in laboratory transgression situations (Bandura, 1969). The characteristics of the model will be important also, so that modelling effects will be dependent on the power, the status, the interpersonal attraction and the ethnic membership of the model concerned. Modelled behaviour which is judged by the observer to be markedly inappropriate to the model will have much less imitative effect than behaviours judged relatively appropriate (Dubanoski, 1967). For example, if a clergyman is observed in the act of robbing a bank, the observer may simply disbelieve the evidence of his eyes, assume that the man is an imposter, or finally, avoid generalizing the observation to all clergymen. Observational learning is particularly relevant to learning transgressions because such behaviours can then be acquired in comparative safety. Thus, all the principles of vicarious reinforcement will apply to the acquisition of transgressions.

Direct Reinforcement

The same is true of the principles of direct reinforcement. Through repeated rewarding experiences, stimuli associated with successful transgressive behaviour (for example multiple stores and open car doors) will evoke future transgressive responses which will become part of the individual's total repertoire of behaviour. Cues which signal the need for caution will also be learned, as will cues which signal that it is safe to act. Environmental stimuli thus acquire discriminative control over transgressive behaviour. Over time, positively reinforced responses are retained and negatively reinforced ones dropped, the process being speeded up by culturally dependent initial opportunities for vicarious learning. O'Leary (1968) and Hartig and Kanfer (1973) both showed in laboratory studies that training in verbal self-instructions (repeating those given by the experimenter) not to respond to temptation markedly reduced transgression during a subsequent period in which there was an opportunity to respond to temptation. The effect was produced whether the instructions related to the positive or the negative consequences of transgressions. There was a suggestion in the Hartig and Kanfer study that older children (5–7) had already acquired the self-instruction (i.e. rehearsal) habit, whereas younger children (3–5) had not. Hence, lack of training in labelling and rehearsing resistance to temptation increases the likelihood of acquiring transgressive behaviours.

Social Settings

Although relevant studies appear not to have been carried out as yet, it seems likely that families exist which train not socially acceptable behaviours (avoiding opportunities to steal, etc.) but instead positively reinforce socially unacceptable behaviours towards those outside the family. Just as a minimum level of nurturance makes possible the use of the more effective love-oriented techniques in the development of pro-social behaviours, so it would enhance the effectiveness of the same techniques in the development of anti-social behaviours. Such an idea may seem bizarre, but it is possible to conceive of the transmission of criminal behaviour within an affectionate family setting both by the modelling of appropriate attitudes and behaviours and by direct reinforcement. A review by Wootton (1959) indicates that on the whole the presence of one offender in a family is associated with an increased probability of another. While there is a general expectation that most parents will train socially acceptable behaviours, there is no such clear onus on peer groups, either before, during or after adolescence; they will differ widely in that some will provide modelled, or direct reinforcement for transgressive, others for non-transgressive, behaviours. The former social groups are learning settings for criminal behaviour. They add to the usual environmental stimuli towards transgression (opportunity, etc.) those of interpersonal and group influences outlined earlier, and do so repeatedly over long periods of time. The importance of the social setting in the acquisition of criminal behaviour is well illustrated by a study by Spergel (1964). He asked children living in three areas of an American industrial city: 'What is the occupation of an adult in your neighbourhood you would most like to have in ten years from now?' In 'Racketville', the most affluent of the three areas, two-fifths of the inhabitants being Italian American, eight-tenths of the children named 'some aspect of syndicated crime'. In 'Slum Town', two-thirds of the inhabitants of which were Puerto Rican and a quarter black, most of the Children talked of 'defending the turf'—i.e. joining a fighting gang—fighting being the major activity of the gangs in that area. Finally in 'Haulberg', where the main crime was car theft, that was indeed the activity which was most frequently mentioned. In all three areas criminal behaviour by teenagers is interpreted by Spergel as a way of demonstrating conformity with the model of a 'big shot' observed in the particular locality. Another instance is provided by Clinard (1952), who describes how businessmen learned black-market practices during World War II from association with existing black-market operators. In Chapter 1 many instances were cited of occupational offending. There can be few occupations which do not, at any one time, contain models for criminal behaviours, and thus provide appropriate settings for the acquisition of such behaviours.

Cressey (1971) has described organized specialist groups of criminals as having existed for centuries. Their areas of activity today include burglary, shoplifting, robbery, confidence games, pickpocketing and car theft, all of which need experience and training, both for carrying out the criminal act itself and for coping with the situation if detected. Skills are developed, like any other occupational expertise, by both example and practice.

The relevance of the wider, political context is argued by Bronfenbrenner (1970), who compared US and Russian educational methods, and stated: 'The peer group need not necessarily act as an impetus to anti-social behaviour. Among Soviet youngsters, it had just the opposite effect. Why? ... The Soviet peer group is given explicit training for exerting the desired influence on its members. In addition, whereas the American peer group is not, The Soviet peer group is heavily, perhpas too heavily—influenced by adult society. ... The American peer group is relatively autonomous, and cut off from the adult world' (Bronfenbrenner, 1970, p. 115).

However, there are considerable difficulties with studies comparing different ethnic groups as social learning settings. For example, Grinder and McMichael (1963) compared Caucasian and Samoan children living in rural Hawaii on the ray-gun task (Grinder, 1961). The subject reports his own score and the game is so programmed that he cannot gain sufficient points to be awarded a prize without falsifying his score; he is tempted to do so by the experimenter absenting himself on some pretext. Hence, cheating is indicated by any score above the minimum level for a prize. The Caucasian children showed more resistance to temptation. In addition, on a story completion task they were significantly more likely to depict remorse, confession and restitution. No sex differences were observed for either group. Whether other tasks would yield similar results was not studied, nor was there any attempt to control for the subjective evaluation of the reward offered for a good performance on the ray-gun task (the Samoan group is probably the least materially affluent of the many Hawaiian ethnic groups, the Caucasian among the most well-off). Finally, the prestige attached to shooting ability may also differ between ethnic groups. In other words, before conclusions can be drawn in terms of one ethnic group—in this case the Samoan—relying more on external controls (and hence displaying less resistance to temptation without surveillance) than another, the factors relevant to the situation must be controlled.

Bacon et al. (1963) carried out an extensive cross-cultural survey. They were able to find data on the rates of crimes against persons and property and on child-rearing practices for 48, mainly preliterate, societies in various parts of the world. They found that as the opportunities for contact with the father decreased, the frequency of both types of crime increased. The higher the level of indulgence—by immediate gratification of the child's wants—the lower the level of theft. The latter two results were trends only, falling below conventional levels of statistical significance. The next finding was that the more highly stratified a society, the higher the level of theft, suggesting the relevance of the concept of relative deprivation. Finally, crimes against persons were positively

associated with anxiety aroused by training for independence and with prolonged sleeping with the mother and negatively associated with amount of
contact with the father. It was not stated how many correlations were *not*
significant; it is possible that the number which achieved statistical significance
may not have exceeded that expected by chance alone. Nor did the authors
indicate the general expectations within each culture concerning personal
aggression and the sanctity of property, or the part played by post-childhood
training in the acquisition of attitudes and behaviours in these two areas.

Transgression: Situational Determinants of Performance

We now review studies of the environmental events immediately associated
with the performance of transgressions. Some studies have typically used
temptation situations such as the ray-gun game (Grinder, 1961) and the various
cheating and lying situations devised by Hartshorne and May (1928, described
in detail by Eysenck, 1964—a more accessible source). Such laboratory studies,
though ingenious, are not as close as one would wish to real crime (for example,
the use of 'theft' situations is rather rare). However, there is a gradual move
towards research situations which have the realism of the field yet are under
strong experimental control. The following are among the situational factors,
variations in which affect the probability of a transgression. The clear prediction
would be that the performance of offences against property would be responsive
to the same factors. (Studies of deterrence, based on official statistics, are
discussed in Chapter 9. Inevitably, such studies are both descriptive only
and poorly controlled.)

Risk of Detection

In a study by Kanfer and Duerfeldt (1968) subjects had to guess numbers
between 1 and 100 that were drawn at random from a box, simply recording
whether they guessed correctly or not. A reward was offered for a high number
of correct guesses; a number above that obtainable by chance was evidence of
cheating. Subjects cheated less when they wrote down their guesses before
hearing whether they were correct or not than when they made mental guesses
and only recorded the accuracy after feedback. However, as the former group
realized that their slips of paper were really thrown away and not checked,
their rate of cheating increased.

Level of Punishment if Detected

A series of studies by Rettig and his associates (see below under the heading
of reward–cost) demonstrated the unsurprising effect of a low level of punishment in increasing transgressions. However, less obviously, it is a well-founded
generalization in experimental psychology that stimuli, whether pleasant or
aversive, are responded to in terms of relative rather than absolute levels.

Hence, it is the contrast between the present and the previously experienced levels of punishment which is crucial, particularly if the previous level was ineffective in preventing transgression.

Level of Incentive (Rettig and Associates)

Again, the greater the incentive the greater the probability of transgression, but contrast effects are again important—between the present level of rewards obtained without recourse to transgressions and the level which could potentially result from crime, both viewed in relation to the level of reward sought. In turn, the last-named variable is influenced by the comparison between one's own material level and that of comparable others. The negative incentive involved is also important—what would be lost if a transgression were not carried out, again in relative rather than absolute terms.

Presence of Models

A number of studies by Blake and associates demonstrated the relevance of models in increasing or decreasing the probability of a transgression (for example Blake, 1958). There was a marked interaction between the presence of a model and the level of incentive to transgression. For example, under extreme temptation subjects disregarded both a non-transgressing model and external surveillance. The status of the model is also important; high-status models are more successful in inducing imitation, despite external surveillance, than are low-status models, particularly when incentives are high (Lippit *et al.*, 1952). It is perhaps the awareness of this effect that leads judges from time to time to hand out 'exemplary' sentences to pop artists found guilty of possessing marijuana (see Schofield, 1971, p. 160, for a pertinent example).

Induced Self-esteem

A number of reports (for example Aronson and Mettee, 1968) suggest that temporarily lowering self-esteem in students by giving them derogatory feedback from a personality test increases the incidence of dishonest behaviour in a subsequent task. Conversely, raising the level of self-esteem reduced the incidence of dishonest behaviour in comparison with a control group given no feedback. This bears on the labelling approach to crime to be discussed in Chapter 8.

The Victim

Feldman (1968) found a difference between honesty to a stranger and to a compatriot in only one of a series of field situations, each created in Paris, Boston and Athens. The situations consisted of overpaying a cashier, dropping money in the street and being overcharged by a taxi-driver. The one exception was provided by the last-named situation, a stranger being more frequently overcharged, but only in Paris. Feldman (1967) found, using hypothetical situations, that both institutional adolescent offenders and secondary schoolboys considered themselves significantly less likely to retain a wallet dropped by an old-age pensioner than one dropped by a businessman and less likely to steal from a friend than a stranger, in both cases irrespective of the likelihood of detection. The judged 'wrongness' of the respective behaviours was in line with the response those questioned expected of themselves (for example stealing from the old lady was judged to be worse than stealing from the businessman). Kiesler *et al.* (1967) found that a commitment to future interaction increased attempts to influence a fellow worker on a laboratory task to behave correctly, implying, although somewhat indirectly, that transgressions are reduced by an expectation that one would have to face the victim again.

Opportunity for Legitimate Gain

McCandless *et al.* (1972), studying an institutional sample of American adolescent boys, found a significant negative relationship between self-reported offending and perceived legitimate opportunity ('Is it hard to find a good paying, honest job in your area'), but only for white inmates, the trend for black inmates being in the same direction but short of statistical significance.

Combinations of Situational Variables: The Reward–Cost Approach

A number of studies exemplify the rational, calculative, approach to the explanation of criminal behaviour, which emphasizes that with the right combination of potential rewards and costs transgressions may be committed by almost anyone. The probability of an offence is also influenced by the person's previous history of positive and negative reinforcements for transgressions (see next section, headed Maintenance); the more similar the present to the previous situation, the greater will be the part played by past outcomes. However, the studies to be cited have typically concentrated on the current variables. The extent to which one can generalize from them to real-life criminal behaviour is also restricted by the fact that they all presented their subjects with hypothetical, questionnaire-described situations, which included more information for decision-taking purposes and did so in a more relaxed atmosphere than is probably typical for persons faced with a real-life temptation to perform a criminal act. Moreover, the range of temptations presented was somewhat restricted. Nevertheless, these studies have demonstrated the general value of the reward–cost approach; an extension to more realistic situations is strongly indicated.

A series of studies by Rettig and his colleagues began with the view (Retting and Rawson, 1963) that the major situational determinants of what they termed 'unethical behaviour' were: the expectancy of gain (Egn); the reinforcement value of gain (= amount of reward, RVgn); the expectancy of censure

($=$ punishment, Ecs); the reinforcement value of censure ($=$ amount of punishment, RVcens); the severity of the offence; and the reference group (the victim of the theft—friends, employers, etc.). Each determinant was included at high and low levels, giving 64 in all. The basic situation presented was that of theft of money. It was repeated in a questionnaire 64 times; in each successive item one of the 64 determinants was changed, the rest remaining constant, until all possible combinations of determinants had been presented. In their later studies, Rettig and associates dropped first the reference group, and then the severity of offence, determinant, giving first 32 and then 16 items, an increasingly more manageable cognitive task for those answering the questionnaire. In all studies subjects were required to state on a scale from 0 (definitely no) to 6 (definitely yes) the decision made (to carry out the offence or not). Rettig's major prediction related to what he termed 'ethical risk', namely, that variations in RVcens would be the major determinant of the decision to carry out the theft or to refrain from doing so. Rettig and Rawson (1963), studying American undergraduates, found that the RVcens variable was, as predicted, the most important determinant of the decision (i.e. variations in the RVcens variable from high to low brought about the greatest change in the stated probability of carrying out the act). Variations in four of the other five determinants exerted lesser, but still statistically significant, effects; only the reference group determinant proved unimportant. Rettig and Singh (1963) repeated the study at the same American university but with Asian students and without the reference group determinant, which was also dropped in all subsequent studies. The results were the same as those obtained by Rettig and Rawson.

Rettig and Pasamanick (1964) then correlated questionnaire responses with cheating on the usual type of simple competitive task (characterized in their study as a 'measure of risk-taking') and found that RVcens was the only determinant to predict significantly to risk-taking behaviour. Rettig (1964) gave his questionnaire, using a situation concerning fraud by a bank employee, to a mixed group of prisoners (mainly sentenced for forgery, or possession of government securities) and a comparison group of students matched with the prisoners for age, sex and socio-economic class. For both groups RVcens emerged as the major determinant, the severity of the offence not influencing either group. The prisoners were less sensitive than the students to the other three determinants. Next, Rettig (1966) studied cheating in group and individual task conditions, found it to be greater with the former and concluded that ethical risk-taking by groups exceeded that by individuals because of the effect of social affiliation in reducing risk-generated anxiety, a conclusion which fits in with our earlier discussion of the 'risky-shift' phenomenon.

Rettig predicted that groups contemplating criminal actions would discourage anxiety-evoking communications between members concerning the risks involved. (In the case of illegal political or commercial actions this is known as 'getting on the team' or 'not rocking the boat'.) In a follow-up study, Rettig and Turoff (1967) had students respond to a 16-item questionnaire (dropping the severity of offence determinant) either as individuals or as members of a group which discussed each item in turn. Once again, RVcens emerged as a major determinant and the level of risk-taking was higher for the group situation.

The story is now taken up by two studies by other groups of workers. Stenfanowicz and Hannum (1971) correlated scores on the 16-item questionnaire obtained from 38 female prisoners with a rating of the level of 'sociopathy' of the prisoners made by the staff. While the correlation between the total risk score and the sociopathy rating achieved a low but acceptable level of statistical significance, none of the correlations with the individual determinants did so. Further in contrast to previous studies the only significant determinant of risk-taking was RVgn, none of the other, including RVcens, displaying significant differences between their low and high levels. This finding suggests that a major weakness in the Rettig studies is a failure to vary systematically the levels of punishment possible. Clearly, if even the upper level had already been experienced and adapted to, it would exert no greater restraint on transgressions than the lower level. Krauss et al. (1972) administered the 16-item Rettig questionnaire to groups of prisoners diagnosed as psychopathic or non-psychopathic. Only the former group was sensitive to Egn, neither group to RVgn (compare the female prisoners above) or to Ecs, but both were sensitive to RVcens (again different from the females). This study reinforces the need to explore prior to a study variations in all the major determinants expected to be of importance.

Feldman (1966) adapted Rettig's approach to younger and less academically able populations. He compared adolescent institutional offenders and schoolboys matched for age and intelligence, but presented only two variables at a time, one a temptation and one a deterrent, making the task cognitively much less demanding. Each pair of 'arguments' was attached to the same situation, that of a teenage manual worker who hears of a house which is empty for the weekend. 'If you were him would you do the job (i.e. break in), yes or no?' The temptation (rewards) were the amount of money stated to have been left in the house (£10 or 50p, at a time when £1 was approximately $2·5); the probability of the money being there (definitely or possibly); how fully occupied was the prospective thief in the evenings (plenty to do, nothing to do); and the purpose for which the money was required (a gift for his mother, or for himself). The deterrents (costs) were the chances of being caught at some time (high or low); the presence of a patrolling policeman (present or absent); the punishment if caught (a correctional institution or probation); and the ease of access (no windows open anywhere in the house, or a first-floor window open). A preliminary analysis revealed that there was no effect in either group of the purpose (gift) determinant, so all items containing it were dropped from further analysis, leaving 48 in all. Although there was much overlap, the approved school group scored significantly higher on average than the schoolboy group both for the overall score (out of 48) and for the subsets of 'high temptation' pairs (temptation high, deterrent low), 'medium temptation' pairs (both temptation and deterrent items high, or both low) and 'low temptation' pairs (temptation low, deterrent high). The order of subsets of pairs was as would be expected—high, medium and then low. That is, the high temptation pairs attracted the greatest number of 'yes' responses, the low temptation pairs the least.

The more detailed results make clear the major importance of the exact combination of rewards and costs in the decision to offend or not to offend. Throughout, the level of cost involved exerted a more powerful effect when rewards were high than when they were low.

For both groups of subjects, the pairing attracting most yes answers was money high and entry easy, and money high and police absent. The pairings attracting the fewest yeses from the institution group were boredom low and police present, and money low and police present: from the non-institutional group they were certainty low and police present, and certainty low and punishment high. For both groups the descending order of importance of the temptations was money, boredom and certainty. For the deterrents, the presence of a policeman, the level of punishment, the certainty of detection and the difficulty of entry were in descending order of importance. (The presence of a policeman is likely to reduce real-life offending, particularly if his appearance is unpredictable by potential offenders—his 'beat' is varied randomly rather than fixed.) The vast majority of yes answers from both groups were 'rational'; subjects rarely indicated yes to a low temptation pairing unless they did so also to the medium and high temptation versions of the same pair of determinants. The fact that this degree of rationality, albeit in hypothetical circumstances, was displayed by two groups of boys both of which were of average or below average intelligence supports the calculative nature of most criminal behaviour on the part of the majority of offenders.

The Rettig studies also support such a view, as do two studies by Piliavin and associates, which used a rather different approach. In the first of these, Piliavin, Vadum and Hardyck (1969) compared self-reported offending, self-reported apprehension and official arrest records with three step-wise 'cost' scales relating to father (ranging from 'being thought well of means everything to me' to 'doesn't matter at all'), to mother (much the same) and teacher (the importance of approval for good school performance). There were statistically significant relationships between most of the cost and most of the offence measures. For example, the lower the weighting placed on father's approval (termed 'low cost') the worse the offence record. Piliavin, Hardyck and Vadum (1969) extended their earlier study by comparing low and high cost boys on a cheating task, the former being found to cheat more, as did boys with a record of police apprehension (compared to those with no such record). Self-reported offending was not used as a measure in the latter study.

Piliavin et al. interpret their overall results as supporting a policy of paying offenders to conform, somewhat of a logical jump, but one which might prove less financially expensive than institutional or probation treatment. It might be even more effective if payments were withheld for further offending (assuming that this was detectable, always the central problem of any non-institutional system of correction).

Concluding Comment

The reward–cost studies have taken little or no account of such 'internal' determinants as the level of moral development and personality variables, considering situational factors to be of overriding importance. As well as comparisons with significant others, people will also use as a point of reference their own previous experiences. The values attached by individuals to the same reinforcers and punishers will thus vary widely between them. Finally, it should be noted that rewards and costs are not absolute. As noted earlier, social comparison processes will play an important part in performance as well as in learning.

Transgression: Maintenance

We noted above that anticipated rewards and costs play a part in determining the performance or avoidance of any particular new transgression. In this section we concentrate on the effect of the outcomes of previous transgressions in maintaining or diminishing such behaviours. Of course, to some extent the distinction between anticipated single outcomes and observed, both single and sequential, outcomes is omewhat artificial; behaviour is determined both by the current situation and by previous outcomes, both single and sequential. Separating out the current situational stimuli (performance) from previous outcomes (maintenance) is both conceptually convenient and assists the presentation of a learning-based analysis of crime. In this section, then, we shall concentrate on the importance of outcomes, the nature and source of those outcomes and the sequence of positive and negative reinforcements.

External Reinforcement

In general, transgressive behaviours are strongly controlled by the prevailing conditions of reinforcement. both those experienced by the offender and those experienced by observed, and significant, others. Again, in general, positive outcomes will tend to maintain transgressive behaviours, negative outcomes will tend to diminish them. Positive outcomes of transgression tend to be expressed in material terms—both money, the universal secondary reinforcer, and property—but improvements in social status may also occur, either directly or indirectly. In the case of an individual whose social contacts are large with professional criminals, status is directly enhanced by a successful, and undetected, transgression of significant size. Status may also be gained in a more long-term way; for example, illegally acquired wealth may be invested in a legitimate business enterprise, the consequent success of which is both a source of social approval for the father and gains access for his children to valued social opportunities.

If all crimes were reported and cleared up, we could expect a rapid diminution in the crime rate. As we saw in Chapter 1, a considerable proportion of offences never reaches the stage of potential action. Even of those which do, many never lead to a conviction—wnen they are termed 'cleared up'. The proportion of crimes known to the police which are cleared up varies widely between different categories of crime, being particularly low for certain property offences. For example, in the UK larcenies from unattended vehicles are cleared up in no more than one-fifth of reported instances (Walker, 1971). The 'odds' are thus heavily on the side of the offender, as they are in the case of shoplifting. Even for the crime of robbery, there is a considerable possiblity that an offender will go undetected. According to McClintock and Gibson (1961), the proportion of London robberies cleared up fell from nearly one-half in 1950 to one-third in 1960. Moreover, the clear-up rate *fell* as the amount stolen *increased*, the trend sharpening over the years surveyed (1950–1960). This suggests that the bigger prizes are sought and won by the more competent offenders. It is clear that both the personal experience of successful outcome and the observed successful experiences of others are widespread. As Radzinowicz (1961) succintly puts it, 'impunity is itself a cause of crime. It attracts new recruits to the ranks of regular criminals; it encourages first offenders to persevere in crime as a profitable source of activity' (p. xi).

Even if a transgression has lead to a conviction, the reinforcement may not be entirely negative. The effect will depend both on the actual return received (typically money or property, but possibly social status) and whether or not the returns were retained by the offender. Clearly, a £20,000 haul which is retained will help to mitigate a prison sentence; the latter will be experienced as more negative if no money was retained from the offence. A significant proportion of crimes cleared up by the police do not result in the offender having to lose the money or property stolen—he may already have spent it or have hidden it in a safe place, etc. Thus the clear-up rate *overstates* the negative side of the long-term reward/cost balance.

The situation is further complicated by the schedule on which reinforcements have been received. It is well known that reinforcements received on an inter-intermittent schedule are strongly resistant to extinction; this general rule can be expected to apply to transgressive behaviour. If an individual carries out six shoplifting offences, all positively reinforced, and then experiences a sequence of six more, all negatively reinforced, it is somewhat unlikely that he will repeat the behaviour again. However, it is much more probable that even if he has been caught six times these will be distributed over a very large number of positively reinforced instances. The result will be an intermittent schedule of reinforcement of the type most calculated to maintain any behaviour—variable interval, variable ratio. The odds in favour of the property offender, particularly those involving shoplifting and larceny from unattended vehicles, are such that *once* the first offence has been carried out, and has been successful, the behaviour is likely to be maintained. Cessation is likely to occur only if there is a lengthy series of negatively reinforced outcomes.

Alternative, legal, sources of money and property are also important. Unless these are readily available, even rather occasional positive reinforcements will maintain transgressive behaviours, except in the face of very severe punishment.

Severe levels of punishment are unlikely to be experienced early in a career of offending. (The prevailing legal wisdom is to proceed through a hierarchy from very mild to very severe penal outcomes.) By the time the severe level is reached the transgressive behaviour may be very well maintained, on a schedule highly resistant to extinction, and particularly so if alternative legal behaviours are not readily available. Finally, as indicated above, positive reinforcements for transgressions obtained by significant social models will help to maintain transgressive behaviours by an observer whose own experienced schedule of reinforcement may tend towards the extinction of the behaviour. Once again, this will be most true when alternative behaviours are unavailable.

Self-reinforcement

As well as being materially and/or socially reinforced for transgressive behaviours, people may also reinforce themselves, for example by accomplishing a self-appointed task, such as theft, requiring a particularly high level of skill. 'Professional pride' is unlikely to be confined to socially respectable activities. Another major cognitive element in the maintenance of transgressive behaviour is pointed to by cognitive dissonance theory.

There have been many approaches to the general notion that people frequently attempt to achieve some form of internal consistency between their beliefs and attitudes about aspects of their world (Berkowitz, 1969). The most vigorous and influential of such approaches is the theory of cognitive dissonance, advanced by Festinger (1957). The overwhelming majority of the studies to which it has led have been carried out in laboratory settings (reviews include Brehm and Cohen, 1962 and Fishbein, 1967) and field studies are rare. As we shall argue below, the phenomena demonstrated in the laboratory are likely to exert more powerful, albeit more complex, effects in field settings.

Dissonance refers to the existence of *non-fitting relations* between cognitions, where 'cognition' means 'any knowledge, opinion or belief about the environment about oneself or one's behaviour. Cognitive dissonance can be seen as an antecedent condition which leads to activity oriented towards dissonance reduction, just as hunger leads to activity oriented towards hunger reduction' (Festinger, 1957). Laboratory studies of dissonance frequently have to resort to complex shifts and devices to induce subjects actually to carry out a discrepant behaviour so that dissonance theory predictions can be tested. In real life, discrepant behaviour occurs frequently in response to all kinds of temptations and threats, some perhaps very great indeed, in which case, as noted above, a linear relationship exists between incentive and attitude change (very high incentive equals very high dissonance equals very high attitude change). There has been much theoretical controversy (e.g. Chapanis and Chapanis, 1964) about whether or not dissonance phenomena can be accounted for within incentive theory, which would expect a positive correlation between incentive and attitude change throughout the range, rather than an inverse one at all but the extreme points of the range. Whatever the outcome of such debates, attitude change does follow behaviour change reliably, and serves the purpose of helping people to justify to themselves, and possibly also to others, behaviours discrepant either with their previous ones or with the standards they are aware their peers expect of them. Inconsistency is experienced as unpleasant; persons will first escape, then avoid, inconsistency by changing either their attitude, their behaviour or their perception of external events. The more important in the life of the person the dissonant elements, and the greater the dissonance, the greater the pressure to reduce or eliminate dissonance. It follows that such phenomena will be more powerful in real life than in the laboratory.

Festinger argues that dissonance is associated not only with discrepancies in actual attitudes and behaviours, but is also the inevitable consequence of a decision to embark on a particular course of action which is different from the present behaviour, due to the 'undischarged tension of the rejected alternative'. The magnitude of post-decision dissonance is dependent on the importance of the decision and the attractiveness of the non-chosen alternative relative to the chosen. Once post-decision dissonance exists, the methods of reducing it include enhancing the attractiveness of the chosen alternative and derogating that of the non-chosen one. It follows that in order to make easier both the process of decision-taking and the escape from or, better still, the avoidance of post-decision dissonance, there will be selective self-exposure to the information on which the decision is to be based, a process enhanced by the cumulative effects of successive decisions in the same area of behaviour.

Dissonance research, of potential relevance to the explanation of criminal behaviour in general, has been carried out mainly in the context of aggression research, as we shall see shortly, but its relevance to transgressive behaviour is clear. Essentially, the subjective sense of discomfort which arises from discrepant behaviours is dealt with by some form of denial or distortion. In the context of transgressions, this means making statements to oneself which derogate the victim ('he's a mug, anyway'), deny the extent of his distress ('he can easily afford it', or 'he's covered by insurance') or assert the universality of the behaviour ('everyone's doing this, why shouldn't I'). Denial or distortion in *advance* of the transgression, rather than afterwards, further increases the probability that it will be carried out, particularly if the justification provided not only avoids dissonance, but is a powerful incentive in itself and accords with the potential offender's most firmly held values. In this way, an action in itself immoral not only may be condoned, but even perceived as positively moral and desirable. A classic recent example is the break-in to the Democratic Party Headquarters in the Watergate complex during the US electoral campaign of 1972. Some of those concerned, with every appearance of genuine conviction, presented the action as one in the highest interests of their country, carried out to seek evidence that the Democrats, once in office, would recognize Castro's Cuba, thus furthering the 'Communist conspiracy' against the USA. The concept of dissonance avoidance, speculative at present (Feldman, 1976a), may contribute considerably to research into criminal behaviour.

A Field Study

In addition to the detailed examination of self-reported offending (Chapter 1) and an enquiry into home settings (Chapter 2), Belson (1975) also asked his sample of London boys questions concerning the positive and negative factors relevant to the acquisition, performance and maintenance of theft. Acquisition was strongly related to an association with boys already stealing. Desire for 'fun and excitement', truancy from school and a belief in a low probability of being caught were related to performance, and 'permissiveness' (how right or wrong stealing was felt to be) assisted the maintenance of stealing. To expand on some of these variables: 'fun-seeking' may instigate the initial few thefts carried out, if these are positively reinforced by material and/or status gains, then such reinforcers will take over from excitement as an instigating stimulus to theft; truancy increases exposure to opportunity; a belief that detection is unlikely is justified by the factual evidence; the actual experience of successful thefts, even if occasional detection occurs, provides a powerful schedule of reinforcement to maintain stealing; 'permissiveness' may be the result of a post-transgression attitude shift as well as a precursor of the first offence. Belson's results amply reinforce the usefulness of a reward–cost approach to the performance of theft, combined with the enhancing effects of certain social settings and the importance of maintenance by positively reinforcing outcomes.

Aggression: Introduction

As a working definition of aggression we shall adopt that given by Bandura (1973, p. 8): 'Injurious and destructive behaviour that is socially defined as aggressive on the basis of a variety of factors, some of which reside in the evaluator rather than in the performer'. The above definition may be explicated and expanded in two important ways.

1. Aggressive acts both damage victims and have consequences for the aggressor, both positive and negative. Among the positive ones are the acquisition of higher social status or the maintenance of existing status.

2. Social judgments of what is aggressive are very important. They depend upon the following: the intensity of the performer's responses; the level of the display of pain or injury by the recipient; the intentions attributed to the performer; and the characteristics of the performer—sex, age, social class, and so on. Finally, the characteristics of the observer himself—the person who is making the social judgment—will determine to some extent the attribution he makes. For example, people interpret observed behaviours in terms of what they might do themselves in a similar situation. A study by Blumenthal and associates (1971) provides some support for this last point. A representative sample of adult American males labelled looting, shooting, student demonstrations and burning of draft cards as violent behaviour. But most men did not believe it was violent if the police shot looters or struck demonstrating college

students. Conversely, a small minority of men who supported the action of demonstrating college students viewed police action as violent. The authors concluded that violence, like beauty, is in the eye of the beholder. A study by Rule *et al.* (1975) further supports the labelling view. In Chapter 1 we reviewed evidence which suggested the contrary view, namely, that violent assaults of all kinds are frowned upon by most, if not all, societies. However, the two approaches are not really in opposition. The labelling view is an assertion about the doubtful boundary area of the legal definition; the legal standpoint is concerned with the great majority of instances of interpersonal violence. As in the case of crime in general, our review of aggression theory and research will be concerned with the agreed-upon majority of instances of violence rather than the disputed minority.

Aggression: Acquisition

Social Settings

To a considerable extent, cultural and subcultural patterns determine the incidence and relevance of violent crimes. Acceptance of the use of violence varies from country to country, from region to region and even by neighbourhood within a single city, as well as by social class, occupation, race, sex and age. Clinard (1968) points out that it is only in the fairly recent past that there has been a decline in the acceptance of murder as a method of solving interpersonal conflict. It was common in nearly all of Europe a few centuries ago, among all classes, the Vikings of Scandinavia being a particularly striking example. The regional differences in the United States are so wide that a general murder rate for the United States as a whole has no close relation to the actual rate of any specific area or section. Murder rates vary a great deal according to ethnic and class lines. Out of 489 cases of criminal homicide in Houston, Texas, over 87 per cent occurred in four areas, not far apart, located near the centre of the city. Nearly all of these occurred in slum areas populated chiefly by ethnic minorities. Wolfgang (1958) comments on the role of subcultural factors among the working class in precipitating violence as follows: 'The significance of a jostle, a slightly derogatory remark, or the appearance of a person in the hands of an adversary are stimuli differentially perceived and interpreted by Negroes and Whites, males and females. Quick resort to physical combat appears to be a cultural expectation, especially for lower socioeconomic class males of both races' (p. 188).

Similarly, a study carried out in London concluded: 'The analysis of crimes of violence according to their factual substance shows that most of the crime is not committed by criminals for criminal purposes but is rather the outcome of patterns of social behaviour among certain *strata* of society' (McClintock *et al.*, 1963). There are manifest differences in the levels of aggression between different cultures (Mead, 1935; Faton and Weil, 1955). Children growing up in one culture may thus be exposed to consistently aggressive, or alternately consistently unaggressive, models. A distressing though valuable research project would be one which compared the readiness to respond aggressively of children growing up in Belfast during the period of civil disturbances in that city (unresolved at the time of writing) and that of those living in a different and undisturbed part of Northern Ireland. The Philadelphia Cohort Study (Wolfgang *et al.*, 1972) described in Chapter 1 noted a much greater rate of *convicted* crime among non-white than white boys. The disparity was more marked for crimes of violence than for those against property, most marked for homicide and rape. The clear impression of the official statistics is that the social setting of the poor non-white American boy is particularly conducive to the acquisition of violent interpersonal behaviours. This impression is reinforced by another study carried out in Philadelphia, this time of rape (Amir, 1972). This is the most careful and useful study of rape to date, but as Amir points out it excludes the 'unknown rapist' who may or may not be a random sample of the total population of rapists. Amir found the rates for forcible rape by known rapists to be the highest for young, single, lower socio-economic, non-whites—exactly as for crimes of violence in general. In addition, rape tended to be an intra-class and intra-racial phenomenon—the victim was also likely to be poor, and non-white. Thus Amir emphasizes a particular subculture as supplying a learning setting for crimes of violence including rape.

Social settings may also be important for the occurrence of murders. A significant proportion of murders are carried out on persons who are well known to the murderer. One survey of 588 male and female criminal homicides in Philadelphia found that a third were the result of general altercations. Family and domestic quarrels accounted for 14 per cent; jealousy 12 per cent; arguments over money 11 per cent; and contrary to popular impression, robbery only 7 per cent (Wolfgang, 1958). Close friends and relatives accounted for over half of all the homicides and four-fifths of those of the females. Only one out of eight murders was the victim of a stranger. Women, as contrasted with men, generally killed someone in their own family (one in two of the murders committed by women in the Philadelphia study as compared with one in six committed by the men). In the British study by McClintock (see above), nearly 80 per cent of all homicides and 'murderous assaults' (attempted murder) were committed against relatives or victims well known to the attacker. Further, homicides and assaults were often precipitated by the victim. Similarly, in Wolfgang's Philadelphia study over one in four criminal homicides were precipitated by the victim in that the victim was the first to show or use a deadly weapon or strike a blow in an argument. Related to this is the finding that a period of aggressive social interaction between the parties frequently takes place before the aggravated assault. Pittman and Handy (1964) reported that 70 per cent of 240 cases studied in St Louis had been preceded by a verbal argument. (NB. In all of the above studies the data cited are based on 'crimes cleared up' by the police; murderers who are strangers are less likely to be detected than friends or family members.)

Classical Conditioning

As is the case with behaviour in general, aggression can be brought under stimulus control by either paired experiences or response consequences, both directly to the individual himself and to an observed model. A number of animal studies have shown that previously neutral situations can acquire aggression-eliciting properties if they are paired with stimuli previously associated with the elicitation of aggression, for example pain (Vernon and Ulrich, 1966) and brain stimulation (Delgado, 1963). Human studies have shown that symbolic and vicarious experiences are also effective. For example, Insko and Oakes (1967) paired neutral with negative words and demonstrated that the former then evoked hostile responses. The latter have been shown to generalize to unpaired words (Das and Nanda, 1963). Berkowitz (1974) has particularly emphasized the importance of associative learning for the acquisition of aggressive behaviours.

There may be two stages in the process whereby cues become eliciting stimuli for aggressive responses: (a) an aggressive attitude is classically conditioned; (b) such attitudes prompt aggression, either following modelling or by direct stimulation of the subject if the circumstances are appropriate (Berkowitz, 1972).

Observational Learning: General

Modelling influences lead to new patterns of aggressive behaviour, strengthen previously learned inhibitions and facilitate previously learned responses. There is evidence of the retention of even briefly modelled aggressive responses over a period of six months (Hicks, 1965), implying the importance of rehearsal processes, as well as that of external reinforcement. Responsiveness to an aggressive model is increased by prior arousal in a competitive situation (Nelson *et al.*, 1969), indicating the energizing properties of emotional arousal. Observed punishment reduces imitative aggression, while observed reward increases it; the greatest effects of both types of outcome follow instructions to reproduce the observed behaviour. General tactics, as well as specific responses, may be modelled, particularly following exposure to several models (Bandura, 1973).

As well as aggressive behaviour, aggressive attitudes and values have been modelled. In one study (Siegel, 1958), children listened to a radio presentation of a taxi-driver resolving a conflict by a violent or non-violent means. The attitudes they later attributed to taxi-drivers in general were related to the behaviour of the original model. According to Bandura (1973), the modelling of attitudes depends more on the success or failure of the behaviours displayed by the person observed than on their intrinsic qualities of 'rightness' or 'wrongness'. Hence the phrase 'nothing succeeds like a winner'. Morally undesirable though this aphorism may sound, the Nazi party did enjoy considerable popular support in Germany. In everyday life this is termed 'climbing on the bandwagon', for example people will scramble to join a manifestly winning political party, partially irrespective of their evaluation of its programme or tactics. Newspapers and television have provided examples for emulation by murderers, kidnappers and hijackers. But it remains true that the overwhelming majority of newspaper readers and television viewers do not carry out such acts, suggesting that other factors are important for those who do, such as previously reinforced illegal behaviours as well as the opportunity available in the current situation, and the possession of appropriate skills as well as the influence of serious psychological disturbance.

What determines which model will be copied when both aggressive and non-aggressive models are available? The relevant variables include the extent of exposure to aggressive, as opposed to unaggressive models, the power and status of the conflicting models, the outcome of the aggressive or unaggressive responses previously made by the observer in comparable situations, success in matching appropriate behaviours to appropriate situations and—a point little mentioned by modelling theorists—the physical attributes of the person concerned. If the spirit is willing, but the flesh is so weak that no appropriate targets are available, even a consistent and sole exposure to aggressive models will lead to little overt aggression by poorly endowed observers. While we have emphasized mainly observational learning in the acquisition of aggression, it is readily apparent that the probability of an aggressive response will be increased by direct positive reinforcement for successful aggression (particularly likely to be received if the victim has been chosen judiciously). Effects which have been attributed to modelling may be partially explicable on other grounds. A number of instances of apparent modelling of aggression by parents were given in the previous chapter (Glueck and Glueck, 1950; McCord et al., 1959; Bandura and Walters, 1959). It was pointed out that the results obtained could have been due to the fact that parents substituted power for love-oriented techniques following the failure of the former with congenitally unresponsive children. Once this had happened, the power techniques were then modelled by parents to their sons. Hence, the process of modelling by parents may be partially initiated by the biologically based attributes of the child. Hoffman's finding (1960) that mothers who used power techniques had children who aggressed towards their peers may be explained in the same way. Evaluations are likely to change in line with such a change of behaviour. Bandura et al. (1963) found that children resolved a conflict over emulating a person behaving badly but successfully towards another by derogating the victim, having previously copied the behaviour of the aggressor. They thus went through the sequence: behaviour change, dissonance arousal, dissonance reduction and attitude change. A familiar example of such a situation is the acceptance by a film audience of questionable tactics providing that they are used by the 'good guy'.

Modelling effects may be rather subtle. Bandura and Walters (1959), confirmed by Bandura (1960), report that parents verbally modelled aggressive behaviour towards people outside the immediate family and positively reinforced verbal reports of its occurrence. A further subtlety in the modelling process is tacitly to condone a behaviour by withholding punishment, rather than to do so explicitly by overt reward. When punishment is expected, its lack is not unlike the reinforcing effects of praise (Mischel and Liebert, 1966). The subcultural transmission of aggression by modelling is widespread, changing even previously peaceable persons into aggressors, as in the case of military service (Bandura, 1973). The process of change is assisted by changing the moral evaluation of aggression, reducing self-censure for aggressive behaviour, emphasing the admiration given to aggression and removing associations with pre-military life by the constant wearing of uniform and the imposition of military routine. Next, simulated battle reduces fear and accustoms the young soldier to the use of weapons, observational learning again playing an important role in this phase. Finally, actual or prospective enemies are derogated, and hence devalued, by calling them 'Krauts', 'Gooks', etc.

The printed materials which have provided the means for the symbolic transmission of aggression for several centuries have now been added to by films, and most recently by television.

Observational Learning: Television

A number of large-scale studies have been carried out on the effects of television viewing on aggression (e.g. Feshbach and Singer, 1971; Liebert, 1972) without leading to a consensus as to whether aggression is increased (the learning view), decreased (the catharsis view, see later in this chapter) or largely unaffected. The evidence is open to considerable variations in interpretation, even when a very long-term follow-up has been used, as in a study by Eron *et al.* (1972). They found that the greater the exposure to violent viewing at the age of eight, the greater the level of interpersonal aggression at the age of 18, even when the level of childhood aggression (at age eight) was controlled for. However, it may be that overt behavioural aggression at age eight (performance) did not accurately reflect the potential level of aggression (learning) at that age, due to lack of opportunity and so on, but that the latter was reflected in a greater self-exposure to televised violence. Hence, the level of aggression at age 18 was not determined by much earlier viewing habits. Instead, both might be due to some common factor operative before the age of eight, such as biological predisposition, parental training, or both.

Major reviews of the literature have come to rather different conclusions. Bandura (1973) has made the following summary statement on the effects of television on aggression: 'Given the evidence for observational learning, there is no longer any justification for equivocating about whether children or adults learn techniques of aggression from televised models. People who watch commercial television for any length of time will learn a number of tactics of violence and murder. Television is a superb tutor. It teaches how to aggress and by the way it portrays the functional value of aggressive behaviour' (Bandura, 1973, p. 271.) It should be noted that Bandura's general argument is logically fallacious. He begins by asserting that observational learning is a major source of learning; the evidence for this statement is indeed strong. Bandura then goes on to say that television viewing is *potentially* an important source of learning by observation. Therefore television *does* exert a major influence on learning. But there is clearly a gap in the argument. A direct test is needed of the assertion that persons seen on a television screen in the viewer's home, and known to be simulating, have as powerful an effect on future behaviour as the direct face-to-face observation of non-simulating individuals both in laboratory and in real-life situations, a point made in the course of a rather more conservative set of conclusions drawn by Singer (1971), as follows.

1. It is true that there is much aggression displayed on the media, but the present evidence is unclear as to how much of a direct impact there is on actual violent actions.

2. Specific persons may be affected, not necessarily frequent television watchers, but those who lack their own imaginative life.

3. A high level of observed, justified, aggression may lower inhibitions against overt aggression.

4. Televised violence is less influential if it is stereotyped and far removed from the real life of the viewer, an example being TV Westerns.

5. The research that has been carried out to date has not yet duplicated the actual conditions of individuals viewing TV in their own home surroundings.

6. The study of the effects of documentary and newsreel depictions of violence would be very worthwhile, as these depictions are much more concerned with real-life occurrences.

The last two points are amplified in a brief review by Leyens *et al.* (1975). First, the film clips used as stimuli in experimental studies have typically been different from most films or TV programmes. Plots have usually been non-existent, and the clips have consisted of uniform series of violent scenes without relief or contrast. Second, in real life people are repeatedly, though intermittently, exposed to violent stimuli rather than a single exposure in a laboratory. (However, the alternative of repeated laboratory exposure might result in a decreased emotional response through satiation unless great care were taken to arrange for exposure to be intermittent—and therefore time-consuming.) Third, the effects of movies have typically been tested immediately post-exposure, and in a similar experimental context rather than in a real-life one.

Leyens *et al.* (1975) tried to overcome these problems in a study of a Belgian private institution for boys lacking adequate home care or who were referred as behaviour problems. The boys, who lived in four cottages, were assigned on the basis of careful observation to two groups, each of two cottage, one relatively highly aggressive, the other relatively low. Every evening for a week aggressive films were shown to one cottage of each group, neutral films to the other member. Observations of behaviour were carried out during the viewing week, and again in the post-movie week. As compared to the pre-movie week, there was a sharp increase in physical aggression in both high and low aggression cottages immediately after exposure to violent films. This was in spite of the presence of the observers. The aggression persisted in the originally high aggression cottage in the post-movie week. Conversely (though unexpectedly), physical aggression decreased in the cottages exposed to neutral films, an effect which persisted in the post-movie week. The explanation may have been a modelling effect by the heroes of the 'neutral' films—in fact, they were 'good, naive and altrustic' (Leyens *et al.*, 1975, p. 357). If so, this is a finding of some importance (see Chapter 4 on help-giving). The authors state that the results confirm those of two American studies (Parke *et al.*, in press). The Leyens and Parke studies point the way to more useful research into the effects of filmed aggression on real-life behaviours.

Aggression: Situational Determinants of Performance

Presence of a Model

This is a convenient point to describe the two sets of experimental arrangements which have been used in much of the laboratory research on human aggression. The first (Buss, 1961) is presented to the subject as a means of studying the effects of punishment on learning. A 'teacher' shocks a 'learner' for his mistakes and can vary the level of the shock (on a scale from one to 10) and its length. In fact, there is no 'learner' and hence no pain, both being simulated. The second approach (Taylor, 1967) takes the form of a competitive reaction-time task. The 'winner' is allowed to shock his 'defeated' opponent, both participants setting their proposed levels prior to each trial. Typically, the experimenter arranges the sequence of winning and losing. The overwhelming majority of laboratory studies have used either children or undergraduates as subjects.

Epstein (1966) found that those exposed to an aggressive model subsequently administered two to three times as many high-level shocks as those not exposed.

Modelling effects differed according to personal attributes: highly authoritarian persons (measured on a standard personality test) were more imitatively aggressive than those lower on the scale used; black models were imitated more than white ones by both levels of authoritarians, but white models were less imitated by low than by high authoritarians. Modelled punitiveness has been shown to disinhibit aggression in children (Hoelle, 1969).

The effects on observers of the model receiving, rather than meting out, punishment have also been studied. The extent to which punishment of an aggressive model inhibits aggression in observers depends on the probability of similar consequences for the observer and his similarity to the model, both as perceived by the observer himself (Bandura, 1973). Finally, the social context is relevant. An observer who is able to justify an aggressive act by a model is more likely to aggress subsequently (Bandura, 1973). This is an interesting sidelight on the effect of television or film aggression by 'good' as opposed to 'bad' guys and suggests that observed aggression by the former is more likely to be copied than is aggression by the latter.

Bandura (1973) considers the laboratory studies of the modelling of aggression to support the following conclusions.

1. The effects of modelled aggression, in descending order of importance, depend on the rewards which follow if the observer matches his response to that of the model, the personal attributes of the model and the personal attributes of the observer.

2. Observers perceive rewards as being greatest for imitating models whom they perceive as intelligent, competent, powerful and of high status. Such attributes are considered by observers to generalize widely over situations.

Prior Emotional Arousal

Several studies have related modelling effects to the prior level of emotional arousal of the subject. Anger enhanced the effectiveness of aggressive modelling in instigating aggression, but anger arousal alone had no effect on a subsequent opportunity for aggressive behaviour (Hartmann, 1969). This finding suggests the relative lack of importance of previously induced arousal, but may depend upon the level of anger aroused—the higher the level, the less is modelling necessary for instigating aggression. Laboratory studies may arouse lower levels of emotions of all kinds than real-life situations. A threat of retaliation significantly reduced aggression only in those not exposed to aggressive modelling (Baron, 1971a). Again, the observed effect of aggressive modelling may be less marked if retaliation is considerable—more likely to be true outside the laboratory. The argument that modelling effects are smaller in the context of high levels of emotional arousal, or external retaliation, is supported by the next two studies to be discussed. Baron and Kepner (1970) reported that aggression was reduced by exposure to a non-aggressive model regardless of how much he was liked, but this kind of exposure was less effective when the observer was previously highly angered (Waldman and Baron, 1971). It can be concluded that high levels of aroused anger reduce the importance of a model in increasing the probability of an aggressive response. Similarly, a powerful modelling situation will effectively incite aggression even in an individual low in anger arousal. Both prior anger arousal and modelling facilitate overt aggression; each will do so alone if present at a sufficiently high level. When the level of one variable is relatively low, the additional presence of the other markedly enhances the probability of an aggressive response.

Berkowitz (1974) has reviewed studies which indicate that several stimuli, for example the presence of a weapon, exert more powerful instigating effects when those exposed to the stimuli are emotionally aroused than when they are relatively quiescent. He suggests that in such states of high arousal aggressive behaviour is a more 'impulsive or involuntary response' than when the individual is less aroused—when attacks are more likely to be designed to produce benefits to him. Because prior appraisal may suggest damaging consequences for imitation, the judgment of outcomes is very important, as is the subjective evaluation of an act. High levels of emotional arousal may distort judgment; hence the premium placed by organized crime on 'stone killers' who kill without emotion, as opposed to 'animals' who kill almost at random (Teresa, 1973). Tannenbaum (1972) and Geen and O'Neal (1969) showed that non-aggressive sources of arousal enhance aggressive behaviour when this is the only response available. At this point drive theory makes an important contribution. Spence (1956) has argued that all dominant responses are strengthened by an increase in drive (arousal). Thus arousal has important energizing as well as directive functions. In line with this view, Christy et al. (1971) found that success in a task increased subsequent aggression as much as did failure. Emotional arousal, which may or may not have been related to anger, is induced by observing fighting between children (Osborne and Endsley, 1971) and between adults (Zillmann, 1971) and augments aggressive responding (Tannenbaum, 1972). In each of the above studies the observation was of actual, as opposed to filmed, behaviour. Whether the same augmentation effect is true for television and other filmed aggression is one of the central points of the controversy concerning the effect of TV violence, as pointed out earlier.

Alcohol

It is commonly assumed that the ingestion of alcohol enhances aggressive behaviour. This is supported by self-reports by alcoholics and by clinical observations, reviewed by Mello (1972), which indicate that alcohol consumption leads to an increase in aggressive feelings and behaviour. However, these effects were by no means universal. Very recently, a number of laboratory studies have begun to examine the rather complex relationship between alcohol and aggressive behaviour. Using an Epstein-type 'reaction-time' competitive task (see earlier), Taylor and Gammon (1975) found that whereas a high dose of alcohol increased aggression, a low one reduced it, the effect being stronger for vodka than for bourbon, possibly related to the shorter absorption time of the former. The authors suggest that a low dose of alcohol produces a 'tranquil state', incompatible with aggression, a high dose an 'excitable state' which is compatible with aggression. This speculation was supported by ratings of 'opponents' made after the task—the high dose vodka group rated their opponents as more hostile than the low dose group. It should be noted that no experimental group was included which received a drink they believed to be alcohol. Such a 'placebo' group was included in a study by Lang et al. (1975). They reported that male social drinkers *led to believe* (my italics) they had drunk alcohol were significantly more aggressive (on the Buss task—see earlier) than those led to believe they had consumed a non-alcoholic drink, regardless of the actual alcohol content of the beverage administered. The authors conclude that it is the *expectation* of alcohol which facilitates aggressive behaviour, and that this may be particularly true for persons who would otherwise find it difficult to overcome inhibitions (socially learned or innate) against an increase in anger arousal resulting in overt aggression. This suggests that believing that one is 'under the influence' may be a socially approved antecedent condition for behaving aggressively in response to appropriate instigating stimuli. However, before we can replace the ingestion of alcohol itself by a belief or expectation type of approach, the Lang *et al.* experiment would need to be repeated for varying levels of alcohol. It may be that a high level of alcohol will increase aggressive responding irrespective of what the individual has been led to believe. Moreover, the outcomes of previous responses to the particular instigating stimuli concerned will be of great relevance. Alcohol may potentiate an *existing* aggressive response; it may be less likely to lead to the performance of such a response which is not already in the repertoire of the person concerned.

Prior Aversive Experiences

Aversive Physical Experiences. Pain and physical assaults enhance aggression by the recipient. Nevertheless, the learning of appropriate responses is a major prerequisite, even in animals. Young ones rarely fight when electrically stimulated unless they have had previous experiences of fighting (Powell and Creer, 1969), and shocking animals within the confines of a small enclosure leads to more fighting than shocking in a large enclosure (Ulrich and Azrin, 1962). Bandura (1973) suggests that pain facilitates but does not inevitably provoke aggression, the probability of which is increased by direct confrontation with the target in a confined space, lack of opportunity for flight and experience of fighting. Indirect pain, such as the threat of long-term aversive consequences which are much worse than the current level of aversive stimuli, may also provoke aggression, but may equally lead to a self-deluding denial of the likelihood of future threat—as witness the appeasement policies of the democracies prior to World War II.

A study by Baron and Bell (1975) looked at the apparent relationship between 'long hot summers' and outbursts of collective violence, such as racial conflicts in American cities. They found that though uncomfortably hot conditions facilitated aggression (administering shocks) by non-angry subjects they had the opposite effect on previously angered persons. The explanation of the apparently contradictory second finding may be some kind of ceiling effect; nevertheless, it is clear that the link between temperature and aggression is far from simple.

Aversive Verbal Experiences. Verbal threats and insults serve as another set of instigating stimuli for aggressive responses. Toch (1969) studied prisoners with a history of violent behaviour and found that the major factors precipitating such behaviour were insults concerning their manliness and general reputation. He found also that those policemen who were most prone to use violence in the course of their duties used strong, as opposed to mild, verbal threats very early in a confrontation with a suspect. If these proved ineffective, possibly because they aroused more hostility than would have been provoked by mild threats, overt physical violence was the only step remaining—the alternative, backing down, would lose too much 'face'. This notion of a hierarchy of aggressive behaviours seems an important one. Insults represent a watershed stage in the hierarchy. If not responded to, they may invite further aggression—the opponent will regard non-response as an invitation to apply further pressure. On the other hand, response in kind may either deter escalation, or if the insult is more serious than that received, provoke escalation. Equity theory (Walster *et al.*, 1973), which we consider in Chapter 4, discusses the relationship between the damage incurred and the reparation paid as compensation for harm done to another person. The notion that if insults match each other honour is satisfied and the combatants may then lower the temperature fits in well with equity theory.

'Aggressive' Stimuli

Berkowitz (1974) has summarized evidence which indicates that a person or gun or movie can intensify an individual's aggressive behaviour because of the prior association of such stimuli with reinforced aggression. However, there are considerable complications in the effect of, for example, a weapon, as is shown by a report by Turner *et al.* (1975). They first established that horn-honking could be used as a dependent measure of aggressive behaviour towards other drivers and then studied the effect of various weapon-related stimuli, associated with the obstructing vehicle, on horn-honking by drivers briefly held up at traffic lights indicating green. The first study showed that horn-honking was decreased by a clearly visible hunting rifle in a rear gun-rack (not unusual in the town concerned). A second study, of the low-visibility condition only, indicated the importance of the relative status (indicated by years on the road) of the respective vehicles—male drivers of new vehicles were much less inhibited by a bumper sticker labelled 'rifle and vengeance' (*versus* no sticker) than were male drivers of older vehicles. No check was made as to whether the obstructed driver was or was not himself armed. As we shall see below, potential capacity for retaliation is an important determinant of aggressive behaviour.

Withdrawal of Reinforcers

There is general agreement by behaviour theorists that withdrawing or sharply reducing well-established reinforcers is subjectively experienced as aversive. The most frequently described responses to such an experience are depression and aggression. The response adopted depends partly on the outcome of previous experiences of such circumstances, and the presence in the person's repertoire of an overt response which may be produced as an alternative to withdrawing into the state of 'learned helplessness' (Seligman,

1975) which is associated with depression. Attack reactions may be precipitated both by withdrawal of reinforcers and by shifting to a more effortful schedule (more output for the same return, Hutchinson, *et al.*, 1968). Aggression between animals has been noted to be enhanced by overcrowding (Calhoun, 1962), partly because of the increased competition for scarce resources and partly because of the closer contiguity of potential opponents, as noted earlier. However, it is likely to be a *shift* from relative spaciousness to relative crowding which is important, rather than crowding itself, which may become adapted to over long periods of time. Crowding may be aversive by contrast, rather than in an absolute sense, because of the difficulty of learning rapidly new social habits.

Frustration

Thwarting goal-directed behaviour has several potential effects, in addition to the typically emphasized enhancement of an aggressive response which is directed towards attaining the blocked goal. These additional and alternative outcomes include an increase in the intensity of responses in general, rather than those concerned with aggression solely (an energizing, rather than a directive effect), as well as helplessness and thus the absence of a response. The last reaction is of great current relevance. Life in the 'inner areas' of large cities may so reduce the expectation of rewarding outcomes for 'trying harder' that their inhabitants may fall into a state of apathy (in behavioural language, non-responding).

The determining factors for a reduction, or an increase, of activity include the success or failure of past attempts— either by oneself or by appropriate social models—to overcome obstacles, and the relative deprivation suffered. If matters have been going well, a check to the flow of rewards may be much more aversive, because of the sharpness of the contrast, than a frustration which is only one of many recently experienced. A further important determinant will be the comparison between onself and others judged to be similar in circumstances (Festinger, 1954). If few of one's peers are being thwarted in their efforts, a frustration experience leads to aggression under conditions in which an aggressive response appears instrumental (effective) in carrying out the task in hand, indicating the importance of the person's interpretation of the effectiveness of his response repertoire.

In sum: 'Frustration is most likely to provoke aggression in individuals who have learned to behave aggressively and for whom aggression has a functional value' (Bandura, 1973, p. 174).

Orders and Instructions

Anyone who has served in the armed forces has experienced behaving aggressively, either in reality or in mock battle, in response to orders from superiors. Immediate obedience to instructions is expected, disobedience is punished. Such newly trained habits rapidly increase the probability of acts which prior to military service might have seemed unthinkably aggressive. The process is assisted by the gradual escalation of aggressive behaviour, as well as lack of direct contact with the victim, derogation of the victim and the approval of a superior for aggression in response to orders. All of these processes combined led part of the way to the Nazi concentration camps, as well as to the many smaller-scale horrors which have attracted public attention from time to time. Whether or not certain persons are more likely than others to carry out such extreme acts, having been exposed to the same past and present experiences, is a question which we shall consider briefly below and more fully in the chapters concerned with individual differences in criminal behaviour. In a most striking series of studies, Milgram (1963; 1964; 1965a, b; overviewed in Milgram, 1974) has addressed himself to the relationship between aggression and verbal orders mediated by 'obedience'. The basic situation he used consisted of an experimenter, an unaware subject and a confederate. The subject was always assigned to the role of 'teacher' in a learning task, the confederate to the role of 'learner'. The assignation of roles was apparently at random, but in fact was prearranged. The task of the teacher was to inform the learner of his 'errors', again pre-planned, by inflicting electric shocks from an impressive-looking but simulated apparatus, the range of shocks available being marked from 'low' to 'highly dangerous'; the voltage levels represented were also clearly visible. The teacher was instructed by the experimenter (firmly, rather than in the peremptory manner of a military superior) to raise the level of shock in response to errors as the experiment proceeded.

In the first study there was no face-to-face contact between teacher and learner; the only feedback of the learner's distress received by the teacher was when the learner pounded on the wall or emitted an occasional moan. In later studies, the promiximity between the two was varied, as was the closeness of the contact between experimenter and teacher and the presence of other (confederate) 'teachers', who were either responsive to the experimenter's requests, defied them or made no comment. The two response measures recorded throughout were the percentage of subjects (teachers) who obeyed orders to give shocks as opposed to walking out of the situation, and the mean level of shock used. After the first study undergraduates, not themselves participants, were asked to estimate what percentage of people like themselves would obey orders in the situation used in the first study (experimenter present, no face-to-face contact between teacher and learner, and a single teacher). The consensus was that only a very small number would do so. In fact, almost 70 per cent of the teachers (Yale undergraduates) both remained in the situation and used the maximum level of shock. To check against the possibility that this was due to undergraduates fearing to disobey a prestigious professor, the study was repeated in a local town, in an innocuous office, using subjects recruited by a vaguely worded advertisement. The results were similar, emphasizing that obedience to an order to inflict pain on another person is a rather frequent response, displayed by substantial numbers of the population at large, given the appropriate set of stimulus conditions. Milgram also varied the degree of proximity between teacher and learner, from the learner being heard banging on the wall but not seen, heard crying out but again not seen, to being both seen and heard and in the same room as the teacher. The greatest proximity was provided by a situation in which the teacher had to hold the learner's hand on to a shock plate in order to inflict punishment. The percentage obeying orders (defined as using the maximum level of shock) was 66 per cent, 62 per cent, 40 per cent and 30 per cent in the above four levels of proximity, respectively. In a further study, obedience was significantly less when the experimenter was on the end of a telephone than when he was in the same room. Finally, the presence of compliant peers resulted in markedly greater obedience than when the others present defied orders or made no comments either way. Elms and Milgram (1965) compared the 20 subjects who were obedient in the two closer-proximity situations with the 20 who were defiant in the two lesser-proximity (heard but not seen) situations on a number of personality tests and questionnaires. No marked differences were found on a widely used test of personality, the Minnesota Multiphasic Personality Inventory (MMPI), but the obedient group was more authoritarian in personality (respectful to authority, derogatory towards subordinates and social and ethnic minorities) on the California F Scale (Adorno *et al.*, 1950). The obedient group described themselves as being less close as children to their fathers and less well disposed towards them currently than the defiant group. A finding of particular interest was that almost the same number (10 'obedients' *versus* eight 'defiants') had done active duty while on military service, but eight of the obedients *versus* only two of the defiants had actually shot at an enemy, suggesting the importance for behaviour in the current situation of previous training in obeying orders to perform highly aggressive acts.

Milgram's research, and similar studies, has been widely criticized as unethical (e.g. Kelman, 1967; 1972), but it serves as salutary evidence that 'psychopathic' behaviours are more widespread than it is comforting to believe, *even in the absence of material rewards* for carrying them out, and despite the evident distress of the victim. The most disturbing implication of this is that many people have learned to pay more attention to the source of an order than the nature of the order they are given. However, there is a further and more hopeful implication; if unquestioning response to orders is a learned behaviour, it should be equally possible to train people both in the set of values represented by Kohlberg and Piaget's highest moral levels (see Chapter 2) and to question orders in terms of these values. An incidental observation by Milgram (1963), which has important implications if confirmed, was that the obedient subjects appeared to fall into two groups: one was apparently cool and unconcerned, the other was manifestly distressed at the victim's pain, but nevertheless continued to obey the experimenter. The behaviour of the former group was not due to guessing that the learner was faking; none of those who served as teachers did so. This observation suggests that some persons obey despite subjective distress; for others there is no conflict.

Interaction between Aggressor and Victim

Thus far we have concentrated separately on aggressors, on victims, or on external influence agents. We now consider aggression as a function of the *interaction* between the major participants.

Sex of Aggressor and Victim. Silverman (1971) found no difference in the level of aggression by males towards females as compared to males, even when monetary incentives were used. Taylor and Epstein (1967) found that while males reacted aggressively to provocation by males, they did not do so to female opponents. However, while females were unaggressive to females, even when provoked, they were as aggressive when provoked by males as males were to each other. They concluded that the departure of one group from its socially sanctioned role ('men are gentlemanly towards women') served as a strong incentive for the other group to become aggressive. In both studies aggression was measured by electric shocks delivered to an opponent. It seems that the stereotype of the unaggressive female—see Gray in Chapter 5—is determined both by social training in sex-roles and by the different capacity for retaliation typically possessed by the two sexes. Given an opportunity to depart from social convention and an equal level of offensive power, females are likely to respond to a male opponent as aggressively as males do to each other.

Status of Participants. In a study by Mosher (1968), delinquent boys competed in pairs, the boys having been nominated as powerful/weak and aggressive/unaggressive by cottage parents. Not surprisingly, weak boys were less aggressive against powerful bullies than against powerful but non-aggressive boys, suggesting that pecking orders relate to the expectation of retaliation as well as to the level of power itself.

Capacity for Retaliation. Both Dengerink and Levendusky (1972) and Shortell, *et al.* (1970) found that subjects reduced their level of overt aggression (electric shock setting) when the opponent was known to possess the ability to inflict a more massive retaliation than they themselves had available. Even if the opponent failed to use this capacity, its threat was sufficient. Subjects who reduced their over aggression attributed more negative qualities to their opponent than subjects not under threat of massive retaliation (Shortell *et al.*, 1970). These authors expected, but did not test their prediction, that this type of attribution would lead to high overt aggression to a later opponent, provided he was perceived as having little capacity for retaliation. An ingenious study by Berkowitz (1965) provides some support for this expectation. Subjects were prevented from winning in a competitive game by the apparent incompetence of their partner. They attributed more unfavourable characteristics to an innocent bystander and inflicted more shocks on him, when allowed the opportunity to do so, if he possessed the same first name as the frustrating partner than if he had a neutral one.

Perceived Intent of the Opponent. Both Epstein and Taylor (1967) and Greenwell and Dengerink (1973) reported that the level of aggression used by a subject was a function more of an opponent's perceived intention to aggress rather than the actual level of aggression he used. Combining this finding with the previous section, it seems that aggression is most sharply reduced in the face of an opponent who not only has a massive retaliatory capacity but is perceived as standing ready to use it, even though his actual aggressive responses are at a much lower level. This exactly describes the situation in the confrontation between Russia and America over the Russian missile sites in Cuba in 1962 (Schlesinger, 1965). In addition, Schlesinger points out, President Kennedy was careful at all times to leave the Russians a clear method of reducing aggression together with potential rewards for doing so (certain political and military concessions). The importance of combining punishment, or potential punishment, for disapproved behaviour with positive reinforcement for approved behaviour has been emphasized at several points throughout this book. In general, the more safely a proposed target may be attacked the more likely is an aggressive act, but the converse is not necessarily true; an early attack, or at least a build-up of demonstrated capacity for retaliation, may be safer than waiting until the aggressor is even stronger, a lesson learned by the Western democracies following the appeasement policies of the pre-World War II period.

Future Interaction. Although there appears to be no study on the effects on the level of aggression of opponents expecting to meet again after the session, it is reasonable to predict that such an expectation would reduce overt aggression. Silverman (1971) found that even sitting together in silence for two minutes prior to the session reduced the level of aggression displayed in the subsequent session.

Punishment

We shall postpone the major part of our discussion on the control of aggression until Chapters 9 and 10, when we discuss the control of criminal behaviour in general, but a mention of an *unintended* effect of punishment— that of instigating aggression—is relevant at this point. First, aggressive tactics may be modelled to the person being punished, for example by parents to children, although other interpretations of the apparent effects of a punitive parent are possible (see Chapter 2). Second, while low levels of aggression may be inhibited by punishment, even without the provision of alternative responses, higher levels are less likely to be inhibited, particularly when the aggression has not yet found its intended mark. Punishment before the aggression has had its intended effect may even lead to an increase in subsequent aggression, as is frequently the case with goal-directed behaviour blocked short of the goal (Amsel, 1962). Reducing the risk of punishment to the aggressor is likely to instigate aggression. Perceived risk is reduced in a number of ways: anonymity, which is likely to reduce the probability of detection; modelling by others in the group; group aggression—which shares responsibility; the condoning of an aggressive act by at least one recognized holder of authority (for example political superiors) even if other powerful bodies remain potentially hostile; and finally, reducing the visibility of the evidence of aggression (hence the use of rubber implements, which leave no marks, by many torturers).

Aggression: Maintenance

In general, aggression, like other behaviours, is strongly controlled by the prevailing conditions of reinforcement, whether experienced by the aggressor himself, or by observed aggressors.

External Reinforcement

Aggressive actions are often followed by outcomes satisfying to the aggressor. The positive consequences of aggression may be material (money, possessions, etc.), or if not directly material nonetheless tangible, such as social status (an advance in the pecking order) or social approval. An advance in status is a more powerful reward than social approval, both in actuality and in anticipaticn (Martin *et al.*, 1968) because both the gain of status and the prospect of its loss have the more far-reaching effects, particularly when there are many competitors. Hence, the man at the top, who can only go down, fights hardest. Social approval, though less effective than a gain in status, is nevertheless effective in maintaining aggression, whether received directly or by aggressive models (Parke *et al.*, 1972, cited by Bandura, 1973) and in field (Bandura and Walters, 1959) as well as in laboratory settings. In certain cultures, such as that of Germany between 1933 and 1945, aggression towards particular groups received unusually sizeable rewards, both of money, social status and of social approval, vastly widening the circle of those displaying specific aggressive behaviours (Hausner, 1967). Some subcultures, reputedly including the Hell's Angels motor-cycle gangs, also attach a very high value to aggressive behaviour. (However, as we shall see in Chapter 8, most aggressive behaviour within juvenile gangs is carried out at a verbal level only.) In general, the standing of a behaviour within the background culture powerfully influences the ease with which it will be evoked and maintained; aggression is no exception.

Rewards received by social models for aggression increase the response rate of aggression by observers, as does the absence of observed punishment for aggression (Bandura, 1965). The level of modelled aggressiveness is directly proportional to the ratio of rewards to punishments received by the model (Rosenkrans and Hartup, 1967). The effects on observers of modelled aggression are more powerful for models of high status than for those of low status. Aggressive behaviour, like most other behaviours, is relatively easy to extinguish when there is a sudden shift from 100 per cent to zero positive reinforcement.

Unfortunately, it is likely that most aggressors experience intermittent schedules rather than a sudden shift. Aggressive responses maintained by intermittent reinforcement generalize well to new situations (Walters and Brown, 1963) and are resistant to extinction. Because the expression of injury from a physically attacked victim may inhibit physical aggression, verbal aggression may be substituted, providing it achieves the same ends. Victim distress is rather disturbing, hence the strictures to victims to 'take your punishment like a man'. However, overt evidence of victim distress may be highly tolerated if it ensures that the aggressors obtain rewards from superiors. According to the *San Francisco Chronicle* (1970, cited by Bandura, 1973), one US battalion in Vietnam received badges in return for the ears of dead Viet Cong soldiers. (How the exact provenance of the ears was established was not recorded.) Displays of suffering by the victim may have either reinforcing or inhibiting effects, depending on their level and the extent to which they serve as evidence of successful aggression. The further removed the victim from the aggressor more his distress can be discounted, and the less its inhibiting effect. The greater the costs of aggression (both victim distress and retaliatory punishment) the greater must be the rewards of aggression in order to more than counterbalance the costs. Overt distress reduces aggression when the level of aggression displayed is relatively low, but may do so much less when aggression is high. Moreover, the more physiologically aroused the aggressor the less able will he be to discriminate victim pain from victim anger. Typically, the effect of the latter would be to enhance aggression unless it signalled an impending and effective retaliation—when the aggressor might resort to flight. Although Baron (1971b) reported that similarity between aggressor and victim did not inhibit aggression, similarity in his (laboratory) study was established only by a pre-session briefing in which the designated aggressor (a student) was informed either that the designated victim was a student with similar views to himself, or an electrician with dissimilar views. In general, common observation would suggest that medium levels of similarity would inhibit aggression more than either very low levels or very high ones—as witness the viciousness of political strife between doctrinally close factions, particularly those on the Left.

Self-reinforcement

As well as being socially or materially positively reinforced for aggression, people also reinforce themseves, for example for accomplishing a self-appointed aggressive task. It is even likely that some people have acquired self-reinforcement systems in which frequent aggressive behaviour is a source of great self-esteem. Bandura and Walters (1959), on the basis of interviews, reported this to be as relatively frequent in habitually aggressive adolescents as its opposite—self-punishment for overt aggression—was infrequent. Hausner (1967) gives a graphic description of Eichmann (one of the main agents of the Nazi 'Final Solution' for the Jews of Europe) as exemplifying a self-reward system in which the destruction of a particular out-group was the greatest source of pride. Finally, overtly visible self-punishment, or self-reinforcement for aggression by models, has respectively inhibitory and facilitatory effects on the behaviour of observers (Bandura, 1973). Self-arousal helps to maintain anger and in turn aggressive behaviour. Self-arousal is itself maintained by thoughts of the intended target (Bandura, 1973). Glass and Wood (1964) have reviewed post-aggression measures of attitude change, obtained in laboratory studies, which demonstrate such dissonance-reduction mechanisms as derogation of the victim, denial of the severity of his pain, attributing to him the blame for the aggressive action (also documented by Piliavin *et al.*, 1967) and selective forgetting of the severity of the victim's distress. Eventually, dissonance will be avoided in advance by the anticipatory justification of the intended act ('he's only a gook' or 'he deserves it for informing'). Dissonance-reduction mechanisms are particularly relevant in those instances in which aggressive behaviour is sharply discrepant with previously held attitudes—the typical case in laboratory studies. Attitudes previously opposed towards aggression may also be changed more slowly through the gradual desensitization of the previously experienced aversion, or by the instigation to gradually more powerfully aggressive behaviour, together with the receipt of positive reinforcement for such behaviours, as well as the successful use of dissonance-reduction mechanisms. The process is helped by the replacement of such evocatively unpleasant terms as 'murder' by the euphemism 'termination'.

The victim may persuade himself that the aggression was less severe than it actually was. Epstein and Taylor (1967) found that subjects rated opponents who displayed the maximum level of aggression less unfavourably, and also as *less aggressive* when they were consistently defeated by their opponents, than when they were victorious, or the honours were shared. Such submissiveness may both reduce the absolute level of aggression suffered (a short-term gain for the victim) and further reinforce and maintain the behaviour of the aggressor (a long-term loss to the victim).

While self-condemnation for aggressive and other anti-social acts is not unknown, particularly in anecdotal accounts of persons later canonised, the use of cognitive dissonance mechanisms to justify aggression is more typical, and has been widely documented both in anecdotal and experimental accounts. The former include the militant students who justified their destruction of a professor's office by comparing it with the 'much greater' destruction wrought in Vietnam, which the professor 'had done nothing to stop', or by appealing to a higher good ('for the eventual triumph of the revolution'). Displacement of responsibility on to superiors (I'm only obeying orders'), as we have seen in the Milgram studies, is another method of justifying to oneself behaviours apparently discrepant with the social norm of not injuring others.

Latané and Darley (1969) have demonstrated the importance of diffusion of responsibility (I'm not the only one here able to help') in explaining the experimentally demonstrated lower frequency of help-giving by groups as compared to individuals (see Chapter 4); a similar phenomenon may operate in the field of aggression but in the opposite direction, with groups acting more aggressively than individuals.

The Catharsis Theory

Before leaving the topic of aggression, it is necessary to consider the catharsis theory, which has been highly influential both within psychology and on the popular view of aggression. According to this approach (Dollard *et al.*, 1939), aggressive behaviour is impelled by a drive consequent on the frustration of goal-directed behaviour. Overt aggression reduces the drive and hence is reinforced. However, there is good evidence (see earlier) that there is no one inevitable effect of frustration on aggression, which may be increased, decreased or unchanged. It follows that antecedent conditions other than frustration are also relevant, including modelling and the anticipated outcomes of aggression. Previous reactions from victims and other actual outcomes of aggression will also be important. Implicit in drive theories is the discharge of unwelcome energy or tension. In the context of aggression this is termed catharsis, which may be achieved directly by the performer of the aggressive act or vicariously through an observed act (for example televised violence). Briefly, it is asserted that the following sequence will occur: instigation → aggressive arousal → aggressive response → reduction of arousal → a *reduced* aggressive response to the next instigation. The most recent version of the catharsis approach (Feshbach, 1970) restricts itself to the discharge of aggressive drive through experiences which enhance and restore the aggressor's self-esteem and sense of power, results which may be achieved even by *non-aggressive* behaviour. However, the onus is still on drive theories both to demonstrate the existence of a 'drive' and to explain the acquisition of aggressive behaviour.

Geen *et al.* (1975) point out that the results of experimental tests of the catharsis theory have been largely inconclusive, frequently because of a failure to control the changes in the external conditions associated with the second opportunity to act aggressively. Thus, a reduction on the second occasion could be due to an increase in external restraints due to the extent of actual hurt inflicted on the victim. Geen *et al.*'s own study, which was very careful to control for possible changes in external restraints, found no support for the catharsis theory prediction of reduced aggression at the second opportunity. However, aggressive behaviour was noted to be followed by a reduction in recorded blood pressure—thus, perhaps, the subjective sense of 'relief'. The learning approach to aggression would relate the expected level of aggression at a second and subsequent opportunity both to the actual outcome of the first opportunity and the instigating circumstances of the second. The considerable evidence cited in this chapter provides much more support for the learning than for the catharsis approach. However, the emphasis of the latter on internal arousal has added usefully to the perhaps overexclusive insistence of the learning approach on external cues to behaviour.

Finally, from the finding (Bandura, 1973) that aggression is as responsive to the expectation of success for aggressive behaviour as it is to the actual impact of aversive experiences, there are implications for attempts to control aggressive behaviour. The major one is that the provision of alternative non-aggressive ways of achieving the same goals is preferable to 'drawing off' aggression by encouraging an aggressive act (the catharsis approach) the most likely consequence of which is repeated aggressive behaviour in the future, particularly if the earlier act was positively reinforced.

Concluding Comment

A number of important areas of social influence research, observational learning, attitude formation and change and two-person and group processes, provide important sources of hypotheses concerning the learning of criminal behaviours carried out against both property and person, the laboratory analogues of which are transgression and aggression. The learning framework common to both classes of crime can be divided for convenience into acquisition, performance and maintenance. In the acquisition of both classes of criminal behaviour, vicarious and direct reinforcement in real life both play major roles. No clear conclusion can be drawn about the effects of filmed or televised models, although the evidence suggests that such effects are neither trival nor crucial. Classical conditioning seems of particular importance to the acquisition of aggressive behaviour. Certain social settings are particularly favourable to the acquisition of criminal behaviour in general; which setting will depend on the particular crime, for example company fraud is more likely to be learned in the institutions of the City of London than in its back streets, the opposite being true for physical assault. The major situational determinants for the performance of transgressive behaviours are: the risk of detection (particularly the physical presence of the police), the level of punishment if detected, the level of incentive, the presence of a transgressing model, the availability of a legitimate alternative, the nature of the victim, the difficulty of the transgression (skills available against skills required) and (possibly) a temporary reduction in self-esteem. Thus probability is greatest when detection is unlikely, punishment minimal, incentive high, alternatives are absent, transgressing models are present, the transgression requires little skill, the victim is both a stranger and unlikely to report the offence, and self-esteem is temporarily low.

The situational determinants for the performance of an aggressive behaviour are the presence of a model, prior emotional arousal, alcohol (though there are complications), prior aversive, physical or verbal experiences, the presence of aggressive stimuli such as a gun, the withdrawal of valued reinforcers (if previous withdrawal has led to positively reinforced aggression), frustration (ditto), orders and instructions to aggress, a lower-status opponent, and an opponent with significantly less capacity to retaliate or one not likely to retaliate irrespective of capacity. Both transgressive and aggressive behaviours are maintained by external and self-reinforcement. The positive reinforcements include both material returns and improvements in social status. The schedule of reinforcement experienced is particularly important; an intermittent schedule will maintain criminal behaviours despite a later sequence of negative consequences. For both broad classes of crime, the human ability to deny and distort perceptions of the victim assists in the shift from previously law-abiding to later law-breaking behaviours. An alternative approach to the explanation of aggression, catharsis theory, has been found unsatisfactory. Thus, the key elements of an explanatory framework for criminal behaviour are appropriate social settings for acquisition, the processes of acquisition themselves, the situations in which the performance of criminal behaviours, once acquired, is more likely, and the conditions which maintain those behaviours. Finally, the ability to account for the learning of criminal behaviours has implications for their control.

Chapter 4

Learning to Limit Criminal Acts: Pro-social Behaviour

In this chapter we turn from the consideration of the major classes of criminal behaviour to research relevant to social behaviours which may counteract or limit criminal behaviour. Two areas, helping behaviour and equity theory, are discussed, both relatively new in the research literature. Whereas helping research is well under way, empirical work stemming from equity theory is only just beginning.

Helping Behaviour

Introduction

The more objective term 'helping' is substituted in this chapter for the every-day term altruism, which carries the implication of self-sacrifice as one of its essential aspects. In fact, the *degree* of loss, or potential loss, suffered by a benefactor is simply one of several antecedent, independent, variables which may be manipulated in order to study their effect on the dependent variable of helping behaviour. Helping is associated with empathy, defined by Stotland (1969) as an emotional response to the observation or the anticipation of an emotional display by another person. As we have seen in Chapter 2 (Aronfreed, 1968), early social training in empathic behaviour is probably relevant to the development of helping behaviour. The essential components of a helping situation involving humans are a distressed victim and a potential helper, the former being dependent on the latter. Benefits many not be entirely oneway. Helping reduces the helper's empathic distress, if only in anticipation of 'feeling worse if I didn't help', or he may live in a society which gives positive reinforcement for helping, particularly if the action becomes publicly known.

We have emphasized the important of the offender–victim relationship throughout, and in the previous chapter we have seen how various attributes of the participants modify both aggressions and transgressions. But other persons may be involved in crimes in addition to the offender and the victim. There are frequently witnesses who might aid the victim, before, during or after the crime, and in so doing might either prevent it, limit its consequences or provide important evidence to the police, assisting an eventual conviction. Bystanders might also come to the aid of the police more directly, as when a policeman confronts an offender, or at least render passive aid by telephoning for help. Finally, there are situations in which the offender has transgressed without prior planning, such as the case of the motorist who has knocked down a pedestrian. Will he come to the aid of the victim, thereby possibly involving himself more certainly in a prosecution than if he quickly drove on, leaving the victim to his fate?

The starting point for much of the current research in helping behaviour was a real-life situation, the murder of Kitty Genovese in New York in 1964. Although the killing took more than half an hour, not one of the many people who heard or watched from the safety of their apartments came out to assist her or even lifted the telephone to call the police (Rosenthal, 1964).

The methods used to study helping experimentally have varied from the cooperative avoidance situation of Miller and his colleagues (Miller *et al.*, 1959) described in Chapter 2 to field studies in real-life settings, such as the New York underground railway system. All such studies have involved the confrontation of a potential helper with a person in distress—the victim.

Theories of Helping Behaviour

Biological. Hogan (1973) lists four 'preconditions' as particularly relevant. First, a disposition to accept authority, seen most vividly in children (Waddington, 1967). Second, a disposition towards altruistic feelings of group loyalty and group compliance (Darwin, 1872; Hamilton, 1971). Third, a disposition to autonomous (akin to internalized) moral conduct (Lorenz, 1966). Fourth, there are said to be critical periods during early development for internalization (Tinbergen, 1968). Hogan states the above as assertions, presenting no evidence. The vast range of human conduct, from the extremes of self-sacrifice to the callous destruction of others, both of which have occurred within the same 'advanced' Western countries, as well as in adjacent primitive cultures (Mead, 1935), suggests that any biological predispositions which exist towards moral conduct are rather easily overlaid by learning experiences.

Learning. As in the case of transgression, but unlike that of aggression, there is no drive theory of helping. Instead, emphasis has been placed on the social training of emphatic responding, and overt helping behaviour which is assisted by the provision of social models and positively reinforced consequences. A major background prerequisite for the development of empathic responding is the childhood contact with adults, or with peers in the absence of adults (Harlow, 1965). In both instances, a close social attachment with others, continued over a significant period of time, appears to be a necessary, though not a sufficient condition for the acquisition of helping behaviours.

The Social Psychological Approach. Berkowitz (1968) has argued that there is a norm of *social responsibility* which is acquired on the basis of moral convictions, and which affirms that help should be given to a dependent other with or without any reward for doing so. Lerner and Mathews (1967) have qualified this view somewhat by restricting the application of the norm of responsibility to victims adjudged to deserve help. Another view asserts the importance of *distributive justice* (if A has harmed B he must act beneficially to C, to D, and so on). A norm of *reciprocity* (A helps B because in the long run he will be repaid) has been proposed by Gouldner (1960). According to Krebs (1970), the bulk of evidence favours the reciprocity view. Persons are most likely to reciprocate when the original benefactor gave the recipient something he needed at the time, even though he had little of the commodity himself and did so voluntarily. People give to others (distributive justice) when the original benefactor cannot be contacted. It is the network of reciprocal relationships implied in all of these views that we refer to by the term 'community'.

There is no real opposition between the learning and the social psychological approaches. The former is explanatory of the latter, which purports to describe the norms of interpersonal behaviour most prevalent in current Western society.

Helping Behaviour: Acquisition

Social Settings

A number of field studies and experimental reports suggest the influence of childhood training in helping in situations in which the victim was both highly visible and very dependent on the potential benefactor. London (1970) carried out unstructured interviews, many years after the events in question, with a number of people who had risked their own lives to help Jews escape death in Nazi-occupied Europe. Three major features of the rescuers emerged: a close identification with parents who had strong views on moral conduct and acted on them, thus serving as both verbal and actual models for such conduct; a zest for adventure; and the personal skills and resources for the task of saving life. In addition, there was frequently a degree of 'social marginality' — either membership of a minority group, or a previous history of being critical of simple patriotism of the unthinking 'my country, right or wrong' type. Rosenhan (1970) compared those who had given financial contributions to 'Freedom Rider' activities in the southern US states during the civil rights campaign of the early 1960's (a form of direct action used in that context) with those who had made only one or two rides (termed the 'partially committed') and those who had made many rides over a period of a year or more (the 'fully committed'). The financial supporters' involvement was mainly due to their present social relationships (keeping up with the liberals), that of both committed groups was influenced by their early relationship with their parents. The fully committed group had close ties with socially concerned parents and followed the models they provided of moral action of a highly risky kind, even at the cost of social stigma and high personal effort. While this was apparently a model of high costs and low payoffs, such an outcome was true only in the short term. In the long run, self-sacrificial behaviour has often resulted in the final triumph of justice. Thus observers have available to them not only models of short-run self-sacrifice but also examples of the eventual success of such behaviours in the long term, a point not mady by Rosenhan. By contrast, the partially committed had poor relations with their parents. In addition, many were being treated by psychotherapy, and tended to use the 'cause' as part of a search for a personal value system and the esteem of others. A questionnaire study by Hoffman (1975) provides further support for the relevance of parental modelling in helping behaviour. The importance of early learning experiences has also been shown in a controlled laboratory setting using the cooperative avoidance situation of Miller and colleagues described in Chapter 2. It will be recalled that monkeys reared apart were markedly inferior, both as communicators of distress and as responders to the distress of others.

Learning: Direct and Observational

The importance of the classical conditioning of affective responses to distress, followed by the direct reinforcement of overt helping behaviours, has been demonstrated by Aronfreed (1968) as well as by Midlarsky and Bryan (1967). Fischer (1963) has shown the importance of external reinforcement for instrumental acts of helping in increasing their frequency. Weiss *et al.* (1971) reported that the speed of the helping response was increased more by immediate than by delayed reinforcement. The acquisition of an emotional response to the distress of an observed other (vicarious classical conditioning) was shown by Bandura and Rosenthal (1966) both to be a genuine phenomenon and to be enhanced by increased physiological arousal. The acquisition of overt helping by observational learning was demonstrated by Aderman and Berkowitz (1970). Berger and Johanson (1968) reported that the communication of overt emotion by the model enhanced the effects of modelling. Midlarsky and Bryan (1967) found that the greatest post-session generosity was displayed by children who had seen a model not only donate winnings to charity but do so with expressed pleasure. Although relevant studies do not seem to have been carried out, the inhibition of helping would be expected to occur in an individual exposed to a non-helping model. In sum, helping behaviour is acquired according to the same learning principles as other behaviours.

One limitation on modelling in the acquisition of helping is pointed to by White's (1972) finding that observing a charitable model enhanced the subsequent private donation of winnings to charity only when the previous level of donation (the base-rate) was low and when there was little real cost to the subject (winnings were in addition to any money they had to begin with). Observation, plus the guided rehearsal of donation, had more effect than observation alone, but following an interval of several days after training there was a decrement in donation and an increase in stealing (from the pile of donated winnings). This study suggests that potential helpers weigh the costs of helping against the gains. However, such calculative behaviour may be reduced in subjects previously trained *not* to count the short-term cost of helping, as the previous section suggested.

Helping Behaviour: Situational Determinants of Performance

Presence of a Helping Model

Krebs (1970) cites many studies which show that exposure to a person displaying helping behaviour enhances the performance of previously learned helping behaviour. He set out a number of functions served by helping models which contribute, separately and together, towards the enhancement effect. (By the same token, modelling *not*-helping inhibits helping; simply insert 'not' before 'helping' in the list which follows.)

1. Modelling increases the salience of a social norm of helping (its 'attention-getting' quality).

2. Modelling demonstrates the appropriateness of helping in the particular situation concerned.

3. Modelling provides information about the helping behaviour of other members of one's group.

4. Modelling provides information as to the consequences of helping.

Instigating Stimuli

Certain perceptible features of the victim influence the frequency and speed of helping. For example, Piliavin and Piliavin (1972) found that a (simulated) bleeding victim received help less often than a non-bloody victim. The effects of such instigating stimuli are likely to interact with the costs of a helping action as perceived by a potential helper. Coming to the aid of the bloody victim of an obviously gangland fight may simply invite assault by his attackers and may have very different consequences from assisting someone, equally bloody, who clearly has been knocked down by a hit-and-run driver. In another study (Baron, 1970) the speed of the helping response (indexed by reaction time) increased as the manifest pain of the victim increased; speed also increased as the level of physiological arousal of the helper increased. From the general finding of a curvilinear relationship between arousal and performance, it would be expected that as the level of arousal of the helper increased beyond the level for optimal performance, *effective* helping (as opposed to frantic but ineffective efforts) would decrease, particularly in situations in which effective helping involved a distinct degree of skill.

Temporary State of the Helper

In general, positive affective states increase helping, negative ones decrease it. Berkowitz and Connor (1966) found helping, particularly of highly dependent others, to be increased by success experiences. It is also increased by the self-perceived competence of the helper (Midlarsky, 1968). Isen (1970) demonstrated in three separate studies that helping, defined as donating to charity, was increased by previous task success and reduced by failure. The effects reported by Isen were largely independent of the attention paid to the 'victim', but at levels of personal failure beyond those achieved in laboratories the attention of a potential helper may be so directed towards his own distress that he simply fails to notice the distress of another person. Isen did not attempt a detailed discussion of the observed effect on helping of what she terms the 'warm glow of success'. One possibility is that there are learned social norms of 'sharing one's good fortune', possibly made more powerful by an associated learned belief that not to do so is to court 'punishment'. In this context, helping becomes a type of *Danegeld*.

Temporary State of the Victim

A series of 10 studies by Berkowitz and his colleagues (for a full listing see Krebs, 1970, p. 278, Table 4) found a consistent increase in helping as the perceived *dependency* of the recipient increased, in a situation in which a 'worker' could help his 'supervisor' win a prize for expanding the output of his group of workers. However, another study (Schopler and Bateson, 1965) found the outcome of a helping situation to depend on the cost of helping (giving up something for helping) and the sex of the benefactor, as well as the level of dependence on the recipient. Both sexes helped more if the cost of doing so was low, but whereas females helped more if the recipient was highly dependent on them, males helped more if the partner was low in dependency. Finally, the more interpersonally *attractive* the recipient, the more is he or she likely to be helped (Daniels and Berkowitz, 1963).

Another attribute of the potential benefactor was studied by Feldman (1968b). He examined the response to requests for help (to mail a letter) from either a compatriot or a foreigner in three cities, Boston, Athens and Paris, and found a tendency for a compatriot to be helped more in all three. It is not known whether situations making greater demands on the potential benefactor would increase or decrease the difference obtained in this study.

Interaction of Helper and Victim

Gaertner and Bickman (1971) used an ingenious 'wrong number' technique: a person calling from a telephone booth identified himself as trying to reach a garage; would the 'unintended' recipient of the call help the caller, who had no money left, by making the call for him? In fact, the number given to the recipient of the call was that of the experimenter's assistant, enabling the recipient's responses to be indexed. The caller's voice was always clearly identifiable as belonging to either a white or a black American. Blacks who were telephoned 'by mistake' helped black and white callers equally, but whites helped whites more frequently.

Gaertner (1973) used two situations, the one described above and one in which subjects varying in race and in political affiliation were asked what they would do after hearing a taperecording of the conversation between the caller and the person asking for help. The result of both situations was that, with age controlled, blacks were helped less by conservatives than by liberals, but conservatives helped whites more than did liberals. In other words, political conservatism is an active attribute, increasing helping of relatively similar others, decreasing the help given to relatively dissimilar others.

Other things being equal, variations in the sex of the helper and the victim do not exert important effects on helping behaviour (Krebs, 1970; Feldman, 1970), but in situations in which there is some danger of retaliation against the helper by a third party it might be that males would be less deterred than females—depending on age, physical prowess and so on. The major point is that neither sex *inevitably* evokes more help or gives more help. The costs of helping *versus* not helping, the distress of the recipient, the possession of the necessary abilities or resources and other situational variables exert more effect than the sex of those involved.

Presence of Others

A series of studies by Latané and Darley (1970) investigated the effect on helping another of the number of potential helpers present, under the general rubric of *bystander intervention*. A typical situation was one in which one subject heard another person in apparent distress. He was led to believe either that he alone heard the victim, or that others, varying in number, could also do so. Most of the studies found that subjects were more likely to help when they thought they were alone, indicating support for Latané and Darley's major explanatory hypothesis: there is a diffusion of responsibility for helping, and of blame for not doing so; the more people are present, the less each individual's share of both.

A number of limitations of the diffusion theory have been demonstrated. Latané (1967) found that hardly any undergraduate subjects intervened to help an assaulted child, even when they were alone. (In fact, when personal danger is a potential cost of helping, and one's companions are known to be handy in a fight, an increase in numbers of bystanders seems likely to *increase* the chances of intervention, indicating the importance of the resources available to potential helpers and the costs to them of helping.) In line with this, Staub and Feagans (1969), cited by Krebs (1970), found that children under the age of 10 were less likely to help another child who had fallen and hurt himself when they were alone than when they were in pairs. However, older children tended to behave more like Latané and Darley's undergraduate subjects. This result again suggests an interaction between the resources available and the number of bystanders present—two younger children may be able to help where one feels inadequate. Kauffmann (1968), cited by Krebs (1970), provides some support for the diffusion hypothesis. He used Milgram's obedience situation, described in Chapter 3, and found that only 11 per cent of those observing a situation by themselves responded to the 'learner's' pleas for help. No difference was made by the assigned status of the bystander, by suggestions of the illegitimacy of the 'teacher's' actions or by indications that the observer would later occupy the role of the teacher. Kauffmann did not study the effect of expecting to occupy the role of the learner at a later stage—a condition which might have provoked more intervention.

Piliavin *et al.* (1969) studied the interaction of victim attributes and number of bystanders in a controlled field situation—the express trains of New York's 8th Avenue independent subway. Four teams of students were used, each consisting of 'victim', a 'model' and two observers, to instigate and record the behaviours of passengers in responding to the 'collapse' of the victim. The speed of responding did not decrease as the number of passengers increased, as would have been predicted by the diffusion of responsibility hypothesis. Victims perceived as ill received more help than those perceived as drunk. The ethnic group membership of victims and helpers made no difference when the victim was ill; when he was drunk his own group was more likely to help. The effect of a helping model in instigating others to help was much more marked when the model helped quickly than when he did so after a delay. Finally, the longer help failed to materialize, the more likely were onlookers to leave the area of the emergency, suggesting that failing to help is experienced as distressing. To reduce his distress the non-helper leaves the scene. (Particularly likely if the existence of the victim cannot be ignored.) Smith *et al.* (1972) confirmed the diffusion of responsibility hypothesis in a somewhat ambiguous situation. (The victim, a female experimenter, staggered away from the subject's presence and into an adjacent room, not being seen by him thereafter.) However, they also found that the difference between the lone bystander and the two-person condition was markedly reduced when the second bystander (a confederate who always refrained from responding) was perceived as dissimilar to himself by the first (naive) subject. Similarity–dissimilarity was manipulated by having the subject and confederate read a report of each other's attitudes to the use of 'pot'. Two studies by Clark and Word (1972; 1973) were concerned with the degree of ambiguity of the victim's apparent distress. Both demonstrated that the diffusion of responsibility phenomenon is much more likely to occur in a situation in which there is room for uncertainty as to the seriousness of the victim's distress. When this was in question (for example the victim was seen but not heard), the speed of helping was not affected by the presence of others. In addition, subjects with skills relevant to the particular situation—the victim in one variation was lying across 'live' electric wires—were more likely to help than those without electrical skills.

Using the Milgram obedience situation, Tilker (1970) found that as he increased the stated ability of an observer to intervene to prevent the teacher continuing to give shocks (implying the observer's responsibility for the learner), so intervention increased, as it did when the level of the learner's distress increased, so that all observers intervened when both responsibility and feedback were maximal. Tilker did not vary the cost of intervention to the observer; in general, it is desirable in experimental studies that the costs of helping and the costs of *not* helping (to both helper and victim) should both be varied.

Darley and Batson (1973) carried out a study which is unlikely to endear them to churchmen. They asked theological students to prepare a talk, either on the theme of the Good Samaritan or on what constitutes a good minister. The students were then asked to go to another building in order to record their talks. They were either instructed to hurry over, or received an indication that there was ample time to get there. Those in a hurry were much less likely to stop and help a shabbily dressed person, slumped by the side of the road, who was encountered by all the students in turn. The theme of the talk they had just prepared made no difference to the frequency of helping. Nor was there any marked relationship between helping and questionnaire measures of 'religiosity'. (No comparison was made with the helping behaviour of atheists or agnostics.) Once again, it seems that the perceived costs of helping play an important part. The students were ostensibly taking part in an enquiry into ways of enhancing the job satisfaction of ministers, hence benefitting themselves in the long run. In addition, in hurrying they were obeying the orders of a person perceived to be in authority.

Restraints Against Helping

We have already identified a number of situational restraints against helping: potential physical injury or financial loss to the helper, lack of self-perceived competence of the helper, uncertainty that the victim was definitely in distress and the presence of others, as well as such attributes of the victim as being of a different race or nationality. Another source of restraint is suggested by Brehm's (1966) concept of reactance. According to this, a person 'reacts' against external attempts to restrict his perceived freedom to engage in a range of potential behaviours by *not* performing the response the other person desires. His goal in doing so is to reestablish, or to safeguard, his threatened freedom of choice—to respond or not to respond as he sees fit. Jones (1970) found support for a number of predictions made by reactance theory: when a person does not feel free to refuse help, the more the victim is dependent the more will he be helped; however, when he does feel free to refuse, increasing the victim's dependence *reduced* helping—because of the greater threat to freedom of a more dependent victim. Reactance is enhanced if the victim's request for help is accompanied by the implication of further requests in the future. (We might call this the 'get off my back' phenomenon.) A series of studies by Goodstadt (1971) also supported reactance theory. Reminding a person that he liked the dependent other reduced helping (making the obligation explicit aroused reactance). Conversely, a reminder of dislike increased helping (as a reaction against the reminder that he should not be helping someone he disliked).

The above 'reactance' studies employed rather mild situations to evoke a need for help; greater victim distress might overcome the helper's resentment of feeling obligated to conform to his stated feelings towards the other. In addition, there are likely to be individual differences in the value placed on being free to respond irrespective of external demands, perhaps related to the locus of control dimension (see Rotter, 1966). Thus, high internals may display more reactance.

People in general help less as the costs of doing so increase, but the reduction is likely to be more marked in those who typically display higher than average levels of behaviours related to those of the classical psychopath-exploitation of others and lack of response to their distress (Wagner *et al.*, 1971). We discuss the concept of psychopathy in Chapter 6.

Helping in Criminal Contexts

Only a few field studies have been carried out which are relevant to the questions we raised at the beginning of this section. Denner (1968) reported that subjects who had witnessed a staged attempted theft and then failed to report it. invariably mentioned that they were unsure of what they had seen and/or feared possible embarrassment (both examples of dissonance reduction by denial following the discrepant behaviour of not reporting an offence when the social norm is that one should do so). An ingenious study by Gelfand *et al.* (1973) followed on from Saul Astor's study of American shoplifting (*New York Times*, 1970). By prior arrangement with a number of drugstores in Salt Lake City, a 'shoplifter' who was dressed alternately in 'hippy' and in conventional clothing picked up an article, tried to make sure that she had attracted the attention of a fellow shopper, and hurried out without paying. All shoppers whose attention appeared to have been attracted were interviewed shortly afterwards. Nearly two-thirds of the shoopers claimed they had not noticed the shoplifter, even though observers on closed-circuit TV recorded at the time that his/her attention had been successfully engaged, and the 'shoplifter', in ratio contact with the observers, never proceeded with the theft until the observer confirmed to her that she had been noticed by one or more shoppers. Males, the middle-aged and those raised in rural environments were more likely to report the shoplifter, whose appearance made no difference to the rate of reporting. The authors interpret the low reporting rate in terms of several variables: diffusion of responsibility because many others might have seen the theft, attribution of responsibility for apprehending shoplifters to the store's own detectives, the possibility of accusing the wrong person and being sued by him, or of the wrong person being convicted on the accuser's evidence. All of these reasons were mentioned by those interviewed. It may be that bystanders would be more likely to report theft from a 'small' shopkeeper; this method of research is worth further study.

Helping Behaviour: Maintenance

External and Self-Reinforcement

Although few relevant studies have been reported, it is reasonable to assume that helping behaviour, like other behaviours, is maintained by its consequences. In a study by Moss and Page (1972), a female confederate asked a subject for a street direction, responding to his information by thanking him profusely (positive reinforcement) or turning away without thanks (negative reinforcement). A second confederate then dropped her purse in the subject's path. It was found that subjects helped less (by picking the purse up, or pointing it out) after negative reinforcement than when there had been no prior encounter (another group of subjects used for control purposes). However, positive reinforcement did not increase helping as compared to the control condition. This seems related to the trivial nature of the first situation, rather than indicating that helping behaviour is an exception to the general rule concerning the maintenance of behaviour. Positive reinforcement tor helping behaviour which is of major importance to the recipient is likely to increase the future display of such behaviour by the donor.

Positive, external, reinforcement, both direct and vicarious, and self-reinforcement would all be expected to maintain helping behaviour. External reinforcement from a third party may take either material (for example financial rewards) or symbolic (medals, mention in newspapers) forms. Reinforcement from the victim is frequently expressive (statements of gratitude, immediate changes in facial expression from distress to relief, etc.). Vicarious reinforcement directly received by observed others (models) would be expected to maintain helping behaviour by observers. Observed behaviours include those portrayed in television and films, as well as real-life examples of pro-social actions. Finally, self-reinforcement will maintain helping behaviour which meets strongly held personal norms of social reciprocity, distributive justice or social responsibility.

The absence of positive reinforcement for helping due to lack of victim feedback, absence of external recognition and so on would tend to reduce future helping behaviour, and the receipt of physical punishment or some other aversive consequence for helping would be even more deleterious. The schedule of positive reinforcements previously received for helping will be of importance. A well-established helping response will be maintained by even occasional positive reinforcements for helping actions, particularly if those reinforcements concerned are highly evaluated by the helper.

Cognitive Consequences of Helping and Failing to Help

Although a great many studies have examined the cognitive consequences of aggression and transgression, usually finding justification of the action as well as derogation of the victim, very few have done so in the area of helping behaviour. Yet, as we have seen, the greater the restraints against helping, the more likely are people to refrain from doing so. How do people deal with such discrepancies in their behaviour from conventional social norms? In tackling this question, Feldman and Callister (1971) made their starting point Zimbardo's (1969) extension of dissonance theory. According to Zimbardo, whether people blame themselves or blame external causes for their own discrepant behaviours depends on the availability of external *justification*, and the degree to which they were free to choose the discrepant behaviour or to refuse to do so. A combintion of high freedom of choice and low external justification was predicted to be the condition most likely to result in derogation of the self, rather than of the other person or an outside authority, etc., when a behaviour discrepant with accepted social norms had been displayed. Feldman and Callister used the cooperative avoidance situation (Miller *et al.*, 1959), appropriately adapted to human subjects. The simulated facial expressions of relief and distress of a display (D) subject, who was a trainee actor, were watched on closed-circuit television by observer (O) subjects. The latter were offered one pound (= 100 pence, about $2·6 at the time) for participating in 'a study of cooperative behaviour'. The situation was set up so that the actor always took the D role, although it was made to appear to O that he was equally likely to do so. O was told that a light signal, visible only to D, would indicate to D that he would receive an electric shock (previously demonstrated to O) unless O operated a response lever to enable D to avoid shock and did so within eight seconds of the light coming on. Half the O subjects (termed high loss = high external justification) were told that they would lose 5 pence each time they enabled D to avoid the shock. The other half (low loss = low external justification) were told that they would lose 1 penny each time. Both groups were told that there would be 20 trials. In this context 'external justification' meant the availability of an 'external' reason—monetary loss—for departing from the assumed social norm of helping a person in distress. During the whole of the 20 trials O had a clear head-and-shoulders view of D. The changes in facial expression of the latter left no doubt that the performance or the omission of an avoidance response by O had direct, and either pleasant or unpleasant, consequences for D.

A large number of behavioural, cognitive and personality measures were taken. The results of present relevance concern the correlations between the evaluative ratings of the D and O subjects (made by the latter before the justi-fication variable was manipulated and again at the end of the 20 trials) and two behavioural measures—the number of trials on which O avoided and the latency of the response on those trials. The results indicated that high-loss subjects who avoided infrequently, or slowly or both, evaluated D worse after the session than prior to the session, but left unchanged their self-evaluation. In contrast, infrequently helping low-loss subjects tended to evaluate *them-selves* worse and left their evaluations of D unchanged. The corollaries of these results also occurred: frequently helping high-loss subjects evaluated D better and left themselves unchanged; frequently helping low-loss subjects tended to evaluate *themselves* better and left D unchanged. It should be noted that the changes in the evaluation of the self and of the other person in this experiment took place after the behaviour of helping or failing to help. The results, which were predicted from Zimbardo's (1969) explication of the justification concept, indicated different methods of achieving dissonance reduction for the two groups. High external justification (high-loss) subjects who helped infrequently dealt with the dissonance between the social norm of helping and their own behaviour by devaluing the other person (i.e. 'I don't like him, hence he was not worthy of help'). Those who helped frequently increased the consonance between helping and evaluation ('I like him, hence he was worthy of help'). Self-evaluations were unaffected because behaviour took place in a context in which the responsibility for one's behaviour could be attributed to an external source—the loss of an appreciable sum of money (for British students at that time). In the case of the low justification subjects (the low-loss group), responsibility rested squarely on the self; failure to meet self-imposed standards led to self-derogation; meeting these standards improved further the evaluation of the self. When external justification for discrepant behaviour is low, the self-administered positive reinforcements for socially approved behaviour are high, but so are the self-administered negative reinforcements for failing to display such behaviour. It may be that the behaviour of those subjects who helped infrequently, despite suffering little financial loss for doing so, is explicable in terms of reactance theory. If so, a reduction in self-esteem seems a rather high price to pay for the retention of freedom. In any event, dissonance reduction achieved by derogating the victim, attributing to others the blame for help not being given or for lack of success if help was attempted but failed to produce the desired effect, is clearly an important aspect of helping behaviour. Whenever means for external justification are available, they will be resorted to, particularly those justifications which enable people to deny that they had any choice in the matter—'I was only obeying orders', etc.

When an attempt to help has been made, has proved unsuccessful and no external justification for this is available, the resulting self-blame may *increase* helping behaviour in the short run—in the same way as frustrating the achievement of any highly prized goal increases the efforts to attain it. But in the longer run, if failure continues, and the cost of repeated attempts are seen to be too great, the individual will provide himself in advance with external reasons for his failures (i.e. he will make sure external justifications are available). Finally, he will avoid stimuli which might lead him into situations in which help will be required. Self-blame is only tolerable in the short term, and only if it has been previously experienced as being succeeded by self-praise, following the success of renewed attempts to help. On occasion, the standard methods for limiting self-blame are inadequate for their task, particularly where external justification is totally unavailable. This is likely to bear particularly hard on individuals biologically predisposed to depression of mood, because of the risk of self-injury, a frequent accompaniment of depression. Self-blame is also likely to have fatal consequences in cultures in which falling badly short of the social norm may be expunged only by suicide—the ultimate self-punishment.

Equity Theory

Overview

We have emphasized that whether people behave 'well' or 'badly' is to a considerable extent a function of previous outcomes and the total pattern of rewards and costs in the current situation. Abstract exhortations to moral actions will fall on deaf ears unless the behaviours which are urged have become part of the individual's repertoire through systematic childhood socialization and have been maintained and strengthened by adult experience. We have seen that the experimental evidence concerning crimes against the person (aggression) and against property (transgressions), as well as the extent to which onlookers prevent or limit them (help-giving), amply supports such a view. Moreover, consistently 'moral' or 'immoral' actions will only occur if training has generalized widely across situations and responses.

Walster *et al.* (1973) have set out this general approach to individual human behaviour as it relates to behaviours between persons in the form of a theory, termed equity theory. The theory is concerned with how people *actually* behave towards each other, as opposed to how they *should* behave. It will be seen to have considerable relevance to criminological problems. The following is a brief selection from equity theory, together with some possible implications for the limitation of criminal behaviour.

Equity theory rests on the basic assumption that man is selfish. The theory does not state whether selfishness is biologically determined or is a learned general response, but this lack of specificity as to its source need not affect our consideration of the theory. It consists of four propositions which predict when persons will perceive that they are unjustly treated and how they will react when they find themselves enmeshed in unjust relationships.

Proposition I. Individuals will try to maximize their outcomes (where 'outcomes' = rewards minus costs).

Proposition IIa. Systems are evolved to distribute equitably rewards and costs.

Proposition IIb. Groups will generally reward members who treat others equitably and generally punish (i.e. increase the costs of the behaviour) members who treat others inequitably.

The story continues in the form of corollary 1·1 of proposition I: 'So long as individuals perceive they can maximize their outcomes by behaving equitably, they will do so. (However) should they perceive that they can maximize their outcomes by behaving inequitably they will do so'. (In plainer language: people will keep the law only so long as it pays them to do so; if it does not, they will break it, particularly when the rewards of doing so perceptibly exceed the costs.)

Walster and her colleagues then ask the question: how do socialized persons react when in an inequitable relationship? They answer it by propositions III and IV.

Proposition III. They become distressed (whether they are the victims or the beneficiaries of the inequity); the greater the inequity, the more the distress.

Proposition IV. Individual who perceive they are in an inequitable relationship attempt to eliminate their distress by restoring equity. The greater the inequity, the more distress, and the harder they try to restore equity. (Thus, by implication, both offenders and victims seek to restore equity.) Equity is restored by restoring either 'actual equity' or 'psychological equity'.

Actual equity is restored by: working less hard, making the employer work harder, demanding a rise, or by stealing or damaging equipment. All of these methods relate to the work situation. In the area of legally defined harm-doing, actual equity may be restored by compensating the victim—through some form of restitution, by the harm-doer depriving himself of some material benefit, even on occasion by self-punishment. The choice of method will depend on the harm-doer's relationship to the victim and on prior self-expectations.

Psychological equity is restored by distorting the perception of one's own and others' inputs (i.e. the total pattern of rewards and costs). For example, the employer of an underpaid worker might say: 'He's stupid, he wouldn't know what to do with more money, he only works to see his friends', etc. A person who has stolen money from another might say: 'He's a fool, he shouldn't have left his money lying around', or, 'We're all bent, I'm no worse', etc. Thus in the area of criminal behaviour psychological equity may be restored by derogating the victim, by denying one's own responsibility, minimizing the victim's suffering, attributing responsibility for harm-doing to another—for example a superior—and so on.

The vast majority of applications of equity theory have been in the occupational context (for example Adams, 1963), but Walster *et al.* also set out some applications to 'exploitative' relationships (those in which a harm-doer damages a victim in some way). They assert that if a harm-doer's outcomes are too high he will feel distressed, as well as anxious concerning retaliation from others (the victim and/or his social protectors), which would restore equity to the situation. For example, a 'reasonable' level of loss due to customer or employee shoplifting may be tolerated by a store; anything in excess disturbs the delicate balance of the conflict between not upsetting customers and employees by too close surveillance and not incurring unsupportable financial losses. Hence, shoplifters may deliberately maintain their depredations against a particular store below the level which would result in too vigorous a counteraction by the management.

Distress may arise from discrepancies between a damaging act and the harm-doer's self-concept as one who does not harm others (or at least his socially learned belief that he should not do so). Even criminal organizations have codes about who should not be harmed—usually members of the organization itself or of coexisting groups with whom there are agreements not to encroach on the other's territories. Harm-doing will be confined largely to retaliation.

Harm-doers' responses to an inequitable situation thus fall into two categories, which are largely, though not entirely, mutually exclusive: compensation and justification. Which category of response will be used will depend on the adequacy of the techniques available for restoring equity and on their cost. The more adequate is a technique in *exactly* restoring equity, the more it will be used. A restraint on its use is cost; the more costly a technique the less likely is it to be used.

Two variables determine the probability of using the justificatory category of equity-restoring responses.

1. The acceptability to the victim of the justification offered by the harm-doer. If little detectable distortion is required and/or the justification is readily believed, then justification will be the method adopted.

2. The amount of contact with the victim. The more contact there is, the less likely is a justificatory technique to be used; it becomes less possible because with increased contact the overt evidence of harm-doing is harder to ignore. Thus some form of material compensation becomes more likely when the less costly (to the harm-doer) justificatory method will not suffice. It follows that the more contact there is between a potential harm-doer and a potential victim, the less likely is inequitable behaviour to occur (because equity can only be restored by actual equity—compensation). If, despite the advance awareness of actual costs, inequity does occur in a situation of close contact, actual equity is very likely to be the method of restoration adopted.

Harm-doers' Choice of Method to Restore Equity

Other things being equal, harm-doers will use the least costly equity-restoring techniques, those that allow both persons (the harm-doer and the victim) to maintain their highest possible relative outcomes; hence, the rarity of self-punishment, particularly when first external justification, and next actual compensation, are available. Hence, unless the dominant power group specifically excludes him ascending a hierarchy of increasingly costly equity-restoring techniques—for example by demanding immediately his resignation for political misdeeds—a politician will first blame his subordinates, then his opponents, for compelling him to resort to doubtful acts. Next he will offer to tighten up the code of behaviour to prevent this happening again', and finally he will fight hard against external punishment (by impeachment, etc.), all before punishing himself by resigning, or, the final step, suicide.

Restoration of Equity by Victim or External Agency

Walster *et al.* assert that when a victim or an outside agency restores equity to a relationship the harm-doer's distress is reduced and he is less likely to use additional equity-restoring techniques. (If this is correct, it would suggest that a thief robs a person he knows to be insured with more equanimity than he would an uninsured person.) The following methods of restoring equity are available to the *victim*.

1. *Compensation*. From an insurance company, from the public purse, etc.

2. *Retaliation*. When given the opportunity, victims retaliate against those who have treated them inequitably. The more inequitable they perceive their treatment to have been, the more strongly will they retaliate (Ross *et al.*, 1971). When the victim retaliates, the need for the harm-doer to resort to compensation or justification is reduced. This may happen, albeit symbolically, in advance of a crime; for example, the potential victim is regarded by the offender as having the police on his side. In a laboratory study, Berscheid *et al.* (1969) showed that derogation of a victim by a harm-doer occurred much more when no retaliation was available to the victim than when he had access to it.

3. *Forgiveness*. This may occur following an apology by the harm-doer. Apologies may take the form of persuasive communications: (i) designed to explain and hence justify the harm-doer's actions ('I hit you first because I thought you were going to hit me', and 'I was starving, you had plenty', etc.); (ii) designed to convince the victim that their relationship is still equitable ('I've been upset ever since it happened'). In the latter case the victim may then conclude that the harm-doer has punished himself sufficiently, so that no further external punishment is necessary.

4. *Acceptance and justification*. The inequity is acknowledged, but nothing need be done to remedy the situation ('let's forgive and forget, and start again all square'). In its extreme form this is the 'learned helplessness' situation (Seligman, 1974)—nothing *can* be done—'we just have to put up with it' (loan-sharking, extortion, etc.). The victim may even justify his misfortune (for example 'God sent it to try me'—'to punish me').

Outside agencies may intervene to restore equity where it is markedly out of balance, using one or more of the following methods.

1. Persuading the harm-doer to give voluntary compensation. This not only restores equity but provides models for the behaviour of other harm-doers.

2. Compulsory compensation if persuasion to voluntary action fails. This is used by both the Norwegian and the Hungarian legal systems. The American system takes restitution into account in fixing paroles (Macaulay and Walster, 1971). The latter point out the formal and informal techniques widely used to induce restitution. 'A police officer may decide not to arrest a shoplifter if the wrong-doer is not a professional thief and if the stolen items are returned; a district attorney may decide not to prosecute if the amounts embezzled are returned' (p. 179). In addition, the state may withhold money from prison earnings.

3. Restitution cannot be elicited. Instead, the victim's suffering may be alleviated, for example, by compensation by the state to the victim of assaults, the British practice for the past few years. It has been argued (Fry, 1956) that this should be extended to the victims of all offences. (Another method of

restitution, not mentioned by Walster *et al.*, might be termed symbolic restitution, as in the phrase 'If I'm caught I'll serve my sentence, it's a risk of the game').

Personality

Walster *et al.* consider that personality variables will relate both to the distress arising from the harm-doer's impaired self-concept and to his fear of retaliation. First, high self-esteem persons will be more inclined to derogate the victim than those low in self-esteem (demonstrated by Glass and Wood, 1964). Second, highly anxious harm-doers will experience more fear of retaliation and hence be more likely to use equity-restoring methods. They will, of course, use the least costly method available, but their interpretation of cost will be stricter than those who are less anxious, so that they will more readily pass from justification to compensation.

Equity Theory and Other Social Psychological Theories

Walster *et al.* briefly discuss a related area of research, that of social comparison theory (Festinger, 1954; Homans, 1961), according to which persons make comparisons of their own outcomes with those of people with whom they are in an actual physical relationship at the time, whom they perceive as similar to themselves in relevant areas of life and who are admired in some way. Hence:

1. inequities arising from harm-doing to relatives, friends, etc., are more strongly avoided than those arising from harm-doing to strangers;

2. if they do occur, equity will be restored more swiftly than following harm-doing to strangers;

3. the self-perception of distress, and the choice of restoratory method, will be by comparison with those adopted by salient others.

In general, as stated earlier, estimates of rewards and costs are strongly influenced by (a) the evaluations of salient others, (b) the levels previously experienced by the person concerned. Hence, rewards and costs are perceived not in absolute but in relative terms by *comparison* with those previously prevailing or available to similar others.

Equity Theory and Criminal Behaviour

If it is correct that the notions of equitable behaviour outlined here are generally learned by members of our society, it follows that the more successfully they are *unlearned*, the more readily will offenders indulge in criminal behaviour against a wide range of victims. Three processes assist the change from behaviour motivated by consideration of equity to totally inequitable behaviour towards the victim: anticipatory derogation of potential victims, lack of contact with the victim and the material rewards of offending. It is likely that the more an individual comes to rely on criminal behaviour for his livelihood, the less will be conduct himself towards his victims according to the principles of equity.

Concluding Comment

We have covered two areas of research into pro-social behaviours: helping behaviour and equity theory. Helping behaviour is seen as relevant to the limitation of criminal behaviour by offenders due to the potential for help given to the victim by bystanders, by witnesses to the police, and to some extent to the victim by the offender. Helping behaviour has been viewed as responsive to the same influences as behaviour is general. Certain social settings increase the probability of acquiring helping behaviours, particularly through the presence of appropriate models. Both direct and observational learning processes assist acquisition. The situational determinants for the performance of helping behaviours include such specific instigating stimuli as a bloody victim (although this may deter help if danger to the helper is implied) and the manifest pain of the victim. Other important determinants are the presence of a helping model, temporary positive affective states of the helper and to some extent a dependent victim (although this relates to the sex of the victim, as well as his/her attractiveness) and a victim relatively similar to the potential helper. The presence of other potential helpers tends to decrease helping behaviour by a particular potential helper, but this depends, for example, on the number of persons required for effective help in the particular situation. Restraints against helping include potential physical injury or financial loss to the helper, his lack of self-perceived competence, uncertainty that the victim was actually in distress, and the possible threat of a dependent victim to the helper's self-perceived freedom of action. Helping behaviour is maintained or diminished by its consequences, which may include both direct and vicarious positive or negative reinforcement—gains or losses in material rewards and/or social status and attention as well as self-reinforcement for reaching learned standards of performance. Persons acquire and use cognitive mechanisms to deny and distort their perceptions of the distress of victims, as well as other salient features of the situation in which the actual behaviour performed failed to attain a socially acquired norm of the desirable level of helping behaviour. Where external justification is less available, self-blame may result for such a failure.

The following conditions seem likely to increase the probability that a crime will be reported by an anlooker.

1. If the report can be anonymous, so that no punishment is likely from the accused person.

2. Complete and guaranteed protection by the police against retribution (related to 1).

3. Not being required to give public evidence. If the subject was wrongly accused, informants who are required also to be witnesses in court will be less likely to inform.

4. The prospect of material or social rewards beyond that of being 'a good citizen simply carrying out his duty', or at least of compensation in the event of financial loss for serving as a witness (for example payment for time off work).

5. A previously held favourable attitude towards the police.

6. The onlooker is similar to the victim or has suffered in a similar way (hence, 'it might have been me', or 'I know what it's like').

7. A previous history of positively reinforced experiences in similar intervention situations. Positive reinforcement by the police may be of particular importance.

In sum, as Berkowitz (1973) points out: 'If we want greater helpfulness we probably have to teach people that this is desirable behaviour, have them rehearse this action, and reward them when they do assist others' (p. 316). The notion that 'virtue is its own reward' means, in behavioural terms, that the individual reinforces himself. This requires first external reinforcement for 'good behaviour'. Such behaviour may then be transferred from external to internal control, given the appropriate conditions for transfer, and maintained by self-reinforcement.

Equity theory research is at a much earlier stage of its development than is research into helping behaviour, but a number of speculations are possible about its potential value. First, it helps to explain the importance attached by sentencing agents (and probably by the public at large) to 'fitting the punishment to the crime' exactly and to the previous record of offences, rather than what is more desirable from the point of view of effectively changing a criminal behaviour—designing a training programme related to the conditions which maintain criminal behaviour by that person. Second, it points to how the police might respond to a relatively provocative behaviour by a potentially aggressive suspect so as to avoid escalation into an actual assault on the police. The prescribed police behaviour would be to match exactly the level of provocation received. Third, equity theory provides a useful supplement to dissonance theory in predicting how offenders can account to themselves for behaviours discrepant from socially learned norms of equitable behaviour. Similarly, it helps to predict the targets of potential offenders—those who offer the least likelihood that the offender will perceive the outcome for the victim as inequitable. Thus he will select, for example, strangers and those believed to be well insured. Finally, equity theory research strengthens the case for victims receiving some form of compensation or reparation.

Chapter 5

Biological Factors

Analogies from Animal Studies

A biological contribution to aggressive behaviour has been argued on the basis of analogies from animal to human behaviour. The older approach, exemplified by Lorenz (1966), sees aggression as essentially instinctual, developing independently of external stimuli, though requiring them for release after aggression has built up to a certain point. Thus Lorenz argues against a learning view of aggression and, by implication, of crimes against the person. According to Lorenz, the problem for man is that biological control is incomplete. Whereas fighting within the same species is well controlled in animals by instinctually based inhibitors, man lacks such controls; hence, murder, wars, and so on. Critics of this approach point out many examples of intra-species aggression among animals (Barnett, 1967) and have demonstrated that both aggression and non-aggression include learned components (Lehrmann, 1953). In a remarkable series of studies, Kuo (1930) raised kittens to respond non-aggressively to rats rather than killing them. Later, he reversed earlier learning by using social modelling procedures to turn cats raised as 'pacifists' into 'killers'.

More recently, Gray (1971; Gray and Buffery, 1971) has combined a broad spectrum of experimental and field studies into a biological theory of two major behaviours, fear and aggression, the latter of which is our current concern. Gray argues that there is a consistent pattern of sex differences in all animals, including man, which expresses itself, for example, in the more aggressive play of male as compared to female children and the higher male rate of crimes against the person. Such sex differences have a biological, specifically a hormonal, origin, the greater aggression of males being due to the markedly higher levels of androgen present in males. These affect brain organization and hence the form and content of behaviour. Male animals castrated at birth (testosterone, related to androgen, is produced in the testes very early in life) are less aggressive than non-castrated males; female animals provided with androgen at birth are more aggressive than females not treated in this way. Next, such biochemically based sex differences in aggression are enhanced by the equally biologically inevitable role played by male animals in establishing and maintaining dominance hierarchies. Gray and Buffery (1971) continue . . . ' it seems reasonably clear that the situation in the human species is not different in this respect' (p. 93). Next, they propose that women have a more highly reactive nervous system for inhibiting socially unacceptable behaviour, so that they are more readily socialized, even given exactly the same social training experiences as men. This is associated with women's greater verbal skills, which assist the cognitive (internal) control of behaviour, known to be more effective than external controls (see Chapter 2). The final evidence of innate sex differences is the division of labour between the sexes, women concentrating on child care and domestic maintenance. Archer (1971) has has made a number of major criticisms of Gray's approach, drawing on extensive animal data to do so. First, a unitary notion of 'aggressiveness' is oversimple—there are several different areas of life in which individuals may or may not be aggressive. There is ample evidence that for many individuals aggressive behaviour, like behaviour in general, is situation-specific. Second, hormones have wide effects, in addition to those they exert on the central nervous system, including the promotion of weight, growth and attention, all of which may affect classes of behaviour other than aggression. Hormonally promoted externally visible effects may shape the responses from other animals. Third, the social roles imposed on males and females may themselves produce, or at least enhance, apparently biologically based differences. This point can be taken further: the relevance of social expectations for sex differences is shown by the vast changes in female behaviour and status in the past 75 years; it is social custom which has changed, not female biology. Fourth, Archer states that the organization of dominance hierarchies is variable; it is not related to reproductive success and appears not to be inevitable—all arguments proposed or implied by Gray. However, Gray's ingenious use of sex differences in developing a biologically based approach to individual differences in behaviour is of considerable heuristic value. We shall return to sex differences as they relate to criminal behaviour in general in a later section of this chapter.

Laboratory studies have also yielded results from which analogies could be drawn. For example, Delgado (1963) showed that electrical stimulation of the hypothalamus evoked attack behaviour in animals, which could equally be brought under control by the same means. However, external stimulus variables are also important. Delgado (1967) reported that electrically stimulated high-status male monkeys would attack subordinate males, but not females. Moreover, low-status males were stimulated, not to attack, but to submission. Hence response outcomes were based both on biological control and on prior learning experiences.

Body-build

The notion that criminals are recognizable by physical features is found not only in popular detective fiction (close-set, shifty eyes, etc.). An association between physical stigmata and crime was asserted by Lombroso (1911), who studied the inhabitants of Italian prisons. He claimed that many criminals physically resembled animals lower in the evolutionary scale than man; for example, those whose arm span exceeded their height and had a flat nose and a sugar-loaf form of skull reminded him of apes. The theory fell into disrepute when many of the 'criminals' were found to have been incarcerated for severaly subnormal intelligence. More recently, attention has turned to body-build simulated by the link between body-build and personality claimed by Sheldon (1942).

Several studies (reviewed by Rees, 1973) have found an association between broad and muscular body-build and crime, but most are marred by serious deficiencies of experimental design. For example, Gibbens (1963) and Epps and Parnell (1952) compared Oxford undergraduates with institutionalized male and female delinquents, respectively. A much better study by Glueck and Glueck (1956) matched 500 each of official offenders and non-offenders by age, intellectual level, racial origin and area of residence. Twice as many mesomorphs (predominantly broad and muscular) and less than half as many ectomorphs (predominantly narrow and bony) were found among the offenders. More recently, McCandless *et al.* (1972) found no association between either convicted or self-reported offending and body-build in 177 adolescent males randomly selected from 500 members of a training school, aged 15–17.

No studies have yet been carried out on self-reported offending and body-build in the population at large. Even if an association is found, it need not necessarily indicate a direct link, for the following reasons. First, well-muscled juveniles may attract greater police surveillance and are more likely to be arrested and charged and, if they appear in court, convicted. Once more, the stereotype may help to create the finding. The social role of offender may be assigned by peers as well as by the agents of social control. Just as physically more mature adolescent females have a higher rate of illegitimate birth (McNeil and Levison, 1963), so more well-developed teenage boys may be more likely to be sought by existing offenders as partners for criminal activities. Second, the influence of offender social models, themselves well built, may be greater on well-built youngsters than on those less well built, because of the greater perceived similarity between the former and the models. Finally, physical attributes can also have several indirect onsequences, as well as being themselves influenced by environmental events (Lindzey, 1965). For example, it may be that mesomorphic physique is the best suited to certain criminal activities, the performance of which is reinforced by a successful outcome. A truer test, not yet carried out, would be an association between body-build and a type of crime in which no advantage is conferred by any particular build.

Sex Differences

It was noted in Chapter 1 that the official statistics of crime indicate that convicted males outnumber convicted females very heavily indeed. However, we also cited ample evidence for the view that the official statistics give a rather biased picture both of offenders; the most satisfactory but rarely attempted method, that of direct observation, indicated that for shoplifting, at least, there was little or no disparity between the sexes. This contradiction to the official statistics is supported by studies of attitudes to criminal behaviour, which show rather small sex differences. Furthermore, even if substantial sex differences in crime survive the introduction of more careful control studies, the explanation for such differences could be *either* biological *or* environmental, or both.

Wright and Cox (1967; 1971) repeated in 1970 a study of the moral attitudes of 16–18-year-old British high school pupils they had originally carried out in 1963. The items included gambling, drinking, smoking, lying, stealing, premarital sexual intercourse and attitudes to coloured persons and to drugs. The data for stealing showed virtually no difference in attitudes between the sexes in either sample. A similar lack of sex difference in attitudes to a number of social behaviours was found in a social survey carried out in Britain in 1964 (Gallup, 1944). The above two studies suggested that if there are real differences in offending between the sexes they are not based on attitude differences, at least in the more well-educated section of the population, but on greater constraints on females and different perceptions by the sexes of their overt social roles.

However, Maccoby (1967) cites eight studies of persons varying in age from preschool to middle years. In all but one, girls or women were found to have a stronger 'moral code' than boys or men. Typical studies included one in which children were asked to state which of two crimes described in a story was worse and why. Girls were significantly more likely than boys to say that stealing was categorically wrong.

Moving from attitudes to behaviour, Maccoby (1967) cites five studies, two of which found no differences between the sexes, two found in favour of the girls and one in favour of the boys. In a more recent study, Medinnus (1966) found boys to cheat more than girls on the ray-gun task, the disparity being greater in sixth-grade (approximately 12-year-old) than in third-grade (9-year-old) children. No differences emerged on another cheating task developed by Grinder (1961)—self-reported rate of reading—at either age, suggesting that the ray-gun finding related to differences in assigned sex-role ('men are better with guns') which become more marked with increasing age. Women who scored high on personality measures of self-esteem (long-term, as opposed to situationally manipulated self-esteem) and on need for social approval cheated more than men high on these two variables. For both sexes cheating was raised by high scores on the two measures separately and more still on the two combined. The most striking finding was that on average men cheated less than women. In general, sex differences in response to temptation are much less clear-cut than the official statistics of crime would lead us to expect.

A number of research workers have believed that an explanation for female crime is required separate from that for male crime. The vast majority of studies of female crime, reviewed by Cowie et al. (1968), have been carried out on females in corrective training institutions. Such groups are heavily biased samples of offenders in general; in the case of female institutions the biasing is even greater because a high proportion of their inmates are sent to them for 'sexual delinquencies' and not crimes against property and persons, as are their male counterparts. This practice simply reflects the pervasive social view of sex differences; promiscuous sexual behaviour is expected for males, hence it is not regarded as deviant. Because no attempt is made in the published researches to separate out 'the care and protection' females (the term applied in Britain to the sexually promiscuous) from the criminally behaving ones, such studies are quite without value. Cowie *et al.* conclude their review of the studies to 1950; 'Delinquency in females is a highly abnormal phenomenon, affecting only a small sub-class of the population, a sub-class eking out its existence in circumstances of extreme deprivation' (p. 24). However, the phenomenon may well be an artefact, created by those officially sanctioned to deal with females, whose stereotype of 'the female criminal' creates the evidence. Cowie *et al.* also argue that psychological problems in girl offenders are more marked than those in boys, and that social learning experiences (for example, learning by observation of others) are of little importance. Moreover, they claim that broken homes are more important as sources of crime for girls than for boys. At the same time, they recognize that selection bias could be responsible for the apparent sex difference in psychological problems and broken homes by noting that girls are sent to institutions, rather than receiving non-institutional sentences, *because* they come from broken homes or are psychologically disturbed, and not because of the severity of the offence or of their past record, as is more likely to be the case for boys. Their own study was of 322 girls, only 81 of whom had been sentenced for offences such as larceny, the remainder being 'sexually delinquent'. Only 48 per cent were deemed 'psychiatrically normal' and 44 per cent were considered to have come from broken homes. They conclude: 'Environmental stress, predisposes to delin-delinquency as a neurotic reaction, sometimes accompanied by psychiatric symptoms; delinquency in the unstressed individual is more likely to be associated with abnormality of personality' (p. 144).

The females in this study were a highly biased sample of female offenders, most of whom were found 'guilty' not of crimes but of sexual promiscuity. No control groups were used, either of other females or of institutional male offenders. It follows that no conclusions of any scientific value can be drawn. The same applies to all the other would-be explanatory studies of female crime, with the partial exception of one by Nye (1958). This is the only study of female offenders to date which used the self-report method. Moreover, and a rarity in criminal research in general, random sampling techniques were used. A seven-item delinquency scale was completed by 2300 children in grades 9–12 in three small towns in the State of Washington, USA. Female offending was considerably less frequent than male. Unfortunately, three of the seven items dealt with behaviours which are not illegal—'defying parental authority', 'cutting classes' and 'sexual behaviour'. No separate results were given for the four remaining items, so that the sex differences in 'crime' obtained are impossible to interpret.

Differences between the sexes in frequency of sexual outlet are much more marked in adolescence than in adulthood; girls start more slowly, then catch up, in recent years more quickly than hitherto (Schmidt and Sigusch, 1972). The same may prove to be correct in the field of criminal behaviour. In order to test for such a possibility, we need self-report studies not only of adolescents, but also of adults. Stratified random samples (random within separate social classes, etc.) of adults in the population at large will be needed to measure the true sex difference in offending and to evaluate explanations of any sex difference which is found to exist. At the present time the only conclusion we can draw is that the research already carried out is quite without value.

If it proves correct that females not only contribute far less to the official statistics than do males but in *fact* offend less, there will be major implications for criminological theories. It will suggest that either innate biological differences between the sexes or the different social learning experiences to which the sexes are exposed are responsible for the disparity. Research would then benefit from concentrating on key biological differences between the sexes and on the different social learning experiences encountered. If sex differences in the true rate of crime occur even between males and females exposed to exactly the same kinds of training experiences, then a biological explanation for crime in general gains support. If, however, such differences disappear as social training becomes more similar, then the biological explanation is weakened and the environmental one is strengthened.

There can be little doubt that certain sex differences once thought immutable are now crumbling throughout the Western world, and are seen to be social rather than biological in origin. Women were once thought too 'delicate' to vote; they do so now without noticeable ill-effect. Only 75 years ago higher education for females was rare, now it is almost as common for females as for males. It is hardly likely that women have become significantly more robust or more intelligent in that short period of time. It is social convention and training which have changed, not female biology. A similar argument applies to the striking national differences still found in occupational distribution between the sexes. Female engineers are commonplace in the USSR. They are extremely rare in the rest of Europe and in the USA. Yet biological differences between the two groups of women are unlikely. The explanation, once again, is to be found in the differing social environments.

Attempts to account for observed differences between the sexes are made difficult because there are two sources of variation for any observed difference in behaviour between males and females of any age almost right from birth. The first is biologically based and implicates genetically inherited hormonal influences during prenatal development, the hormonal environment being different for genetically male and female organisms. However, biological predisposition is not the only explanation possible. We cannot assume that the post-natal environment, from birth on, is exactly, even approximately, the same for the two sexes. Indeed, it is rather more likely that male and female children are given systematically different training experiences. Barry *et al.*

(1957) found a consistent tendency across many societies for parents to induce self-reliance in boys and conformity to external demands in girls. Porteus and Johnson (1965) found that in 15-year-old Honolulu children girls showed more advanced moral development, suggesting that parental training is carried on for longer periods with girls than with boys, who may be influenced by the peer culture from an earlier age, so that girls eventually catch up with and pass boys.

Some interesting data are supplied by Rosanoft et al. (1941), who carried out a twin study of behaviour problems including offending (see below). Prior to adolescence there was no difference between the numbers of male and female twin pairs in which one twin was a problem. During adolescence the disparity was 7 : 3 in favour of male twins and in adulthood was 5 : 1. Two explanations are possible for the increasing sex difference: physiochemical changes during adolescence and (more probably) the cumulative effects of strict social training given to girls.

It may or may not make good social sense to train physically female and physically male persons for the different roles currently assigned to the two sexes. But from a scientific point of view it makes extremely difficult any attempt to separate out biological and social influences on sex differences observed in the adult or even in children. Any potential differences, based on biological predisposition, which are present at birth may well be amplified by social training. We do not know to what extend this is so, but the recent reduction in disparity between the sexes in several areas of behaviour makes it likely that it was rather large in the past. It may still be significant, but we have little firm evidence.

It should be noted that a largely environmental explanation for whatever sex differences in crime survive more adequately controlled research does not entirely eliminate the explanatory importance of hormonal influences during prenatal development. That mean differences between the sexes may well be less than thought does not necessarily mean that differences in behaviour between individuals of the *same* sex will be found to be due entirely to social training. It is equally likely that human beings, irrespective of sex, are exposed during the prenatal period to varying hormonal influences which predispose to differences in behaviour. *On average*, men may differ from women in the level of exposure to these influences, but with considerable overlap. It is the case that, given equal training opportunities, many women are stronger than the average man; in the same way, many will prove to be more aggressive. We cannot predict the behaviour of *any given individual* in any area other than reproduction and lactation from a knowledge of physical sex alone. The conclusion is that all individuals, of both sexes, carry hormonally mediated predispositions which interact with social training experiences. As far as male–female differences are concerned, we can expect a gradual reduction in the apparent disparity in the crime rate as the social roles allowed the two sexes become more similar.

Using the Rokeach (1968) measure of values—defined as broad preferences which underlie a large number of attitudes—Cochrane (1971) compared male and female prisoners with previously obtained control data on non-prisoners. but there was no difference between prisoners and non-prisoners in the valuation placed on family security. The female prisoners had a more masculine value system than did female non-prisoners, but this difference may have developed after institutionalization and not before. It would be of considerable interest if 'masculine' value systems predicted to future offending in females who had not yet begun an offending career.

Whether or not disparities in crime between the sexes reduce, differences between human beings, irrespective of sex, will remain and may require both biological and social explanations. Whether *separate* explanations for the criminal behaviour of each sex are necessary is a quite different question. The general argument of this book is that criminal behaviour is not special to any social class or age group, so that the same explanatory principles will apply to all. In accordance with this theme, a separate explanation of female, as opposed to male, crime will not be required.

Chromosome Abnormalities

Biological inheritance is transmitted genetically, the genes being organized on chromosomes, of which there are 23 pairs in men, 22 homologous pairs of autosomes and the sex chromosomes, XX in females and XY in males. Several sex chromosome anomalies are known, the one which has aroused the greatest interest in criminological studies being the presence of an extra Y chromosome in males, first described in a letter to the *Lancet* in 1961 (Owen, 1972). In the next few years several reports appeared of a raised incidence of the XYY anomaly in institutionalized male psychopaths. A biological basis for the 'aggressive psychopath' seemed to have been discovered.

A detailed and comprehensive review by Owen (1972) makes it clear that this is now doubtful. His major conclusions are as follows.

1. Subjective judgments often enter into karyotyping (the technique used for identifying the extra Y chromosome).

2. The combined prevalence of XYY males in institutions is 4–5 times that *presumed* to have been the prevalence in the general population. Recent studies of the *actual* rate in the newborn show it to be 'not very different from that found in institutions'. It follows that: 'Whatever support the aggressive XYY hypothesis might receive from a differential rate among prisoners will not be confirmed by the rate of incidence among the newborn—unless they all grow up with a history of imprisonment' (Owen, 1972, p. 222).

3. The median height of XYY prisoners reported to date is markedly higher than average, but height may have been the reason for seeking karyotyping in the first place. (Moreover, aggression by a tall person is more likely to be successful, and hence repeated. The link would then be between height *per se* and aggression, mediated by social reinforcement. The argument applies to body-build in general.)

4. Case reports of the behavioural characteristics of XYY males range from

'schizophrenia' to 'serious and hard-working', but the general picture is of seriously disturbed behaviour, tending towards severe aggression. Controlled studies using objective measures are much less striking. For example, Hope *et al.* (1967), studying the inmates of the Scottish institution, Carstairs, assessed 44 variables. For only five were the XYY inmates significantly different from their controls, and two of these were in the relation of part to whole. Owen comments, 'The lack of any definitive finding with what psychometric data have been collected should call into question the validity of the aggressive XYY stereotype. Because of the clear selection bias operating and the high expectancies in many reports, impressionistic data should be questioned' (p. 244).

5. Sexual offences are the most common among XYY individuals in institutions Crimes of violence *per se* are significantly *less frequent* than in suitably matched control groups (Price and Whatmore, 1967a, b; Griffiths *et al.*, 1970). Owen summarizes: 'Little can be concluded from the data at hand about the phenotypic behavioural characters more likely to result from XYY than XY chromosomes' (p. 228). Perhaps most important of all, the majority of reported offences are against property, not persons, and the overwhelming majority of those responsible, even for the latter, are of normal chromosomal constitution. Even if Owen's review had supported the stereotype of the aggressive XYY male, the vast majority of offending would still have required a non-chromosomal explanation.

Genetic Inheritance

Family Studies

Prior to the introduction of the twin and adoption methods (see below), the typical research procedure in studies of human genetic inheritance was to find persons showing the behaviour of interest and then to study their families to determine the frequency and distribution of the behaviour concerned. A study by Robins (1966) is a frequently cited example of this approach. She carried out a follow-up study of children referred for 'anti-social behaviour' to a psychiatric clinic. Only 36 per cent of the sample had both parents at home. The percentages of the fathers displaying a variety of problem behaviours were as follows: excessive drinking, 32 per cent; non-support or neglect, 26 per cent; desertion of wife and children, 21 per cent; poor work habits, 20 per cent; physical cruelty, 20 per cent. In addition, 48 per cent of the mothers and 23 per cent of the fathers were psychologically disturbed or intellectually handicapped. Such studies are inevitably open to criticism because the original diagnosis of 'anti-social behaviour' may have been influenced by knowledge of parental behaviour and family circumstances. A recent study by Clonninger *et al.* (1975) is also poorly controlled. They studied (by interview in half the cases) 387 first-degree biological relatives of male and female convicted offenders who had been diagnosed 'sociopathic'—in effect a synonym for psychopath. Relatives themselves were termed sociopathic if they had shown repeated anti-social and illegal behaviour by the age of 15. There were two main findings. First, a much higher proportion of male than female relatives were thought sociopathic. This is the usual finding concerning the disparity between the sexes. The second finding is of particular interest. A significantly higher proportion of the relatives of the *female* sociopaths were judged sociopathic as compared to the relatives of the male sociopaths. This higher familial incidence suggests a greater genetic contribution to female than to male sociopathy. However, there are several critical comments to be made. The female sociopaths had a more criminogenic environment (a higher proportion of their relatives were sociopathic). The opposite conclusion could thus be drawn: that the genetic contribution to female sociopathy is *less* than that in males. Both interpretations suppose that males and females have an equal chance of being assigned a diagnosis of sociopathy given equal behaviours. This is unlikely because the *criteria* for assignation are different: females tend to be labelled deviant for sexual, males for social deviancies. This is a criticisim which vitiates most studies of crime or sociopathy involving females (see earlier). More specifically, although approximately half the relatives of both the male and female sociopaths were available for interview, the authors do not indicate whether the non-responding half were similar for social-class composition. It is at least possible that the interviewed relatives of the female sociopaths were more sociopathic than the average of the group from which they were drawn, the opposite being true for the relatives of the male sociopaths. In general, the family study method is so fraught with methodological difficulties that it is likely to be replaced by the two next methods, which, potentially at least, make it easier to separate out genetic and environmental contributions to the behaviour in general.

Adoption Studies

Typically, the adoption study involves tracing the children of biological parents displaying the behaviour of interest given up for adoption, preferably early in life, by adoptive parents who are also assessed for the behaviour. A comparison for criminal or 'psychopathic' behaviour is then made between the index group and a suitable control group, or between their relatives. There are three recent adoptive studies relevant to inheritance of criminal behaviour. Schulsinger (1972) drew from a Danish adoption register 5000 children adopted at an early age between 1924 and 1947, of whom 57 had received the diagnosis of psychopath. He compared them with 57 controls from the same register, matched for age, sex, social classes, age of adoption and 'in many instances for neighbourhood of rearing' (this incompleteness is an unfortunate failing— as we have seen, social settings play a major part in the environmental acquisition of behaviours labelled criminal; the same is likely to be the case for behaviours labelled psychopathic). Schulsinger found the frequency of diagnosed psychopathy among the biological relatives of the index cases to be $2\frac{1}{2}$ times that of the control group. However, because of the size of the samples this was just short of the 0·05 level of signifance. Although Schulsinger was 'blind' as to which group of relatives the index and control cases belonged to, no such control operated on those who originally assigned the diagnosis psychopath to the index cases—who may have been well aware of the case histories of the biological relatives of the index cases. That is, given that the diagnostician takes a biological view of the causation of psychopathy, children who are behaving in ways which might attract the label psychopath are more likely to do so if they originate from a 'bad' family. (The history of the biological family is supposed to be unknown to adoptive parents, but such a restriction appears less likely on psychiatrists, social workers, etc.)

The Schulsinger study and both family studies reviewed earlier were concerned with psychopathy, a concept of doubtful reliability and therefore of uncertain value for research. The next adoption study, that by Crowe (1972), is much more satisfactory as it deals with actual offences, albeit as indicated by official records. Forty-one female offenders who served in a reformatory between the years 1925–56 gave up for adoption 52 children, who were aged 15–45 at the time of the study. The control group were drawn from the state index of adoptions and were matched for age, sex, race and age of adoption, though not for neighbourhood of rearing. Only two control group members, as compared with eight index cases, had an official arrest record. Both figures seem rather low: for example, as we noted earlier, the Philadelphia study by Wolfgang *et al.* (1972) found a recorded contact with the police by *the age of 18* in one-third of those surveyed. Nearly one-fifth had a record of 'index' offences (the more serious ones, approximately equal to Part I offences—see Chapter 1). Thus a smaller proportion of the children of imprisoned mothers had an arrest record by the age of 45 than a complete age cohort of the Philadelphia boys by the age of 18. Admittedly, the Crowe group was not divided by sex, but even so, doubt is cast on the completeness of the information on the sample. Despite this, the disparity in arrest records between eight index cases and two controls remains. This may have been due to quite mundane reasons: the arrest policies of the respective police forces in the areas in which the two groups grew up and lived; differential surveillance towards boys known to be children of criminal mothers and those not so known; perhaps most important of all, a different adoption policy for the children of offenders and those of official non-offenders—no data are provided on the criminal records of the adoptive parents of the two groups.

That such a differential adoption policy may well be operating is indicated by the last study to be considered. Hutchings and Mednick (in press), cited by Rosenthal (1975), compared 1145 male adoptees with an equal number of matched non-adopted controls. The authors then compared the rate of criminology in the biological and adoptive fathers of the 143 adoptive subjects with a criminal record and 143 matched non-criminal adoptees. The results are shown below.

Adoptees	Rate of criminality Fathers	
	Adoptive	Biological
Criminal	22%	49%
Non-criminal	10%	31%

At first sight, the marked disparity in criminality between the biological fathers of criminal and non-criminal boys (49 per cent *versus* 31 per cent) is a result which supports the genetic inheritance of criminality. But we must also note that the *adoptive* fathers of criminal adoptees have a rate of criminality more than twice as high as the adoptive fathers of non-criminal adoptees (22 per cent *versus* 10 per cent). This is most embarrassing for a genetic view of criminality, which can be retained for these results only if we assume that the 'genetically predisposed' youngster leads into crime his adoptive father, whereas the non-predisposed does not! The alternative explanation is more plausible: children of fathers with known criminal records are more likely to be placed with adoptive parents with known records than are the children of those without a record. The same explanation may also apply to the children of mothers with no criminal record (see the report by Crowe, 1972, above).

To date there appears to be no adoption study of crime which even approximates to the most satisfactory design in this context—namely, the cross-fostering method (Rosenthal, 1971), a method which, with additional controls, enables genetic and environmental contributions to be separated out. Cross-fostering requires that half the children of fathers known to be offenders are adopted by adoptive parents with little or no record of offending and half by known offenders. A similar division is made of the children of fathers not known to be offenders. The prediction would be of a higher rate of offending in the children of criminal fathers adopted by non-criminals than in the children of non-criminals similarly adopted by non-criminals. The highest rate would be found in those who are criminal both by genetics and by rearing, the lowest in those for whom both types of influence are non-criminal. There are obvious ethical objections to the full application of the design, but a partial application is readily possible. It requires a comparison between two groups of adoptive parents *matched* for criminal records with whom are placed respectively the children of non-criminal and criminal parents. The genetic theory would predict a high rate of offending in the latter. To reduce, so far as possible, a parental environmental contribution, it would be preferable for both groups of adopting parents to have a very low, preferably zero, rate of offending. To control for a peer environmental contribution, the group should be matched for neighbourhood of rearing. Finally, self-reports should be used in addition to official arrest records.

It cannot be concluded that the adoption method has yet yielded clear-cut results which bear on the genetic inheritance of crime, but an ethically and scientifically acceptable design is readily available.

Twin Studies

The existence of two types of twin, the identical (monozygotic—MZ) which are genetically identical and the fraternal (dizygotic—DZ) which are not, enables the genetic contribution to a variable to be assessed with some accuracy. However, a major assumption is required in studies comparing the members of MZ and DZ pairs reared together. This is that the amount of variance contributed by the environment is the same on average for the members of the two types of twin pairs. However, it cannot be assumed that parents treat both types of twin in the same way or that any differences in treatment are randomly distributed, not being more marked for either type of twin pair. For this reason, the most satisfactory studies (until the recent development of biometrical genetics, see below) are those of twins reared apart from as near birth as possible. If the concordance (roughly the similarity) between the members of the MZ twins reared apart is as great as between MZ twins reared together, and greater than that between DZ twins reared together, a strong genetic contribution to the behavioural variable in question is indicated. Unfortunately, only a few twin studies have used this design for any area of behaviour, and none for criminal behaviour. However, a strong contribution of genetic inheritance to extraversion has been demonstrated by Shields (1962) using the separated twins method, and extraversion appears to be related to offending, as will be indicated in Chapter 6. Hence, some weight can be placed on the studies of concordance for criminal behaviour which compared MZ and DZ twins reared in the same environment which are discussed below. More precise estimates of the heritability of any trait relating to criminal behaviour would require the combination of the self-report method and the highly developed statistical methods of biometrical genetics (for example Jinks and Fulker, 1970). As yet these have largely been applied to plant and animal characteristics, but are beginning to be applied to human behavioural variables.

Table 5.1 collects together the studies of criminal behaviour in adult MZ and DZ twins which have appeared to date. Much the most complete and

Table 5. 1. Twin studies of criminal behaviour

| Authors | | Monozygotic | | Dizygotic | | P |
		No. of pairs	Concordance (per cent)	No. of pairs	Concordance (per cent)	
Lange (1929)		13	76·9	17	11·8	<0·005
Rosanoff and co-workers (1941)		37	67·6	28	17·9	<0·001
Kranz (1936)		31	64.5	43	53·5	
Stumpfl (1936)		18	64·5	19	36·8	
Christiansen (1968)	MM	67	35·8	114	12·3	<0·001
	FF	14	21.4	23	4·3	
	MF			226	3·5	

M, male; F, female.

satisfactory is that carried out by Christiansen (1968). It is based on the 6000 pairs of twins which were born in the Danish islands between 1880 and 1910, where both twins survived to the age of 15. The other series may have over-represented the concordant pairs—because they had a greater likelihood of attracting police attention than the less conspicuous discordant pairs—hence the lower concordance rate for Christiansen's group than for most of the others in Table 5.1. The data shown refer to convicted adult criminal behaviour. It can be seen that the majority of the studies, including Christiansen's, indicate a significantly higher concordance rate for MZ than for DZ pairs.

Christiansen (1968) not only looked at concordance rates for convictions in general but also at the rates according to severity of sentence, social class and area of birth. Concordance was lower for both MZ and DZ twins for offences dealt with by fines than for those which led to imprisonment. He found a higher twin coefficient (a somewhat different method of estimating similarity) for MZ than DZ pairs in middle-class subjects and those born in rural districts than in working-class pairs and those born in urban districts. According to Christiansen, these results fit in with the higher rates of crime in working-class and urban populations, because higher overall rates of crime increase the relative importance of social variables and decrease those of (genetically based) personality factors which express themselves in increased concordance in twins. However, detection rates may be greater in rural areas for MZ than DZ twins irrespective of class (because of the greater 'visibility' of the former). Despite the difficulties in collecting reliable data, the weight of evidence (see Chapter 6) which suggests a contribution to offending of geneti-cally influenced personality variables makes such a study very desirable.

Concluding Comment

A reasonable appraisal of biological influences on criminal behaviour would be that they are probably less important than their extreme proponents would urge but of greater importance than those wedded to a solely learning account would allow. Biological variables may predispose to certain behaviours, then interact with learning experiences. The most scientifically tenable approach is an *interactionist* one which bears in mind the length of the chain which succes-sively links genes, enzymes, biochemical processes, structural development and response potentialities (Corning and Corning, 1972).

Chapter 6

Personality and Crime

Introduction : Consistency Versus Specificity

The typological model (for example persons are *either* extroverts *or* introverts) was largely abandoned in personality research many years ago, and was succeeded by the dimensional model, which suggests that a relatively few dimensions of personality account for individual differences in behaviour. The positions people occupy on variables such as extraversion and neuroticism are assumed to be relatively constant over time and to reflect either genetic influences or experiences early in life, or both. It is further assumed that people will respond to new situations in ways which are predictable from their position on the dimension of personality concerned. Questionnaires, typically self-report in nature, are used to give a quantitative score for each dimension. A detailed account of the development and structure of one of the major systems of personality measurement, that of H. J. Eysenck, and its relationship to other dimensional approaches is given in Eysenck and Eysenck (1969).

Eysenck's view is that while previous learning experiences and current situational stimuli are both important, long-term, largely inherited, predispositions play a major role. In fact, one of the central elements of his approach is that people respond differently to the same learning experiences according to the position they occupy on the major dimensions of personality. Eysenck's approach, an example of the *consistency* model of personality, would expect the same persons to behave rather consistently in different situations and at different times. The *specificity* model of individual differences has been active only in recent years although it was first made explicit by Watson's (1919) forceful exposition of the behaviourist position. It emphasizes the extent to which learning experiences and current situational stimuli interact to produce differences between individuals, so that behaviour is largely, even entirely, predictable from an exact knowledge of the individual's learning history and of the current situational stimuli which impinge on him. In short, the specificity model attributes individual differences in behaviour to external events and not to 'personality'. A particularly well-argued account is given by Mischel (1968), who cites a good deal of evidence in favour, in several areas of behaviour. Later in this section we shall suggest a compromise between the consistency and specificity models which may have important implications for explanations of criminal behaviour.

Essentially, the controversy will be settled by the extent to which individuals are *in fact* consistent in a broad area of behaviour, such as criminal behaviour, irrespective of variations in learning history and in the current situation. The occurrence of criminal behaviour and its frequency might be entirely related to situational variables and previous learning, and not to 'personality'. If there is little cross-situational and cross-temporal consistency in criminal behaviour then there is no basis for expecting personality measures, based on the assumption of consistency in behaviour in general, either to correlate with criminal behaviour or to discriminate between people according to frequency of offending.

Unfortunately, attempts to study the consistency of criminal behaviour, or of related areas, have been rare. The earliest and still much the most ambitious and comprehensive is that of Hartshorne and May (1928), who studied the consistency of cheating, lying and self-control in nearly 11,000 children who were administered a large number of tasks. A very full account is given in Eysenck (1964). The correlations between, for example, the cheating tasks averaged around 0·2, a finding considered by both Hartshorne and May (1928) and Mischel (1968) to support the specificity view. However, Burton (1963) made a very careful reanalysis of the original data, using statistical techniques largely developed since the original study, and arrived at rather stronger support for a consistency view. Nevertheless, there was still very considerable variation within individuals, which indicated, as Hartshorne and May put it, '. . . as we progressively change the situation, we progressively lower the correlations between the tests' (Hartshorne and May, 1928, p. 384). More recently, Nelson *et al.* (1969) found a 'low to moderate' consistency of response to temptation by 100 sixth-grade (mean age 11 years) boys and girls, suggesting an intermediate level of consistency.

Miscellaneous Studies

Several reviews have found little or no support for an association between personality and criminal behaviour. Metfessel and Lovell (1942) concluded that sex and age were the only constants and that no clear-cut picture of a criminal personality could be drawn. Similarly, Schuessler and Cressey (1950) reviewed 25 years of research on 30 different personality tests. They concluded: 'When the results are considered chronologically, there is nothing to indicate that the personality components of criminal behaviour are being established by this method. On the contrary, as often as not, the evidence favours the view that personality traits are distributed in the criminal population in about the same as in the general population'. (*Note.* They are not denying the 'existence' of personality traits, but that such traits are related to individual differences in criminal behaviour.)

More recently, the personality approach has fared a little better (Silver, 1963; Hathaway and Monachesi, 1956; Gottfredson and Kelley, 1963; Pasewark *et al.*, 1971). The last-named compared institutionalized male and female adolescent offenders with non-offenders on the Edwards Personality Preference Schedule (Edwards, 1959). They found a greater similarity between the male and female offenders than between male and female non-offenders, implying personality features common to offenders which override sex differences. Hindelang (1972) has criticized studies which have focused on personality differences between offenders and non-offenders on such widely used personality tests as the Minnesota Multiphasic Personality Inventory (Hathaway, 1951). His major point is that such studies have compared institutional and non-institutional persons. Thus, they may reflect the effects of institutional life. Would personality measures taken before commitment have shown similar differences? More pertinently still, because the personality variables concerned might predispose, not to offending, but to being caught, would self-reported offending relate to personality measures? Hindelang (1973) correlated scores on the Psychopathic Deviate Scale of the MMPI and on three scales of the California Psychological Inventory (Gough, 1957) which had previously been found to discriminate institutional offenders from non-offenders with the frequency of offences self-reported by self-described solitary and group offenders. The assumption of several personality approaches is that solitary delinquents would be more disturbed, as indicated by the various scales used. Only two of the 76 comparisons were significant at the 0·05 level—about what would be expected by chance alone—thus casting doubt on the assumption of several personality workers that solitary delinquents would be more disturbed.

Another long-established theme is the greater '*impulsiveness*' of offenders, a trait which would be revealed by laboratory measures of various psychomotor tasks, particularly in the form of errors due to overhasty responding. Between 1957 and 1958, Kelly and Veldman (1964) tested the entire seventh-grade (approximately aged 13) male populations of four Texas towns (884 pupils in all) on symbolic language tests, four psychomotor tests and several self-report measures of 'surgency' (roughly, higher scores indicate a lack of interest in detailed and exacting tasks). In 1962, 424 of the original sample were recontacted; 32 were officially labelled offenders, 52 had dropped out of school and the remainder were still in school. The three groups were then compared for their scores on the original measures. With social class controlled there was no difference on the symbolic language tests, but both the offender and drop-out groups had obtained higher surgency scores and had made many more errors on the psychomotor tasks than the other children. The results were interpreted as indicating the greater impulsiveness of the offender and drop-out groups. It is unfortunate that self-report measures of offending were not used. 'Impulsiveness' may simply predict to getting caught. The same criticism vitiates other studies using psychomotor tasks (Anthony, 1959; Gibson, 1964; Martin and Warde, 1971). Erickson (1966) compared on the Porteus maze test matched pairs of offenders selected on the basis of conforming, or not conforming, to the rules of the institution in which they were housed and found that the former made significantly fewer errors. (Data on the frequency of offences which were detected would have been valuable.) The suggestion was that the more impulsive the individual the less amenable he would be to social training in the environment concerned. However, the groups, although matched for IQ and ethnic membership, were not matched for previous offence record, arrest record or previous institutional experience (i.e. for total relevant learning experience prior to the present institution). Schalling and Holmberg (1970) also reported that higher scores on personality questionnaires thought to relate to impulsiveness were higher in offenders than in non-offenders. Once again, the offenders were an institutional population.

Because impulsiveness might influence the decision to commit an offence, as well as the care with which it is carried out, studies relating measures of impulsiveness to self-reported offending would be valuable. We shall shortly review studies concerning offending and extraversion, one of the two major components of which is impulsiveness, the other being sociability (Eysenck and Eysenck, 1963). Separate scores for the two components have rarely been reported. Finally, a study by Litt (1972) of perinatal complications in 2000 Danish males (particularly during delivery, and thought to relate to minor brain damage) is of some interest for theories of impulsive behaviour and crime. There was no support for the relationship of perinatal difficulties with criminal behaviour in general, but some evidence of a link between criminal acts described as impulsive and delivery complications. Once again, the study compared convicted offenders with non-offenders, and not self-reported offences in an unselected population.

A number of studies have looked for personality correlates of officially recorded aggression, based on the assumption that aggression is a general trait, varying between persons, and that behavioural aggression is predictable from standard self-report measures of personality. This is a particular instance of the overriding consistency–specificity controversy. Blackburn (1972) has carried out a useful ground-clearing operation by analysing the interrelationship of scores on 17 personality scales, frequently used in aggression research, which were obtained from 165 male patients in a British maximum security hospital for psychiatrically disturbed offenders. Four major sets of personality variables (factors) emerged: aggression, hostility, extraversion and a fourth, interpretable as anxiety. The first two were largely independent of each other and may indicate that the readiness to engage in overt aggression is at least partially unpredictable from subjectively experienced hostility. The remaining two factors are reminiscent of the two personality dimensions consistently isolated by Eysenck (1967), namely, extraversion–introversion and neutroticism–stability. *If* personality test scores do indeed help to predict to aggressive behaviour, at least in some individuals, then the Eysenckian system of personality dimensions appears promising. As we shall see shortly, this is true of criminal behaviour in general.

The possible *interaction* of overt aggressive behaviours and the habitual level of provocation required before a violent response is made has been studied by Megargee (1966). He hypothesized two broad types of physically aggressive persons. The first, the commonly held stereotype, is chronically low in self-control. The second, and much less obvious group, is chronically *over*-controlled, having rigid inhibitions against overt aggressive behaviour which they do not display until the level of anger aroused is high enough to overcome their strong inhibitions. (Megargee adds that they have not learned other means of expressing aggression, such as verbal responses, implying, though not following through, at least one alternative explanation, namely, lack of verbal skill.) His theory suggests that what he terms a 'moderately assaultive' group will be less hostile and aggressive and more controlled (measured by standard paper-and-pencil self-report measures) than other criminal groups. He tested this hypothesis on several groups of adolescent offenders and found some support, although 'all extremely (i.e. as opposed to "moderately") assaultive delinquents were more aggressive and less controlled than other delinquents' (Megargee, 1966, p. 18). Behavioural measures of operationally defined self-control, correlated with the level of provocation to overt aggression, would be preferable. This experimental approach was adopted by Osborne and Mackay in a small-scale unpublished study (carried out in 1971 at the University of Birmingham) of the hypothesis that violent offenders would be less competent in verbal communication than other offenders—hence when provoked they lash out. No differences were found on several objective measures of communication between violent and other offenders.

Extraversion, Neuroticism, Psychoticism

Introduction

In the earlier years of the development of Eysenck's comprehensive theory of personality (approximately from 1947 to 1967) only two major himensions of personality were postulated: extraversion (E) and neuroticism (N).

More recently (Eysenck and Eysenck, 1968) a third dimension, psychoticism (P), has been added. E and N were measured successively by the Maudsley Personality Inventory (MPI, Eysenck, 1958) and the Eysenck Personality Inventory (EPI, Eysenck and Eysenck, 1964). The latter also includes a lie scale (L) designed to pick out individuals answering the questionnaire in general in a socially desirable way rather than as a true reflection of their long-term behaviours. A more recent development is the PEN questionnaire, which measures all three dimensions as well as including a lie scale. There are also parallel versions for younger (under 16) populations, the Junior MPI (Furneaux and Gibson, 1966), the Junior EPI (Eysenck, 1965) and the 'Junior PQ' (unpublished at the time of writing) which measures P,E and N in children. Although extraversion consists of two semi-independent components, impulsiveness (I) and sociability (Soc), certain items of the E scale being more related to one than the other (Eysenck and Eysenck, 1963), scores are usually given for E overall rather than for the I and Soc components separately, and only a few of the many studies relating E and crime have separately related the latter to I and Soc. The E dimension runs from high extraversion to high introversion (i.e. low extraversion), the N dimension from high neuroticism to high emotional stability (i.e. low neuroticism.) No name has yet been given to the low end of the P dimension. The E and N dimensions are almost uncorrelated in non-patient populations, but tend to be somewhat negatively correlated in patient populations, (i.e. high N is associated with low E). In the population at large, the P and N dimensions are correlated about 0·3. Whereas both the E and the N dimensions approximate in the general population to the classical 'bell-shaped' distributions, scores on the P dimension tend to be 'J-shaped', most people obtaining low scores (Eysenck and Eysenck, 1968).

In idealized form, the high E scorer displays sociability, activity, optimism and outgoing and impulsive behaviours, the low E scorer the opposite of all of these. The person high on N is likely to be variable in mood, sensitive to insult and hurt, anxious, restless and rigid; once again the opposite applies to the person low on N. Eysenck (1970) describes the high P scorer as being characterized by the following features: solitary (not caring for other people); troublesome (not 'fitting in' with others); inhuman and cruel; lacking in feeling (insensitive to others' troubles); sensation-seeking; hostile to others; liking unusual things; disregarding danger; liking to make fools of others. It is tempting to regard P as standing for *psychopathy*, rather than *psychoticism* in the usual sense of psychotic behaviour. Eysenck himself has noted 'the description derived from the pattern of traits observed seems very close to that of certain types of prisoners' (Eysenck, 1970, p. 198). Certainly, there is some similarity between the disparaging attitudes of offenders to victims, the relative lack of feeling for others (usually cited as the central feature of psychopathic behaviour, see Chapter 7) and the behaviours which comprise the P dimension.

Eysenck has postulated a physiological basis for E and N, but has not yet done so for P. Extraversion is deemed to be related to the general level of cortical arousal, with extraverts having a lower level than introverts. They are also quicker to develop inhibition, due to repeated responding, and dissipate it more slowly. Inhibition builds up during any conditioning or learning process. It follows that extraverts should learn less rapidly and less strongly than introverts. This applies to all types of conditioning and learning. A vast number of studies have been carried out, using a wide variety of tasks, a consideration of which is outside the concerns of this book (see Eysenck, 1967). By no means all the evidence favours the predictions made by Eysenckian theory (for example, see Feldman, 1964). According to Eysenck, socialized (i.e. rule-keeping) behaviour rests on the childhood conditioning of learning, through punishment, *not* to perform behviours considered undesirable by parents and teachers. This is a key point. In fact, as we have seen, socialization tends to be less efficient when physical punishment (imposition of an aversive stimulus) as opposed to love-oriented (withdrawal of positive reinforcer) techniques are used. In addition, positive previous learning, through rewards for offending, probably plays an important part in the acquisition both of attitudes favourable to offending and of actual offending behaviours. Eysenck's own theory has very little to say either about the relevance of the type of child-training technique or the part played by the positive learning of criminal behaviour.

To return to Eysenck's thesis: with equal opportunity to acquire avoidance conditioning it is predicted that extraverts will respond less well. Hence they will perform more illegal acts, both in childhood and later on ('. . . a failure on the part of the person to become conditioned is likely to be a prominent cause in his running foul of the law and of the social mores generally', Eysenck, 1964, p. 120). The clear prediction follows that higher E scores will be associated with higher levels of offending.

The physical basis for N is considered by Eysenck to be the autonomic nervous system (ANS); persons high on N are considered to have a highly labile ANS and to react strongly, with excessive fear reactions, to painful stimuli. When N is high it interferes with the efficient learning of responses, particularly to unpleasant stimuli, because of the irrelevant anxiety evoked. The clear prediction for social training (considered by Eysenck to be achieved by fear-arousing stimuli) is that it will be interfered with by a high level of N. Individuals high on N as well as low on E have a strong capacity for acquiring conditioned fear reactions; persons equally high on N but also high on E show labile reactions but fail to acquire fear responses because of their poor conditionability. For any given level of E, the higher is N, the higher the level of offending which is expected. The stable introvert (en) will be the *most* effectively socialized person; he conditions well, and overanxiety does not interfere. The neurotic extravert (EN) will be the *least* effectively socialized; he is a poor conditioner in any event and his high level of N interferes still further. Neurotic introverts (eN, low on E and high on N) and stable extraverts (En, high on E and low on N) will be intermediate for socialization and hence for level of offending, because in each case the position on one dimension hinders socialization, the position on the other assists it.

The prediction for the P dimension follows directly from the content of the P-scale items; the higher the P score, the higher the level of offending. In brief, the Eysenckian view would expect that levels of offending would be directly proportional to scores on each of the E, N and P dimensions. All three dimensions have been studied for both sexes and in groups of non-offenders (by the self-report method) as well as in institutional offenders. However, because of the recency of the addition of the P dimension, the majority of reports have measured only the E and N dimensions. The following is a brief overview of the studies published up to and including 1975. Several reports, either unpublished or in press, will also be referred to.

Results

1. Adult male prisoners. The comparison has been with the E and N scores obtained by non-prisoners. Representative studies are those by Bartholomew (1959; 1963), Fitch (1962), Eysenck and Eysenck (1971a) and Burgess (1972). Neuroticism scores are consistently higher in prisoners. There is a trend for N to increase from non-prisoners through first offenders to recidivists.

In the previous chapter we noted a similar trend for interview-assessed psychological disturbance and suggested several explanations in addition to, or instead of, the view that psychological problems predispose to offending. The difference between the Eysenckian view and the psychodynamic view is that the former relates N to failure to learn *not* to offend, the latter considers offending as a positive act which arises from, and indicates the presence of, 'underlying' psychological problems.

In general, the prediction for E has not been supported, although Eysenck (1974) reports some confirmatory evidence. Prisoners are little more extraverted than non-prisoners. It is of interest that they tend to be *higher* on impulsiveness and *lower* on sociability; the combination yields approximately the same overall score for E. The higher score for impulsiveness may indicate either that impulsiveness confers a higher likelihood of offending, or of being caught, or both. The lower score for sociability may simply reflect the reduced opportunity of prisoners for mixing with their fellows; E scores, like self-report personality test data in general, are likely to be a composite of long-term behaviours and those currently displayed. It is of note that there is a marked over-representation of prisoners in the EN quadrant.

2. Younger male prisoners. Again, the comparison has been with E and N scores obtained by groups of non-prisoners. Representative studies are those by Hoghughi and Forrest (1970) and Gibson (1967a). For N the prisoners scored higher than the non-prisoners, and N scores rose with the degree of misbehaviour within the institution. Extraversion scores appear to be *lower* than in non-prisoners. Impulsiveness and sociability have not yet been analysed independently.

3. Self-report studies in schoolboys. (There are as yet no self-report studies relating E and N to self-reported offending in non-prisoner adults.) In these studies E and N scores are correlated with self-reported offending, measured by a variety of anti-social behaviour (ASB) questionnaires. Some of the behaviours listed involve infringements of school rules which are not in themselves illegal. The studies by Gibson (1967b) are representative; there are also several unpublished studies carried out at the University of Birmingham by Allsopp (1968) and Saxby *et al.* (1970). The results show rather clearly that self-reported offending is positively related to *both* E and N, separately and combined. There is a suggestion that it is the impulsiveness component of E which is more important.

4. Female prisoners. The studies include Bartholomew (1963), Eysenck and Eysenck (1973) and Saxby *et al.* (1970). The prisoners have tended to score higher on both E and N than controls, but much more markedly so for N.

5. Self-report studies in schoolgirls. A study by Allsop and Feldman (1975) also included the P dimension, and is described below.

6. Psychoticism and offending. Rather little work has yet been published. From that which has (Eysenck and Eysenck, 1970; 1971b; 1973) it is clear that P scores are very much higher for both male and female prisoners than for male and female non-prisoners.

7. The lie (L) scale. There are complex interactions between L scale and P, E and N scores. In general, it is necessary to control for the influence of L, because of the possibility that certain individuals are less influenced than others by considerations of social desirability and thus *report* offences more readily. It will be recalled that Gold (1970) found his adolescent schoolchildren to vary in how readily they admitted offending. Whether the obtained differences between introverted and extraverted subjects discussed above are in the true level of offending or relate merely to the reporting of offences remains to be studied. It is the core of the descriptive question concerning E and offending. A repeat of Gold's study using other informants to validate self-report, together with the E and L scores of the individuals giving reliable and unreliable self-reports, is indicated. It is also possible that high N subjects may report more than low N subjects. This might be expected on the basis that increased anxiety leads individuals to report events about which they feel some guilt.

8. The separate and combined effects of E, N and P. Only two studies (Allsopp and Feldman, 1975; 1976) have related self-reported offending to all three of the Eysenckian personality dimensions. Nearly 200 Birmingham secondary schoolgirls, ranging from 11–15 years in age, were administered by Allsopp and Feldman (1975) a 48-item questionnaire (ASB) composed of both illegal behaviours and infringements of school rules. This study did not report separately on the two groups of prohibited behaviour. However, a study of the ASB reports of schoolboys (Allsopp and Feldman, 1976) showed levels of self-reported offending to be very similar for the two sets of offences, justifying combining them into a single ASB score. A rating of school behaviour by teachers ('naughtiness' = Na) was also available. ASB scores were positively and significantly related to P, E and N in descending order of significance, and Na scores to P and N, although only the former achieved statistical significance. The P, E and N scores were then divided at the median points and the mean ASB and Na scores plotted for those high (i.e. above the median) on all three, any two, only one, or none out of P, E and N. The results, which are quite striking, are shown in Figure 1. They suggest the usefulness of combining personality scores when analysing self-report data. Adding a high N score to the combination of high P and high E had rather less effect than adding either high E or high P to high scores on the other two dimensions. A replication of this study, in schoolboys, has been carried out by Allsopp and Feldman (1976) and has obtained very similar results.

9. E and N and type of offence. Hindelang and Weis (1972) used cluster analysis to gether into seven groups 26 offences self-reported by 245 Los Angeles middle-class high-school males. They then correlated the scores on each of the seven clusters with the four possible combinations of E and N. The expected descending order of frequency of offending—EN, either En or eN, and en—was obtained for 'general deviance' and 'traffic truancy' and partially obtained for two other clusters, concerning 'drug-taking' and 'malicious destruction', respectively. No differences between the combinations of E and N was found for theft (a rather disappointing result—theft is the most frequent offence) and the

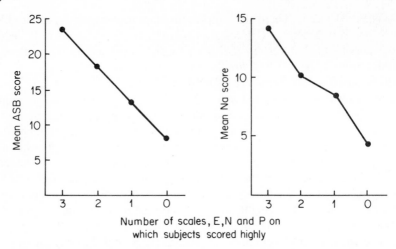

Number of scales, E,N and P on
which subjects scored highly

Figure 1.   Mean ASB and Na scores for all subjects combined
in upper level on three, two, one, or none of the personality scales
E, N and P. From Allsopp and Feldman (1975).

second of two clusters concerning drugs. For the 'aggressive' cluster the En combination was the highest (contrary to prediction). Hindelang's study provides a partial model for future work. Certainly an empirical division into offence types is required, as is the use of the P and L measures, as well as those of E and N, both separately and in combination.

Accidents and Personality. The importance of the impulsive component of extraversion for offending, certainly for making mistakes which increase the possibility of getting caught, seems rather clear. Getting caught is similar to making a serious error in the performance of a skilled and potentially dangerous task, the consequence of which may be an unpleasant 'accident'. Several studies have reported an association between E, N and accidents. Fine (1963) found that the most extraverted one-third of nearly 1000 Minnesota students had significantly more traffic accidents and violations than the other two-thirds. Willett (1964) cited several studies in which accidents were associated with extraversion (particularly impulsiveness), aggression and emotional instability. In his own sample of serious motor offenders, Willett found accidents to be related to impulsiveness, sociability and low 'reflectiveness'. (None of the studies cited or carried out by Willett used the Eysenck-developed measures of E and N, but the use of the terms in these studies appears similar to that of Eysenck.) Finally, Craske (1968), using the EPI, found certain E items (all relating to impulsiveness) and certain N items (concerning guilt and depression) to be associated with industrial accidents. There is thus a strong case for analysis for the relationships between impulsiveness, sociability and offending which control for getting caught.

Conclusions

1. E. The prediction relating E and offending has been supported in female but not in male prisoners, and strongly supported in self-report studies of adolescent non-offenders of both sexes. It may be that the impulsiveness component of E is more important than the sociability component in increasing the probability of performing an offending behaviour. Impulsive behaviours may also increase the probability of being caught, so that the interpretation of a positive correlation between E and offending in samples of prisoners must be in doubt. A positive correlation in self-report studies is much more likely to indicate actual performance of offences as opposed to merely being caught; however, high E scorers may be more likely to admit offences.

2. N. The prediction relating N to offending has had support in both prisoner and non-prisoner samples. The correlation for the former may be at least partially due to the effects of imprisonment and partially to the decreased efficiency of anxious offenders, leading to a greater tendency to be caught. The correlation in self-reporting samples may be contributed to by a greater tendency for anxious persons to admit deviant behaviour more readily.

3. P. The predicted correlation for P and offending is found in both prisoner and non-prisoner samples. While the finding for the former could be accounted for by the effects of prison life (increasing the behaviours related to the P dimension), this explanation cannot hold for the self-reporting samples.

4. The combination of the above median scores on two or three of E, N and P is more strongly associated with criminal behaviour than any one dimension alone. The association is strongest for individuals scoring above the median on all three dimensions. Expressed another way, those scoring high on all three *tend* to be consistent in carrying out a range of illegal behaviours; those scoring low on all three *tend* to be consistent in not carrying out a range of such behaviours. Bearing in mind that the results of self-report studies may be accounted for by a greater tendency to confess of persons high on E, N and P, we can conclude, until it is possible to record accurately actual as opposed to self-reported offending behaviours, that there is some support for the Eysenckian position. Those who score high on E or P (N is rather more doubtful) appear more likely to offend than those who score low, those who score high on both being particularly likely to do so. Thus, extreme self-reported scores are *correlated* with relatively consistent offending or non-offending behaviours. But what is the cause of these differences between individuals? Is it consistent and different prior experiences, or is it different levels of some predisposing influence or influences which led to different outcomes, despite similar experiences? Both explanations concern events earlier in the life of the persons under study; a retrospective study requires that we reconstruct those earlier events, so that a prospective study is preferable. The constraints of time, however, have resulted in very few such studies being carried out and these, as we have seen earlier, are typically marred by the poor recording of 'experiences' or a failure to exercise the appropriate controls on observers.

However, although it is very difficult to reconstruct earlier actual experiences with any accuracy, the role of another earlier event, that of genetic inheritance, can be assessed more exactly.

The Inheritance of Personality

We have seen that P, E and N tend to be related to the performance of prohibited behaviours in non-institutional populations of adolescents, at least as indicated by self-report. Earlier (see Chapter 5), we found evidence from twin studies that criminal behaviours appeared to be partially related to genetic inheritance and we suggested that personality factors might provide the link between genetic inheritance and criminal behaviour. In fact, there is good evidence that both E and N have considerable genetic components. A detailed review of the evidence concerning the inheritance of scores on questionnaire-measured personality dimensions and of objective tests of behaviour is provided in Eysenck (in press). The best-known early study is that by Shields (1962), who compared 44 pairs of MZ twins reared apart from infancy, a similar number reared together and 28 pairs of DZ twins reared together. The correlations he found for E and N are shown below.

| | MZ | | DZ |
	Reared separately	Reared together	
E	0·61	0·42	− 0·17
N	0·53	0·38	0·11

It can be concluded that the MZ twins reared apart are even more similar than the DZ twins. A reexamination of Shields' data by Jinks and Fulker (1970) using more advanced techniques of statistical analysis largely confirmed his results. They suggest that there is a substantial contribution of both genes and environment to E, and that rearing separately makes little or no additional contribution to the environmental differences experienced by twins reared in the same environment. Eaves and Eysenck (1975) have reported a correlation for E of 0·57 between a large number of monozygotic twins reared together, again confirming Shields' earlier results. With respect to P, Eaves (personal communication, 1975) has obtained results for a large number of monozygotic twins, as follows. The number of twin pairs in each group appears in brackets.

| MZ | | DZ | |
Male (79)	Female (241)	Female (133)	Opposite sex (74)
0·578	0·413	0·332	0·217

Eaves (personal communication, 1975) suggests that these results and other evidence he has collected imply substantial contributions to P of both genes and environment, and that P consists of two dimensions, one of items associated with psychopathy as the term is traditionally used and one of items with psychotic behaviours.

Fulker and Eaves (1973) showed that the heritability (roughly, the influence of genetical as opposed to that of environmental factors) both of E and N was much greater for those scoring high or low on the E and N dimensions than for those in the middle range, for whom environmental influences were much more important. This is a finding of some significance for the discussion which follows, in which we return to the consistency–specificity controversy, seek a compromise and relate it to the findings concerning personality and criminal behaviour.

Consistency versus Specificity: A Compromise

Both the proponents and the opponents of the consistency view tend to assume that a given degree of consistency in a particular population (usually rather low, Mischel, 1968) means that *all* individuals in the population contribute to it equally. An alternative approach is that *some people are more consistent than others*, a possibility which has been raised recently at the theoretical level by Alker (1972). Yet Hartshorne and May (1928) noted that when they arranged their schoolchildren in order of consistency, some always behaved honestly, others always dishonestly, the majority sometimes honestly, sometimes dishonestly, according to the particular situation. It is this large middle group of whom it is most appropriate to state, 'their behaviour varied according to the exact specifics of the situation' (Mischel, 1968). In the case of a minority, it can be suggested that environmental variables have to be rather powerful to exert a significant control over behaviour. For such persons, their extreme scores on the personality variables of E and P, and possibly N, more strongly under genetic control than the average scores of the majority, will be of substantial importance. These arguments are likely to apply more strongly with the increasing age of those studied; Hartshorne and May found that consistency was greater in the older children, and it should be borne in mind that the vast majority of the studies cited by Mischel as indicating rather low levels of consistency were carried out on rather young children. A study by Olweus (1975), carried out in Norway, provides further support for the view that individuals vary in the consistency of their behaviour. About 90 per cent of a group of 13-year-old boys were neither consistently 'bullies' nor consistently 'whipping boys'; the remaining 10 per cent were divisible into one or the other, at least as judged by teachers, and maintained the consistency of their behaviours over the year for which observations were taken.

It is concluded that our ability to make confident predictions from personality measures to offending behaviour is likely to be greater for extreme-scoring individuals than for those who score in the middle range. Even for the extreme scorers, predictions from personality scores to behaviour may be more accurate in situations marked by certain common features, termed 'moderator variables'

(Alker, 1972). An example is provided by the Machiavellianism Scale (Christie and Geis, 1970), which is broadly concerned with holding cynical and non-altruistic beliefs about the world in general. Persons scoring high on the scale successfully manipulate low-scoring persons, but only in situations which permit face-to-face interaction, allow the participants to improvise and contain elements which arouse distracting emotion (Christie and Geis, 1970). Similarly, there will probably prove to be limitations on the situations in which we can predict the offending behaviours of persons scoring particularly high, or particularly low, on the dimensions P, E and N. Applying the above agruments to the Eysenckian system leads us to the following summary statement. Those who score high, particularly on all three dimensions, would be expected to break rules and cause harmful consequences to others in order to achieve their own ends in rather consistent ways. Those who score particularly low on all three dimensions would be expected to avoid such behaviours equally consistently, except in the most extreme combination of relatively high potential gain, mild punishment even if detected and high opportunity. The majority, scoring in the middle ranges, would be expected to be inconsistent in their offending behaviours and to depend on the total pattern of situational temptations and constraints. In short, there is no doubt that some people are more consistent in their offending or lack of offending than are others; E and P (and possibly N) may help us to predict who those individuals will be.

These are useful descriptive hypotheses which might then be succeeded by an attempt to set up detailed *explanations*, from which follow testable predictions. Before we can proceed to the latter stage of research enquiry (and to some extent we have done so already through the heritability studies), there are two questions to be discussed concerning Eysenck's theory of personality as applied to crime. The first concerns the fact that the theory largely relates to *learning* rather than to *performance*, the second that not only does the theory emphasize learning, but it is largely concerned with one variety of learning, namely avoidance, as opposed to approach, learning.

Eysenckian Theory and the Acquisition and Performance of Criminal Behaviours

Learning and Performance

Briefly, a response may be learned but not performed. On the other hand, to be performed it must be in the repertoire of the individual concerned. In humans, most responses so present have been acquired by learning; some are innate or depend only on maturation to appear. The personality research thus far surveyed has been concerned with the *performance* of offences, indexed either by convictions or (preferably) by self-report. Yet Eysenck's theory is specifically concerned with the *learning* of behavioural responses. In order to test the theory properly, we would need either to study the initial acquisition of attitudes to offending behaviour, and of offending behviours, themselves, or create experimental conditions which would reliably translate into performance whatever learning had occurred, so that measures of performance would truly represent the responses which had been acquired. As the matter now stands, in testing Eysenckian theory, performance indices are used to *infer* previous learning; however, the match may be far from exact. Although there have been many investigations of both moral attitudes and the variables affecting the performance of offending behaviours, the acquisition of such attitudes and behaviours has not been related to personality measures. In that sense it can be said that Eysenckian theory as applied to criminal behaviour has not yet been tested in the most satisfactory way possible. Those tests made to date depend on the assumption of a one to-one relationship between learning and performance.

Learning to Offend or Learning not to Offend

Eysenckian theory emphasizes avoidance learning—learning *not* to offend— as the key type of learning relevant to criminal behaviour. Offenders are seen as those who are predisposed against the rapid acquisition of social rules by avoidance-learning experiences. Yet, as we have seen in Chapter 3, there is powerful experimental evidence of the role of positive reinforcement in controlling such analogues of real-life offending as aggression and transgression. Extraverts are deemed by Eysenckian theory to learn less adequately by *both* types of learning, both positive and negative, although it is only negative learning experiences that are considered relevant by the theory in the context of criminal behaviour. If the positive learning of offending is a key source of criminal behaviour, the Eysenckian prediction would have to be that extraverts would offend less, not more, as the theory does, in fact, predict. However, as we shall see, this objection could be overcome if extraverts mix socially so much more frequently than introverts that they have a great many more positive learning experiences, so many more that they attain a higher level of learning. We have seen that extraversion is related to the performance of offending behaviour. For the purposes of this discussion, it is convenient to assume that there is a close relationship between learning and performance. How can we account for the observed differences in offending between persons high and low on E, N and P? The following explanations are possible, and are set out for E, N and P in turn. In each case the straightforward Eysenckian explanation is given first. It should be emphasized that the discussion is speculative, and is intended to suggest useful lines of research.

Extraversion 1. If both groups are given the same number of avoidance-training experiences, those low on E will be more responsive than those high on E. Thus low E persons will, on average, be more likely than high E persons to acquire attitudes unfavourable to offending and less likely to acquire offending behaviours. This explanation assumes *equal* exposure to training experiences which teach people *not to* offend.

2. High E persons are more likely to mix socially than low E persons. If

such social mixing exposes them to social models of offending behaviour, then high E persons are more likely than low E persons to acquire both attitudes favourable to offending and offending behaviours. This explanation assumes *unequal* exposure to training experiences which teach people *to* offend. A variation on 2 is that high E persons may interact socially no more frequently than low E persons but, because they are more responsive to social reinforcement, they will be more likely to acquire offending attitudes and behaviours.

3. Both 1 and 2 are correct and are not in opposition. High extraverts may be less responsive to positive, as well as to negative training experiences, but because they mix socially very much more frequently, they attain a higher level of learning of criminal attitudes and behaviours.

It should be noted, in connection with explanation 1 above, that Eysenckian theory concerning differences in response to avoidance training has been concerned exclusively, with noxious physical stimuli. In real-life situations parents and other training agents may use such stimuli (conveniently termed physical methods) or the non-physical methods of withdrawal of affection and induction, both of which involve the use of social, as opposed to physical, reinforcers. It may be that high extraverts are indeed less responsive to training by physical methods, but in view of their greater tendency to seek the company of others, will they be equally unresponsive to social methods of training? Moreover, can we equate the two social methods? Whereas love withdrawal involves the loss of a social reinforcer to the person being trained—i.e. it is his *own* distress which is being manipulated—the induction method attempt to train the social perception of the distress of the *other* person—the trainer.

Perhaps explanation 1 will hold only for those persons typically trained by physical methods and not for those trained by social methods? It may be that working-class parents are more likely to use physical methods (Hoffman and Saltsztein, 1967). If this is so, the prediction relating extraversion to offending may hold more powerfully for working-class than middle-class persons.

We must also consider the case of the introverted child predisposed to be responsive to physical punishment but who is trained, inappropriately, by one of the social methods, to which he is predisposed to be relatively unresponsive. The parents of such a child may either turn to physical punishment or (particularly if they are strongly opposed to the use of physical punishment) they may continue to use social methods, possibly at reduced levels of intensity and frequency, which further reduces their effectiveness. Bell (1968, see Chapter 2) has suggested that children congenitally low on 'person orientation' will receive less affection from their parents, and hence will become even less likely to respond to social cues. Therefore, Bell concludes, they will be less likely to develop moral attitudes as socially defined and (by implication) be more likely to offend.

Neuroticism. As in the case of extraversion, Eysenckian theory concerning N is a theory of learning and not of performance. Yet the available data concern N and performance. Moreover, there are doubts concerning both types of data: those concerning prisoners *versus* non-prisoners may reflect the effects of prison life in increasing N, as well as the increased likelihood of high N persons to be caught; the positive relationship between N and self-reported offending may simply indicate that high N persons offend no more but are more likely to confess. Putting aside these doubts for the moment, what sort of explanations might be adduced to account for a positive association between N and the acquisition of offending behaviours?

1. A highly labile autonomic system (high N) interferes with efficient avoidance learning. Whether this would hold true for both physical and social methods may depend on the position of the high N person on the extraversion dimension.

2. High N persons are more likely than low N persons to acquire attitudes favourable to offending and offending behaviours through social learning experiences, either because they are more likely to mix socially or are more responsive to equal social exposure. Social mixing may be both anxiety—reducing—because it presents a potential source of approval—and anxiety—provoking, because the response might be disapproval rather than approval. An alternative, which is very persuasive, is that the behaviour of high N persons is particularly responsive to those reinforcers which assist them to cope with their emotional problems. If such reinforcement is given for offending behaviours, such behaviours will be more likely to be acquired. On the other hand, offending behaviours are possible sources of punishment, and are thus anxiety-arousing and likely to be avoided.

Thus there is a complex of conflicting influences concerning the positive acquisition of offending behaviours by high N persons. However, when high N is combined with high E, the increased social interaction (or increased responsiveness to social reinforcement) will tip the balance of the conflict in favour of greater social exposure/social responsiveness by EN as opposed to eN individuals. The consequence might be an increased likelihood of acquiring offending attitudes and behaviours. The conclusion is that high N persons are more likely than low N persons to acquire such attitudes and behaviours when they are also highly extraverted.

Psychoticism. This is the most recent addition to Eysenck's list of major dimensions of personality and has not been closely related to the learning aspects of the theory. However, it can be assumed that P would be expected by Eysenck to affect the response to learning experiences. Recalling the learning—performance distinction and assuming that higher scores for prisoners as compared to non-prisoners do not reflect the effects of prison, or that the positive relationship between P and self-reported offending indicates merely increased confession by high P persons, what explanations can we advance for a link between P and the acquisition of offending behaviours?

1. High P persons respond less well to avoidance training. From the content of the P items—see earlier—we might expect that this would be particularly true of avoidance training by induction, which emphasizes the acquisition of

an empathic response to the distress of another. The social method of love withdrawal might also be inappropriate for persons predisposed to high P scores because the withdrawal of a social reinforcer may be less disturbing for a high P person than for a low P person. However, there is no obvious reason why the response to the use of physical punishment should discriminate high P from low P persons.

2. High P persons respond more strongly to positive learning experiences concerning offending attitudes and behaviours than do low P persons. The composition of the P scales is partially concerned with rather bizarre behaviours, some of which are solitary, others group, activities. Some high P individuals will thus be more exposed to learning from other people, either directly or vicariously, than others. The fact that P scores tend to be positively correlated with E suggests that the former predominate. The alternative possibility, that high P persons are more socially responsive given the same exposure to learning experiences than are low P persons, seems less likely, because of the presence in the P scale of items concerning lack of responsiveness to others.

Social Settings

We have mentioned two broad classes of explanations for all three dimensions, one in terms of response to avoidance training and one in terms of response to positive training by either behaviour-contingent or observational learning experiences. (However, as we have seen, it may be that for the E dimension, *both* sets of explanations may relate to individuals.) Both explanations emphasize variations—in individual predispositions to rapid or slow avoidance learning and to high or low social responsiveness—and in the intensity, frequency and content of training experiences. The first group of emphases concerns *individuals*, the second concerns *social settings*. We have already specified that Eysenckian predictions will hold much more strongly for persons scoring at the extremes of the E, N and P dimensions, and most strongly of all for persons scoring at the extremes of all three. The behaviour of such extreme scorers is likely to be under a marked degree of genetical control.

The majority of persons score in the middle ranges, the minority at the extremes of any one dimension, and an even smaller minority at the extremes of more than one. The implication of this discussion for the consistency–specificity controversy is that both views are correct, but for different people; the consistency view is of some relevance for the extreme-scoring minority, the specificity view of considerable relevance for the medium-scoring majority. What can we say about variations in social settings? First, it follows from the general discussion on consistency *versus* specificity that situational variations are likely to be much more important in the acquisition of criminal behaviours for medium scorers (the majority) than for extreme scorers (the minority). Second, such 'social', as opposed to 'personality', control will be greater in social settings in which either parents use ineffective methods of training, or there are plentiful social models of offending, or both, than in settings in which parental methods are effective, or social models are rare, or both. It follows that even extreme *high* scorers on P, E and N will be less likely to acquire criminal behaviours if both optimally effective methods of training (for their particular personality mix) are used and exposure to social learning experiences of offending is rare than if less than optimal methods of training are used and exposure to social experiences is frequent. Conversely, even extreme *low* scorers will be more likely to acquire criminal attitudes and behaviours if training methods are suboptimal and exposure to learning experiences is frequent than if the opposite is true. As indicated earlier, which training method is optimal may depend on the innately determined attributes of the child, particularly in the case of those at the extremes of dimensions of personality, although the general finding has been that the social methods of training are on average more effective than are the physical ones. Examples of less than optimal methods of training for particular types of extreme scorers are the use of induction for high P persons and of physical punishment for high E persons. The former would be more likely to respond to physical punishment, and the latter to the withdrawal of affection. Beyond this it is not possible even to speculate. Moreover, it will not be possible to assign an appropriate method to a particular young child until we have reliable methods of designating extreme individuals from a very early age (i.e. well before people are able to answer personality questionnaires). However, there is much less difficulty in matching personality and training method in the case of older children.

Conclusions on Acquisition

It is obvious that learning experiences favourable to criminal attitudes and behaviours are more likely to occur in social settings in which offending is frequent than in those in which it is infrequent. The relationship between personality and criminal behaviour is likely to be much closer in the latter settings than in the former—in which situational sources of influence are pervasive. It follows that the Eysenckian theory of the acquisition of criminal behaviour will be more strongly supported in relatively low-crime social settings than in relatively high-crime settings. In order to test this prediction, exact information concerning the true frequency of offending will be required. It would also be desirable to relate personality scores to the acquisition of different types of offence rather than offending overall (see Hindelang and Weis, 1972, mentioned earlier). Finally, it would be necessary to compare persons exposed to different methods of training.

In sum, the following variables are likely to be relevant in constructing groups of persons to compare in studies concerning the *acquisition* both of attitudes favourable to crime and of criminal behaviours.

1. E, N and P scores (and L scores if offending is indexed by self-report rather than direct observation).
2. The type of offence.
3. The true frequency of offending in the particular social setting.

4. The training method used—physical punishment, love withdrawal or induction.

While such studies typically will be concerned with children—the older the individual the more likely he is already to have acquired criminal behaviours—they might also be appropriate for those older persons who have either not acquired criminal behaviours in general or have not done so for a particular class of offence, possibly due to effective earlier training, by parents, teachers, etc., or to limited exposure to criminal social models. Such persons might encounter in their work context models who carry out a category of offence mainly found in that context—for example, a professional group, or in political life. Such a group of adults would provide an appropriate context in which to test out the Eysenckian predictions concerning acquisition.

We can combine the above discussion with our earlier one to make the following clear-cut predictions.

1. In a social context in which the level of crime is high, the individuals least likely to acquire criminal behaviours will be those who are low on all three of P, E and N and have been exposed to appropriate methods of social training.

2. In a context in which criminal behaviour is low, those most likely to acquire criminal behaviours are those who are high on all three of P, E and N and have been exposed to inappropriate methods of social training.

Conclusions on Performance

In Chapter 3 we reviewed the evidence that a number of situational events evoke the performance of criminal behaviours. It would be expected that once such behaviours have been acquired, then their performance on any particular occasion would be under the control of such instigating stimuli. Nevertheless, there might still be differences between two persons with the same previous history of criminal experiences in the probability of a particular set of stimuli, to which they were both exposed, evoking a criminal behaviour. Insofar as P, E and N scores are related to such differences, the following tentative predictions may be made.

1. E. Highly extraverted persons who are particularly high on the sociability component of E may be more likely to perform an offence than those very low on that component when the offence is carried out in a group, the information concerning the possibility of doing so is socially conveyed, or when social, as well as financial, consequences, will follow a successful outcome. Those particularly high on the impulsive component may be more likely to perform an offence than those low on the impulsiveness component when the opportunity for the offence is immediate than when it is distant.

2. P. High scorers may be more likely to perform an offence than low P scorers when the proximity of the victim is high and his distress is evident. When proximity is low, so that victim distress is not evident, P scores seems unlikely to predict to the performance of an offence.

3. N. It is not easy to envisage circumstances in which N will relate to the performance an offence, except that on balance high N persons seem more likely to be deterred by the prospect of an unsuccessful outcome and so would be less likely to offend when the risk is high.

The above predictions rest on the assumption of a one-to-one relationship between learning and performance. Yet whether or not a learned 'offending response' is translated into performance will depend at least in part on the reward–cost balance operating in the particular situation concerned. When the balance is very unfavourable (low relative potential gains, low opportunity, high probability of detection, and severe punishment, etc.), rather few people will offend; such persons, according to Eysenckian theory, are likely to be high on E, P and N. When the balance is favourable (high gain, high opportunity, low probability of detection and mild punishment), many will do so—some of whom will have average, possibly even low scores, on E, P and N. Combining these statements, it can be concluded that the situational balance of rewards and costs interacts with previous learning experiences, the outcome of which may be influenced by personality variables, to produce a behavioural response to that particular situation. When the balance is unfavourable, a person *high* on P, E and N may be less likely to perform a well-learned offending response than a person *low* on P, E and N, but with a relevant criminal behaviour already in his repertoire, who is exposed to a particularly favourable combination of rewards and costs.

As noted in Chapter 3, it cannot be assumed that rewards and costs have an objective existence independent of the learning history and current social context of the individual concerned. Indeed, it is rather likely that people will differ in their *interpretation* of the same constellation of rewards and costs. To a considerable extent, interpretation will be influenced by previous experiences and the current life situation in reaching a decision to offend or not to offend. Extreme personality scores might also contribute both to the interpretation and to the consequent decision. It may be, for example, that persons high on both E and N would be more likely to perceive a particular reward–cost balance as favourable than those low on the E and N dimensions. There is some inferential evidence to support such a view. Merbaum and Kazaoka (1967) found that questionnaire-defined (Byrne, 1964) repressors (R) reported more positive emotion than sensitizers (S) but negative emotions more frequently. Correlational studies by Byrne (1964) suggest that the R and S ends of his RS scale are identifiable with EN and eN, respectively, so that in a simplified sense, EN persons are 'optimists', eN persons are 'pessimists' in their evaluations of the same reward–cost balance.

Conclusions on Maintenance

As in the case of behaviours of all types, maintenance will relate to the consequences experienced for the performer of that behaviour. Might we expect personality differences to play a part? In general, it is difficult to see how persons will differ according to personality in their perception of how rewarding has been the outcome of a successful offence. However, personality differences might relate to the perception of how *punishing* has been an unsuccessful offence. In the same way that those high on both E and N may be more 'optimistic' in advance of a crime (see above), so they may be more able also to reduce the perceived aversiveness of an actual punishment and to continue to perceive optimistically the next opportunity. We might also expect personality differences to affect the perception of the victim. To some extent the P dimension is concerned with 'lack of feeling' and with related cognitive responses. We might expect that high P scorers would be less responsive to the distress of victims and so more likely than low P scorers to carry out repeatedly offences in which victim distress was particularly evident. However, as we described in Chapter 3, the processes of cognitive-dissonance reduction assist offenders *in general* to derogate the victim and distort their perception of his distress, thus justifying offences, first after the event, and then in advance. The extra 'advantage' conferred by high P will be most evident early in an offending career (i.e. in the acquisition phase, see above) and in the commission of offences in which victim suffering and distress are particularly evident.

Concluding Comment

This ends our discussion on the relationship between Eysenckian personality dimensions and the acquisition, performance and maintenance of criminal attitudes and behaviours. However, a brief mention is required of the methods used to measure personality.

It is necessary to remind ourselves that questionnaire scores are simply the quantitative total of items endorsed by those filling in the questionnaire—persons report on those areas of their own behaviours represented by questionnaire items. Such behaviours are, of course, under the control of the persons' everyday experiences, so that personality scores may well change over time, the extent depending on the degree of change in actual experiences. For example, it is well established that depressive illness increases scores on the N dimension, the scores returning to their previous level after recovery (Sperlinger, 1971). In brief, personality scores reflect experience, in addition to the possibility of individual predispositions to experience. There will be a continuous interaction between behavioural experiences and self-reports of 'personality'.

In discussing the differences obtained in P, E and N scores between groups of prisoners and non-prisoners, we raised the possibility that the personality scores obtained by the former might reflect the effect of prison life, thus distorting the comparison. It follows that items comprising the sociability components of E are less likely to be endorsed positively by prisoners, who inevitably have little opportunity for social life, than by non-prisoners, so that E scores may, overall, decline with increasing prison experience. On the other hand, both N and P scores may increase, the former because of the emotionally distressing effects of prison life, the latter because of those features of prison life which enhance 'lack of feeling' and other behaviours represented in the P dimension. Because of the complicating effect of prison experience, we have argued in favour of studies of personality and criminal behaviour being carried out on the non-prisoner population. But just as the prison experience may affect personality scores, so may the experience of successful but undetected offending, particularly when this has been more than merely occasional. Scores on all three dimensions may reflect such a personal history. If the consequences of offending include marked financial gain, thus increasing the social attractiveness of the individual concerned, the result may be an increase in social mixing, a consequent increase in the sociability component of E, and thus an increase in the overall E score. The continued experience of 'getting away with it' may either increase or decrease N scores, depending on how easily detection is evaded; easy evasion may lower the general level of subjectively experienced anxiety, thus decreasing N scores. Difficult evasion may increase anxiety, so increasing N scores. Continued derogation of the victim, and denial of his distress, may be reflected in increased P scores. A history of frequent but undetected offending (or offences sometimes detected but leading to punishments of a non-institutional type, thus maintaining the person in the non-prisoner research population) may itself bring about the predicted positive association between P, E and N and the performance and maintenance of criminal behaviours.

The above suggest that personality test scores may be determined by the social and personal consequences of criminal behaviours rather than determining their performance and maintenance. If self-reported personality scores change in response to behavioural experiences, particularly consistent experiences, then the specificity–consistency controversy, at least so far as it is concerned with performance and maintenance of behaviours, might resolve very powerfully in favour of the specificity model, the central feature of which is that behaviour changes as the situation changes. Consistent experiences will produce consistent behaviours, which are then reflected in extreme personality scores. Thus, rather than such extreme scores resulting in consistent behaviours, extreme scores are simply a report by the respondent that he behaves consistently. It will be exceedingly difficult to design experiments which will be able to disentangle the complexities of such reciprocal relationships, but the attempt seems worthwhile.

In conclusion, it can be said that the Eysenckian personality dimensions are likely to make a useful contribution to the explanation of criminal behaviour, but more to its acquisition than its performance or maintenance, and much more in the case of extreme, than in the case of median, scorers. Even in acquisition, by extreme scorers, personality will be only part of the story; situational variables will play a significant role.

Chapter 7

Mental Disorder and Crime

Introduction

First, we shall outline briefly the historical development of the current British legal approach to 'mentally disordered' offenders (the American approach appears not dissimilar). A comprehensive review has been given by Jacobs (1971).

In ancient Rome, an offender deemed mad was treated with leniency because it was thought morally unacceptable to add another punishment to that imposed on the sufferer by the 'madness' itself. A powerful argument was put forward by a noted British jurist, Mathew Hale, in his *History of the Pleas of the Crown*, published in 1736, that the insane should not be punished because they do not know the nature of their actions. The notion of diminished responsibility seems to have made its first appearance in the trial in 1800 of Jonas Hadfield, who was accused of shooting at George III. The powerful advocacy of his counsel, that he was suffering from a delusion and so should not be punished even though he was 'not wholly insane', secured an acquittal.

Probably the most famous and influential trial in the history of legal definitions of mental abnormality is that of Daniel M'Naghten, which took place in 1843. He was charged with the murder of the Secretary to the then Prime Minister, Sir Robert Peel. (He intended to assassinate Peel himself.) M'Naghten claimed an extreme and complex set of paranoid delusions, one of which was that he was persecuted by Peel. The defence argument was that he had lost 'control', having been unable to resist his delusions. His acquittal led to considerable controversy and several years later to the statement by the Law Lords which constitutes the 'M'Naghten test', a set of principles widely used by the courts in both Britain and the USA. The key section is: 'To establish a defence on the grounds of insanity it must be clearly proved that, at the time of committing the act, the party accused was labouring under such a defect of reason, from disease of the mind, as not to know the nature and quality of the act he was doing; or if he did know it, that he did not know that what he was doing was wrong'.

The statement clearly places on the defence the onus of showing a causal link between a 'disease of the mind' and the crime committed. The British courts followed the M'Naghten ruling in general terms until 1957; they did not accept the Roman view that insanity was punishment enough. Instead the accused was found 'guilty but insane', a form of words introduced in 1883, and was to be kept in strict custody. Because acceptance of a plea of insanity in 'mitigation' typically meant an indeterminate sentence in a mental hospital, it was generally used only in cases of murder—in which a guilty and sane verdict led to death by hanging. In 1953 the Royal Commission on Capital Punishment proposed an extension of the M'Naghten rules to include the capacity of the person to stop himself. The proposal was not accepted at the time, but the 1957 Homicide Act introduced into English law the defence of 'diminished responsibility' due to a variety of causes, already admissible in Scotland under the rubric 'substantially impaired responsibility'. Thus the legal concept of responsibility developed from one that was all or none in nature to one which implied quantitative variation. In the language of psychology, the shift was from a typology to a dimension. It is tempting to extrapolate and suggest that the way is now open to a further extension from a dimensional to a situational view of causation. However, a further shift must also occur in the law's view of behaviour, from abstract notions such as 'responsibility' to an acceptance of causal explanations which are either biological, or environmental, or both.

The most crucial recent development in Britain is embodied in section 60 of the 1959 Mental Health Act, according to which *any* offender committed by a higher court may be detained in hospital or made subject to a guardianship order. It makes no *requirement* for a causal link between the abnormality and the offence.

Section 4 (1) of the 1959 Act defines 'mental disorder' as meaning 'mental illness, arrested or incomplete development of mind, psychopathic disorder, and any other disorder or disability of mind'. 'Mental illness' denotes a disorder which has not always existed in the patient but has developed as a condition overlying the sufferer's usual personality. It seems that depression and schizophrenia come under this heading. Arrested and incomplete development of mind refers, in effect, to mental (intellectual) handicap, a more or less permanent feature of the person concerned. 'Psychopathic disorder' is defined in the act as a 'persistent disorder or disability of mind (whether or not including abnormality of intelligence) which results in abnormally aggressive or seriously irresponsible conduct on the part of the patient, and requires or is susceptible to medical treatment'. Finally, the meaning of 'Any other disorder or disability of mind' appears to be rather unclear. It *could* be interpreted as including all 'mental disorders' not covered by mental illness, subnormality and psychopathy, for example, brain damage and the neuroses (anxieties, obsessions, etc.). The 1959 Act gave power to detain for treatment only those persons who fall into the categories of mental illness, subnormality and psychopathy. Nevertheless, we shall look briefly at some data on brain damage and the neuroses as they relate to offending. We shall also include an overview of the evidence concerning sex offences and offenders, a category which is increasingly likely to be considered (for example by the Butler Committee, see below) as different from the general run of offences against persons. It is included in the present chapter for convenience, without any necessary implication that 'sexual deviants' are 'mentally disordered'.

At the present time (1975), the Butler Committee on Mentally Abnormal Offenders has just reported on, amongst other matters, 'to what extent and on what criteria, the law shall recognise mental disorder or abnormality in a person accused of a criminal offence as a factor affecting his liability to be tried and convicted and his disposal'. In addition, the Committee has considered unfitness to plead, criminal and diminished responsibility, and alternative arrangements for dealing with mentally disordered or abnormal offenders. The Report of the Committee will contribute, among other sources, to a revision of the 1959 Act.

Are people who suffer from psychological disorders, either permanently or temporarily, more likely to carry out criminal acts as compared with people who are not disordered? As is the case with other areas of research, studies testing this possibility have been carried out almost entirely on convicted offenders, housed in penal institutions. Careful surveys (for example, Smith, 1971) suggest that less than 10 per cent of imprisoned offenders are describable in terms of formally labelled psychological disorders. At best, therefore, the 'disorders' theory of offending can account for only a small minority of offenders. Does this proportion exceed that which would be expected in the population at large? Even if it does, the disparity could be due to several reasons other than a true increase in the likelihood of criminal behaviour by psychologically disordered persons.

1. Disordered persons may carry out an offence less skilfully, plan it less carefully or choose more difficult targets than stable persons, all failings which increase the risk of detection. There is ample evidence of an impaired performance on motor skill tasks associated with many psychological problems (Yates, 1973).

2. The police may charge a disturbed person more readily, if only with the laudable aim of ensuring official recognition of the disorder, and hence the provision of effective help.

3. Guilty pleas may be made more frequently by those who are disordered, because mitigation is more readily available; this is a species of plea bargaining. The sentence given may specify treatment, but in custody.

4. Penal institutions may increase the incidence of psychological disorders among those placed in them; certainly, they are hardly likely to be so pleasant as to reduce it. A comparison of studies of different age groups of offenders in institutions (Gibbens, 1963, late teenagers; West, 1963, habitual prisoners aged 30 plus) suggests an increasing incidence of disorder with increasing age. As West's group had a mean of nearly nine previous imprisonments, it could be either that disordered individuals in fact reoffend more than others, irrespective of all other factors, do so because their psychological problem makes it more difficult to keep a job, or that they are caught more often. In this last connection it is of interest that in West's study the sum of money involved in the latest offence immediately prior to imprisonment was much

less for those judged deviant in personality than for those judged normal. It will be recalled that McClintock and Gibson (1961) found that the 'clear-up rate' fell as the sum of money involved increased. Combining these two findings suggests that disturbed persons both carry out smaller crimes and are caught more often. Having been caught several times they receive institutional sentences, the cumulative effect of which is hardly likely to improve their psychological functioning.

It follows from all of the above that studies of offenders in penal institutions which show an association between offending and any given psychological problem must be in doubt unless all the necessary controls have been exercised.

Two types of study of the relationship between offending and psychological problems are technically satisfactory. First, self-report studies carried out on random samples of the population at large and not on psychiatric patients or institutionalized offenders, both of which would be inevitably biased, one due to self-selection, the other due to social selection. Even in this case, a positive association between the presence of psychological problems and offending indicates *correlation*, not *causation*. Moreover, it may be that individuals who are suffering from psychological problems are more likely to confess to offending behaviour than those who are not. However, if it is possible to carry out an observational study which would reveal the true occurrence of offending, and if it is shown that the individuals under study offend when the problem is active and not when it is in remission, then a *causal* link may be said to exist. Such a link would also be shown if the successful treatment of the problem removed both the problem and future offending. An analogy is provided by Walinder (1965), who cited several reports of sexual deviation, particularly fetishism (sexual arousal to objects, such as clothing, rather than to persons), which occurred together with cerebral dysfunction involving convulsions, in which both the convulsions and the deviant sexual behaviour disappeared following surgical intervention. Following the above general comments we now turn to studies of particular problems. All the studies cited are of convicted offenders, often in penal institutions. Few have used even minimal controls. We retain the terminology of the 1959 Mental Health Act (see above), concentrating particularly on psychopathy.

Mental Illness

Kloek (1968) reviewed his own (Dutch) research, as well as other studies, and concluded that there was no special association between *schizophrenia*, the most psychologically incapacitating of the psychoses, and crime. West (1966) found that in the UK the incidence of murder in association with *depression* was high—one in every three English murderers killed themselves immediately after the crime. These were most often men who had killed their wives or women who had killed their children. Nevertheless, the vast majority of depressed persons do not commit murder, so that explanations *in addition* to depression must be sought for murders by depressed individuals. The relative frequency of depressive murder is much less in the USA than in Britain due to the very much higher rate of murder and violent death in general. We discussed in Chapter 3 the importance of social setting variables for aggression. It is such variables, together with those relevant to aggression in general, which will help to give a complete explanation of murders during states of depression.

Psychoanalytic theory (for example Friedlander, 1947) suggests that a great deal of crime is motivated, not by personal gain, but by 'deeper' causes, such as a search for affection and a 'need' for punishment for forbidden, and hence guilt-inducing, thoughts. Particular emphasis is placed on shoplifting, which is viewed as an indication of psychological disturbance and not as a means of self-aggrandisement. Gibbens et al. (1971) studied the rate of admission to mental hospitals during the years 1964–69 of 1525 women shoplifters convicted in 1959. They found it to be 8·4 per cent—three times as high as the figure during the same period in the population at large, of the same age and sex. Half the admissions—usually for depression—followed suicide attempts. It is unfortunate that no data on admissions were available for 1959–64, in which case the then obtained rate of 8·4 per cent may have been higher. However, even if this were so, it would not necessarily support unequivocally the thesis that shoplifting is a symptom of psychological disorder, likely to continue unless the psychological problems are successfully treated. There are at least two additional explanations. The first, mentioned by Gibbens et al. (1971), is that the disturbance followed conviction, and was a response to it, rather than preceding and causing the offence. The second is that only a small proportion of shoplifters are apprehended (see Chapter 1). Disturbed persons are likely to shoplift less efficiently and hence are more likely to be caught. What is needed is a study relating psychological disturbance to self-reported—or better still observed—shoplifting, and not to convictions for shoplifting.

Intellectual Handicap

There is consistent evidence that a major contribution to intellectual functioning, at least as measured by formal psychometric tests of intelligence, is made by genetic inheritance (Shields, 1973). An association between intelligence and crime, if found, would then give some support to a biological view of the causation of crime. Once again, research has been concentrated on convicted offenders. The early studies suggested that they were of markedly lower IQ than the population at large (Woodward, 1955). More recent studies reviewed by Woodward (1955, and revised in 1963, see also Prentice and Kelly, 1963) have indicated a disparity of no more than eight IQ points between convicted offenders and non-offenders. Even this rather small disparity may indicate no more than that intellectual dullness impairs both the performance of criminal activity, as it does that of all types of skilled performance, as well as the success of attempts to avoid detection and conviction. We have already seen that lower social class membership systematically biases towards appearing in the official statistics of crime, as opposed to the actual commission of offences. There is a positive association between social class and intelligence, with low intelligence heavily over-represented in the working class. The greatest selection bias will thus operate against those offenders who are both members of the working class and dull in intelligence. Until studies are carried out relating intelligence to self-reporting offending, no firm conclusions can be drawn. Such studies may even produce the opposite finding from the older view that offenders are of low or average intelligence compared with the population at large, particularly in the case of offences in which considerable skill is required both for committing the offence and avoiding detection. McClintock and Gibson (1961) showed that whereas 50 per cent of robberies which involved less than £10 were cleared up, only 15 per cent of those involving over £100 were cleared up (London Metropolitan Area, 1957). The more intelligent would both be more likely to be positively reinforced for crime by successful outcomes and less likely to be detected, and hence more likely to continue offending.

Is there an association between low intelligence and particular *categories* of offences? Walker (1965) compared the indictable offences of all male offenders aged 17 and over dealt with by the English courts in 1961 with the offences of 305 males of similar age committed to hospitals by criminal courts as being 'subnormal' or 'severely subnormal'. The percentage of the 305 sentenced for sexual offences was six times as great as that found for other offenders. There was no difference in the categories of violent offences and property offences. Rather little weight can be placed on the finding for sexual offences until we know how accurately this reflects the true rate of offences committed as opposed to those reported and detected. Walker also suggests that the sexual offending of the intellectually handicapped may reflect their lack of ability to make socially acceptable sexual approaches; social ineptitude is interpreted by the 'victim' as indicating criminal intent.

Other Disorders

Brain Damage

Demonstrable brain damage is sometimes found to be the source of a particular problem of behaviour. The electroencephalogram (EEG) measures the electrical activity of the brain. Hill and Pond (1952) found a higher proportion than expected (on the basis of their incidence in the population at large) of abnormal EEG's in murderers labelled 'irrational' and 'legally insane' than in those labelled 'incidental', 'motivated' and 'sexual'. Subsequent studies have been less successful in associating EEG abnormalities with major disorders of behaviour. Gibbens *et al.* (1959) studied the offence records of diagnosed psychopaths with abnormal EEG's at the time of diagnosis, and found them to be no worse over the next 10 years than those of psychopaths without EEG abnormalities. Loomis (1965) found no significant relationship between EEG abnormalities and continued criminal behaviour by adolescent females. It seems that EEG data add little to behavioural findings in either diagnosed psychopaths or adolescent offenders.

A related interest has been in the extent to which impulsive aggression is linked with epilepsy—a problem frequently associated with an abnormal EEG. Gunn and Bonn (1971) carried out a national survey of British penal establishments in which 158 unequivocally diagnosed epileptics were compared with 180 nonepileptic prisoners matched for sex, institution and length of time in the institution. No differences were found between the two groups for the most recent offence (against property or against persons), for the nature of previous offences, or the degree of violence employed in offences against persons, but, the idiopathic epileptics (no focal lesion) had a disproportionately higher share of previous convictions for violence, whereas those with focal lesions tended to have a disproportionately small share. However, as the authors point out, the sentencing practice of the courts (based on assumption about different types of epilepsy) may have been a confounding factor. Finally, on a rating of 'impulsivity' of previous offences, epileptics were rated higher than controls. Although the scale used was somewhat crude and the raters knew the diagnostic category of the offender, the 'impulsiveness' of an offending behaviour may be of some importance. Relatively unplanned offences, carried out on the spur of the moment (i.e. instigated largely by situational stimuli), seem *a priori* more likely to be detected. Whether individuals who consistently display impulsive behaviour are in fact more likely to offend, as against being more likely to be caught, is a matter for the self-report and direct observation types of study' as we noted in Chapter 6.

The connection between criminal behaviour and brain damage occurring, or suspected of having occurred, at widely differing ages has been studied by Roth (1968) and Douglas (1960). The former pointed to the general decline in old age (when cerebral disease is most frequent) of crime in general, and of violent crime in particular. He suggested that the decrease in sexual offences such as sexual association with a minor (paedophilia, see below) is less marked and that there may be an association between cerebral degeneration and the first occurrence of such offences. Feldman (1973) has pointed out that middle-aged and elderly persons interviewed (typically rather briefly) about sexual offences when in custody have much to gain if the legal authorities accept a claim that the offence which led to a court appearance was also the first occurrence of the behaviour. Persons interviewed in therapy settings, at greater length, who have less incentive to claim a sudden onset in middle years, tend to report a lengthy history, often dating from adolescence, of such illegal sexual behaviours as paedophilia and exhibitionism (public exposure of the genitals, typically by males, see below).

Douglas (1960) carried out a very large-scale British survey relating premature birth (associated with a greater incidence of minor brain damage than normal birth) and 'bad behaviour' as rated by primary schoolteachers. He found significant correlations between the two variables, but only in working-class, not middle-class, children. Douglas concluded that 'unsatisfactory' mothers are more likely both to give birth prematurely and to rear children badly. An alternative explanation is that premature children are on average more difficult to rear successfully (in the sense of effectively controlling unacceptable behaviours), perhaps because of biologically based abnormalities (Joffe, 1969). The social resources of middle-class mothers may be more able to cope with the added difficulty than those available to working-class mothers. It was pointed out in Chapter 2 that there is typically an interaction between the behaviours of the trainer (parent) and of the trainee (child). The direction of effect is thus twoway (Bell, 1968).

Psychopathy

Introduction

According to Eysenck (1964), 'the psychopath presents the riddle of delinquency in a particularly pure form, and if we could solve this riddle in relation to the psychopath, we might have a very powerful weapon to use on the problem of delinquency in general' (pp. 55–6).

This suggests that the psychological variables which are relevant to the behaviour of the 'delinquent' are also relevant to that of the 'psychopath'. However, the notion of '*the* psychopath', as a separate type of individual, may well be as erroneous as that of 'the delinquent' as a separate type, so that we shall argue for the study of psychopathic *behaviour*, just as we argued for the study of criminal *behaviour*. We may conclude that some individuals are, indeed, either qualitatively or quantitatively different from people in general, but this should be the conclusion of a sequence of description and explanation, and not an initial assumption. Moreover, while it is likely to be true, as Eysenck implies, that experimental psychology has a major contribution to make, the variables which have been studied to date in order to explain 'the psychopath' may well be less important than others which have attracted almost no research interest. Thus, two major errors mark research in this area to date: the assumption of a separate type of person and the choice of phenomena studied. Both errors influence strongly the most thorough review of the research literature to date, that by Hare (1970). Hare's book will be drawn on considerably in the review which follows, both to set out the research which has been done and to illustrate its errors. Following a review of current research, we shall argue for a very much closer relationship of 'criminal' and 'psychopathic' behaviours than is usually accepted, and hence for the major relevance to the latter of the experimental literature reviewed in earlier chapters in connection with the former. Briefly, for the moment, the term 'criminal' emphasizes the commission of an offence, the term 'psychopath' emphasizes the (low) degree of remorse of the offender, particularly in response to the distress of the victim. In fact, offences against legal norms inevitably involve victims, however remote. (We are excluding from our consideration, as we have done throughout this book, the so-called victimless offences.) The behaviour of 'criminals', as well as that of 'psychopaths', results in the distress of a victim. Relative lack of empathic response to such distress is an important part of criminal as well as of psychopathic behaviours. In fact, it is simpler to consider the behaviours as so intertwined as to be very difficult, if not impossible, to separate out. It seems fair to conclude that the terms 'criminal' and 'psychopath' are social responses to two behaviours or sets of behaviours which are, in fact, much the same. We shall return to this theme after discussing descriptive and explanatory studies.

There is no doubt that great social anxiety is aroused by the undoubted distress to victims caused by those currently labelled psychopath. This is summed up in the appellation 'dangerousness'. A small number of those released from institutions such as Broadmoor in Britain and Atascadero (California) in the USA which specialize in mentally disordered offenders, particularly psychopaths, reoffend after release, sometimes to the extent of murder. The Butler Committee defined 'dangerousness' as 'a propensity to cause serious physical injury or lasting psychological harm' (p. 59). The term is to be reserved for those likely to *repeat* the damaging behaviour. How do we predict such persons? Butler admits the difficulties but concludes 'men with several convictions of violence are considerably more likely than their peers to be convicted of violence in the future' (p. 60). They do not define 'several' and, indeed, offer no clear guidance to assist prediction. A review by Steadman and Cocozza (1975) indicates that the overwhelming majority of murderers released from Broadmoor-type hospitals both in Britain and America do not kill again and concludes that a great many 'false positives' (people who will not kill again if released) remain incarcerated because of the social pressure to err on the side of caution. Both Butler and Cocozza and Steadman urge both recurrent and frequent reviews and a move away from a sole concentration on personality to the study of the person interacting with situational stimuli. Such an approach will also assist the design of treatments matched to a particular person with a particular learning history.

Definition

The term 'psychopath' is widely used by students of psychopathology. In the classical German psychiatry of Schneider (1959) it is a generic term for personality disorder of any kind, whether it is the individual himself who suffers, or whether his behaviour causes others to suffer. In American and British psychiatry 'psychopath' is reserved for the latter individual. Restricting ourselves now to the Anglo-American usage, research workers in different countries have emphasized different features as key elements. The Americans frequently stress charm, social skills and vanity, as well as more socially damaging attributes. In Germany there is a considerable emphasis on emotional coldness and lack of feeling for others, and in Britain impulsiveness and aggression are given weight as major traits (Craft, 1966). According to

Craft, the two major defining features, common to most published accounts, are lack of feeling for others and impulsiveness. The latter may relate to getting caught rather than to actual offending, so that we shall emphasize feeling for others, particularly victims, as the key behaviour of interest.

Authorities differ on the prognosis for diagnosed psychopaths, the Germans particularly emphasizing unmodifiability and failure to learn from experience. It is this last feature, which strictly relates to the response to attempts at treatment rather than the pre-treatment behaviours themselves, which has been the major question tackled by research to date. Yet it is a question which is clearly circular in nature: those who fail to respond to treatment are the 'true' psychopaths; the 'true' psychopath is the one who fails to respond to treatment. In fact, the fault may lie with the treatment used, which may be quite inappropriate, rather than with some *permanent and unchangeable* deficit in the individual concerned. Even the notion of 'unmodifiability' in response to *currently* used methods may be false. Gibbens *et al.* (1959) compared diagnosed psychopaths with a sample of other offenders for frequency of future offending and found it to be the same in the two groups. This study is worth repeating. If confirmed on larger groups, using self-report measures, it would make even more doubtful the value of further research designed to explain 'unmodifiability'—usually in terms of some deficit in individual avoidance learning (see below).

Type, Dimension and Situation

Hare (1970) discusses whether we should postulate a type (the psychopath) or a dimension (psychopathy). He concludes: 'Both views are appropriate, representing...different sides of the same coin...research...can be fruitfully carried out without a formal commitment to a particular view' (p. 12). He goes on to cite almost exclusively research of the typological kind, which has compared psychopaths with non-psychopaths. The vast majority of research has been carried out on institutional individuals. The notion of 'type', with each group being quite separate from each other group, has been largely abandoned in personality research, yet it continues to influence psychopathy research, despite the fact that the defining attributes are themselves personality variables, which are generally acknowledged to be continuously, rather than dichotomously, distributed. The typological view is that people are either affectionate or lacking in affection in some all-or-none way. A dimensional view is that they vary on a quantitative dimension of feeling for others. Hare goes no further towards the dimensional view than to state: 'In principle it would be possible to use modern statistical techniques...to yield a single score indicative of a given individual's degree of psychopathy' (Hare, 1970, p. 12). Yet the dimensional view, expressed in the notion of a 'degree of 'psychopathy', implies a belief in a high degree of consistency across situations in the 'amount' of psychopathy possessed by any given individual. The view that behaviour is similar across quite different situations is now under heavy attack (Mischel, 1968), as pointed out in Chapter 6. There is considerable support for the contrary view, namely, that behaviour is specific to the given situation. To remind ourselves of the conclusion we reached earlier: the pendulum will probably settle midway between the consistency and the specificity views. At the very least, situational variables will interact with previous outcomes in the same situations and with 'personality' to determine behaviour. In sum, we should be studying *psychopathic behaviours* rather than psychopaths or psychopathy. We may come to the conclusion that some persons are consistently psychopathic, others consistently the opposite, with the majority falling between, the view that we argued in Chapter 6 concerning criminal behaviour in general. Conversely, we may find either stronger support for the specificity or for the consistency view than the middle-of-the-road position. However, at the present time common observation suggests that very few individuals are likely to be consistently psychopathic or non-psychopathic in all situations and towards all persons. As an example of the former we may cite Eichmann, one of the major figures in the design and execution of the plan to exterminate European Jewry, who was known to be a tender husband and father (Hausner, 1967). The same appears to be true of many Mafia leaders (Teresa, 1973).

Research Populations

In discussing criminal behaviour we noted that incarcerated offenders may be largely unrepresentative of offenders in the population at large, a considerable degree of bias having entered into their selection. The same is likely to be true of institutional psychopaths, but to an even greater extent. There is some overlap between behaviour which damage others and those which are defined as illegal. However, for example, the police will hesitate to interfere in family matters, such as severe physical violence by one spouse against another. Nor does deliberately damaging the career of a rival count as a legal offence, unless a specific law has been broken, yet such behaviour is far from unknown in business and the professions, to say the least. Indeed, there can be no doubt of the widespread occurrence of psychopathic behaviours—defined as those which damage others, either physically, materially or psychologically, usually to the benefit of the offender, and are accompanied by relatively little remorse, operationally defined as the performance of equity-restoring behaviours—see Chapter 4). The trials of German and Japanese war criminals and the excesses of police forces and soldiers in many parts of the world supply considerable evidence of the frequency of such behaviours and of their responsiveness to situational influences as well as a suggestion of individual differences in their probability of acquisition and performance. It is almost a matter of chance whether psychopathic behaviours coincide with legally defined offences. Yet unless they do, the individual concerned remains outside even the biased selection process which leads to the production of a sample of incarcerated offenders.

There is still a further source of selection bias. Some studies select their psychopath group from the total population of the prisoners in the particular institution, so that all have an equal chance of appearing in the 'psychopath' and in the 'non-psychopath' groups. In other studies the group of psychopaths is composed of those previously diagnosed, the diagnosis having been made by a psychiatrist in connection with an appearance in court. However, the frequency of requests for psychiatric examinations varies, not only from country to country, but within countries, so that a proportion of the 'non-psychopath' group, of unknown size, might have been both referred for examination and diagnosed as psychopaths, if such a procedure had occurred more frequently in their geographical area than actually was the case.

Moreover, the reliability of diagnosis, particularly of behaviour problems such as psychopathy, is low (Davison and Neale, 1974). Even when groups of 'psychopaths' and 'non-psychopaths' have been selected from a general sample of prisoners, the measures used for selection vary widely between different groups of research workers, even in the same country. Differences in experimental findings may be due either to different criteria for selection, to procedural differences, or some mixture of both. Comparability of results is possible only within those of the same group of research workers, for example that led by Hare. Even if common selection criteria were agreed upon, a further objection to research on institutional groups arises. This is that the results obtained may tell us more about the effects of life in the institution than about the behaviours which led to incarceration. It is a problem which may work two ways: on the one hand, it may reduce real differences between psychopaths and others—both have been incarcerated; on the other, it may increase them—those who are selected as psychopaths for research purposes may already have been so identified, unofficially, and have received different handling by the staff, possibly enhancing preexisting differences. Perhaps most telling of all the criticisms of the exclusive use of institutional populations in research into psychopathic behaviour is one provided by Hare himself. He cites evidence (Robins, 1966) that 'only a small proportion of the psychopathic population is actually referred to psychiatrists' (Hare, 1970, p. 115). We might add that even in the case of those referred, their apparent 'recidivism' may be partially due to other factors, such as increased police surveillance and an increased probability of complaints by other persons following successful earlier complaints.

We turn next to descriptive and explanatory studies of 'psychopaths' compared to 'non-psychopaths', retaining the conventional division into the two groups used by the studies which will be cited.

Descriptive Studies

Learning. 1. Avoidance learning. Studies on avoidance learning stem from two related sources. The first, already critically discussed, is the view that psychopaths are unusual in failing to learn from experience, particularly the experience of punishment. The second is that this is due to an inability to learn, rather than a lack of opportunity to do so. Cast into the language of experimental psychology, the prediction is that the psychopath will be particularly poor at learning avoidance responses to painful stimuli such as electric shock. Several studies, from Lykken (1955) to Scura and Eisenman (1971), have found this to be so (reviewed by Trasler, 1973, who also cites a minority of contradictory evidence). However, there is very considerable overlap in avoidance learning scores between groups of psychopaths and others (usually 'non-psychopathic' institutionalized offenders).

Hare considers the key element to be a relative failure to acquire anticipatory fear responses to cues indicating the onset of noxious stimuli, cues which do seem to serve this purpose for non-psychopaths. Another associated finding is that while the majority of non-psychopaths choose immediate over delayed shock, only about half of a group of psychopaths did so (Hare, 1966). While this finding is of interest, it is somewhat difficult to relate it to the major defining feature of psychopathic behaviour, the lack of response to distress expressed by *others*. At the least, it would have to be shown that slowness in anticipating pain to oneself is related to lack of perception of pain to others. Only one study has been reported to date which is even potentially relevant. As mentioned earlier, Miller *et al.* (1967) compared monkeys reared apart from both their own mothers and other infant monkeys with normally reared monkeys, both in avoiding shock to themselves and in enabling another monkey to avoid shock. Whereas the reared apart monkeys were markedly inferior to the normally reared ones in responding to the distress of the other monkey (in a cooperative avoidance situation), there was no difference between the two groups in prior individual avoidance learning. This suggests that it may not be possible to predict from relative lack of avoidance to noxious stimuli to oneself to response to the pain expressed by another. In any event, a direct study of cooperative avoidance, and other help-giving situations, is indicated in man. (See Chapter 4 for some preliminary studies towards such a programme.)

2. Reward learning. A number of studies of reward learning, usually of verbal conditioning, have failed to find differences between psychopaths and others (Bernard and Eisenman, 1967; Bryan and Kapche, 1967). However, Stewart (1972) found that social reinforcement increased the production of both dependent and aggressive responses in non-psychopaths, but not in psychopaths, the differences being enhanced by prior frustrating experiences. The groups were constructed on criteria laid down by Quay (1965) and all subjects were from a penal type of institution. This result suggests that psychopaths are relatively unresponsive to the rewards provided by another person—approval, attention, and so on. However, a study by Sutker *et al.* (1971) appears to suggest the opposite conclusion. They found psychopaths learned a serial verbal task faster than non-psychopaths, but superiority was shown only on items which had a high social content (for example, FUN, SEX) and not on those with a low social content (for example, KEY, MUD). Once again, we need studies of responses to positive emotions displayed by others in situations which are as realistic as possible.

Physiological Correlates. Hare (1970) has reviewed EEG studies which suggest that 'the widespread slow-wave activity often found in psychopaths bears a certain resemblance to the EEG patterns usually found in children' (pp. 35–6). However, he also points out certain deficiencies in the 'cortical immaturity' hypothesis which will be considered shortly, together with another theory which is partially based on EEG findings, that of low cortical arousal creating a search for heightened external stimulation.

The search for differences in autonomic functioning (heart-rate, skin resistance, etc.) between psychopaths and others has been a persistent line of enquiry. Hare (1970) summarizes evidence to suggest that the resting levels of several indices of autonomic activity and the levels of response to external stimulation are both lower in psychopaths than in others. More recently, Fenz (1971) failed to find differences between psychopaths and others in heart-rate responses to a stressor, a result confirmed by Hare and Quinn (1971). However, the latter found psychopaths to be markedly poorer in the acquisition of conditioned anticipatory electrodermal responses either to a stimulus followed by shock or to one followed by slides of a female nude. According to Hare (1972a), it is the electrodermal response system which is the major site of autonomic differences between psychopaths and others.

McKerracher (1969), studying diagnosed psychopaths, found complex relationships between electrodermal and several other autonomic indices. He suggests that the data on conditioning and autonomic measures in psychopaths are best interpreted as indicating differences in activation rather than conditionability, i.e. psychopaths are as conditionable as others, provided they are sufficiently aroused. This relates to the importance of sensation-seeking by both offenders and psychopaths which has been asserted by several theorists. Clearly, autonomic functions are both complex in themselves and relate to behaviour in complicated ways (Venables, 1976). Future descriptive research should concentrate on overt behavioural measures of interpersonal behaviour. Only when these are clearly delineated and related to the real-life performance of psychopathic behaviours should the autonomic correlates of the latter be studied.

Interpersonal behaviour. There have been few studies of the interpersonal behaviours of diagnosed psychopaths and none using the ingenious experimental arrangements developed by Milgram (1963), Miller *et al.* (1963; 1967) and others which appear useful for that purpose.

Sutker (1970) found that 'sociopathic' subjects (a frequently used synonym for psychopath) were *more* autonomically responsive (on the galvanic skin response, one of the electrodermal measures) to a stimulus paired with immediate shock to *another* subject than were non-sociopaths. Sutker interprets this result as indicating that sociopaths are at least as sensitive to social cues as others. An alternative interpretation would be that the sociopaths found the receipt of shock by another to be highly pleasurable. It is not simply *sensitivity* to social cues of distress but *responsiveness* to them which is likely to be of importance for the explanation of psychopathic behaviours.

Hare and Craigen (1974) carried out a study of mutual shock administration, in which subjects took it in turn to inflict and receive shock. Their psychopath subjects differed from the non-psychopath group in giving smaller skin conductance responses both to self-receipt of shock and the anticipation of shock to the other person. In general, there was no difference in heart-rate responses in either situation. However, on the first trial (10 were used in all) the anticipatory heart-rate for shock to the self in the psychopath group accelerated significantly more than that of the non-psychopath group. Hare and Craigen interpret this as indicating a greater defensive behaviour (thought to be indicated by heart-rate acceleration) by psychopaths than by others. The biphasic heart-rate pattern (acceleration followed by deceleration) was more marked in response to self-receipt of shock in the psychopaths than in the controls. If, as they suggest, acceleration helps a person to cope with aversive stimulation to the self, then acceleration associated with shock to another should be lower in psychopaths than in others. (The distress of another person is supposed to be less disturbing to psychopaths.) However, there was *no* difference between the two groups in their anticipatory heart-rate to shock to the other participant in the situation. In this connection Miller (1967) found the biphasic pattern much more marked both in those monkeys who helped in the cooperative avoidance situation and in those who learned to avoid shock to the self than in those who did neither. Pending further research, preferably using the cooperative avoidance type of situation, it is thus difficult to interpret Hare and Craigen's findings with confidence. We shall return later to the importance of using interpersonal situations in research into psychopathic behaviour, where this is taken to mean response to victims.

Explanatory Studies

The construction of explanations of psychopathic behaviours has run well ahead of the collection of reliable, empirical data concerning the situational and dispositional (i.e. personality) variables which increase the probability of occurrence of such behaviours. The explanations considered below all concern antecedent experiences or predispositions, and thus assume that some persons consistently behave in a psychopathic manner; by implication, the majority consistently behave in a non-psychopathic manner.

Deficient Avoidance Learning. This theory has been developed by Hare. He suggests that a major element of psychopathy is a low level of the capacity for experiencing anticipatory fear of noxious stimuli both to the self and to others. This is associated with a low electrodermal response to shock both self-received and received by others. Hare combines this with the greater cardiac acceleration noted in trial 1 of the Hare and Craigen study (1974, see above) as follows: 'The small electrodermal responses preceding aversive stimuli reflects the relative *absence* of fear arousal...anticipatory cardiac activity is an adaptive response...(which) reduces the emotional impact of the situation' (Hare, 1972a, p. 11). It is not apparent why, if psychopaths are already deficient in 'fear arousal', they should further 'reduce emotional impact' (it seems reasonable to categorize fear as an emotion). Moreover, if they are indeed deficient in fear arousal, hence failing to avoid shocks and other noxious stimuli as efficiently as those less deficient, it would seem to be more 'adaptive' to *increase* the emotional impact of stimuli rather than reducing them. In any event, it is largely irrelevant to the central question concerning psychopathic behaviour—response to the distress in others— to study the failure to learn from punishment to oneself, as was pointed out earlier.

Chronic Adrenalin Sensitivity and Verbal Labelling. Schachter and Latané (1964) postulated that psychopaths are constitutionally sensitive to adrenalin. (An increase in adrenalin flow is associated normally with strong emotional stimulation.) The fact that the 'true' psychopath is low in anxiety does not necessarily mean he is low on autonomic reactivity—*both* low and high anxious persons are considered by Schachter and Latané to be highly reactive auto- nomically. However, whereas anxiety neurotics verbally label their emotional experiences in cognitive terms, the equally reactive psychopaths learn to ignore emotional arousal. Schachter has demonstrated in a number of studies (collected together in Schachter, 1971) that the relation of sympathetic arousal to an emotional state is at least partially dependent on the verbal labels available in the surrounding situation. He claims that sociopaths do not discriminate between emotional states. Because they are poor at verbal labelling, they label only very high autonomic levels. In effect, they have learned to apply 'emo- tional' verbal levels only to those levels of arousal encountered in the most extreme situations.

Schachter and Latané (1964) found that sociopaths made more errors than non-sociopath criminals on a complex avoidance task on which errors led to shocks. When adrenaline was administered the sociopaths made signi- ficantly fewer errors than previously, the non-sociopaths more, the previous difference between them being eliminated. Schachter and Latané also found that adrenaline differentially affected heart-rate, that of the sociopath to a greater extent than the non-sociopath. Finally, they suggest that sociopaths will commit 'cool' crimes such as burglary and forgery rather than 'crimes of passion' such as manslaughter, murder and sex crimes. However, the vast majority of reported offences are 'cool', but rather few offenders are labelled 'psychopaths'.

Goldman *et al.* (1971) successfully replicated Schachter and Latané's findings on the effects of adrenaline on heart-rate only for psychopaths with low scores on Lykken's Activity Preference Questionnaire (1955). Hare (1972b) recalculated the Goldman *et al.* data and found this latter result to be statistically non-significant. He failed also to replicate the Schachter and Latané (1964) finding on the autonomic effects of adrenaline, even for psycho- paths low on the Lykken scale.

Chronic underarousal. Quay (1965) has associated chronic underarousal with a high level of stimulus-seeking by psychopaths. He cites studies indicating psychopaths to be low on indices of autonomic arousal and to make a more than usually rapid return to those low levels after stimulation. This is related to Hebb's optimal stimulation approach. Hebb (1955) suggested that individuals differ in the level of external stimulation they find optimal; those functioning at a lower basal level of arousal will tend to seek further stimulation, those at higher levels will tend to avoid it. There is a good deal of support for this view, particularly from studies of sensory deprivation (Schultze, 1965). However, there is little direct evidence, as yet, either for or against the view that diagnosed psychopaths tend to seek increases in stimulation more than do non-psychopaths, or that damaging others is a *more* potent source of such stimulation than other possible sources. However, there is some (very) indirect evidence. Farley and Farley (1972) found that institutionalized adolescent girls scoring high on the sensation-seeking scale (S.S.S., Zuckerman, 1964) made significantly more attempts to escape from the institution and engaged in more fighting than those low on the scale. High scorers on the S.S.S. tolerate the sensory deprivation situation rather poorly (Zuckerman *et al.*, 1968). Farley and Farley (1967) reported that 10 of the 26 items of the S.S.S. correlated with extraversion (measured by the Eysenck Personality Inventory), all at beyond the 0·05 level of significance, suggesting that extraversion is associated with sensation-seeking. As we noted earlier, there is a marked tendency for high extraversion to be positively related to antisocial behaviour. Finally, there is evidence that stable extraverts are lower on EEG measures of cortical arousal than are stable introverts (Winter *et al.*, 1972), and persons diagnosed as psychopaths are likely to be extraverted in personality (Eysenck, 1964). A study relating EEG-measured cortical arousal to operationally defined measures of such behaviours as response to distress carried out on people in general, rather than on diagnosed psychopaths *versus* non-psychopaths, would be of interest.

Socialization Theories. An overview of the evidence relating criminal behaviour to childhood emotional deprivation or separation was given in Chapter 2. According to Hare (1970), most persons who come from disturbed backgrounds do not become psychopaths. Moreover, Cleckley (1964) states that a large percentage of his psychopathic patients came from backgrounds conducive to 'happy development and excellent adjustment'. In addition, with the exception of a study by Robins (1966), all the reports relating psychopathy to disturbed childhood have been retrospective in nature (Hare, 1970). An interviewer accepting the theory which relates disturbed childhood to psychopathy is rather more likely to interpret as 'disturbed' the childhood of a psychopath than that of a non-psychopath. Robins found that children later diagnosed as psychopaths were more likely than those displaying other disturbances to have 'psychopathic or alcoholic fathers'; they were also more likely to have displayed various anti-social behaviours as children. However, it is not clear to what extent the adult diagnosis of 'psychopath' was made independently of a knowledge of his childhood behaviour and circumstances (see Chapter 5 for a critique of this study). We need prospective studies of the subsequent adult behaviours (not the diagnostic label) of children whose behaviours and home circumstances are accurately and objectively described at the time.

Attribution of Negative Intent. Attribution theory (Kelley, 1973) is a recent development in social psychology. It is concerned with how people make causal inferences about events, how they answer the question why. Both 'cause-seeking behaviour' and the process of doing so are likely to be explicable in the same terms as behaviours in general. The current point is a descriptive one—at least in Western society, people do attribute causes to events. Causes may be attributed to one's own behaviour, to that of others, or to the non-human aspects of the situation. Attributions may vary from situation to situation or they may be rather consistent, the ambiguity of the cause of many events assisting the development of consistencies. For example, aversive consequences to oneself may be attributed consistently to the punishing intentions of others. Howells (personal communication, 1975) is carrying out at Broadmoor Hospital a programme of research based on the proposition that diagnosed psychopaths tend to make attributions of negative intent to other people in general—that is, they consistently perceive others as a source of negative, rather than positive, reinforcement. Rather than wait to test their expectation, they tend to 'get in the first blow'. This results in a hostile response from the other, confirming the original prediction. This programme of research is still in its very early stages; moreover, it is essentially a descriptive programme and does not seek to establish, at least at present, explanations for any generalized attributions of negative intent which may be revealed. Nevertheless, because it concerns interpersonal behaviour, it is potentially of considerable relevance and particularly so when comparison studies within the attribution framework are carried out in the population at large.

Cognitive Rehearsal. In Chapter 2 we referred to the part which may be played in the development of socially acceptable behaviours by the cognitive rehearsal of social training experiences. It was expected that individuals would be found to differ both in the frequency and intensity of their cognitive rehearsal behaviours. 'High rehearsers' may learn social rules particularly effectively. Psychological processes are, of course, neutral as to content. Frequent and intense rehearsal may increase the probability of performance of socially undesirable behaviours as well as socially desirable ones, depending on the content of the individual's experiences. Thus, if an individual with well-developed habits of intense and frequent rehearsal is exposed to highly deviant material, and has little exposure to more conventional behaviours and/or to the opportunity to carry them out, the result may be a potentially 'psychopathic' act. Once carried out, this may be maintained by subsequent frequent rehearsal and intermittent performance. Paradoxically, it may be that the cognitive rehearsal of deviant material is particularly likely by patients housed in institutions for diagnosed psychopaths—which typically provide little or no opportunities for the normal social experiences which might provide alternative non-deviant material for rehearsal. Like attribution theory, the rehearsal approach appears to have heuristic value, particularly if studies are carried out both on diagnosed and control populations.

Conclusions

1. At the descriptive level, experimental research has failed to demonstrate clear differences between labelled psychopaths and others. At the explanatory level, little support has emerged for the theories tested. The remainder of the conclusions set out the reasons for this lack of progress.

2. There is a clear discrepancy between the widely agreed description of the behaviours which attract the label 'psychopath' and the experimental studies of persons labelled as displaying those behaviours. Whereas the description emphasizes interpersonal behaviour, implying studies of the appropriate behaviours using two or more persons, in practice experimental studies have been much more concerned with single-person situations.

3. Thus, the lack of progress is related to the general framework within which experimental research has been carried out. Clinical descriptions are associated with the assumption that the 'psychopath' is a separate type of individual. Experimental research has typically followed that assumption by comparing 'psychopaths' with 'non-psychopaths'. Those studies which have moved from a typological to a dimensional model are based on a similarly untested assumption: that although individuals lie on the same quantitative diemension, they are divisible into those who are consistently 'more psychopathic' and those who are consistently 'less psychopathic'.

4. Studies of criminal behaviour carried out on those confined in institutions are vitiated by a strong bias in the legal process by which certain groups of offenders are more likely than others to be sentenced to confinement as well as by the effects of the prison environment. The same is true of the studies of psychopathic behaviour, but to a still greater degree. Whereas the definition of a particular behaviour as contravening the law is clear, that of the behaviours which attract the *additional* label psychopath is far from clear, and variations between official labellers are considerable.

Progress is likely to be more rapid if we apply the principles of behaviour acquisition, maintenance and performance, applied in Chapter 3 to the two major areas of criminal behaviours, offences against persons and against property. While environmental events play the major role in any satisfactory account of such behaviours, biological predisposition towards broad differences in behaviour might exert some effect (Chapter 5). In Chapter 6 we suggested that such predispositions might be expressed by the personality dimensions of extraversion, neuroticism and psychoticism, and that these would be much more important for the extreme-scoring minority than the average-scoring majority. Any research programme which seeks to take into account the possibility of gene–environment interaction should begin with descriptions of the behaviour of interest and proceed to index the differing situational stimuli which result in variations of that behaviour. If certain individuals appear more consistent in their behaviour than others—who typically change as the current situation changes—we should look for the explanation of such differences in consistency first in their respective previous learning histories and then, such an explanation failing, at the possibility of different genetic predispositions.

Before embarking on such a research programme into psychopathic behaviour, we have to ask two questions. Firstly, what are the behaviours to to studied? Secondly, if we succeeded in answering the first, are such behaviours different from those that we have already discussed under the respective headings of aggression and transgression? In general (omitting 'victimless offences'), criminal behaviours are those legally proscribed behaviours which, if successful and unpunished, are positively reinforcing for the person carrying them out (the offender) and aversive to the other person, or persons, who suffer as a consequence (the victim). Such behaviours are divisible into two broad groups: against persons (aggression) and against property (transgression). At any one time, legal prohibitions are likely to cover only a proportion of all examples of these two groups. For example, a particular financial manipulation may occur for a number of years before it is defined as illegal; assaults by husbands on wives (or *vice versa*) have an uncertain status in the criminal law—depending on the cultural context, they may or may not be defined as illegal. From the point of view of experimental psychology, the only substantial difference between injurious or acquisitive behaviours defined as criminal and those not so defined is that legal proscription increases the probability of aversive consequences for the 'offender' and decreases their probability for the 'victim'. For research purposes, particularly those associated with the development of control methods, it is convenient to confine studies of criminal behaviour to legally proscribed behaviours, but it is important to note that research might usefully include, even largely consist of, injurious and acquisitive behaviours not legally proscribed.

Criminal behaviour, then, typically involves offenders and victims, and may concern actual physical injury and/or financial loss or the threat of such consequences. The term 'psychopathic behaviour' appears to relate to 'lack of feeling for others'. In behavioural language, this becomes 'a low probability of responding so as to reduce, or stop completely, the aversive consequences for another person, either of one's own behaviours or those of someone else'. Translated into everyday terminology, we are talking about damaging another person and continuing to do so despite the obvious distress of the victim, or failing to prevent damage by another person. Many instances of 'psychopathic behaviour' also represent infractions of the criminal law, others do not. From the point of view of experimental psychology, the only difference is that, if criminal in addition, psychopathic behaviours have an increased probability of aversive consequences for the 'psychopath' and a decreased probability of such consequences for the victim. Thus, 'criminal' and 'psychopathic' behaviours have a great deal in common. In practice, if there is any distinction, it is that the term 'criminal behaviour' cues us to concentrate on the offence-related aspects of the behaviour. It is perhaps the case that we apply the label 'psychopathic' when the victim is in particularly close proximity to the offender and the aversiveness of the consequences for him are particularly visible to the offender. But both proximity and visibility are continuous rather than dichotomous variables. Moreover, we are dealing with dimensions of situations and not of persons. Thus, the term 'psychopathic' draws our attention to the victim-related aspects of injurious or acquisitive behaviours.

Do we then need separate research programmes on criminal and on psychopathic behaviours if they are simply related aspects of the same behaviour? In general, the answer must be that we do not. However, the existence of the medico-legal label 'psychopath' reminds us that a complete programme of research into criminal behaviour must give proper weight to the victim-related aspects of such behaviours.

Sexual Offences

We shall discuss only those sexual offences in which there is a *victim* (either non-consenting or below the legal age of consent), which do not involve an actual physical assault on the victim, which are likely to remain offences, and concerning which research findings exist. Thus we shall concentrate on sexual relations between an adult and a minor (paedophilia in psychiatric terminology) and indecent exposure (exhibitionism), and exclude rape, homosexual relations and incest. Rape, which obviously involves an assault, was discussed briefly in Chapter 3. Homosexual relations between consenting adults in private, while it does not involve an assault, is no longer an offence in most countries of Europe. Changes in the law are also likely in the United States or have already begun. It can be envisaged in the future that the law may be more or less similar for both homosexual and heterosexual behaviour. Finally, incestuous acts (roughly, sexual intercourse between father/daughter, mother/son or brother/sister) are prosecuted very rarely in Britain or the USA. As there is no 'victim' in the usual sense of that word, complaints are unlikely to come from either participant, and in fact the true incidence is entirely a matter for conjecture. At present, quantitative research on any aspect of incest, whether causes or consequences, is very sparse.

The Social Context

Clinard (1968) points out that what is an unimportant sexual act in one social context may become a serious breach of law in another. He notes the different consequences of a pat on a waitress's rear by a truck-driver in a transport café, a diner in a middle-class restaurant and a man in the street who encounters her by chance. The first is regarded as perfectly normal in the context, the second as an offensive display of bad manners, the offender being asked to leave, and the third, if reported to the police, may lead to a charge of sexual assault. Gebhard *et al.* (1965) give the following definition of a sex offence, combining both cultural and legal aspects: 'A sex offence is an overt act committed by a person for his own immediate sexual gratification which (i) is contrary to the prevailing sexual mores of the society in which he lives, and/or is legally punishable, and (ii) results in his being legally convicted' (cited by Clinard, 1968, p. 345).

Wheeler (1967) points out that the strongest legal sanctions are directed towards controlling the degree of *consent* in the relationship, with many states (in the USA) allowing the death penalty for forcible rape. Other bodies of sex law place limits on the nature of the object. For example, while there is an increasing tendency in different parts of the world to allow homosexual relations between consenting adults, there is little move anywhere to allow them between an adult and a person under 16, even if he (or she) appeared to consent. There are parts of the USA in which legal restrictions are also placed on the *nature* of the sexual act, so that full legality is restricted largely to acts of heterosexual inter-course other than oral-genital contacts, digital manipulation and anal entry, all of which are technically illegal, even when they occur by consent between a married couple. Finally, the law attempts to control the *setting* in which the act occurs. Acts which are legal when they occur in private may be proscribed when they occur publicly.

Wheeler (1967) lists four criteria for the establishment of sex legislation: the moral condemnation of the wider community; the perceived social danger of the offence; the psychopathology characterizing the offender; the increasing recognition of the important practical criterion of enforceability. The last reflects the lack of visibility of most forms of sexual relations between consenting partners so that detection and arrest are nearly impossible in the vast majority of instances. Wheeler concludes: 'It is no surprise that our sex laws are inconsistent and contradictory. A consistent criminal code for sex offenders is unlikely to emerge until there is agreement on the fundamental aims of criminal law in this area' (p. 83). He also points out that until the consequences for society of various types of sex relationships are better known, changes in sex legislation will have to be based largely on changes of attitudes and ideology, rather than on compelling evidence. Wheeler notes that between 1937 and 1950 thirteen states of the USA passed legislation defining sexual psychopaths and established administrative procedures for their custody, treatment and release. Procedures leading up to the legislation were similar in the various jurisdictions. There was a sequence characterized by: arousal in the community of a stae of fear as the result of a few serious crimes; agitated community response, leading to the appointment of a committee to gather information and make recommendations which, generally, were uncritically accepted by the legislature. The assumptions that were implicit included the notions that all sex offenders would be potentially dangerous, and were very likely to repeat their offences, but could be accurately diagnosed and effectively treated by psychiatrists.

Clinard (1968) cites a good deal of evidence to support the view that sexual offenders are not usually recidivists. For example in England, of a group of 1985 convicted sex offenders who had been released for four years, 85 per cent had no subsequent conviction (Radzinowicz, 1957). However, it is very difficult to know what to make of such figures. The majority of offences of most kinds are either unreported or remain undetected by the police. This is likely to apply with particular force to sex offences. Hence, it is highly likely that the low apparent proportion of reoffending among convicted sex offenders considerably understates the actual percentage which reoffend. The finding that a considerable proportion of convicted sex offenders do not attract a psychiatric label is of some importance because individuals who are disordered are likely to be less 'efficient' offenders (in the skills which avoid detection) than are less disturbed persons. Hence, those offenders who remain uncaught are likely, if anything, to be even less disturbed, on average, than those who are caught.

Paedophilia

Introduction. In Britain heterosexual intercourse is illegal between a male and a female under 16. Homosexual intercourse is illegal when either partner is under 21. In practice, prosecutions tend to be brought more in the homosexual than in the heterosexual area, and when one partner is an adult and the other under 16 than when both are adolescent. In such instances the adult attracts the label 'paedophiliac'. There are no data on the proportion of the adult population whose preferred sexual partner is a pre-adolescent. Convictions reflect many factors, including complaints by the 'victim'. It is quite unknown what proportion of habitually paedophiliac individuals are ever convicted. Even the definition itself is inconsistent between research studies. One of the few major surveys, that of Mohr *et al.* (1964) carried out at the Toronto Psychiatric Clinic, included all paedophiliac referrals (55 in number) between the years of 1956 and 1959. They defined paedophilia as 'the expressed desire for immature sexual gratification with a pre-pubertal child', where pre-pubertal meant before the development of secondary sexual characteristics. Because the average age of onset of puberty is well under 16, many of those in the sample would seek as partners children aged 13 and under. By contrast, another survey, carried out in Britain by Schofield (1965b), defined as paedophiliacs those whose preferred sexual object was under the age of 16. Hence, some of Schofield's sample would not be regarded by Mohr *et al.* as paedophiliacs.

The behaviour. Whereas Mohr *et al.* emphasized 'immature' sexual gratification, meaning sex acts appropriate to the age of the victim (used throughout this section instead of 'partner'—which may, or may not be, more accurate depending on the 'willingness' of the child concerned) such as mutual genital display, fondling, etc., Schofield made no such limitation. However, six of the 26 homosexual paedophiliaces in Mohr's sample used fondling as their major sexual act; by contrast, in 14 cases the major acts consisted of undoubted overt adult sexual behaviour, including fellatio, anal intercourse and masturbation. In addition, Mohr *et al.* cite other studies, including that carried out by Radzinowicz (1957) in which only nine per cent of the homosexual offences recorded consisted of fondling, and a California study (Department of Mental Hygiene, California Sexual Deviation Research, 1954) in which the vast majority of paedophiliac acts consisted of overt sexual behaviour. In the case of heterosexual paedophiliacs, only a minority of the acts with the victim involved 'immature' behaviour such as fondling or display. However, no definite generalization to the total population of paedophiliacs can be made from these samples of offenders seen in prison or in psychiatric centres, as it may be that complaints are not made either by the victims or their parents unless sexual behaviour of a more active kind than fondling or display is involved.

Schofield (1965b) summarized as follows the major differences which achieved statistical significance between 50 convicted paedophiliacs (PC) and 50 convicted homosexuals (HC—offences with adults aged over 21, still illegal at the time of the study). The majority of both groups were interviewed in London prisons.

The HC group were more likely than the PC group to have had their first homosexual experience before the age of 21, to have 'come to terms with their condition', to have told their friends about their sexual interests, to have visited homosexual meeting places, to have had a venereal disease and to have been arrested for non-sexual offences.

The PC men tended to look more masculine than the HC men, were more likely to be living in small towns than rural areas, to be married, to have had regular heterosexual intercourse at some period in their lives, to have strong feelins of guilt after a homosexual experience and to 'go out of their way to avoid temptation'. They also had lower frequencies of total sexual outlet.

A majority of the paedophiliacs in the Schofield sample were married. However, there was a strong tendency for the marriage to break down, the same tendency being noted by Mohr *et al.* Both Mohr *et al.* and Schofield reported that homosexual paedophilia began relatively late in life. Mohr *et al.* described three peaks, one in puberty, one in the mid-to late-thirties and one in the mid- to late-fifties, 'only a small minority being paedophiliacs from childhood onward'. Twenty-two of the Schofield series reported no sexual experience with boys before the age of 21, 15 of whom claimed none until the age of 30 and six none until well over the age of 50. By way of contrast, Feldman and MacCulloch (1971) found that all seven of the paedophiliac patients whom they treated by aversion therapy had an unbroken history of paedophiliac behaviour from adolescence onwards. The difference between the findings of the latter authors and those of Mohr *et al.* and Schofield may reflect the different degrees of thoroughness of interview used. Feldman and MacCulloch interviewed their patients, in hospital, for several hours in each case. By way of contrast, Schofield's interviews were carried out in prison, and lasted no more than 50 minutes. Although the prisoners were assured that the information would be confidential, Schofield himself doubted whether the prisoners behaved as if they believed this assurance. Similarly, the Mohr *et al.* group had all been apprehended.

One of the few systematic reports concerning the personality of paedophiliacs is that by Fisher and Howell (1973), who administered to groups of homosexual and heterosexual paedophiliacs the Edwards Personal Preference Schedule (EPPS, Edwards, 1959). The EPPS consists of a number of scales designed to indicate the level of a particular 'need'. Both groups had been convicted (in California) of sexual offences against children. It was found that heterosexual and homosexual paedophiliacs were more like each other than either were like the heterosexual male comparison group (a large normative sample reported by Edwards, 1959). Both homosexual and heterosexual paedophiliacs were higher on *intraception* and *abasement*, and both were lower on *autonomy* and *aggression* (all at the 0·01 level). The homosexual paedophiliacs were higher than the heterosexual paedophiliacs on *heterosexuality* and lower on *order* and *endurance*. The authors consider the finding concerning heterosexuality might reflect a tendency for homosexual paedophiliacs to fake a stronger interest in heterosexual sex than they actually feel (supporting the doubts of Feldman and MacCulloch that male paedophiliac behaviour is a substitute for heterosexual behaviour adopted by some middle-aged men). In sum, both homosexual and heterosexual paedophiliacs tended to be rather more neurotic and introverted (to simplify the terminology of the EPPS) than the population at large. It is unknown whether these personality features preceded the beginning of paedophiliac behaviour or were responses to the social disapproval of such behaviour.

Explanations. The general finding that behaviour is maintained by its consequences and the availability of alternative behaviours is likely to apply also to paedophiliac behaviour. (Most instances of the behaviour are undetected and hence unpunished; the behaviour is pleasurable enough for paedophiliacs to be seemingly unaffected either by prospective or actual punishment.) The performance of the behaviour will be elicited by opportunity and appropriate instigating stimuli. The antecedent conditions for the behaviour are less obvious. Their specification will be assisted if the problem of the most usual age of onset of the behaviour can be cleared up. The central aspect of the behaviour seems to be the attraction of an adult to sexually immature persons, whether of the same sex or his own sex. Moreover, the attachment is frequently more than a solely sexual one. There may be a generalized and life-long inability to form emotional attachments to adult persons of the same age, but in that case why have some paedophiliacs married? There are no reported studies of the wives of paedophiliacs.

The Effect on the Victim. The extent to which the victims of paedophiliacs are affected by their experiences has been looked at by several authors. Mohr *et al.*

review evidence to show that there is little tendency for the victims to show sexual pathology, as adults, of a gross kind, but that there is a tendency for some individuals to experience problems in their social and emotional adjustment. Unfortunately, in none of the surveys cited by Mohr *et al.* were control groups used. Gibbens (1957) reports that there was no difference in the percentage of borstal boys of known homosexual trends who reported 'being made a pass at' by a stranger as compared with those without homosexual tendencies. Doshay (1943) followed up 108 boy victims of sex offenders aged from seven to 16. In the whole group there was not a single instance of a paedophiliac offence when they were themselves adult. Similarly, Tolsma (1957) followed up 133 boys who had homosexual experiences with adults. All but eight were married and had not continued homosexual practices. Finally, Schofield (1965b) reporters that three-quarters of a non-patient homosexual group had started homosexual practices before the age of 17, most of them with boys of the same age. Only a relatively small proportion (16 per cent) had a homosexual initiation by an adult. It would be desirable to compare over a long period the victims of paedophiliacs with other children, the two groups, if possible, being matched for variables such as degree of psychological disturbance at an age equivalent to that at which the victims were attacked. In conclusion, there are few reliable descriptive findings concerning paedophiliac behaviour, and hence little on which to base explanatory theories which would enable the development of well-grounded methods of treatment. Yet the behaviour is most unlikely to be legalized, and the courts will continue to have before them many hundreds, even thousands, of cases per year. Many will be sent to prison, where they are exposed not only to the criminalization and prisonization experienced by prisoners in general, but also to the hostility and contempt reserved by their fellows for sex offences, particularly those concerning children.

Exhibitionism

Introduction. As far as the official statistics are concerned, exhibitionism is one of the most frequently encountered sexual deviations in the United Kingdom. The offence 'indecent exposure' formed one-quarter (490) of Radzinowicz's total of 1985 sexual offenders in his 1957 study, and represented approximately one-third of the sexual offenders found guilty in 1965. However, as pointed out by Schofield (1965b), the likelihood of the very much more common homosexual behaviour resulting in a conviction was so minimal prior to the change in the law as to be almost non-existent. Hence, one cannot argue from the frequency of a sexual behaviour in the criminal statistics to the frequency of the behaviour in the population at large. In the case of exhibitionist behaviour, the only source of information is the complaint of the victim (used throughout this section as a less clumsy term than 'exposee'). The frequency of complaint will depend upon the degree of personal distress experienced by the victim and her previously learned manner of responding to exhibitionist behaviour ('ignore it', 'report it', etc.).

Definition. The simplest definition is: 'The exposure of a part or the whole of the body for sexual or non-sexual rewards' (Evans, 1970). A variation is given by Rosen (1964), who defines an exhibitionist as a man who exposes his genitals to someone of the opposite sex outside the context of the sexual act. When this serves as the major source of sexual pleasure, or is compulsive or repetitious, Rosen regards exhibitionism as a 'perversion'. Mohr *et al.* (1964) define exhibitionism rather similarly, except to add as an important feature: 'Not leading to an aggressive act'. The behaviour is almost entirely confined to males, even in non-Western cultures (Ford and Beach, 1952). In those few societies in which women deliberately expose their genitals, exhibitionism appears to be a stage of courting behaviour.

Classification. Both Mohr *et al.* and Rosen (1964) divide exhibitionist acts into two groups. In the first, the act follows as the result of some rather obvious social or sexual trauma, disappointment or loss, or as an accompaniment to a severe mental or physical illness. The second is associated with an obsessive–compulsive personality. The individual may try to resist the compulsion to expose himself, but finally gives way to it. Rosen describes two types of precipitating events. In the first there is an internal describes two types of precipitating events. In the first there is an internal sexual excitement arising spontaneously as in the adolescent, or instigated in the adult exhibitionist by sexually arousing visual stimuli. In the second type exposure occurs as a result of a non-sexual tention situation.

Description. Evans (1970) states that the act of exposure will vary according to the timidity or the boldness of the offender and the urgency of the compulsion. Some expose from behind a curtained window or while seated in a parked car. At the other extreme the offender may totally undress and spring out before his victim. The act is, as often as not, carried out in a public place. Some exhibitionists expose repeatedly in the same spot.

Mohr *et al.* (1964) report that in only four of 54 cases were neighbours exposed to instead of strangers, and in three of these instances the neighbours were inadvertent victims. Both Mohr *et al.* and Radzinowicz (1957) report that exhibitionists exposing to adult females tended to expose to them individually, while those exposing to children were more likely to do so to groups of children. Some exhibitionists are extremely specific in their choice of victim—she must wear certain clothes, must appear educated and sophisticated, or have other virtues.

A central feature appears to be that no further relationship is sought between the offender and the victim. In only a few instances does exposure constitute a frank sexual invitation. For most exhibitionists the intended reaction of the victim appears to be of three kinds: fear and flight; indignation and abuse of the exhibitionist; pleasure and amusement. However, it is also true that a 'victim' who responds favourably is not likely to complain to the police. Once again, research has been confined to those who have been convicted. The usual age of onset of exhibitionism is at puberty and the period ranges between the ages of 15 and 30. Onset after the age of 45 is extremely rare, except when it is the result of organic factors (Evans, 1970).

Personality and Other Individual Differences. The intelligence quotients of the Mohr *et al.*(1964) series were normally distributed, but there was some tendency to educational underachievement. However, as no data were provided on social class the specific importance of educational factors cannot be estimated. While the majority of the Mohr *et al.* series had good work records, the authors also state: 'They seem to have difficulty with their supervisors'; no evidence for this statement is supplied. Exhibitionists tend to marry, according to Mohr *et al.*, at a normal age, the majority being married in their early twenties, with the peak age at 22 to 23. In most series the proportion who were married varies between 50 and 60 per cent (Evans, 1970). Mohr gives an anecdotal description of the nature of the relationships with the wife and the personality characteristics of the wife; the latter are said to include considerable difficulty in the sexual area, but no clear data are supplied. The characteristics of the wife are said to involve dependence and ambivalence; again the evidence is anecdotal.

Mohr *et al.* cite personality assessments by Rickles (1950) to the effect that exhibitionists tend to be: 'Tense, compulsive, with a rigid control over emotions'. No quantitative data or data for comparison groups are given, but there does seem to be general agreement in the literature that the exhibitionist act has the phenomenological quality of a compulsion (the 'urge' to perform a behaviour is first resisted, then the resistance is overcome). Rosen, reviewing a series of 24 exhibitionists who received psychoanalytic therapy over a two-year period, considered that there was a functional equivalence between exhibition and the expression of aggression. He drew this conclusion because: 'It was possible to deal indirectly with the sexuality of the patients a great deal of the time by discussing their aggressions'.

Associated Problems. Several organic conditions have been reported to be associated with a consequent exhibitionism. Evans (1970) sees some exhibitionist acts as a consequence of confusion and the loss of self-esteem and moral values present in conditions that involve damage to the central nervous system. Typical examples are brain damage in degenerative conditions of the central nervous system, such as brain tumours, presenile psychosis, senile arteriosclerosis and general paralysis of the insane. Diabetics have exposed when their blood sugar is poorly controlled. Often an exposure occurring in a person with a previously blameless character is a warning that something is greatly wrong and, indeed, some cases appear in court before the true source of the problem is realized (Evans, 1970).

Explanations. The early childhood of the individual is a favourite candidate for the explanation of almost any behavioural problem. One-third of the Mohr *et al.* (1964) series had fathers absent for prolonged periods of time and also claimed to have had more distant feelings for their fathers than for their mothers. In the absence of control data the importance of this finding cannot be assessed. Evans (1970) pursues two lines of speculation. The first, which is behavioural in nature, is that the exhibitionist act is acquired by classical conditioning as a chance association with another behaviour and is then reinforced by masturbation to the deviant fantasy. Evans cites a case in which the individual was urinating in an alley when a young femle chanced to pass and notice the act. This was followed by the individual becoming an habitual exhibitor. Evans thinks it likely that the act was reinforced by the ensuing pleasure of masturbation to orgasm to the recalled fantasy. The behaviour is maintained by similar outcomes following subsequent exposures, and performance is in response to readily available instigating stimuli. The importance of both anticipation and subsequent cognitive rehearsal is suggested by the frequent reference to the obsessional nature of the thinking of exhibitionists. Evans also cites a case, reported by Bandura and Walters (1963), in which vicarious learning in the home appeared responsible for the acquisition of the deviant behaviour. Next, Evans speculates that exhibitionism may be understood in terms of the concept of displacement. This is well defined and understood among lower animals. For instance, if males are fighting, they will often break off the encounter and go through the motions of seizing food or copulating with the nearest female or other substitute. Energy displacement will thus 'spill over' from one basic drive to another and particularly between the sex drive and aggression, which appear to be constitutionally linked in the male. This harks back to the view of Rosen (1964) mentioned earlier.

At present, the behavioural approach, perhaps combined with a predisposition to obessional modes of thinking and poor heterosexual social skills, appears the stronger explanatory candidate. Cognitive rehearsal of the relevant deviant behaviour, particularly when combined with a lack of opportunity for alternative, socially acceptable behaviours, may help to maintain both paedophiliac and exhibitionist behaviours, in combination with the reinforcement received for their overt performance.

Chapter 8

Sociological Approaches

Introduction

Sociological approaches to behaviour tend to emphasize external influences which affect large number of people They point to the broad brush of economic and political changes, of power relationships, of class and status, rather than the fine grain of individual behavioural experiences. Thus we shall look, briefly, at economic explanations of offending, at approaches which focus on working-class experiences and at subcultural settings, and at the relative social power of control agents and certain offenders. However, sociologists have worked also with both learning and cognitive concepts and we shall consider examples of these attempts.

This book is principally an attempt to apply experimental psychology to crime; a review of sociological approaches is inevitably brief and non-specialist, but it will be seen to serve a useful purpose. We shall conclude that at least one sociological approach, labelling theory, adds an important complementary component to a view of crime otherwise solely concerned with learning experiences and individual differences.

Economic Explanations

General Prosperity

Thomas (1925) correlated the British business cycle for the years 1854–1913 (the cyclic fluctuations in several economic indices) with a variety of social indices including the criminal statistics and 'found that prosecutions for drunkenness increased with prosperity, whereas burglary and other forms of "breaking and entering", showed a strong tendency to increase in the lean years; ordinary larcenies showed a weaker tendency of the same sort' (Walker, 1965, p. 90). Walker notes that similar correlations held in the USA during both the 1920's and 1940's. While there are positive correlations between unemployment and police arrests (Glaser and Rice, 1959) in the USA, this is far from indicating a causal relationship. In addition, as we have noted earlier, arrests are far from a random sample of offences. Finally, as Walker points out, 'observations (such as those above) ... have been overshadowed by the more spectacular long-term trends of both economic conditions and crime, in which a steep and steady rise in the standard of living of practically all social classes in Western Europe and the Americas has been accompanied by a steep and steady rise in the rates of crime, including property crime' (Walker, 1965, p. 91). He argues that affluence increases both the awareness of material possessions, particularly through the communication media, as well as the opportunity for gaining them illegally—for example, theft from unattended vehicles increases as vehicle ownership increases. Opportunity is also related to urban–rural crime differences; shoplifting, for instance, is made more possible by shops large enough to walk around.

Poverty and Social Disorganization

Poverty is difficult to define. There is a difference between being poor and a self-perception of being deprived. In the view of some investigators, 'poverty' may be caused by what they regard as unwise spending. Burt (1923), for instance, found that 56 per cent of his delinquents came from poor or very poor homes—the highest of whose families' 'small, but constant' earnings did not 'suffice to maintain a constant level of physical health, because, though theoretically above the minimal standards for necessities, much of it was absorbed by other expenditure, useful, needless, or unintelligent'. He was not, however, much impressed by poverty as a causal factor. 'Since of the total inhabitants of London no more than 30 per cent belong to the lowest social strata . . . the amount of delinquency coming from those lowest social strata is, beyond question, disproportionate; nevertheless, in the higher and more prosperous ranks, its frequency is still unexpectedly large. And, when nearly half the offenders come from homes that are far from destitute, poverty can hardly be the sole, or more influential, cause.' In his opinion, 'in only 3 per cent of the male delinquents, and in not 1 per cent of the female, could the effects of poverty be called the prime contributory factor'. He continues: 'Our general conclusion, therefore, on the influence of poverty must be this. If the majority of delinquents are needy, the majority of the needy do not become delinquents'. Indeed, in Burt's view, it is more remarkable that 42 per cent come from those classes 'designated by Booth as "comfortable"'. He adds, 'this figure will probably surprise those familiar with the industrial school type. The explanation is clear. In the better kind of home, the parents and interested friends more often desire—and more successfully attempt—to debar their children's petty mis-demeanours from becoming a subject of official enquiry and action; the official agency in its turn, when appraised of all the facts, is more reluctant to banish a child from a good home to an industrial school'. A similar study carried out today might lay even less emphasis on poverty as a major causal factor.

Both mental illness (Buss, 1966) and crime have been associated with the 'areas of social disorganization' in the centres of large cities. It is likely to be the *events* which occur in such areas, rather than their physical ecology *per se*, which are relevant, if at all. This topic will be returned to shortly under the heading of subcultural theories. Walker (1965) finds it 'striking' that crime rates remain the same in rehoused juveniles as in the slums from which they came (Ferguson and Pettigrew, 1954). But this should be no great surprise; there is no reason to suppose that people inevitably change their attitudes and behaviours along with their dwellings, particularly in areas of behviour, such as offending, which are not directly concerned with housing itself. The original models for the observational learning of criminal behaviour have simply transferred to a new physical setting.

Unemployment

A review by Wootton (1959) of the employment record of convicted offenders indicated that the level of unemployment among offenders depended partially upon the general level of unemployment. While offenders were more frequently out of a job than controls, this may have been because they were less employable (i.e. skilled) and hence the first to go when times were hard, because they were less likely to seek work, or because having lost a job a new one was harder to obtain by someone with a criminal record. Wootton also found that offenders changed their jobs about twice as often as the controls. This may have been because they are more impulsive, because they are less suitable for the jobs they take up, or because when their record is discovered by an employer they are dismissed. Those with previous convictions seem more likely to commit an offence during periods of unemployment than at other times. N. Morris (1951) found that at a time of full employment over 72 per cent his 270 'confirmed recidivists' were unemployed the last time they recommenced their criminal activities. This would be expected by a behavioural view; a well-learned response (offending) will be performed for an expected reinforcer when an alternative response (paid employment) is either unavailable or requires more effort to obtain than a criminally attained goal. Once a behaviour is acquired, it *may* be performed; unemployment is best seen as a potential instigator for the performance of an already acquired criminal behaviour. Will unemployment increase the likelihood of a first offence, all other sources of influence (environmental and biological) being held constant? A reward--cost approach to this question suggests a different effect according to the probability of reemployment in general and the relationship between reemployment and detection. When the probability of the particular individual being reemployed is very low and detection is irrelevant to those chances, unemployment will probably be an important positive instigator to crime. Conversely, when unemployment in the relevant area of occupational activity is perceived as temporary, and reemployment would be made unlikely by detection, the individual concerned may be even more law-abiding than when he is employed. Clearly, the blanket term 'unemployment' must be analysed in terms of the probability of reemployment for the particular individual at the particular time and place.

Theories of Social Failure and Alienation

Merton and Anomie

Several sociological approaches trace their descent from the concept of 'anomie' originally described by Durkheim (a recent edition appeared in 1970) in the nineteenth century. Merton (1969) conceives of anomie as a 'disjuncture between the cultural goal of success and the opportunity structure by which this goal might be achieved'. Since the lower strata were discriminated against in educational and occupational marketplaces, this was the group least likely to realize the 'American dream' ... 'No wonder that from these strata so many pursued deviant activities; only such activities offered an available route to success' (cited by Box, 1971, p. 105). As Box points out, Merton, and several similar 'strain' theories, has set out to explain one of the major facts of *officially* designated criminal behaviour—that it appears heavily concentrated in the lower social groups.

Cohen and Adolescent Status Problems

According to Cohen (1955), a large section of working-class children experience status problems because of their lack of success in meeting middle-class standards of successful school performance. The consequent frustration and anxiety is dealt with by a 'reaction formation' whereby middle-class values and norms (previously accepted) are now rejected. Instead, working-class adolescents display a contempt towards property expressed by destructive acts rather than theft. Several criticisms may be made of this theory. First, it applies explicitly only to the relatively rare acts of destruction against property, and not to the much more frequently occurring offences concerning the material acquisition of property. Second, it assumes, without supporting evidence, that working-class children almost inevitably accept middle-class values, at least initially. Finally, the theory relates only to those working-class adolescents who do accept middle-class values yet fail to succeed educationally. This last criticism applies both to Cohen's theory and to that of Cloward and Ohlin, to which we now turn.

Cloward and Ohlin and the Role of Alienation

As set out by Cloward and Ohlin (1960), this theory differs from Cohen's and is an improvement on it in several ways. First, it equates criminal behaviour not with destructive, but with acquisitive behaviour. Second, it avoids the problem posed by the reaction formation concept, substituting the 'withdrawal of approval from middle class norms'. It retains Cohen's notion that middle-class norms are initially accepted but later rejected when they fail to lead to educational success, as well as his emphasis on the juvenile gang as providing psychological support.

A study by Gordon *et al.* (1963) clarifies the matter somewhat. They found that middle- and lower-class offenders and non-offenders of both classes do accept middle-class *pre*scriptions of the desirable goals of life. However, the degree of acceptance of middle-class *pro*scriptive norms (behaviours that are not allowed in order to achieve the agreed goals) declines as the social level goes down.

Both Cohen's and Cloward and Ohlin's theories apply only to lower-status boys with high ability but low actual, or expected, educational achievement. If this is correct, studies of working-class self-reported offenders should show: (a) that they both have *higher* levels of ability—as measured by formal tests of intelligence—and originally had higher educational aspirations than non-offenders; (b) despite (a) they have relatively low levels of actual achievement; and (c) that their lack of success is due to the poverty of opportunities provided by the social system within which they live. No studies of this kind appear to have been carried out as yet, although a number of studies have supported the view that poor school performance is *correlated* with juvenile offending. This is by no mean the same as the assertion either that poor performance *causes* offending, or that offending is a substitute goal for an original goal of academic success reasonably held on the basis of superior ability. An example of such a study is one by Hargreaves (1967). He found the percentage in each 'stream' of a British secondary school who admitted having been recently involved in stealing to be as follows: A stream, 7 per cent; B stream, 43 per cent; C stream, 73 per cent; and D stream, 64 per cent. (In passing, the reduction from C to D does not fit in with the general theory; moreover, the disparity between the A stream and the rest is much greater than Belson's findings—see Chapter 1—would lead one to expect.) Hargreaves also found that upper stream boys had similar values to their (middle-class) teachers; those in the lower stream did not. In the upper streams, high status among peers was positively associated with academic record; in the lower streams, the most popular boys were the most anti-school and anti-authority. Hargreaves suggests that the behaviour of each group of boys is a response to the educational aspirations held for them by their teachers—high for the upper streams and low for the lower streams—and this situation exemplifies the consequences for behaviour of the social labelling process (see below). There is a readily available alternative explanation for the above findings. As each boy enters the school he joins an existing social learning situation. The apparently brighter boys are placed with bright boys, duller ones with the dull boys. The former are already offending more frequently and are thus more likely to provide social models for such behaviours. In other words, boys may learn a variety of behaviours, including criminal behaviours, directly by observing those of their peers with whom they most frequently associate, at least as much as they learn indirectly in response to the label assigned them by teachers. This approach suggests that any boy, whether dull or bright, assigned to a stream with an existing high level of criminal activity will be more likely to learn criminal attitudes and behaviour than if he were assigned to a stream with a low level of activity. Conversely, any boy would be less likely to learn criminal activity in a stream with a low level of activity than in one with a high level. Hargreaves's theory would suggest that it is the dull boy only, placed in a dull stream, who will learn to offend. The approach argued for thus emphasizes learning contexts concerning criminal activity, that of Hargreaves emphasizes the intellectual level of the boy concerned. The clearly contrasting predictions are readily testable.

In addition, it could be argued that Hargreaves has applied his theory to the wrong boys. A sense of failure and rejection can only be experienced if a target has been set and accepted. Experiencing a sense of 'failure' is potentially more likely for bright than for dull boys because their educational targets are more likely to be explicit and high achievement more emphasized. Hargreaves's theory should therefore predict that criminal behaviour would be greatest in those *bright* boys who fail to achieve the levels of educational success of which their ability suggests they are capable. It follows that statistics of criminal behaviour which compared educationally successful and un-successful bright boys would provide a more precise test of Hargreaves's theory than those which he actually collected. Moreover, measurements of social attitudes should be taken on entering school and again after educational assessment and teacher feedback to pupils. A causal relationship, supportive of the theory, would be suggested by the following sequence: high ability; high expectation held out; educational failure; a change in values away from those held by teachers; and an increase in offending.

It has been suggested above that the 'strain' theories might be tested more appropriately on bright than on dull boys. The criticism can be extended. A criminal response to low achievement should surely be more likely by low-achieving *middle-class* boys than by low-achieving working-class boys— the former seem *a priori* both more likely to have acquired middle-class values and to be rejected for failure, both by parents and teachers. It follows that the 'strain' theories should have been applied to bright middle-class, rather than dull working-class, boys! Yet they seem specifically restricted to the latter.

The Subcultural Approach

The subcultural, or cultural diversity, approach (for example Mays, 1963) asserts that members of a subculture in which offending is highly frequent will typically be offenders simply by conforming to the prevailing social norms. There is no need to postulate either 'strains' or 'reaction formations'. The offender subculture socializes its members into what is 'normal' by its own standards but deviant by those of the middle class. Because not all families in the subculture are offenders, neither will all the boys in that subculture be. Differing frequencies of delinquent behaviour are accounted for by differing degrees of 'resistance to contagion' (Morris, 1957).

The subculture view is (albeit unwittingly) an assertion about the learning process. It states simply that people learn from others, without saying how this occurs. But our empirical knowledge of the learning process is such as to make unnecessary such vague medical analogies as that of 'resistance to contagion'. Moreover, although it discards the notion of 'strain', the sub-cultural approach is again confined to socially disadvantaged settings, and says nothing about the acquisition of criminal behaviours by those in more advantaged subcultures. (There is, of course, no reason why it should not do so. We would then have a theory which states that new offenders have learned criminal behaviours from those who have already offended—i.e. by observational learning.)

Research on Delinquent Gangs

The sociological theories considered so far have in common the belief that the offender element of the working class transmits its anti-social values through the teenage gang. According to Hood and Sparks (1970), 'In the last ten years...research...has challenged basic assumptions...of the concept of the highly organized gang...as a "criminally orientated" sub-culture... with internal solidarity and group loyalty within gangs...and the idea that delinquency is simply negative, maliciously and consciously in opposition to middle class standards' (pp. 86–7). They also point out that sociological views about gangs, now more doubtful following recent research, were largely developed in the USA and presumably were intended to apply most particularly to that area of the world.

Studies which have shown that offences by early and mid-adolescents tend to be carried out in small groups have used samples of convicted offenders. Whether the self-report method would show the same result is not known, but the greater attention paid by the police to group offences was noted in Chapter 1 (Erickson, 1971). However, even these small 'groups' (of twos and threes), though they may be loosely associated in 'gangs', are not in themselves gangs. It seems to be the case that 'although a potentially large "membership" may be mobilised at times of external threat...gangs usually have a relatively small core' (Hood and Sparks, 1970, p. 89). Nevertheless, there is evidence from a study of Los Angeles teenagers (Klein and Crawford, 1967) that (official) delinquency rates were higher in those sections of the gang between whom there was the greatest amount of social contact. In itself, this is not surprising; people with similar interests and beliefs tend to see more of each other than do people with dissimilar interests and beliefs. What this study does suggest is that it was criminal behaviour which was the core activity of this particular gang, and which provided it with its *raison d'être*. However, no other activity which they might have had even more in common was surveyed.

In line with the possibility that gangs exist for purposes in addition to, or even rather than, criminal behaviour, Hood and Sparks cite studies which suggest 'a mixture of theft and violent activity, rather than a commitment to either' (p. 97). Even violence 'although discussed a good deal, does not seem to be the only, or even the primary goal of the group members...nevertheless, at the core there may be cliques who are especially involved in planned and persistent theft' (p. 98). There is a clear need for studies of adolescent social groups in general, middle-class as well as working-class, the activities they carry out and the short- and long-term psychological and material functions they serve. As a general prediction it would be expected that, irrespective of the content of what is learned in such groups, it would be found that one of the major ways in which adolescents acquire their behaviours is through the observation of other adolescents. The behaviours modelled by the most admired and most successful adolescents will be copied by their fellows; if criminal behaviours achieve the most valued outcome it is these which will be imitated. Adolescent social groups will be found to exemplify the general tendency for the observation of the behaviours of others and of the outcomes of these behaviours to be a major source of learning.

Theories of Crime in all Social Classes

Matza and the Similarity of Criminal Behaviour in all Adolescents

Matza (1964) rejects both the view that criminal behaviour is peculiar to the lower class and that it arises out of conflict and strain. He suggests that adolescents see themselves as pushed around by forces outside their control. In 'desperation', in order to register their protest and restore the 'mood of humanism in which the self makes things happen' (Matza, 1964, p. 191), they carry out criminal acts. This is reminiscent of the concept of locus of control (Rotter, 1966), according to which individuals differ in the extent to which they expect outcomes directly consequent on their own actions. The implication of Matza's theory is that individuals who consider themselves externally controlled *resent* this and therefore commit criminal acts as the only ones of whose consequences they feel themselves in control. The next stage is that adolescent offenders learn techniques of 'neutralization' to enable them to avoid guilt, an example of which is to justify violence as anticipatory self-defence. Matza suggests that neutralization techniques are used both prior to and after criminal acts. The notion of neutralization is very reminiscent of dissonance reduction following cognitive or behavioural inconsistency. Scores of laboratory studies have been carried out within the framework of dissonance theory, many of them concerned with aggression, transgression and helping, topics which were reviewed earlier. It can be seen that there is nothing uniquely sociological in Matza's theory: the concepts of 'desperation' and 'neutralization' are well researched in the experimental psychology of personality and social behaviour under the headings of locus of control and dissonance theory. A great deal of clearly specified theory and careful experimentation is available for application to the study of criminal behaviour. Unsupported assertion, however appealing its humanist 'message' and however persuasive the literary style in which it is couched, is quite unnecessary. Finally,

Matza's approach appears confined solely to adolescents, rather than to people of all ages, and is thus limited in its application.

Differential Association Theory

First propounded nearly 40 years ago by Sutherland (1937), the theory of differential association sets out to explain how criminal behaviour develops, and in what circumstances. Its central emphasis is on learning, as the following nine statements (taken from Sutherland and Cressey, 1970), which contain the core of the theory, make very clear.

1. Criminal behaviour is learned.
2. Criminal behaviour is learned in interaction with other persons in a process of communication.
3. The principal part of the learning of criminal behaviour occurs within intimate personal groups.
4. When criminal behaviour is learned, the learning includes (a) techniques of committing the crime, which are sometimes very complicated, sometimes very simple, (b) the specific direction of motives, drives, rationalizations and attitudes.
5. The specific direction of motives and drives is learned from definitions of the legal codes as favourable or unfavourable.
6. A person becomes criminal because of an excess of definitions favourable to violation of law over definitions unfavourable to violation of law.
7. Differential association may vary in frequency, duration, priority and intensity.
8. The process of learning criminal behaviour by association with criminal and anti-criminal patterns involves all of the mechanisms that are involved in any other learning.
9. While criminal behaviour is an expression of general needs and values, it is not explained by those general needs and values, since non-criminal behaviour is an expression of the same needs and values.

Statements 1 and 8, in particular, clearly identify the differential association approach as emphasizing learning as the central explanatory principle of offending behaviour, rather than the surrounding social conditions, biological predisposition, unconscious motives, or any of the other alternative causal views. Sutherland's theory consists of a set of assertions, largely unanchored in empirical findings and imprecise in its language. It has been formulated very much more briefly by DeFleur and Quinney (1966); 'Overt criminal behaviour has as its necessary and sufficient conditions a set of criminal motivations, attitudes and techniques, the learning of which takes place when there is exposure to criminal norms in excess of exposure to corresponding anti-criminal norms during symbolic interaction in primary groups' (p. 4).

Burgess and Akers (1966) have translated the first eight of the above statements into the language of the operant approach to learning. But it is questionable whether it is necessary to do so, any more than the development of a behavioural approach to abnormal behaviour required the initial translation of psychoanalytic theory into the language of the psychology of learning. Dollard and Miller's (1950) text which carried out the latter translation is an intellectual *tour de force*, but a behavioural approach to psychopathology could have proceeded directly to the basic phenomena as observed; using psychoanalytic theory as a stepping-stone simply gave an extra legitimacy to that theory, and may even have delayed the systematic and direct application of behavioural principles to abnormal behaviour. In the same way, there is no need to translate Sutherland's conceptually naïve psychology into contemporary psychological language. Doing so is an interesting intellectual exercise, but it is much simpler to apply learning principles directly to the observed phenomena of criminal behaviour.

Control Theory (Hirschi, 1970)

Differential association theory is concerned with the positive learning of criminal behaviours. Control theory (Hirschi, 1970) is concerned both with positive learning and with learning *not* to offend. It starts with the question: 'Why don't we all break the law?'. It argues that the law is kept only when special circumstances exist, so that there is no need for a special motivational account which assumes strain. The success of social training is considered to depend on *attachments*, *commitments* and *beliefs*.

Attachments refer to 'the emotional intensity of one human being's involvement in another'. They are low when a representative of the social order, such as a teacher, rejects an adolescent by assigning him to a lower stream. In his turn the boy, who feels insulted, rejects the teacher, the source of the insult, and the values for which he stands. It seems that 'attachment' is another way of talking about interpersonal attraction (Berscheid and Walster, 1969); the greater the attachment the more effective is, for example, a teacher as a social reinforcer of approved or disapproved behaviours. Commitment refers to 'the rational element' in the social bond. Individuals do not persist in lines of activity unless there is something in it for them. This is similar to an analysis of behaviour in reward–cost terms. The greater the overall gain from a behaviour the more likely is it to be carried out; the greater the overall loss the less likely. Individuals make subjective evaluations of the elements in the reward–cost matrix. In fact, Hirschi largely leaves out the reward side (potential gains following deviant acts), concentrating mainly on the losses which follow apprehension. Beliefs refer to the extent of acceptance of law-abiding norms. The other situational variables increasing the probability of deviant behaviour are *skills*, *supply*, *group support* and *symbolic support*. Special skills are essential to perform many crimes. Supply refers to the availability of the special tools and equipment which may be needed for certain criminal behaviours. Group support appears to refer to the fact that deviant attitudes and behaviours are more likely to be learned in the settings of some social groups than in others. Groups supply both discriminative stimuli for responses and reinforcement for appropriate performance. Symbolic support appears to be another term for mechanisms of dissonance reduction.

Thus translated, control theory adds little to the psychological concepts of interpersonal attraction, attitudes, positive and negative reinforcement for behaviours, discriminative stimuli, responses, decision-taking and the reward–cost matrix and dissonance reduction. Control theory is, in large part, a reward–cost approach to the performance and maintenance of deviant behaviours, but says nothing about their acquisition. Norm-containment theory (Reckless, 1962) which we consider next is another sociological version of the reward–cost approach.

Norm-containment Theory

This theory has a double aspect: the capability of groups to transmit norms effectively and hold their members within bounds and the retention of norms by the individual as an inner control over behaviour. Two constraints on deviant behaviour are postulated, external and internal. External controls are those exerted by the police and other agents of the legal system; internal controls are those within the individual, his total set of attitudes against carrying out deviant behaviours. Both reduce the probability of such behaviours. Individuals who can be classified as strong–strong (both in external and internal containment) will have a very low probability of committing crime or delinquency (becoming a legal deviant), whereas individuals who are classified as weak–weak will have a very high probability of committing crime and quency. Norm-containment theory also suggests that the acquisition of deviant behaviours is due to differential associations (see above).

The last two theories both suggest the usefulness of regarding the performance of offending behaviours as the outcome of the rewards and costs contingent on performance. In Chapter 3 we considered psychological research carried out within a reward–cost framework and in Chapter 2 we gave a detailed account of research on internalization.

It is appropriate at this point to mention two studies, one relating to control theory, the other to norm-containment theory. Jensen (1969) reported that belief in the inevitability of law-breakers being caught and punished was negatively related to both self-reported and official offending in adolescents of both sexes and races aged 13–17. The relationship was stronger for the less serious (for example under $50) than the more serious (over $50) thefts. Jensen also stated (his Table 7, p. 197) that belief in apprehension and punishment was positively related to the closeness of the father–son relationship, to the level of educational aspiration and to attachment to the law (interpretable as attachment, commitment and belief, respectively). In discussing the correlations between belief in apprehension and respect for the law by school grade and self-reported delinquency level, Jensen notes that they are higher among the younger than the older pupils. Unfortunately, he did not test the statistical significance of even those of his results which he submitted to quantitative analysis. Voss (1969) studied self-reported and official offenders, differential association (friendship with offenders) and a shortened version of the socialization scale (So, Gough, 1957) in 284 seventh-grade Honolulu schoolchildren. According to Gough, the So scale indicates the 'degree of social maturity, and integrity...the individual has attained'. Both the So scores and differential associations were significantly related to the various measures of offending, the latter more strongly. Combining the two measures resulted in a stronger association than either alone. Nevertheless, over half of those categorized as being in the 'most vulnerable' (on the Gough scale) and 'most associative' (with other delinquents) quadrant reported no offences, and 80 per cent of them had no official record of offending either. However, membership of the opposite quadrant 'least vulnerable' and 'least associative' correctly predicted non-self-reported offending in 90 per cent of those in the quadrant.

Despite weaknesses in conceptual and statistical analysis and in experimental design, the above studies suggest the general usefulness of both the differential association and the control theory approaches to crime (and hence of the learning approach outlined in earlier chapters).

Social Labelling Theory

In Chapter 1 we noted some similarities between criminology and the study of abnormal behaviour and mentioned labelling theory as an important approach. A key influence has been that of Lemert (1951), who argued for transferring attention from the behaviour itself to the reactive pattern it elicited. There are acts to which reactions are *possible*, a pool from which control organizations may select those to be labelled deviant—as 'criminal', or as 'mentally ill', etc. The aim of 'explanation' should be to uncover the process by which labels are acquired and accepted, and the focus thus shifts from those who receive labels to the activities of those given the power to label. Thus, the central theme of social labelling theories is that deviant behaviour arises from attempts at control; it is a response to activity on the part of those officially designated as 'labellers' and 'controllers'. Social labelling theory has strongly influenced psychological research in the field of abnormal behaviour. For example, Ullmann and Krasner (1969) place heavy emphasis on labelling concepts in their explanatory theory of sochizophrenia, filling in the gaps in labelling theory with the use of operant learning principles. They begin with two general axioms: any behaviour, even the most bizarre, may be learned; persons frequently take on the roles they have been assigned by others. Next, Ullmann and Krasner cite studies which indicate that patients convey the impressions the physician seeks (in learning theory language: the patient emits responses which are reinforced by physicians; it is *only* bizarre responses which are so reinforced, non-bizarre ones are ignored and so are extinguished). Certain officially sanctioned labelling agents, psychiatrists, psychologists, etc., are thus *responsible* for the *maintenance*, if not the initial appearance, of 'schizophrenic symptoms'. Ullmann and Krasner somewhat overstate their case, for example there is substantial evidence for inherited predispositions to schizophrenia (Rosenthal, 1971). Nevertheless. a study by Rosenhan (1973) provides powerful support to the paradoxical contribution of the social apparatus ostensibly set up to treat the problem to both its maintenance and enhancement, if not its origin.

Rosenhan and seven carefully trained colleagues, termed 'pseudo-patients', presented themselves to a dozen institutions, all complaining of a single symptom, that of hearing voices that said words like 'empty', 'hollow' and 'void', thus suggesting that the patient found his life futile. All the pseudo-patients were admitted to all 12 hospitals, in almost all cases with diagnoses of schizophrenia. As soon as they gained admission they resumed normal behaviour and sought to convince staff members that they should be released. Eventually (in some cases it took up to 52 days) they were all discharged, typically with a diagnosis of 'schizophrenia in remission'. During their stay their behaviour was consistently interpreted by the staff in ways which fitted that expected of schizophrenics. The only ones who realized that the experimenters were not schizophrenics were other patients. In a further experiment, carried out in a teaching hospital, Rosenhan began by informing the staff of the findings of the first experiment, and then told them that a pseudo-patient would attempt to gain admission within the next three months. The staff accepted the challenge to their ability to detect normality. Over 10 per cent of nearly 200 successive admission during the three-month period were diagnosed 'normal'. In fact, Rosenhan deliberately did *not* send any pseudo-patients to the institution concerned. Clearly, both 'normality' and 'insanity' are to some extent in the eye of the beholder.

The expectations of caring agents strongly affect the outcome of encounters with them. Do people who have been led to believe that they are deviant behave differently from others who have been led to believe they are 'normal'? Freedman and Doob (1968) operationally defined deviance by artificially manipulating the results of personality tests taken by small groups of under-graduate male subjects. After each test the subjects were shown a predetermined distribution of scores. Those of the subjects randomly assigned to the 'deviant' condition appeared near the ends of the distribution, those of the remainder, designated as non-deviant, clustered around the middle of the distribution. The effect of being made to feel deviant was checked by a self-rating test on the deviants, who reported themselves 'more different from others' than did non-deviants. A variety of ingenious and well-controlled experiments was carried out following the deviancy manipulation, several of them some weeks afterwards. Manipulated deviancy was found to have significant effects on affiliation behaviour (like preferred to associate with like) and on aggression (like chose like for reward and unlike for punishment), but not on several social variables such as conformity. The fact that a single manipulation of deviance exerted effects, at least on certain important areas of behaviour, and did so after an interval of up to several weeks, is of considerable relevance, because it indicates that the effect of labelling by others is enhanced by the acceptance of that label by the individual labelled deviant. There is thus some evidence for the usefulness of labelling as at least contributing to the maintenance, and possibly to the performance, if not the acquisition, of abnormal behaviour. By inference the labelling approach may also be of relevance to the explanation of criminal behaviour. Welford (1975) distinguishes three key hypotheses of labelling theory as applied to criminology. (1) No act is intrinsically criminal. (2) The sequence of events from surveillance to the type of sentence received is a function of offender rather than offence characteristics. (3) Labelling is a process that produces eventually identification with a deviant image and sub-culture. (That is, the labelled individual finally applies to himself the label originally applied by the agents of social control and taken up by significant others such as employers.)

Hypothesis 1 was discussed in Chapter 1. We concluded that property and personal offences were proscribed in most, if not all, cultures and times. While it may be a key hypothesis for the labelling approach to victimless offences, we have to conclude that for offences involving victims it is either not a key hypothesis or the theory suffers a damaging blow. Essentially this is a matter for the proponents of the theory, but the former possibility allows us to discuss the next two hypotheses.

We considered hypothesis 2 at some length in Chapter 1 and concluded that the agencies of social control are more likely to index certain offences and offenders than others—the 'working-class offences' and young, working-class, black, males. Severity of police disposition was greater for the latter group than for the others (Wolfgang et al., 1972). Severity of disposition (together with seriousness of offence) was related to an increased probability of re-offending. Thus we have the possibility that attempts at control have a counter-productive effect—instead of dimishing offending, there may be an overall enhancement. This is perhaps the core of the labelling approach. The evidence is too clear to be ignored.

It is this process of 'selective attention' which, according to Ullman and Krasner (1969). amplifies the existing bizarre behaviour of schizophrenics and extinguishes non-bizarre behaviour. In the field of crime, two studies (Hirschi, 1970; Gold, 1970) tend to support the theory that police apprehension increases future offending, that by Gold being particularly persuasive (the Hirschi study did not control the crucial factor of the time of the offence relative to the time of apprehension). However, other interpretations are possible. First, increased criminal activity following apprehension, whether indexed by arrest record or by self-report, could be due to frustrative non-reward (Amsel, 1962). There is considerable experimental evidence that blocking progress towards a goal has as one of its effects an increase in the activity to attain the goal. Second, subsequent increased criminal activity, as indexed by arrest record alone, may simply reflect increased police surveillance, rather than being caused by it. Nevertheless, the line of research is a promising one. and further studies would be of value. They should use self-reported offending as the dependent variable and should measure the time relationship between offending and apprehension, should this occur, the outcome of offences in terms of economic or other reinforcers, and the level of police surveillance.

The label applied by control agents may become known to others in society. Their reactions to the labelled individual may help to maintain his deviant behaviour, possibly even to enhance it, by reducing the possibility of alternative behaviours. A number of studies support this assertion. Christiansen (1969) studied the recidivism rates of wartime Danish collaborators sent to prison following the end of the war for a minimum of two years. The rate of recidivism was markedly lower for those who returned to South Jutland, an area of strong Nazi sympathies, than for those returning to other areas where such sympathies were less marked. This result may be interpreted as indicating that post-prison social rejection was less severe for the South Jutland group than the rest, thus they were less likely to turn to other crimes. Such studies would be improved by direct measures of social rejection rather than an indirect inference from recidivism rates.

As well as differences between communities, some crimes such as motor offences (Willett, 1964) and occupational offences by businessmen (Clinard and Quinney, 1967) seem to attract less post-sentence sigmatization than others. Studies are needed which not only measure the responses made to returning prisoners, but do so in terms of the type of offence committed.

The response of the immediate family circle of the ex-prisoner may be as important as that of the wider community. Box (1971) suggests that returning to a broken marriage may render 'normalization' harder than returning to a stable one. The literature on organized crime (for example Messick, 1971; Teresa, 1973) indicates that the 'organization' frequently 'looks after' a professional criminal's family during his time in prison, assisting the stability of the marriage; in return, the organization retains the 'loyalty' (i.e. the silence) and the continued services of the criminal concerned. Fordham (1968), writing about the participants in the 'Great Train Robbery', stresses the compatibility of the roles of good husband and father and major criminal.

There is evidence of a correlation between recidivism and unemployment (Reitzes, 1955), but the relationship could be due either to those with a worse record being less likely to seek employment, to obtain it despite earnest efforts, or both (see earlier in this chapter). A study which controlled for the variable of employment-seeking was carried out by Schwartz and Skolnick (1964). They found that the potential employers of unskilled workers, when presented with the files of imaginary applicants, were markedly less likely to offer employment when the file mentioned a police record than when it did not. Even when an acquittal, confirmed by an exonerating letter, followed a recorded charge, the probability of an offer of employment was reduced as compared to a file free of any police involvement.

It should be noted that Lemert (for example 1972) distinguished between primary and secondary deviants. The latter *define themselves* as deviants, the former do not. The self-definition of the secondary deviants is consequent on the reaction of others to their offending activities. Secondary deviants are primary deviants who have been selected and 'transformed' (learning theorists would say 'successively shaped') into behaving in the ways in which society 'expects' of criminals. Some deviance theorists, for example Matza (1969), consider that taking on a 'deviant identity' need not be confined to those who are sent to penal institutions but could also follow apprehension and non-institutional punishment, such as fining or probation. Both labelling theory and learning theory would predict that both deviant identity and deviant behaviour would be enhanced by the customary social response to crime (only deviant behaviour is attended to and hence reinforced, non-deviant behaviour is ignored and so tends to extinguish).

Thus hypothesis 3 concerns the final stage of becoming deviant—self-labelling as 'criminal'. The deviant's self-concept changes to bring his total set of attitudes in line with his deviant behaviours—which have been shaped and maintained by social reactions to initially trivial behaviours (minor eccentricities in those later labelled schizophrenic, minor offences by those who later carry out a major crime). The self-label is seen as serving a positive purpose: by identifying with a subculture, the deviant is able to maintain a favourable self-image—a purpose assisted by the process of 'rejection of the rejectors' (Schrag, 1971). We have seen in Chapters 2 and 3 that the search for cognitive consistency is likely to help the maintenance of criminal behaviour, but more in the early stages of the shift from noncriminal to criminal behaviours. Moreover, we emphasized the major importance for maintenance of positive reinforcements for criminal behaviour and the scheduling of those reinforcements. Finally, a distinction may be drawn, at least in theory, between the possible effects on self-labelling of an institution for the mentally ill and a prison. In the former, many of the inmates have sought help and most are confused and distressed, the staff have high status as experts ascribed to them by the patient, and there is little or no inmate subculture to provide patients with an alternative source of esteem and approval. By contrast, prisoners have not sought help, their 'distress' is likely to be due to being in the institution rather than to the reason for their entry, and the staff are not seen as 'helpers' and are not ascribed high status by the prisoners. Finally, there is an on-going prisoner subculture to supply status and self-esteem. Most important of all, the hypothesis of self-labelling as deviant seems not to have been empirically tested. Until it has been we cannot draw conclusions about it except that it may not be a *key* element of the labelling approach—at least not for all offenders. We must also note that some persons, at least, may not seek the consistency between behaviour and self-perception which is the core of the hypothesis.

We have discussed, briefly, the importance of labelling theory for the sequence from surveillance to reoffending. We can conclude that it makes an important contribution to the explanation of the development and maintenance of criminal behaviour. The reactions of powerful others must be included in the outcomes of offending behaviours, as well as the direct and vicarious positive and negative reinforcements for offending to which the learning approach tends to be restricted. However, we have not discussed an important link in the chain of becoming a 'reoffender', namely, the learning setting provided by prisons and other penal institutions. It is appropriate to regard exposure to such settings as one of the consequences of the detection and sentence— albeit it is the reaction of labellers to the offender as well as the severity of offence and detection which combine to lead the individual into prison. In the next chapter we discuss, under the overall heading of the current penal system, the possibility that the prison setting increases criminal behaviour, rather than decreasing it, as is intended. If it appears that prison experiences increase criminal behaviour, at least for some offenders, we can consider this as one of the *secondary* effects of the labelling of particular groups.

The labelling perspective thus makes an important contribution. But *why* does labelling occur? Two explanations will be considered: the political and the psychological.

The political explanation was anticipated in our discussion of the 'strain' theories concerning offending by young working-class males, the notion being that they offend because they are denied legitimate means of access to the goal of affluence held out as desirable in our society. A further stage is to ask *why* these groups are denied access, and what is the role played by social control agents? An answer has come from sociologists working within a Marxist frame of reference (for example Quinney, 1974). Briefly, they assert the following: economic processes are the major means of social control; the capitalistic economic model is the central cause which generates, and must therefore control, excess labour; this control is exerted by means of the criminal justice system which generates crime and criminals. Thus, the lack of opportunity for affluence, for certain groups, is an essential feature of capitalism.

The above political view seems to have led to rather little empirical work, but it should not be impossible to design appropriate studies, as we discussed at the beginning of this chapter.

An alternative political view has been set out by Box (1971). It states that even if none were poor or oppressed there would still be crime because of the latent social function crime serves. Box asserts that deviant behaviour, of which legally defined offences are examples, is actually tolerated, even encouraged, by the controlling group in *any* society (we may assume both capitalist and non-capitalist) because it maintains their control over the conforming majority. He goes on to argue that the fact of deviant and unacceptable behaviour forces a continued definition of what is acceptable; thus deviance both clarifies and maintains the social rules and sharpens the authority of the norm. The examples of deviant behaviour provided by deviant individuals are used by those in authority, as it were, *pour encourager les autres*. Deviance can be presented as a threat to the way of life of the majority. For example, homosexuality is a threat to heterosexual married people; this helps to legitimize the unpleasant ways in which homosexuals are treated by society. In order for a particular offence to be noticed and punished, the boundaries between deviant and non-deviant behaviour must be clear and unambiguous, and Box notes the considerable publicity given to deviance in general and crime in particular. Examples of ways in which deviance can be used to serve an *instructive function* are provided by such heavily publicized trials as those of political offenders in Russia—and to some extent in the USA. for example the 'Chicago trials' (concerned with alleged offences during the 1968 Democratic Convention). According to Box, deviance can also be seen as a social barometer, almost a harbinger of change, so that when deviant behaviour is extremely widespread it eventually results in a change in the rules. Finally, deviants are *selected* by authority figures to carry out the above functions. Thus the occurrence of deviance acts can be seen as a part of the political process, both maintaining the rules and fostering change.

On close inspection, Box's analysis applies very much more to victimless offences, such as consenting sexual behaviours, drug-taking and gambling, and to offences definable as 'political' (conspiracy, etc.) than to the offences against persons and property which form the great bulk of prosecuted crimes, concerning the undesirability of which there is little disagreement, and certainly there is no pressure to remove them from the list of offences. Moreover, it is very questionable whether giving heavy publicity to an example of a particular offence necessarily reduces the frequency of that offence. Research findings concerning the effects of modelling support the view that the opposite might well occur. For example, hooligan behaviour in football grounds is likely to increase rather than decrease following television newsfilm of 'fans' who had invaded the pitch, evaded pursuing police and regained the safety of the crowd. Box asserts that the criteria the police use to make decisions about the disposition of suspected persons relate to their own social class (most frequently upperworking) and educational background (most frequently high school, but not college), their political values (typically right of centre) and their comparative social isolation (friendships tend to be with other policemen). He argues, though without providing evidence, that the anxiety of the police to be accepted as middle class, despite their social class of origin and relative lack of education, results in a bias in their pattern of arrests against young working-class males (and blacks in the USA). Yet the low arrest rate for 'middle-class' offences is likely to relate more to their low visibility than to police leniency. Moreover, there is no evidence that senior police officers, presumably accepted as middle class, change their views about the association between crime and certain social groups as they achieve promotion from the lower ranks.

Experimental psychology provides an alternative approach. There are two aspects of this. The first, mentioned in Chapter 1, is that the 'cooperativeness' and general social skills of the middle class increase the chances of a caution as opposed to a formal charge and a court appearance. The second explanation, related to the first, is that *once* the stereotype exists that the middle class is more law-abiding it will determine where the police will look when no-one has been suspected. It follows that the likelihood of detection will be higher for offences committed by the supposedly 'more criminal' classes and that once detected, the less socially skilled are more likely to be prosecuted.

As mentioned earlier, there is an intended positive side to police bias; it is assumed that the home circumstances of certain offenders are more capable of preventing reoffending than those of others. But this is an assumption of quite unknown accuracy. It might well be true, but on the other hand it may also happen that a 'respectable' home labels an offender as irretrievably bad in order to explain the difference from the behaviour of the rest of the family, thus making further offending more likely. It would be preferable for the police not to set up its own sociological guidelines, but in fact all official persons (and unofficial ones also) tend to view the world through stereotyping blinkers, the purpose of which is to simplify the conduct of daily life. Mischel (1968) has argued persuasively that trait views of personality—which go far beyond the actual evidence concerning behavioural consistency—can be explained in terms of the general human tendency to think in categories, rather than in subtle specifics. Much earlier, Bartlett (1932) showed how human perception and memory dealt with evidence not easily assimilated into existing cognitive categories by the processes of 'labelling' and 'sharpening' (ignoring inconsistencies and heightening congruities). How much easier to carry out both processes *in advance*—by constructing a stereotype of the 'typical' criminal which then influences the pattern of surveillance and arrest. In that their professional behaviour is partially determined by categorical and stereotypic modes of thinking, the police are simply demonstrating that they are responsive to the same psychological processes as are other human beings (including those persons, equally blinkered, who regard all policemen as 'fascist pigs'). Preexisting categories serve to control not only responses but also the perception and evaluation of incoming information. The labelling approach helps to account for the excess of young black working-class males in the official statistics of offenders. It is silent about the explanation of criminal behaviours by members of other groups (middle-class males and females, etc.). By contrast, the learning-based account we set out in Chapters 2 and 3 helps to explain the activities of offenders of *all* groups, both those detected and those undetected, and particularly so for the latter. However, the labelling approach, by drawing attention to the reactions of others, as well as to the actions of offenders, makes a significant contribution to a satisfactory explanation of criminal behaviour, particularly by those members of '*excess*' groups who are detected and processed by the criminal justice system. We have also seen that some persons may be more likely than others to acquire criminal behaviours.

Thus a complete explanation of crime will draw on the experimental psychology of learning and of individual differences, as well as on the labelling approach. The heading of this chapter implied that sociological explanations of crime provided an alternative to those suggested by the psychology of of learning and of individual differences. In fact, we have seen in this chapter that some sociological approaches are basically assertions about the processes whereby crime is learned, or social rules fail to be learned, and about the settings in which learning occurs. Thus they add little to the material discussed in Chapters 2, 3 and 4. The labelling approach, the most interesting and potentially most fruitful sociological contribution, can be seen as complementary to psychological approaches, rather than an alternative explanation.

Chapter 9

The Current Penal System

Methods and Results

Introduction

In passing sentence on a convicted offender the courts have a choice of sentence ranging from a conditional discharge to a term of imprisonment varying from a few months to life. The selection of type of sentence and of severity within type depends on a variety of factors, as we saw in Chapter 1. One factor which we did not discuss is that of the intended effect of the sentence. For the most part this is either remedial (corrective) or deterrent. In the first case it is hoped that the offender will be so changed by the sentence received that he will not reoffend. Ostensibly, at least, punishment by some form of deprivation does not play a major part. An intended corrective effect is more likely to be found in the sentences given to young offenders and to adult first offenders, for whom a change in response to training is thought to be more possible than for older recidivistes. A deterrent effect implies a hope that the sentence received will be *unpleasant* enough to deter the offender from repeating his illegal behaviour. An element of positive training, if present at all is secondary. As well as the offender himself being deterred from re-offending, it is hoped also that those who have not yet offended will be deterred from doing so by the example of the unpleasant fate of those convicted and sentenced. A further element which may sometimes influence the behaviour of sentencing agents is that of retribution. This is the view that the offender should suffer as the caused others to suffer. Finally, an offender deemed 'incorrigible' may be imprisoned for many years for purely preventive reasons with no hope of personal 'reformation' or deterrence.

It is desirable that any sentence should be evaluated in terms of efficacy, efficiency and social acceptance. The test of efficacy is well established, that of efficiency is increasingly used, and that of social acceptance may be of overriding importance, particularly in Western countries. Both 'corrective' and 'deterrent' sentences can be evaluated, potentially at any rate, in terms of objective outcome measures such as reconviction rate and financial cost per unit of time to achieve a given outcome. A sentence framed with retribution in mind rather than the future behaviour of the offender can be evaluated logically only in terms of the subjective satisfaction of members of society, an outcome which has not been studied. Research has been largely confined to corrective and deterrent effects—with the exception of a study by Clarke (1974) on the effects of incarceration in preventing offending, which we consider later. In practice, corrective and deterrent effects overlap considerably because the test of the efficacy of a particular sentence is that of reconviction rate, an outcome which applies to both types of effect. However, there are two major differences which justify a separate consideration of the two effects. First, the corrective effect is often tested by setting up special experiments (type A prison *versus* type B prison, etc.), whereas the deterrent effect is typically tested by inference from the official statistics. Second, by definition, whereas studies of the corrective effect are confined to convicted offenders, deterrent effects may extend to those who have not yet offended.

Corrective Effects

The array of methods conventionally used by the penal system includes probation, fining and various types and time periods of institutional confinement. Detailed accounts will be found elsewhere (for example Walker, 1965). Such methods have developed empirically and have not been influenced to any great extent by the findings of sociological or psychological research.

There is a tendency for the reconviction rate to decrease with increasing age of the offender; for example, that for 14–16 year olds in Britain exceeds that for 17–21 year olds. At first sight this might suggest that incarceration succeeds eventually, a second 'dose' proving more effective than a single dose, particularly as the second institution has to cope with boys with whom the first has already failed, apparently a more difficult task. But there are several alternative explanations. First, the boys who were reconvicted after approved schools (for those of 16 years of age and less, and now termed community homes) but not after borstal (the 17–21 year olds) might have ceased offending at the older age even without institutional care, due to increased opportunities for the legitimate acquisition of goods from earnings or the increased perceived costs of offending, a change in perception which might occur in boys generally with increasing age. Second, and more important, we do not know that they have ceased *offending*, merely that they have not been *reconvicted*. It is possible that boys who have passed through approved schools have learned skills which enable them to evade detection more readily and/or have learned which offences carry the least risk of detection.

Walker (1971) has discussed the problems associated with the measurement of corrective efficacy, problems which are common to estimating the efficacy both of the conventional penal methods, which we discuss below, and the psychological and other non-penal methods of correction, which are covered in the next chapter.

1. It is essential to define what is being 'corrected'—is it overt lawbreaking, 'immoral attitudes', etc.? What is being corrected inevitably relates to the choice of the measure of outcome used: reoffending, moral attitudes, family

care, job performance, evaluation by others, and so on. 'Moral improvement' may be asserted as a valid measure of change, particularly when formal reconvictions are as great after the treatment under test as the comparable base-rate method.

2. There are problems in using the criterion of subsequent reconvictions.

(a) Should we confine ourselves to the same specific type of offence as that which led to the sentence treatment, or is it a fair test of treatment to include all types of offence? Hence the question: what is the intended range of generalization of the corrective method?

(b) Are all subsequent offences noted, reported, indexed and detected?

The same arguments apply to corrective efficacy studies as to the explanatory studies of crime (see Chapter 1). If the official statistics are systematically biased, then so are the results of corrective efficacy studies. It is more accurate to term the success rate the *known* reconviction rate. Provided that post-treatment surveillance is equated and offenders have been randomly assigned to different treatments, we can talk with reasonable confidence about the relative efficacy of two or more methods of correction.

3. The length of the follow-up should always be stated. There are a number of general rules as to length.

(a) The more first offenders (strictly, first convicted) in the sample, the longer should be the follow-up.

(b) The more recidivists in the sample, the shorter follow-up may be. In both cases the objective is to include as many reoffenders in the net as possible. A cumulative analysis of the trend over time will show the point in time at which the differences between the groups being compared have become statistically significant.

4. The 'spontaneous' recovery rate should be known (those who do not reoffend despite not being exposed to any formal method of correction). One method of estimating this is to follow up persons who have both offended and have so reported themselves, but have not been officially detected. Subsequent offending requires a similar self-report. Such a design has not yet been used in the field of offending, but is relatively often used in the study of the efficacy of treatments for psychological problems. For example, a frequent finding has been that an untreated group recovers to the same extent as one treated by some variety of psychotherapy (Rachman, 1972).

5. There are a number of findings concerning variables relevant to the official reconviction rate.

(a) The fewer the previous convictions, the lower the subsequent reconviction rate.

(b) The older the offender during follow-up, the lower the reconviction rate.

(c) The more time an offender has spent in a custodial institution, the more likely is he to be reconvicted.

(d) Women and girls have lower reconviction rates than men and boys, when matched for age and penal history.

(e) Reconviction rates vary by offence.

It follows either that studies of corrective efficacy should control for sex, age, previous criminal career, type of offence and the time previously spent in custody, or that offenders should be randomly assigned to treatment groups. In the latter case the number of individuals in each of the groups under test should be sufficiently large to make sure that all the variations are likely to be present equally in all the groups.

Deterrent Effects

As indicated above, whereas the corrective effect has often been tested by setting up special experiments (frequently inadequate in design, as we have seen), the deterrent effect is typically tested by inferences from the official statistics of offending. This is acceptable providing that a number of assumptions are met (Walker, 1971).

1. The statistics of crime are collated and listed in a uniform way over a substantial period of time.

2. During this period, the penalty for a given offence is *changed*.

3. The change is publicized (and a check made of potential offenders' knowledge of the change). In practice, this is rarely even attempted, let alone attained.

4. During the period of time in question no other social change has occurred, such as an increase or decrease in the opportunity for carrying out the offence, or in the level of police surveillance, which could be equally responsible for any change observed in the level of offending. In practice, such a degree of experimental control is probably unattainable. If so, the 'other changes' should be measured and their effect controlled for by appropriate statistical techniques.

5. The probability of being detected for the offences should be known to potential offenders, or at least the level of their knowledge should be measured.

In practice, according to Walker (1971), very few of the above criteria have been attained and we have to conclude what we can concerning the variables relevant to deterrence from unsatisfactory studies. A review by Rosser (1975) drew a number of tentative conclusions.

1. Very broadly, it is the certainly of punishment rather than its severity which has a deterrent effect. However, this is much more true of assault and robbery than of murder.

2. It is essential to distinguish between pre-offenders and reoffenders. Even the certain prospect of a particular punishment will not deter a reoffender if the punishment concerned has previously been found easily tolerable.

3. There is a difference between the objective certainty of detection and the objective level of punishment to be expected and the subjective beliefs of potential offenders.

4. In general, the research carried out under the heading of reward–cost (see Chapter 3) seems relevant to a study of deterrent effects. Within each group—pre- and reoffenders—deterrence seems partially specific to the given

situation and the given individual. The prospect of an inevitably publicized appearance in court for a particularly 'shameful' offence may be a very important deterrent to a preoffender holding an important social position, but not to one occupying a more obscure place in society.

The implication is that for convicted offenders a penal sentence should be matched to the particular individual. Unfortunately, this runs contrary to current beliefs that the sentence should be matched with the crime and to the previous criminal record and not to the offender himself. Paradoxically, as we have seen, offender characteristics, albeit largely irrelevant demographic attributes such as age, race, class and sex, do enter into the sentence received. Instead, the reward–cost approach would argue for matching the sentence received to the history both of criminal and non-criminal behaviour and the current social situation of the individual concerned.

Prevention by Incarceration

A study by Clarke (1974) tried to measure the extent, if any, to which incarceration prevents criminal acts which may have occurred but for the imprisonment of the offender concerned. Clarke confined himself to juvenile offenders, using the Philadelphia cohort of Wolfgang *et al.* (1972). He calculated that about 0·6 index offences were prevented per incarceration at a cost conservatively estimated at $1100 (including food, laundry, etc.), but excluding the substantial and probably greater cost of correctional and court personnel. Clarke comments that 'this seems an expensive way of preventing crime, although it may be less expensive than other preventive policies' (pp. 533–4). For example, a study by Chaiken (1974) estimated $35,000 as the cost of detering one felony by increasing police patrols in New York City subways. However, in rebuttal of the apparent ineffectiveness of prevention by incarceration, Clarke agrees that removing the threat of prison may remove its deterrent effect—both on existing and on potential offenders. He suggests that this consequence would be gradual but provides no supporting evidence. Clarke's study was concerned only with juvenile offenders. An extension to adult offenders, particularly 'professional criminals', would be of value. Moreover, the economic calculation should attempt to cost the loss suffered by the victim, both in material and subjective terms. The last calculation will be very difficult, but a start has been made in the compensation given in a number of countries to the victims of criminal assault.

Penal Methods: Conclusions on Efficacy

A number of attempts have been made in several countries to compare the effectiveness of the various penal methods. As summarized by Hood and Sparks (1970), the major findings of those analyses which are statistically acceptable are as follows.

1. For many offenders a period of probation is likely to be at least as effective in preventing reoffending as an institutional sentence.

2. Fines and discharges are more effective than either probation or imprisonment for both first offenders and recidivists of all age groups. However, giving non-institutional sentences would probably raise the *current* crime rate (but see Clarke, 1974, above); while offenders are in confinement they are unable to offend.

3. Longer sentences do not reduce the reconviction rate as compared to shorter sentences.

Schur (1965) was if anything even more pessimistic in his conclusions as to the effects of conventional penal methods: 'No research has been done to date that enables us to say that one treatment programme is better than another or that enables us to examine a man and specify the treatment he needs. There is no evidence that probation is better than institutions, that institutions are better than probation, ... (so) much of what is now being done about crime may be so wrong that the net effect of the action is to increase rather than to decrease crime ... none of the researches conducted to date answer these questions'.

It is partly this lack of demonstrated success of any conventional penal method which has led to experiments in a variety of psychological treatments, which we consider in the next chapter. The apparent lack of overall success may mask two opposing effects: *some* offenders may be deterred from reoffending; others may actually be more likely to reoffend following punishment. A similar argument has been applied to the treatment of psychological problems by Bergin (1971). He suggests psychotherapy helps some people significantly but equally significantly worsens the outcome of others, in both cases as compared to an untreated group. Combining those helped and those worsened averages out the opposite effects. If this is correct, the next step is to identify which individuals respond positively and confine treatment to them. Only very limited progress has been made towards this end in the areas either of psychological problems or of criminal behaviour, as we shall see in the sections on prediction studies later in this chapter, and in Chapter 10.

Penal Methods: A Psychological Critique

Essentially, behaviour is changed most effectively either by positive or negative reinforcement or the two in combination. The current penal system contains attempts at elements of both approaches, although the latter tend to be more prominent. It is likely that behaviours which benefit those carrying them out are changed more effectively by a combination of positive and negative reinforcement than by either used in isolation from the other. Under the heading of positive reinforcement come the attempts to retrain offenders in non-criminal ways of earning money and the efforts of institutions for young offenders to train such socially desirable attributes as 'team spirit' through sports and games. Positive reinforcement for the development of approved behaviour tends not to be applied in any systematic sort of way and there appears little or no attempt to develop and reinforce behaviours alternative to, and preferably incompatible with, criminal behaviours, other than by trade training. Nor is the development of alternative behaviours associated *systematically* with the reduction, perhaps by negative reinforcement, of criminal behaviours.

The current penal system places more emphasis on negative than positive reinforcement, usually (but inaccurately) using the term 'punishment'. Strictly speaking, 'punishment' is reserved in learning theory language for the actual application of an aversive stimulus, something rarely if ever done in the present penal system, which almost exclusively uses negative reinforcement in the technically correct sense of the term—the withdrawal of a positive reinforcer. Withdrawals include the loss of money involved in fining and imprisonment (due to loss of earnings in the latter case) and the deprivation of access to valued social reinforcers (friends and family, heterosexual activities, etc.) due to imprisonment. Within the custodial institution there may be further negative reinforcement—solitary confinement, a reduced diet, etc. It is difficult to characterize probation as either a negative or positive reinforcer—the social contact with the probation officer may have either consequence (or neither). As in the case of positive reinforcement, the current penal system makes inefficient and ineffective use of negative reinforcement. A full listing of the features of negative reinforcers which increase the probability of a change of behaviour in the desired direction is given in Chapter 10 in the context of a general discussion of psychological approaches to changing criminal behaviour. However, 3 broad points may be made. First, the sequence of punishment experienced by repeated offenders typically proceeds through conditional discharge, fines and probation, and thence first to brief and finally to longer institutional sentences. This is akin to increasing the level of a noxious stimulus, such as electric shock, to which an individual is exposed from very low to gradually higher levels. Gradual exposure enables people to tolerate a much higher level of shock than when a relative high level is the first to be used. In the latter case, the individual typically first escapes and then avoids shock, and then subsequently avoids even *lower* levels. One of the crucial tests of any method of negative reinforcement is whether or not it results in the undesirable behaviour being avoided; if avoidance does not occur, the effectiveness of the immediately higher level of punishment is inevitably decreased. However, giving a first offender a stiff sentence, such as a heavy fine, is rather contrary to current notions of 'fairness'—which means matching the punishment to the severity of the previous offence record and of the current offence rather than to the probability of its effectiveness in securing a change of behaviour. Second, negative consequences are rarely contingent in time with the performance of the criminal behaviour. This is inevitably unless the prisoner is apprehended at the time of the crime, but is contributed to by the very lengthy delay before sentence. Finally, in the discussion of punishment which follows, the obvious must not be lost sight of—only *apprehended* offences are available for negative reinforcement. Unless the very great majority of their offences are detected, the result for most offenders is an intermittent schedule of positive and negative reinforcement and the probable maintenance of the undesired behaviour, particularly if the positive reinforcements gained have been substantial and negative ones relatively mild.

The current penal system seeks to control offenders by negative reinforcement, both in the 'natural environment', i.e. outside prison, by such means as fines and probation, and within a special environment, that of the penal institution. The latter setting has been heavily criticized, not only for failing to achieve the desired positive outcomes of deterrence or correction, but also for having unintended harmful consequences.

Harmful consequences of Imprisonment

The potentially damaging effects on inmates of a period in a correctional institution have been asserted frequently at the anecdotal level and are beginning to be studied by a number of methods. Two broad categories of harmful effects have been described. The first suggests that the experience of prison actually increases the likelihood of reoffending after release. The second arises from the possible damaging effects on human beings of institutional life in general and of prison life in particular. Thus the first is essentially concerned with the wellbeing of society as a whole, the second with the wellbeing of the prisoners themselves.

Schools for Crime: Prisonization and Criminalization

Institutions are not only formal organizations but are also informal social systems, with well-defined codes of behaviour which provide environments for learning new social responses and for strengthening or inhibiting old ones. Many of the behaviours approved of by society at large, and by their representatives, the prison officers, are likely to be punished by other prisoners, the converse also being true. In short, the value system to which the inmates are exposed is a more completely criminal one than the outside world, inevitably so, because all inmates have offended. Evidence concerning 'countercontrol' by offenders which operates against the efforts of behaviour therapists is given in the next chapter. It should be no cause for surprise if attitudes favourable to offending become strengthened and skills and expertise relevant to crime more developed following a period in a corrective institution. The process is termed *criminalization*. According to Erickson (1964), 'such institutions (i.e. prisons) gather marginal people into tightly segregated groups, give them an opportunity to teach each other the skills and attitudes of a deviant career, and often provoke them into employing these skills by reinforcing their sense of alienation from the rest of society' (pp. 15–16).

Just as the psychiatric in-patient is removed from the normal world in which at least some of those he would meet (other than the staff) behave in non-bizarre ways, so the prisoner is removed from social contacts with non-prisoners. All prisoners are exposed to an 'inmate code of behaviour'

(Tittle and Tittle, 1964) the acceptance of which eases their adjustment to life in an institution. As in any group, new members learn the rules and general culture of the community, a process termed *prisonization* (Clemmer, 1940). The two processes, criminalization and prisonization, are really related aspects of the broad training effects of prison life. The relationship between length of stay in prison and acceptance of norms of behaviour set by prison staff tends to be U-shaped (higher early in the sentence and before release than in the middle, Wheeler, 1961). This holds more for certain groups of prisoner than others (Garabedian, 1963). Some prisoners may become *more* law-abiding as a result of enforced association with particularly unpleasant criminals who serve as clearly defined discriminative stimuli for behaviour to be avoided (Sykes, 1958). It is also possible that prison officers exert some remedial effect. Clearly, there is a considerable variety of social stimuli and reinforcers to which prisoners are exposed, and which must be indexed by research studies of the effects of the prison experience with much more precision than hitherto.

There is very little reported research on the *post-prison* effects of confinement. Bondesen (1969) found that knowledge of prison *argot* (used as an index of socialization into the inmate culture) by adolescent female offenders increased as their time in a training school lengthened, and was positively correlated with reoffending in the five years following release. Bondesen should have studied the self-reported offending of those *not* arrested to overcome the objection that police surveillance and hence arrests of offenders assessed as more criminally socialized might have been greater than it was of those assessed as less socialized.

Thomas (1973) has provided evidence which has some relevance to the possibility that adaptation to the prisoner community reduces the likelihood of not offending after release. He suggests that prisons contain two conflicting systems of social control: the formal system, set up by the authorities, aims at 'resocialization'; the informal system, set up by the prisoners and transmitted to successive new entraints, has the effect of 'prisonization'—training the inmate in a social code hostile to the attempts of the authorities. Success for one implies failure for the other. Thomas predicted that many of the variables affecting the outcome of the struggle would be external to the prison, examples being the frequency of letters and visits from friends or relatives. He found that scores on scales of prisonization (higher scores indicated acceptance of the inmate code of loyalty to other inmates and manipulation of prison officers) and on a scale of post-release expectations ('I will stay out of trouble', etc) were negatively correlated with the number of letters and visits. (The more letters and visits, the less prisonization and the more optimism about staying out of trouble.) He reported no data on the relationship between letters and visits and actual reconviction rate. Such a study would be the obvious next step.

Prisoners deprived of contact with the outside world are literally 'locked in' to a world in which offending is the norm. This is likely to be true even in institutions which are avowedly therapeutic in purpose, such as those for adolescent offenders. If a psychologist were asked to design a system for training adolescents to offend he could hardly improve on our present system of 'correctional' institutions. The only social contact the young inmates have with non-offending norms is with those exemplified by the adult staff, by definition much older, typically better educated and with quite different social interests. If it is true that peer groups train adolescents in social attitudes and behaviours, then it would make more sense to 'sentence' young offenders to boarding-schools, in which the vast majority of the students were official non-offenders, than to maintain them in the present correctional institutions. The results in terms of official reconviction rates could hardly be worse than those currently obtained, and the recurrent economic costs might even be less. (The cost per inmate at a British community school is greater than that per place at even the most expensive boarding-school.) It might be objected that the law-abiding majority would be 'infected' by the minority of offenders, but if this is true, it should be even more true that to allow such boys to mix only with each other would make 'contagion' almost inevitable. An intermediate approach would be provided by hostels, situated in towns, in which boys lived, but from which they left during the day to occupy ordinary jobs, returning in the evenings. Thus they would have some contact with official non-offenders. In the next chapter we review the information at present available on such 'half-way houses' (more typically used for older offenders as a way back from prison).

Psychological Damage

A second potentially harmful effect of imprisonment, particularly in those institutions whose main stated purpose in incarceration rather than treatment, has been asserted by a number of writers, the best known of whom is Goffman (1968). He sees prisons as examples of 'total institutions', others being mental hospitals and prisoner-of-war camps. Such institutions are self-contained and are largely or totally isolated from the rest of society. All activities of the inmates are carried out to an imposed schedule and under an imposed set of rules, in the same place, under the same authority, and as part of a single overall plan designed to fulfill the official aims of the institution. These aims may be laudable—to care for patients, or reform prisoners. However, in practice, the intention of returning the inmates to the outside world, but improved in some way, is likely to be subordinated to, and taken over by, the requirement that the institution be run in the manner most convenient to those in charge. Typically, also, total institutions are marked by a sharp dichotomy between staff and inmates. The total institution is deemed to have effects on its inmates which are said by a number of critics to be psychologically damaging but are usually not clearly described.

Several attempts have been made to study the effects of prison life on inmates. A number of different measures were used in a study of 175 prisoners in British prisons, all serving long sentences, who were divided into four groups by increasing length of sentence. Two reports have appeared from those concerned in this study. Bannister *et al.* (1973) found no decline in general intellectual performance with length of imprisonment, although some reduction was noted in perceptual-motor speed. Personality assessment showed some increase in measures of self-directed hostility and neuroticism. Hessin *et al.* (1974) administered a large number of scales to measure evaluative concepts. They found a general lack of change due to length of imprisonment, although there was some decline in self-evaluation. The results of Bannister and colleagues can be interpreted in several ways: imprisonment makes its effects felt early in the total period of exposure to prison with rather little later change; long-term imprisonment does not have damaging psychological effects or, if it does, these were not picked up by the measures used. This group of workers used quantitative, questionnaire-administered measures. A very different approach was adopted by Cohen and Taylor (1972), who provide an account of a qualitative study of prisoners serving up to 20 years in the E wing of Durham prison, set aside for 'particularly dangerous' prisoners. They were invited to give a series of evening classes on sociology, the format of which rapidly changed to unprogrammed discussions of writings on prison life. The classes provided the basis for a 'collection of observations, anecdotes and descriptions, rather than a table of results' (pp. 32–3) which form the material for their book. Cohen and Taylor rejected questionnaires and structured interviews, and instead carried out unstructured interviews and collected the prisoners' letters and 'writings'—essays, stories and poems related to the content of the evening class material—through which, they assumed, by a process of 'literary association' the men would reveal their own responses to prison life and hence its effect on them. A further method was to ask the prisoners to correct the authors' research papers. Cohen and Taylor's general view was that the prisoners appeared to be affected rather little by their environment. Hence, they suggest as key questions: how do people survive in the extreme situation of prison? how do they give life meaning and pass their time? how do they resist their environment rather than resign themselves to it? They conclude that the isolation of the prisoners in the wing from the general run of prisoners and from staff, and their mutual proximity to each other, assisted high internal solidarity, as did the fact that (in their own eyes) they were more intelligent, urbane and sophisticated than the officers. In addition, they were high in the status hierarchy of prisoners, having carried out daring and highly lucrative robberies.

In contrast to Goffman's predictions and to many other reports, the prisoners are described as actively resisting the damaging effects of the deprivations associated with prison life by adopting one of the following methods: 'self-protection'—from hobby-type activities such as body-building to challenging the rules; 'campaigning' by writing to the press (for example, one prisoner wrote 545 such letters in 10 years, all of which required smuggling out); attempting to escape; going on strike; and active confrontation, such as rioting. Cohen and Taylor emphasize the importance for the prisoners' survival of sustaining an ideology, for example a belief that their friends outside cared about them. Their book is written in a much more pleasing literary style than the usual academic text, and is thus persuasive, an effect assisted by the authors' modest disclaimer that any weight should be placed on their findings. The research methods used are open to bias of all kinds; their assumption that literary writings function as projective tests is highly doubtful, and in any event the reliability and validity of such tests are both so low that their research use, even by previously committed practitioners, is rapidly declining; no quantitative data are provided concerning the differing methods of 'resistance'. Nor are we given any information as to the effect of holding an ideology as compared with not doing so. Finally, it is of interest that the authors consider that some of the E wing prisoners some close to certain romantic anarchists: 'In common (to the two groups) is an idea that life cannot be lived fully within present day society and that one can only make out by taking on orthodox society in a direct manner' (p. 168). But they provide no evidence for this view of the prisoner as a hero: it might be expected that bank robbers, having made their romantic gesture, would return the money (as did the protagonist of the film 'The Thomas Crown Affair' following his second successful bank raid) rather than retaining it and spending it on consumer goods and other products of the capitalist society.

In contrast to the studies of actual prisons, a most striking 'simulated prison' experiment has been carried out by Haney et al. (1973). They began by noting two current explanations of 'documented evidence on the deplorable conditions of our penal system and its dehumanizing effects upon prisoners and guards' (note the inclusion of the latter). The first is the 'dispositional' hypothesis, which implies that confinement with irredeemably bad criminals damages those who are remediable; hence, isolate the former. A corollary is that it is initially cruel persons who are more likely to seek jobs as prison guards. In this case, the remedy is more careful selection. The second hypothesis implies that the fault lies in the prison environment, which 'brings out the worst' in people.

In order to test these competing hypotheses (the authors regard the general charge of 'dehumanization' as proven), a simulated prison situation was set up in the cellars of the Psychology Department of Stanford University for an intended period of two weeks. From 75 undergraduates who responded to an advertisement for 'volunteers for an experiment on prison life' to be paid at the rate of $15 per day, 24 were selected on the basis of several personal questionnaires and interviews as being the most stable and mature, and as having the least severe histories of antisocial behaviour. All were college-educated, middle-class and white and were strangers to each other. They were randomly assigned to serve as either guards or prisoners and given a battery of personality measures. The 'prison' consisted of three small cells, containing a cot for each prisoner and a closet. Each cell was occupied by three prisoners for 24 hours per day. The other rooms were used as guards' quarters; guards worked eight-hour shifts in rotation throughout each 24-hour period, going home when not on duty.

The prisoners received contracts guaranteeing them adequate diet, clothing, housing and medical care. They were told that as they were under surveillance some civil rights would be lost, but there was to be no physical abuse. The assigned task of the guards was to 'maintain the reasonable degree of order in the prison necessary to its effective functioning'. How this was to be done was not specified, but the details of the administrative system were laid out. The guards were told that the purpose of the experiment was to study the behaviour of the prisoners and that they were not to use violence of any kind. They were issued with uniforms and bations. The prisoners were clothed only in smocks (without underclothing) and a nylon cap, and were allowed no personal belongings, the combined purpose being to reduce the prisoners' sense of 'individuality, power and masculinity'.

To increase the realisim of the study, the prisoners were arrested at their homes by genuine policemen, who first informed them of their rights, then fingerprinted, searched, stripped, deloused and photographed them. They were placed in their cells, given work assignments, and told they would have two visiting periods during the two weeks, as well as daily exercise periods, and would be counted three times per day.

The data available for qualitative and quantitative analysis included videotape recordings of meals, visits and all other regular events, and audio-recordings of conversations between prisoners and guards, both separately and together. The guards made daily reports, the experimenters kept informal diaries, and all participants were interviewed one month after the end of the study.

The experiment was stopped after six days, eight days sooner than the two weeks intended, because of the growing distress of the prisoners, five of whom had to be released even before six days had elapsed, mainly because of 'extreme depression and anxiety'. Whereas the remaining prisoners were delighted when the experiment ceased prematurely, the guards were not. During the six days, all guards came to work on time, and some worked overtime without extra pay. Despite the attempt to exclude deviant individuals, the behaviour of the guards varied widely, some being 'tough but fair', others 'cruel', still others 'passive'. Only one described himself as 'upset' by the prisoners' distress; he made no attempt to ease their situation.

Analysis of the videotape recordings showed that most of the behaviours of guards towards prisoners were negative, consisting of threats, physical aggression and insults. As time passed, the prisoners initiated fewer exchanges with the guards and became more passive. The taperecordings revealed considerably more negative than positive statements about themselves by both guards and prisoners, particularly by those prisoners who sought an early release. In addition, 90 per cent of the conversations of both groups, even in the guards' rest-room, consisted of prison topics. The prisoners were frequently uncomplimentary and deprecating towards each other. The picture of negative feelings among both groups was confirmed by the self-reports of mood which were obtained by the check-list method several times a day. The major findings from the personality questionnaires were that the early released prisoners were more extraverted and less empathic, conforming and authoritarian than those who stayed until termination.

The final interviews yielded a number of striking statements, although no quantitative analysis is provided by the authors which would enable us to see how representative were such remarks by guards as: 'Looking back I am impressed by how little I felt for them', and 'Acting authoritatively can be fun, power can be a great pleasure'. Examples of prisoners' comments included: 'My prison behaviour was often less under my control than I realised ... I was operating as an isolated self-centred person ... rational rather than compassionate', and 'I learned that people can easily forget that others are human'. The authors list the following conclusions.

1. Prisoners' rights, including even eating and sleeping, were rapidly redefined by the guards as 'privileges', and were subject to withdrawal.

2. Prisoners sided with guards against 'trouble-making' prisoners.

3. The most hostile guards served as social models for the less hostile ones, rather than the reverse.

4. The passive and helpless behaviour of the prisoners was assisted by the loss of personal identity and the arbitary rule-system.

5. The experimenters witnessed the transformation of 'ordinary, American students' into 'cruel guards and passive, self-deprecating prisoners'.

Both sets of behaviours were 'elicted rather easily' in persons deliberately chosen as not having either unusually 'hostile' or 'dependent personalities'. Thus the 'abnormality' resided largely in the institution (i.e. in the demands of the situation) and not in those placed in the institution, a conclusion which is similar to that drawn by Milgram from his studies on obedience described in Chapter 3. (However, if more extreme-scoring persons had been chosen the effects observed in both groups might have been even more extreme. Thus in real life prisons 'dispositional' variables may interact powerfully with situational ones.)

6. The observed effects would appear even more dramtically in real-life prisons. In the simulated prison there was no involuntary homosexual behaviour', no beating-up by guards or physical violence between prisoners.

7. Finally, they discount explanations in terms of explicit role demands (Rosenthal, 1966), citing the fact that prisoners were prepared to lose earnings in order to be released early and accepted without argument the decision of the experimenters concerning requests for early release. The reality of the situation was attested to by a 'prison consultant' and by priests widely experienced as prison chaplains.

To what extent can we generalize from this study to a conclusion that real prisons actually damage, in a variety of ways, the human beings, both prisoners and guards, who spend time in them? Three important differences between the simulated and the real-life prison should be noted.

1. There is typically an existing 'inmate culture' (see earlier in this chapter) which provides a set of behaviours approved by other prisoners and thus

social support. It is organized in a hierarchical fashion so that those occupying senior positions can continue to enjoy considerable self-esteem. Many prisoners will have experienced this culture in previous prisons and some will have had preparatory experiences in institutions for juveniles. In contrast, the 'prisoners' in the Haley study were middle-class students, few of whom, we may assume, had previous experience of prison life.

2. Similarly, real-life guards are trained, however minimally, rather than merely given verbal instructions, and there is an administrative structure of senior guards and officials which, potentially at least, provides guidelines and restraints for the behaviours of the less experienced guards.

3. Typically, prisoners are allowed a number of activities to fill the day rather than having to merely sit and pass the time as best they can. In addition, the clothing worn by the inmates was somewhat bizarre and was certainly different from the uniforms usually worn by prisoners.

At a more theoretical level, the authors imply that the behaviours they observed were simply 'released' in some way by a pathological stimulus. Yet the same principles which govern behaviour in general are likely to apply also to prison behaviour. Both 'guards' and 'prisoners' are likely to have learned previously appropriate responses (possibly from the mass media). The initial performance of such responses by the prisoners was reinforced by their fellows, because it avoided trouble, as well as by the guards. Similarly, the behaviours of guards which most readily achieved the stated objective of 'maintaining order' were positively reinforced by other guards. The most effectively behaving prisoners and guards served as social models for their colleagues, further contributing to the behaviours noted.

Shortcomings aside, the prison study reinforces the several demonstrations already provided in this book that civilized behaviours of all kinds only occur following appropriate antecedent learning conditions, and when they are positively reinforced. Perhaps, then, the study is a hopeful one. Correctional institutions may not *inevitably* become destructive. Whether they do so depends on the extent to which deleterious antecedent conditions exist and behaviours damaging to the self and others are positively reinforced. The extensive literature on the effects of institutional care on child development (see Chapter 2) suggests that institutions may be designed which are not harmful. Turning penal institutions into settings which positively reinforce desired, rather than undesired, behaviours would require that we abandon the notions both of retribution and of deterrence, or at least that, if an element of punishment remains, the prisoner is provided with socially acceptable and positively reinforced alternative responses.

Clearly, carefully controlled research is necessary in a wide variety of real-life correctional institutions, from those ostensibly most oriented towards therapy to those containing 'high-risk' prisoners who receive custodial care only. Such studies should also follow up prisoners on release to ascertain any long-term consequences. The research required should be concerned with behaviours of real importance in the lives of the prisoners and their guards, yet be carefully controlled and quantified. Perhaps more important, particularly in the case of 'incorrigible' prisoners, from whom society is being protected through long sentences, if achieving a change in their criminal behaviour is beyond our present expertise, ways of mitigating any deleterious effects of the prison experience must be developed. This is particularly important for those sentenced to life imprisonment, the number of whom is rising rapidly. Fifteen years ago there were 133 'lifers' in Britain, but the expected total for the next decade is more than 1400. The British authorities have started a 10-year career plan ('lifers' usually are released after this period of time) whereby there is a steady progression from a high-security training prison to an open prison.

In fact, attempts have been made in several countries to design prison settings which would avoid both psychologically damaging consequences for their inmates and the development of an inmate culture marked by criminalization and antisocial attitudes. The first aim was particularly prominent in the design of Grendon Underwood, Britain's first psychiatric prison, which was established over 10 years ago. Prisoners are transferred to it from other prisons and borstals and are not admitted directly from the courts. It has as many staff as inmates (150 of each) and is organized as a 'therapeutic community', the emphasis being on staff–prisoner and prisoner–prisoner relationships. The aim is a supportive, warm and permissive environment in which the prisoners are encouraged to talk about their own problems and those of others. All prisoners meet daily in groups, each of which has a therapist, the whole community meeting once a week. In addition, there are programmes of occupational therapy, work, arts and education, sports and religion. The prisoners' rooms are heated and adequately furnished, with views over the countryside (Parker, 1970). Grendon may be considered to differ from a Goffmanian 'total institution' both in the above ways and also because the scheduling of the day is less rigid and authority is less omnipresent. However, authority is *omnipotent*, as indicated by the phenomenon of the 'ghost train' (Parker, 1970), a term used by the prisoners to denote the transfer elsewhere of 'undesirables' in the middle of the night. Parker (1970) provides many striking quotations from the prisoners, including the following:

'. . . at the moment I am doing life, plus three years, three years, four years, and another life, I think' (Norman, one of the sex offenders at Grendon, p. 217).

'It's just another nick. Only here they're a bit cleverer than most places . . . if you give people good food and a certain amount of permissiveness, they are much more likely to behave themselves' (Ron, p. 70).

'You mustn't overdo it of course; you must let them think you are making progress, but slowly' (Archie, p. 59).

Without a quantitative study, there is no way of knowing how many of the prisoners agree with the comments of Ron and Archie, if so, how strongly, and to what extent their participation in group therapy represents a search for a solution to personal problems as opposed to conformity to the requirements of the regime. Nor are there reports as to how Grendon compares with other institutions in its actual as opposed to intended effects on the psychological wellbeing of its inmates, or the degree of development of an inmate culture and other features deemed undesirable by the prison authorities. Highly relevant information is likely to come from Swedish studies by Bondesen, not yet translated into English at the time of writing, reported in the *Guardian* (1974) by Michael Zander. Bondesen studied 13 institutions representing the full range of Swedish penal methods and mostly described as 'small, open and treatment orientated' and included in her study 90 per cent of all inmates. In all 13, 'criminalization, drug addiction, institutionalization and alienation outweighed any positive effects' and 'were found to increase in proportion to the length of time spent in the institutions, in all of which there is a strong criminal subculture'. Criminalization, which was the most serious negative effect, was measured by attitudes to crime and criminals and to inmate solidarity, and by a test of knowledge of criminal slang. The major topics of conversation in all institutions were crime, alcohol and drugs (but not sex). The lack of difference between ostensibly different institutions is seen by Zander as confirming Goffman's theory of the negative effect of 'total institutions'. Only three per cent of the inmates said they had been greatly helped by their term in custody compared with 63 per cent who said they had been greatly harmed, and 'the constant theme was the desire to get away from anything that reminded them of prison'. Finally, Zander writes, 'Professor Bondesen concludes that treatment in institutions seems to be largely ineffective and that all institutions of whatever kind are more likely to increase than to decrease criminal tendencies'.

Prediction Techniques

Introduction

It has been argued frequently that if future offenders could be picked out at an early age there would be no need to expose them to the possibly damaging effects of the penal system because it might be possible to 'correct' them, as it were, in advance. There is a second purpose behind the use of prediction techniques. Even if an offender's 'potential' for crime was missed and he offended and was convicted, it would be desirable to assign him to the sentence most likely to prevent future offences. Thus prediction techniques have two major uses.

1. To assess the probability that a person who has not offended will do so in the future. The prediction is concerned with *onset*.

2. To assess the probability of reoffending (more precisely of redetection, if official records are used as the dependent measure). The prediction in this case is concerned with *relapse*.

In both cases, full assessment of the accuracy of the prediction technique under test requires both that no attempt at intervention is made, and that police surveillance is no greater than it otherwise would have been. The accuracy of a predictor always has to be compared with some base-rate. For example, if

70 per cent of offenders are reconvicted, by chance alone *any* predictor will be correct seven times out of 10. A particular predictor, to be of value, has to be correct significantly more often than seven times out of 10. The higher the known reconviction rate, the more difficult is it for a predictor to be significantly more accurate than chance alone. It is usual that a number of variables predict more effectively than any one of them alone, so that they are combined by an appropriate statistical technique, such as the multiple regression equation, to form a combined predictor. An early example is provided by Mannheim and Wilkins (1955, see below).

Walker (1971) has listed some of the arguments against the use of prediction technique, as follows.

1. They encroach on civil rights, particularly those of the person who has not yet committed an offence. (We shall return to this theme in Chapter 11.)

2. Predictions may become self-confirming prophecies, for example through increased police surveillance of 'bad risks' (and/or decreased surveillance of the 'good risk' ex-inmate).

3. It is undesirable to argue from group means to individual cases. (For example, while it may be correct that black Americans on average obtain lower IQ scores than white Americans, it is certainly not correct that any *particular* black American will necessarily score lower than any *particular* white American; some will do so, others will score the same, others again will score higher.) However, providing that the prediction equation is derived properly, it may be possible to assign a *probability* to any given individual—of offending, or reoffending, and so on. Typically, as we shall see, the accuracy of prediction for extreme individuals (very highly likely, or very highly unlikely, to reoffend) is much greater than for those in the middle ranges. Unfortunately, the majority usually obtain intermediate scores.

Predicting Future Offenders

The best-known attempt to identify future offenders is that carried out over several decades by Sheldon and Eleanor Glueck. In their 1964 paper they overviewed their work to date, citing three major predictive factors available at ages 5 and 6: family cohesiveness; supervision by the mother; discipline by the mother. They claimed that 96·4 per cent of the children they identified in 1952, on the above criteria, as of being of low 'delinquency potential' had not become offenders. In contrast, 85 per cent of those identified as high in delinquency potential had subsequently offended. They considered that accurate identification of 'predisposing' personality traits (extraversion and suggestibility) would have accurately identified the 'middle potential' group, 50 per cent of whom became offenders. Eleanor Glueck (1964) claimed that comparable accuracies of prediction had been obtained by measures taken at age 2–3. However, Michael and Coltharp (1962) reported that the predictive scale developed by the Glucks failed to discriminate accurately, and Voss (1963) challenged the applicability of the Glueck scale to a normal population which consisted largely of medium-risk children. Rose (1967) reviewed a large number of prediction methods, including that of the Gluecks. He found that all of them predicted least well in the most numerous middle-risk range. Rose also points out that children identified as being at high risk are also more likely to be of low socio-economic class, and hence under greater surveillance. Conversely, 'low-risk' children tend to be of higher socio-economic class, and less under surveillance. Thus, offending by the former has a much greater chance of detection than that by the latter. It is, of course, detection, and not offending, which is typically used as the test of a prediction method. The apparent confirmation of a differential prediction of a high probability of offending by the poorer, and a low probability for the better-off, children may thus be little more than an example of the self-confirming prophecy. Finally, Rose raises the most important question: even if high-risk children can be identified accurately, can anything be done to prevent future offending? We consider that question in the next chapter, which concerns non-penal methods of control.

Predicting Reconviction

A number of studies (for example Wilkins, 1958; England, 1955) have tried to isolate the variables which correctly predict reconviction. They are unanimous in finding the most accurate predictor to be the previous criminal record of the person concerned. This finding may be seen either as exemplifying the principle that the most accurate predictor of future behaviour is past behaviour in the same general situation (Mischel, 1968) or as a further example of the self-confirming prophecy (the worse the previous record, the higher the level of police surveillance following sentence—immediately when this takes the form of a fine or probation, or after an interval of incarceration when the sentence is to a penal institution).

One of the earliest, and best-known, studies in this area is that by Manheim and Wilkins (1955), who measured the relationship between a number of pre-bostal factors (for example, drunkenness, prior convictions, living with parents) and the post-borstal outcome for several hundred youths. A prediction table successfully predicted the outcome in 57 per cent of cases, the predictions being much more accurate for the high- and low-risk cases than for those in the middle range. It can be concluded, at the very least, that a spell in borstal did not reduce the chances of reconviction of the high-scoring boys; it might even have made them worse. It could *not* be concluded, without the use of control groups randomly assigned to another form of treatment and to no treatment at all, that the success of the low-scoring boys was due to their spell in Borstal; they might have fared equally well with any treatment, or with none. An approach to this design was reported by Benson (1959). He used the Mannheim–Wilkins prediction index to identify comparable groups of young offenders who had been sentenced to borstal, or prison, respectively. No difference in reconviction rates was found. This was, of course, a retrospective study. A prospective design, involving random assignation to groups, is preferable. Finally, the predictive value of two well-known personality questionnaires has been studied. Smith and Lanyon (1968) found that the use of MMPI profiles failed to improve the accuracy of prediction of post-probation reoffending when added to data on the previous criminal record. Tyler and Kelly (1971) reported that the high School Personality Questionnaire (somewhat similar to Cattell's Sixteen Personality Factors Questionnaire) made only a marginal improvement in the accuracy of ratings of behaviour at intake in predicting behaviour in a juvenile institution.

Perhaps the most fundamental criticism of all of attempts to predict response to treatment is that there is little point in carrying out such exercises until it is shown that *any* one method is more effective with a particular subgroup of offenders than other available methods. As we have seen, this is not the case so far as the current penal system is concerned.

The Penal System and Social Policy

The Efficiency of Methods of Control

The cost of methods designed to control criminal behaviour has to be met from public funds. Monies used for one purpose means less for others, perhaps equally worthy. It follows that when faced with a choice between two equally effective and equally socially acceptable techniques, the more efficient (in financial terms) should be chosen. The more difficult cost–benefit decision is that between two programmes of control, one of which is less effective, the other more efficient. It is not only the short-term costs of treatment per successful boy which are important in evaluating a particular method. The long-term cost to society of unsuccessful boys must also be taken into account. Richmond (1972) has estimated at $34,481 (about £17,000) the cost to the American public of a person making his first appearance in a juvenile court at the age of 16, and who is then in and out of trouble for the next 25 years. (It is worth pointing out that the great bulk of the money does not go to the direct upkeep of the imprisoned offender, but to pay the salaries of those who enforce the law and operate the penal system. A major reduction in both first and subsequent offences would free monies for other social agencies but might result in less work for the police force, the probation service, the judiciary, the legal profession and the prison service.)

A study by Adams and Vetter (1971) illustrates a further element which might enter into a cost–benefit analysis. They compared the outcome of probation assignment to high case-load (61 per person) or low case-load (30 per person) probation officers. After a six months' follow-up, the boys assigned to the former had a significantly higher reconviction rate than those assigned to the latter. However, the difference, while statistically significant (albeit not at a high level), fell far short of being two to one, indicating that the successes of the low case-load officers were more expensive than those of the high case-load officers. Even had the cost per successful boy been less for the former, we would need to know how generalizable were the results (i.e. to young offenders overall; those in this study were white, first offenders, aged 14–16).

However, the benefit to the taxpayer is not the only important element. High case-loads may so reduce the appeal of the job to probation officers that they seek other employment. If the job is so unattractive that there are always many vacancies, those who do remain have even higher case-loads, resulting in a further twist in the spiral of decreasing job satisfaction. Moreover, those who leave any job are likely to be the more able—who can more easily find employment elsewhere.

The Police

In Chapter 1 we concluded that the police tend to share the general stereotype of the typical offender as young, male, working-class and black (in the USA), and that members of such groups are more likely than those of other groups to proceed to the stage of imprisonment following the same offence. Earlier in this chapter we reviewed the strong evidence that prison may increase the possibility of reoffending—rather than decreasing it as intended by the authorities. Thus it might follow that it is desirable to change the stereotypic beliefs and consequent actions of the police, so reducing the number of persons reaching the stage of imprisonment. Weiner (1974) examined the possibility that college-educated policemen might be less likely to hold biased stereotypes than their non-college-educated colleagues. He found this not to be the case, and suggested that membership of the police force exposes policemen to a pervasive set of learning experiences which overcome any previous more 'liberal' education. An attempt from within the police force would be necessary to overcome stereotypic thinking.

Bandura (1973) has suggested that rather than trying to change police attitudes an attempt should be made to influence their behaviour, particularly towards those who exemplify the unfavourable stereotype. The police should be trained to use aggressive methods as a last rather than a first resort, thus avoiding escalation and a possible charge leading to a prison sentence (assaulting the police, etc.). A study by Werner et al. (1975) indicates that juveniles may be trained to display behaviours acceptable to the police (see Chapter 1). Three juveniles with a police record, but still living in the community, were trained to behave appropriately—in terms of facial and other non-verbal expressions, general cooperativeness and mode of answering questions. Police officers showed films of the boys before and after training judged that they would have been less likely to take the boys into custody after than before training. Such training in 'conning' might, of course, reduce the deterrent effect of prospective police contact; a controlled study is indicated.

In general, there is no doubt that the police play a critical role in the legal process. They have wide powers of discretion and often exercise them without direct supervision or evaluation of the correctness of their decision. The police would assert that their job is to maintain the peace rather than enforce the law, for example, by making the minimum response possible, perhaps even turning a blind eye. If exercised with maximal effectiveness, police discretion may play a major role in reducing criminalization. The limited evidence to date suggests that further studies would be very worthwhile.

Formal Intervention Programmes

Wolfgang *et al.* (1972) asked the question 'at what point in a delinquent boy's career an intervention programme should act' (p. 254). They concluded that because (in their Philadelphia study) '46 per cent of young offenders stopped after the first offence, a major and expensive treatment programme at this point would appear to be wasteful' (p. 254). They go so far as to suggest that intervention be delayed until the third offence, because an additional 35 per cent of second-time offenders desist at that point. 'Thus one could reduce the number of boys requiring attention in this cohort from 3,475 after the first offence to 1,862 after the second offence, to 1,212 after the third offence, rather than concentrating on all 9,945' (p. 254). The strictures concerning the ineffectiveness of conventional intervention programmes noted earlier in this chapter would still, of course, apply, but if the resulting improvement were only in terms of a lower financial outlay and reduced criminalization it would still be well worthwhile to follow the Wolfgang *et al.* suggestion, providing that the deterrent effects of earlier intervention were not lost by postponing formal programmes until after the third offence.

In conclusion, it is essential that official policy—both of the police and the courts—should be determined by carefully defined and measured considerations of efficacy and efficiency, operating within a humane framework of minimum, but substantial, civil rights (see Chapter 11).

Concluding Comment

The current penal system may have some *deterrent effect* on those who have not yet offended, and may also deter some first offenders who have been caught from repeating their offence. However, an overpunitive response to a first offender may even increase the probability of further offences. There is little clear evidence for a deterrent effect on those who have offended more than once. It can be concluded that the current system has little or no *training effect* and imprisonment may even have negative consequences, two forms of which have been identified: firstly, deleterious effects on the within-prison behaviour of both prisoners and guards—some of whom may be much more affected than others; secondly, an increase in skills and attitudes relevant to the maintenance, even enhancement, of criminal behaviour. Both combine to reduce the probability of avoiding post-prison criminal behaviour. The attempts which have been made to reduce criminalization seem relatively ineffective. They include the provision of specially designed prison environments and attempts to predict which offenders would be most responsive to which training procedure. The carefully planned use of police discretion might reduce criminalization but might also reduce the deterrent effect of police contact. In general, there is a strong case for experiments with methods different from those of the current system.

Chapter 10

Psychological Methods of Control

The 'treatment' approach to offenders raises major questions of ethics and personal rights as well as, by implication, the beliefs of those carrying out treatment as to the explanation of criminal behaviour. These questions will be considered in the next chapter in the course of a discussion on the social context of attempts to control criminal behaviour. For the present, we shall review the psychotherapeutic, social, psychiatric and behavioural literature on the treatment of offenders.

Psychotherapeutic and Allied Methods

These include many variations, from simple reassurance to a full-scale psychoanalysis. Although the psychotherapies vary in their techniques and therapeutic aims as well as their explicit theoretical formulations, they all rely on verbal communication of some kind, although this may be carried out individually or in a group setting. The most ambitious and intensive form of psychotherapy is represented by *Freudian psychoanalysis*. This may last up to several hundred one-hour sessions, administered four to six times per week for several years. The intention is to afford the individual insight into the unconscious motivation of his behaviour and to allow the development of a 'healthy' personality structure. Frequently, the aim is not the removal of the symptom, rather it is to solve the unconscious problems which have led, according to psychoanalytic theory, to the development of a particular symptom. The major technique is that of free association, in which the individual is asked to say everything which comes into his mind without any effort to select or suppress. This material, together with the individual's reports on his dreams, is then explored and interpreted by the analyst. One of the major points to make about the method is that it can be available to only a very few individuals because of the amount of skilled manpower involved. Hence, psychodynamically oriented therapists have sought shorter methods which would still embody the major therapeutic principles of psychoanalysis. Analytically oriented psychotherapy may, although seeking the same ends as full psychoanalysis, take a much shorter time, because the therapist plays a much more active role in directing the content of the treatment session to those areas that are thought to be the most significant in understanding the underlying sources of the patient's problem.

Perhaps the best known of the other schools of psychotherapy is that of Carl Rogers, termed *client-centred* therapy. The therapist is supposed to be active but non-directive and the aim is to allow the patient to resolve his own problems by the use of the 'healthy' part of his personality. There is much evidence, cited by Bandura (1969), that Rogerian therapists influence, by verbally reinforcing the appropriate comments of the individual in therapy, the psychological direction in which he proceeds. Such evidence supports the view that, far from the individual in treatment choosing the therapeutic goal, this tends to arise from the particular theoretical orientation of the therapist concerned.

A considerable body of evidence has been marshalled by Eysenck (1960) and by Riachman (1972), both of whom throw doubt on the therapeutic efficacy of the various forms of psychotherapy. At the present time there is a move towards regarding the psychotherapeutic situation, whether it involves the individual patient and the individual therapist or a therapist and a group of patients, as lying within the overall ambit of experimental social psychology, so that work on interpersonal attraction, attitude change and social influence all became highly germane (Goldstein *et al.*, 1966; Feldman, 1976a). This development is likely to continue with increasing emphasis in future years. Both the psychotherapies *and* the behaviour therapies may involve an interpersonal relationship.

The Treatment of Predicted Offenders

As indicated earlier, this approach seeks first to identify potential young offenders and then provide them with a treatment which would sharply reduce the probability of later offending. Four studies are available for appraisal.

1. *The Cambridge–Somerville youth study.* This is the earliest (carried out between 1937 and 1945) and still the largest study. It is described in detail by Teuber and Powers (1955); see also Eysenck (1964). Welfare workers supplied the names of 650 'underprivileged' pre-adolescent American boys judged by them likely to become offenders. They were then individually matched for such variables as age, IQ, school grade and ethnic and socio-economic background. By the toss of a coin, one boy in each pair was assigned to the treatment (T) group or the control (C) group. T group boys were assigned to counsellors, all of whom adhered either to the psychoanalytic or the client-centred approach and treated their clients by means of individual face-to-face contact. The follow-up extended from 1945, when treatment had lasted between two and eight years in individual cases, to 1948, when the outcome was evaluated. In terms of number of appearances before the courts or before the Court Prevention Bureau, and of number of recorded offences, the T and C groups were almost identical. The C group had offended slightly less if the less serious offences were considered, slightly more where the more serious ones were concerned, neither trend reaching statistical significance. Quite clearly, prolonged individual psychotherapy had failed to reduce the frequency or incidence of offending in those treated by it. Interëstingly, the therapists had been much

more optimistic about their efforts than the quantitative figures actually demonstrated. Moreover, when informed of the results both the analytically trained and the client-centred trained therapists asserted that the results would have been much better had their own principles of therapy been applied by all therapists! While it is fair to note that many clients reported that they had enjoyed the contact with their therapists, it is possible that the systematic provision of any form of friendship or social support would have been equally appreciated.

2. *Hodges and Tait (1965)*. Seventy-three children living in a high-crime area of Washington, DC, and assessed as potential offenders were divided into treatment and control groups. The former group were treated by social case workers under the guidance of psychonanlytically trained psychiatrists. Twelve interviews held with each mother and 12 with each child over a period of one to two years between 1954 and 1956. At follow-up in 1962, 69 per cent of the treated and 65 per cent of the untreated children had been convicted. The application of the Glueck prediction system suggested that the treated children had, if anything, a better prognosis at the beginning of treatment than had the control group. This finding may either cast further doubt on the Glueck system, or suggest that treatment actually increased the likelihood of offending, or both. It is important to note that treatment was not solicited by the families concerned, and that the parents of treated children who were convicted were rated as less cooperative than those of the non-convicted ones, indicating the importance of the total environment within which intervention programmes take place.

3. *Meyer et al. (1965)*. Four hundred teenage New York girls described as displaying problem behaviour in school were randomly assigned to treatment by youth counsellors or to a control group. At follow-up, there were no differences between the two groups on any of the outcome criteria employed (academic progress, teachers' ratings and official criminal record). As in the case of the Cambridge-Somerville study, both clients and counsellors thought that the treated group had advanced in confidence and social maturity. No quantitative comparison between the groups was made for these latter variables.

4. *Craig et al. (1965)*. A sample of 'potential delinquents' living in New York matched with a control group for age, IQ, ethnic group and score on the Glueck scale was treated in a child guidance clinic for a period ranging from 30 months to four years. At follow-up 10 years later, there was no difference between the groups for official criminal records.

It can only be concluded that a range of psychotherapeutic techniques, carried out by a variety of therapists, have failed to prevent the development of criminal behaviour more effectively than the passage of time alone and the events which occurred during that time.

The Treatment of Convicted Offenders

There are now a large number of studies reporting the results of treating convicted young offenders by various forms of psychotherapy and counselling.

The majority figured in a review by Logan (1972) of 100 outcome studies, covering a variety of methods. The largest group involved some form of psyhotherapy, the next largest conventional penal methods, particularly probation, and the remainder were vocational training programmes of various types. We shall first summarize Logan's review, and then survey individually some of the best-known psychotherapy treatment reports, all of which were included in the review, before briefly mentioning a few studies not covered by Logan.

The scientific acceptability of outcome studies of corrective efficacy was evaluated on the basis of the following 10 criteria. (Logan's main point is that unless these criteria are met the meaning of a 'successful outcome' is uninterpretable, and hence there is no clear justification for applying the technique to other offenders.)

1. An adequate description of the technique or training programme was provided. If it were not, the method, however successful, would not be repeatable by others.

2. (Associated with 1) The method can be made systematic and repeatable.

3. A control group was provided.

4. Assignment to treatment or to control group was random (preferable to control by matching). If random assignation was used, was it within a single offence group?

5. If assignment was not random, careful matching should have been used. Thus studies should meet either criterion 4 or criterion 5, preferably the former.

6. Only the treated group received the active elements of treatment. (This implies, although does not state, the desirability of a pseudo-treatment group as well as a no-treatment group.)

7. Comparisons were made on a before and after basis, so as to ensure that any change which took place within the treated group did so over the defined period of time covered by the treatment programme.

8. Success was operationally defined in behavioural terms and its measurement was quantitative, valid, reliable and repeatable.

9. The definition of success was compatible with that typically used by criminologists, namely, the official rate of reconviction. (Logan did not discuss the severe problems of bias associated with the use of official statistics; supplementation by a well-controlled self-report method would be desirable.)

10. A reasonable period of follow-up was allowed, and took place within a real-life setting.

Logan failed to include two criteria usually considered of major importance.

1. The assessment of change should be carried out without the assessor knowing whether the subject had received treatment or not, or, if more than one treatment was used, which he had received.

2. Post-treatment surveillance by law enforcement agencies should not be greater for one group than the other; hence, those agencies should also be unaware of the treatment, or lack of treatment, received.

Applying only his own criteria (which he regarded as *minimal*) to the 100 studies he was able to trace, Logan drew the following conclusions.

1. Not one study met all the criteria.

2. Forty-two used some kind of control or comparison, but only 31 met either the matching or the randomization criteria.

3. By the most generous interpretation of criterion 1, only 12 studies employed a clearly defined method.

4. Only four studies, at best, met criteria 2 and 3.

5. Adding in criteria 8 and 9 eliminated all but one study.

6. Adding criterion 10 eliminated the one remaining study.

Finally, the overwhelming majority of studies failed to control for the two additional requirements (blind assessment and police unawareness) mentioned above.

Thus, no psychotherapy study of those cited by Logan, however optimistic its conclusions, can be considered unequivocally to support the view that some form of psychotherapy will reduce the probability of reconviction. Below we describe briefly the best-known of the psychotherapy programmes for young offenders. The majority have been carried out in California, much the most active state of the USA in research into the control of offending.

Grant and Grant (1959). The authors developed a system for assessing 'level of maturity' (to do with the manner of handling personal relationships) which ranged from level 1 (that of the small infant) to level 5 (awareness of others' feelings, and sympathy with them). The original system was administered by interview and scored qualitatively. A quantitative, questionnaire, version has been developed by Gottfredson and Kelley (1963). Grant and Grant (1959) studied the response to treatment of three groups, each of 20 military offenders (mostly desertion), which were respectively high, low and of mixed level of maturity. Treatment was by group psychotherapy, each group being run by supervisors for nine weeks. The high-maturity group are said to have responded significantly better overall on the criterion of return to military duty. However, the study failed to meet any of Logan's criteria except for 3, 7 and possibly 9, and the Grants' own conclusion was: 'No significant differences were found which could be attributed to supervisors' predicted effectiveness'. In short, this was a study of poor design and uncertain outcome which used a predictive instrument of unknown validity and reliability. In connection with the last two failings, Beker and Heyman (1972) concluded that the typology had not yet been shown to be reliable, valid and effective in planning treatment programmes for offenders and characterize it as a 'rudimentary clinical tool', unrelated to socialization theory in general (see Chapter 2).

Adams (1962, the Pico project). This study compared the conviction record, three years after release, of 200 juvenile offenders who had received individual psychotherapy for one or two sessions per week in a Californian institution, with that of 200 untreated juvenile offenders. Those initially rated amenable (50 per cent) and treated did better than those rated amenable and untreated.

There was no difference between treated and untreated 'non-amenables'. Amenability was assessed by 'pooled clinical judgments' at intake, and was defined as being 'bright, verbal, anxious, insightful and desirous of change'. Logan found this study deficient on his criteria 1, 2 and 7, so that the meaning of the reportedly greater change in the treated 'amenables' and the nature and the reproducibility of the treatment are both unclear.

Empey et al. (1964, the Provo experiment). An attempt was made to modify the value system of a group of persistently offending 15–17 year olds, all of whom were members of a 'delinquent subculture', by giving them intensive group counselling for 4–7 months in a non-residential centre. A control group was placed on probation of the usual type. No difference in outcome was found, and in any event this study was faulted by Logan on his criteria 2, 6, 7 and 10, while the achievement of criteria 8 and 9 was in considerable doubt.

Jessness (1965, the Frico Ranch study). The effect of residence in a 20-boy lodge on boys previously classified as belonging to one of eight offender subtypes was compared with that of residence in a 50-boy lodge, the former being assumed to allow more staff–inmate interaction and less peer-group influence. On the basis of a 15-month follow-up it was concluded that boys of three neurotic subtypes did better in smaller than in larger units (14 per cent had their parole revoked after living in the smaller units, as against 51 per cent of those who lived in larger ones). However, there was no difference in outcome for the other five types of boy, and after three years the earlier differences obtained for the neurotic types no longer held—80 per cent of both the larger and smaller unit neurotic boys had been returned to the reformatory for parole infringements. In terms of Logan's criteria, this study failed on 1, 2, 6 and 10.

Warren et al. (1966, the community treatment project). This study compared intensive treatment in the community of a group of boys classified into eight subgroups by two levels of maturity (high and low) and four types of personality (neurotic, non-neurotic, etc.) with equally intensive treatment in an institution of boys similarly subdivided. The results suggested, on the basis of a 15 months' follow-up, a more favourable outcome for the community treated neurotic subgroups as compared to their institution treated counterparts. Only trends were observed for the other subgroups. This study failed on Logan's criteria 1, 2, 6 and 10. In addition, Hood and Sparks (1970) made a number of cogent criticisms.

1. There was no difference in outcome when the comparison was by maturity level alone, and the reliability of the maturity classification is in any event doubtful (see above, Beker and Heyman, 1972).

2. They cite Warren herself in support of their doubts as to the equality of supervision exercised: 'It has proved impossible to operate the programme without the experimental or control status of the subjects being known, not only to the decision making personnel in the Youth Authority, but also to the school systems and to some extent the law enforcement agencies' (p. 206).

3. The treatment programmes used were constantly modified over the course of the project, so that even if any difference in outcome occurred it would

be very difficult to identify the active elements of the treatment programme which were responsible.

Persons (1967). Forty-one adolescents housed in a correctional institution were matched for IQ, arrest record and mean length of stay in the institution with an equal number of control subjects. The former group received 20 individual sessions of psychotherapy over a 20-week period. The treated group behaved better in the institution, had fewer post-release parole violations and a better job record. Moreover, those boys considered by the therapists to have been successfully treated did better on all post-treatment criteria than those judged unsuccessful, suggesting the possibility of developing indices predictive of a successful outcome. The apparent success of psychotherapy in this study stands in sharp contrast to the lack of success in the studies cited earlier. As Logan found Persons' study deficient for criteria 1, 2, 6 and 10 (and of doubtful adequacy for criterion 9), it cannot be considered to remove, to more than a slight extent, the overall impression of the ineffectiveness of psychotherapy in the treatment of young offenders.

Weeks (1962, Highfields project). This was a comparison between boys in two New Jersey institutions, in one of which (Highfields) there was deliberately created a 'therapeutic climate'. Assessment after a six-month follow-up found no difference in reconvictions between the white boys in the two institutions. However, the black boys housed in Highfields had a lower reconviction rate than the black boys in the control group. It is not clear why this was so, particularly as no concomitant changes were obtained on measures of attitude to law enforcement agencies. Logan faulted this study on criteria 1 and 2 and in addition assignation to institution was non-random, although an attempt at *(post hoc)* matching was made.

Miller (1970, Southfields). An attempt was made to replicate the therapeutic atmosphere of Highfields. However, the post-treatment recidivism rate of the treatment group was no lower than that of a similar group placed on probation, casting further doubts on the Highfields 'atmosphere' as achieving anything over and above the much less expensive probation method (and, as we noted in Chapter 9, there is considerable doubt as to whether probation has any greater effect than does the passage of time alone).

Cornish and Clarke (1975, Kingswood). A British study, published after Logan's review, compared over a 10 year period the effects of two regimes at the Kingswood Training School, one of the traditional type, formal and highly structured, the other a 'therapeutic community' involving twice-daily group discussions. Both systems resulted in a reconviction rate of 70 per cent. This is likely to be a minimum estimate of reoffending.

Treatment of Offenders by Psychotherapy: Conclusions

Hood and Sparks (1970, pp. 211–5) summarize as follows the 'values and limitations of the research to date' (i.e. on the treatment of offenders).

1. No typology of offenders or treatment has been shown to be either reliable

or valid. (The notion of 'types', as opposed to the interaction of dimensional position, learning history and current situation—see Chapter 6—is itself very doubtful.)

2. Considerations of justice and of security impose severe limitations on the (desirable) random allocation of offenders to treatments.

3. Some offenders may fail with all existing methods. (This seems somewhat overgenerous; in fact, there is no evidence that *any* offender will be less likely to reoffend when treated by any psychotherapeutic method as compared to any conventional correctional method, such as probation, or, indeed, by the passage of time alone.)

An even more fundamental consideration is the clear evidence (Rachman, 1972) of the *lack of success of any psychotherapeutic approach*, over and above spontaneous recovery, with individuals suffering from a wide variety of neurotic and personality problems. If the psychotherapies fail to help individuals who both undoubtedly suffer from their own problem behaviours and have sought help for them, there is no reason to expect them to succeed in changing the behaviours of individuals who are not complaining of personal distress and have rarely sought therapeutic assistance. It follows that changing the behaviour of persons (such as offenders) who typically benefit from their deviant behaviours is likely to be much more difficult than changing that of those who do not benefit (such as neurotic patients). Psychotherapeutic techniques fail with the latter; they are even more likely to fail with the former. This takes us to the heart of the problem of the treatment of offenders. Although offenders 'suffer', they do so only when caught (and they may have become so habituated to punishment that it is seen only as a normal and acceptable occupational hazard). The low probability of detection means that offending is frequently rewarded, and hence maintained. Even when the offender is apprehended he may have enjoyed the fruits of his crime before he was caught. Moreover, the psychotherapy treatment studies, discussed above, have been carried out solely with young offenders. If they had demonstrated a well-documented level of success as compared with control groups (and this is clearly not the case), replication with adults, presumably more difficult to treat, would still be necessary. It can only be concluded that further studies of the effects of psychotherapeutic methods are unlikely to be of any value in advancing our knowledge of how to change the behaviours of young offenders. This is not to say that specific medical and psychiatric techniques for the treatment of the specifically medical and psychiatric problems of a minority of offenders may not reduce their future offending. The logical requirements for demonstrating a connection between offending and psychological disturbance were set out in Chapter 7. The relevant, and rather scattered, literature is reviewed below

Treatment of Offenders Diagnosed as Suffering from Psychiatric Disorders

We shall concern ourselves not with the normal provision of medical and psychiatric health care services to residents of penal institutions—in any group some individuals will be in need of such services at any one time—but with the specific application of medical and psychiatric techniques in an attempt to reduce the probability of reoffending.

It is possible that many recidivists suffer from psychiatric disturbances which incapacitate them from holding down normal jobs for any period of time. The same incapacity may hinder the skilled performance of offences, as well as effective attempts to avoid detection, so that an important contributory source to the psychologically disturbed section of the total prison population is likely to be a higher detection rate for the offences carriéd out by disturbed persons. Life in penal institutions is likely to have a deleterious effect on behaviour, and the longer the cumulative experience of institutional life the more severe are its effects likely to be. It would follow that at the very least the penal system and its institutions should be so organized as not to reduce the probability of a successful adjustment to non-prison life after release. Moreover, it is highly desirable that there be an adequate provision of skilled care for offenders found to be suffering from psychological problems, both during the period in prison and after release. It has become clear that long-stay patients discharged from mental hospitals need adequate after-care facilities to bridge the massive gap between a protected environment and real life. Similar facilities are necessary for released offenders treated during confinement by psychiatrists or psychologists. In the next section we shall discuss the question of hostels, half-way houses and other community-based provisions for resocializing offenders in general, as well as the possibility of reducing the difference between life in the penal institution and life outside.

Craft (1968a) has described a four-tier pyramid of resources for offenders who have received a diagnosis of 'psychopath' in Britain.

1. The security hospitals, for example Broadmoor, provide *compulsory* psychiatric treatment—which even prisons are not allowed to require. They contain psychopaths adjudged particularly severe. Treatment is described by McGrath (1966) as training for conformity, using rewards and punishments.

2. NHS general psychiatric hospitals. These are non-security and include a wide variety of treatment practices.

3. A small number of open, psychiatric in-patient units, especially set up for psychopaths. The best known is the Henderson Hospital, Survey, which was begun as a voluntary treatment group by Maxwell Jones in 1947. About 30 per cent of the entry are court referred. All hospital events are discussed in groups. It is assumed that verbal exploration increases socially responsible behaviour. Tuxford (1962) reported a 40 per cent reconviction rate for the Henderson Hospital. Craft (1966) set up a similar regime at Balderton Hospital, Notts., (the patients in which are more likely to be dull normal in intelligence) and compared the outcome with a more authoritarian regime. At follow-up, the latter regime was superior in terms of reconviction rate. Craft (1968b) then compared Balderton with two other (Welsh) units, which were also authoritarian. The results again tended to favour the authoritarian method. However, there may have been differences in the communities to

which the patients were returned. The importance of the after-care agent has been shown by Davies and Sinclair (1971) and is referred to below in the context of a discussion on half-way houses.

4. Out-patient clinics (this is the most common of the four types of provision). A particularly well-known example is the Portman Clinic (London). This is a psychoanalytically oriented centre and tends to be rather selective. Few outcome data appear to have been reported, except in the special category of those convicted for homosexual offences (Woodward, 1958; Coates, 1962).

Not included in the survey by Craft was Grendon Underwood, which was described in Chapter 9. No official results for Grendon have yet been released by the authorities. However, the *Sunday Times* (1975) carried a report of a study by a Home Office psychologist which compared 87 Grendon inmates with 87 from the nearest local prison (Oxford), matched according to age when convicted, year of release, amount of time in prison and number of previous convictions of the type of offence for which they had been most recently convicted. Four years after release 60 per cent of both groups had been reconvicted (an inevitable underestimate of reoffending). The *Sunday Times* report notes that whereas Grendon is only just over half full, Oxford, like most local prisons, is very overcrowded. In addition, as stated earlier, Grendon is much more heavily staffed than the other prison. Thus the results obtained indicate Grendon to be much less cost-effective. In favour of Grendon we must note a serious deficiency of the study: Grendon inmates are selected as being psychologically disturbed, those at local prisons are not. The appropriate comparison group would thus have been a group of equally disturbed offenders, matched with the Grendon group as in the study described above, but exposed to a normal prison regime. Nevertheless, it seems reasonable to conclude that in terms of reconviction Grendon fails with a *minimum* of nearly two-thirds of its inmates. Supporters of the regime would argue that other benefits, such as improved psychological functioning, are also relevant outcome criteria; studies to test such claims remain to be carried out.

In general, outcome data are sparse. Stürup (1968) has reported a 10-year follow-up of 960 'mentally abnormal' criminals released from Herstedvester (a well-known Danish centre for offenders diagnosed as psychopaths). Eighty-seven per cent had remained in the community. The rates in the United Kingdom for a variety of methods are much lower (about 30–60 per cent). In all cases reported, including the Danish results, official statistics were relied upon.

It was argued in Chapter 7 that a distinction between 'psychopaths' and 'criminals' is likely to be largely artificial, and that both 'groups' consist of persons who have damaged others in some way, although not always (i.e. in the case of some 'psychopaths') so as to infringe the law. It follows that methods of changing the undesired behaviour need not differ widely between the two groups, and that behaviour modification generally requires first an analysis of the behaviours concerned and then a programme of training designed to result in a change in those behaviours. A detailed discussion of behavioural methods of controlling criminal behaviour (which is applicable, as argued above, to 'psychopathic behaviour') follows shortly. In this context it is of interest that the Butler Committee (1975) has recommended that training units be set up in prisons, not hospitals, for the treatment of 'antisocial psychopaths' (Butler suggests replacing the term by 'personality disorder'). Such units should have as their objective modifying the social behaviour of their inmates and 'clinical psychologists with specialist knowledge and experience of behaviour therapy will have a particularly important part to play' (p. 99). Butler also concluded that 'medical treatment has not been successful in treating psychopaths' (p. 199).

The outcome of psychiatric treatment for offenders placed on probation in Britain overall has been surveyed by Grünhut (1960) for the year 1953, and by Woodside (1971) in the city of Edinburgh for the years 1966–68. Grünhut reported that almost half of those put on probation with a requirement to submit to treatment had committed offences against property, and about one-third sexual offences. Nearly half the total of 636 cases surveyed had been assigned a prognosis of their likelihood of responding to treatment, that for the property offenders being on average much worse than for other offenders. This was borne out by the respective reconviction rates, but the rate of complaint is likely to be so much higher for property offences than for sexual ones—in which the 'victim' is frequently a consenting partner, for example in the case of homosexual acts—as to render reconviction rates useless as an index of treatment outcomes for sexual offenders.

Woodside's report of 55 offenders recommended for treatment at the Royal Edinburgh Hospital in 1966–68 is similarly inadequate. Sixteen of the group 'completed probation satisfactorally', but what this meant in terms of actual reoffending was not stated. Moreover, in the absence of an untreated control group there is no way of knowing whether psychiatric treatment reduced, increased or left unchanged the post-treatment offending of those concerned. Ogden (1959) claimed that cosmetic surgery for minor deformities freed from chronic embarrassment young offenders on whom he had performed such operations, made them more amenable to training and hence lowered their reconviction rate. No control data were provided. Insofar as low self-esteem and low esteem from others increases the likelihood of criminal behaviour, cosmetic surgery for those offenders in need of it might be worth a careful trial. However, it would first be necessary to establish that the rate of offending was indeed greater among those with minor deformities, all other factors being held equal. A particularly drastic form of surgical treatment, namely, castration for rapists, is reported by Stürp (1968). This was the fate of nearly half of 38 rapits received at Herstedvester in the years 1935–61. Stürup reports that the majority of the *castrati* did not subsequently attempt rape. In the section on behaviour therapy of offenders we shall discuss aversion therapy, a rather less drastic method than castration, which has been applied to a number of sexual offences, including paedophilia and exhibitionism, though more frequently to the treatment of voluntary clients seeking to change from a homosexual to a heterosexual preference.

Social and Job Training and Half-way House

On the assumption that if habitual offenders possessed job skills and regular work habits they would not return to offending after discharge, it has frequently been argued (for example Gunn, 1972) that workshops should be set up in which exprisoners could be equipped with occupational skills and get used to regular market wages. There appear to have been no controlled studies set up to investigate such claims. What is probably the most advanced prison regime in the world (*Guardian*, 1973), the open prison at Tilberga, Sweden, in which prisoners receive normal wages and pay normal sums for food, etc., selects its participants very carefully on the basis of probability of escape, ability to do the work and requirement for supervision. Such a selection procedure would be acceptable for post-discharge comparison purposes if half the prisoners so selected were randomly assigned to the Tilberga regime and half to a more conventional one. The availability of base-rate figures for the reconviction rate of the Tilberga type of prisoner would be less satisfactory but still of value. At present neither control appears to have been exercised. However laudable its aims from a humanitarian point of view, the Tilberga system is not designed as an experiment in the usual scientific sense of that term. (See also Chapter 9 for Bondesen's survey of Swedish prisons.)

Both the mental hospital and the prison systems are now experimenting with 'half-way houses', community-based hostels which provide some training in social skills and a sheltered contact with the outside world, so permitting a gradual rather than a sudden readjustment after discharge. Grygier *et al.* (1970) surveyed Canadian half-way houses and concluded that there was little difference in the rate of recidivism between the half-way house and the parole system, and that the former inevitably was more expensive. A similar conclusion was drawn by Shoham *et al.* (1971) concerning the effects on recidivism of the after-care system in Isreal. Both the above reviews argue that the after-care approach is potentially beneficial if properly utilized. The problem of defining what 'properly' means is well demonstrated by the statement by Grygier *et al.* that 'in a half-way house rules are at minimum . . . because it is not a prison'. This has echoes of the psychodynamic view that the repressed conflicts which 'underlie' disturbed behaviour, including antisocial behaviour, can only be resolved in a permissive and accepting atmosphere, rather than one in which approved behaviours are positively reinforced and thus strengthened, and disapproved ones go unreinforced, if not actually punished, and thus become weakened. It is the latter which is the view of behaviourally oriented psychologists, who would argue that the acquisition of appropriate social behaviour requires the systematic provision of carefully planned learning experiences, albeit against a background of general concern and caring for the individual. This was one of the main conclusions which emerged from the review of the literature on socialization in Chapter 2.

Thus far we have concentrated on what happens to prisoners within the agencies of the penal system in determining reconviction rates. In Chapter 8 we discussed the importance of the non-prisoner community in labelling prisoners as deviant and thus maintaining them in that role. Davies and Sinclair (1971) studied the effect on the reconviction rate of young offenders of the type of social training 'atmosphere' provided by the home to which the boy returned.

It was found that the best outcome occurred when both parents were 'firm but kind', as opposed to the situation in which one parent was firm and the other lax. Similarly, the reconviction rate for boys housed in hostels after confinement was lowest when the warden was 'firm but not distant'. Once again we have an emphasis on a combination of a clear system of rules and a general background of caring as optimal for retraining. In addition, Davies and Sinclair's findings suggest the desirability of carrying out training procedures in the individual's natural environment—in his familiar surroundings of home, friends and work. Several behaviour therapists have placed a similar emphasis, as we shall see below.

Experimental Psychology and the Control of Criminal Behaviour

Introduction

The psychology of learning has been much the major source of the behaviour therapy approach (also termed behaviour modification and behavioural intervention) to the treatment of problems of behaviour. Other areas of experimental psychology, such as social and cognitive psychology, have been drawn on to a lesser degree, but are likely to make greater contributions over the next 10 years than they have done in the recent past (Feldman and Broadhurst, 1976).

The aim of the behaviour therapies is to modify the current, behavioural responses ('symptoms') of the individual. Principles derived from the psychology of learning are used to account for the development of the problem behaviour as well as to design techniques of modification. The major behaviour therapy techniques include desensitization, in which the reduction of subjective anxiety and of avoidance behaviour is achieved by gradually bringing the patient into contact with the stimuli of which he was previously fearful; operant conditioning, which for the most part employs positive reinforcement; aversive training, in which the individual is trained to avoid a previously attractive stimulus. Evidence is growing that the direct observation of a model successfully treated by a behaviour therapy method may be as effective in helping a distressed individual as experiencing the treatment himself (Bandura, 1969). A conservative view of the very short history of the behaviour therapies (the major developments started only in the 1950's) would be that their therapeutic efficacy and efficiency is encouraging, particularly for the more clear-cut problems, such as phobias and obsessions, and for sexual difficulties. An excellent high-level overview of the behaviour therapy approach is provided by Bandura (1969). A very useful handbook, which reviews the psychotherapies as well as the behaviour therapies, is that edited by Bergin and Garfield (1971).

Whereas desensitization has been the most frequently employed of the behaviour therapy approaches in the clinical field, it has rarely been used in the control of criminal behaviour. Much the most frequently used approach has been an operant one, particularly in the form of the token economy.

Whatever the behavioural methods employed, they all have in common an initial analysis of the behaviour concerned. The following statement (Baer et al., 1968) was made with particular reference to operant conditioning, but it applies in its essentials to all behaviour therapy procedures: 'An applied behaviour analysis will make obvious the importance of the behaviour to be changed, its quantitative characteristics, the experimental manipulations which analyse with clarity what was responsible for the change, the technologically exact descriptions of all procedures contributing to that change' (p. 97). The methods reviewed below indicate the variety of behavioural approaches already adopted, sometimes as yet only in analogue studies and often involving only a single piece of work. However, we review also two sustained programmes of treatment research, at Kansas and at Hawaii, both of which have drawn on many of the specific methods which follow.

The Token Economy

The earliest site of application of operant principles in the clinical field was in the wards of large mental hospitals, which usually house long-stay patients with many deficits in social skills, possibly due to their original psychotic illness, but frequently exacerbated by social conditions in the institution.

The solution adopted for the problem of retraining was that of the token economy (Ayllon and Azrin, 1968), a system of reinforcers applicable to virtually all behaviours, which could be readily distributed or removed in response to desired or undesired behaviour. Briefly, the medium of exchange in the ward is not money, as in the world outside, but a system of tokens, much as gamblers play not with real money but with the more convenient poker chips which are exchanged for money at the end of the game. In the same way, the patient in a token economy programme exchanges his tokens for a wide variety of goods and privileges. Winkler (1971) has related token economies to general economic concepts and theories. The following characteristics of tokens, all of which relate to their usefulness in behaviour change programmes, are listed by Krasner and Ullman (1973, pp. 281–3).

1. Tokens are concrete and worthwhile indicators of social approval, which is backed up by exchanging them for goods.

2. They open up a limitless world of reinforcers, both primary and secondary.

3. They provide a time bridge between the performance of an act and a later explicit reinforcement consequent on the act.

4. Tokens can be given or withdrawn flexibly, frequently and without interfering with on-going behaviour.

5. Tokens can be paired with social approval, eventually enabling material reinforcers to be replaced by social reinforcers, so assisting the generalization to the outside world of the acquired or restored behaviour.

6. They can be used to shape and develop chains of behaviour.

In order to set up a token economy it is necessary first to designate which behaviours are desirable and which are changeworthy, and then to observe and record the existing level (the base-rate) of the behaviours which are to be changed, increased or reduced in rate, as well as their consequences in the actual environment. (The criteria by which 'desirability' and 'changeworthiness' are judged, and who is socially sanctioned to operate such criteria, lie at the heart of the ethical dilemma of the clinician turned criminal behaviour modifier (see Chapter 11)).

Examples of token economy (t.e.) systems applied to young offenders include reports by Burchard (1967), Karacki and Levinson (1970), Lawson et al. (1971) and Sloane and Ralph (1973). Burchard (1967) carried out two experiments, both of which used tokens, as well as time-out from positive reinforcement (see below) used as a punisher. His subjects were 12 intellectually retarded offenders in an institution. The first experiment attempted to increase the time spent sitting at a desk in school, and the second sought to control fighting, cheating and other disapproved behaviours. Both experiments achieved some degree of control over the behaviours concerned, but no attempt was made to generalize control to the outside community. Generalization was considered by Burchard to be the central problem because of the considerably lower predictability of reinforcers for behaviour in the natural environment as compared to the control possible in an institutional setting. He argued, therefore, for a series of intermediate hostels, in which the system of tokens and time-out would gradually be faded out, and verbal and other social reinforcers of the kind encountered in the natural environment faded in.

Karacki and Levinson (1970) established a t.e. programme for two groups of adolescent offenders at the Kennedy Youth Centre, West Virginia, one described as 'immature', the other as 'psychopathic'. This is an interesting departure from the usual lack of emphasis on individual differences in personality which is characteristic of the operant approach to behaviour. Tokens are earned for good general behaviour and for classroom progress. Karacki and Levinson emphasize the need for detailed and accurate observation of inmate behaviour in order for schedules of reinforcement to be administered as planned.

According to Gerard (1970), 80 per cent of those who had passed through the programme had not been reconvicted, as compared with the general average of 60 per cent for other institutions. No separate figures were given for the 'immature' and 'psychopathic' groups. Lawson et al. (1971) established a t.e. system at Dannemora State Hospital for 41 males committed there because of their disordered behaviour while in the state correctional system. The mean age of the group was 47, and their median length of stay in Dannemora, at the outset of the study, was 10 years. Nearly half had originally been in prison for murder or manslaughter, and the majority of the rest for robbery. Three-quarters of them had been diagnosed as suffering from schizophrenia. The objective of the exercise was to establish the inmates on regular schedules of activities, using a system of tokens which was carried out by the existing staff.

One-third of the patients were able to be transferred to higher graded wards in the hospital, suggesting a limited degree of success. This study is of particular interest because it is one of the very few behaviour therapy-reports involving an adult population which was, moreover, an unusually difficult one due to the high frequency of severe psychotic disturbances and the length of time spent in an institution.

Sloane and Ralph (1973) reported on a very detailed t.e. programme which has been set up in the Nevada Youth Training Centre. Observation of the social behaviour of the boys in the Centre was carried out each day at regular and frequent intervals. Progress was rewarded by increased privileges. No outcome data had been reported at the time of writing.

Cohen and Filipczak (1971) set up a token economy linked to the acquisition of basic educational skills (reading, writing and artihmetic) by adolescent offenders in an institution. The tokens received for progress could be used to purchase better than the basic levels of accommodation, services and commodities. A 'banking' system was also set up, inadequate progress leading to requests for 'loans' being refused, as well as the loss of privileges already attained, such as a private room, better food, and so on. The boys each planned their own work rate and educational programmes, so that a poor performance was one by comparison with the norm that the boy had set for himself. There was no direct attempt to change the behaviours which had resulted in entry to the institution. A comparison with an ordinary training institution showed that a stay in the experimental one resulted in a lower rate of recidivism after discharge. However, the longer the period of follow-up the smaller the superiority of the experimental programme, so that the greater efficacy of the method used as compared to an ordinary institution must be in doubt.

Attempts have been made by McKee (1971) and Parlett and Ayers (1971) to improve the educational performance of offenders using the method of programmed instruction (a very systematic step-by-step approach to teaching, with progress to the next stage contingent on attaining a given level of performance at the previous one). McKee (1971) demonstrated that a given rate of progress on an experimenter-managed programme was maintained in a later self-managed phase. Parlett and Ayers (1971) reported that following exposure to a programmed learning situation several personality scores on the Cattell Sixteen Factor Personality inventory changed away from the profile stated by the test manual to be typical for prisoners. Neither study reported the effect on the rate of recidivism of the attempt to improve educational attaintments.

Behaviour Modification in the Natural Environment

The major premise of this approach is stated by Tharp and Wetzels (1969, p. 7) as follows: 'The environment in which the individual is embedded is principally responsible for the organization, or disorganization, the maintenance or change, the appearance or disappearance, of any behaviour'. It follows, according to the authors, who go on to give many illustrative and well-analysed examples, that intervention and prevention should occur in the individual's 'natural environment' (family, school, friendship group, etc.) and not in the artificial environment of an institution. They urge also the use as intervention agents of non-professionals, albeit under the general guidance of professionals. Several of the University of Hawaii studies, described below, exemplify both the natural environment approach and the systematic use of non-professionals. Buehler (1973) points out that attempts to control behaviour in the natural environment are prone to some of the same problems as those encountered in institutions, particularly the powerful and contrary control exercised by the peer group of the offender, which is opposite in intention to the goals held by the change agents. He suggests that the problem can be reduced by a careful initial behavioural analysis, thoroughly training the trainer in the principles of behaviour modification, keeping small the number of the group under treatment, and retaining the control of all positive and negative rein-forcers in the hands of the trainers and those who interact directly with the offender group. Buehler also recommends establishing the desired behaviours in the 'nuclear group' (i.e. the first few members of the group) before adding new ones. This is a crucial point which unless attended to inevitably undermines attempts at changing the behaviour of offenders which are made on a group basis. It is essential that the offender is provided with consistent, rather than contradictory, models and sources of positive reinforcement for approved behaviours. The problem is how to begin the process—to establish the 'nuclear group'; it is common to all control attempts carried out on a group basis, whatever the theoretical orientation of the change agents.

At present, the probation officer is the change agent who operates in the 'natural environment' of offenders. Thorne et al. (1967) have very clearly set out for probation officers the principles of behaviour modification and describe how, once conversant with these principles, they could teach parents to control the behaviour of their own children. This is a good example of the 'triadic' approach on which Tharp lays great emphasis: the psychologist trains the professional (probation officer, teacher, etc.), who then trains those, such as parents or press, who are the most salient elements of the natural environment of the offender (or schoolchild, preschool child, etc.). Jamieson (1965), himself a judge, has enthusiastically taken up Tharp's general approach, arguing that judges should be trained in behavioural principles, which they should then apply in drafting the conditions of probation orders so as to increase the likeli-hood that the behaviour of offenders would actually alter, as opposed to this being a pious hope. A number of reports are of some relevance. Hall et al. (1972) trained parents in behviour modification principles and procedures and then encouraged the parents to develop techniques specific to the problem behaviours of their own children. These were rather different from those associated with offending behaviour, including, for example, failure to wear orthodontic devices or to carry out household tasks. Nevertheless, it might be possible to apply the same procedures to the control by parents of the offending behaviour of their children. Patterson (1974) has reported a programme concerning behaviours closer to actual offending. The parents of 27 children referred by 'community agencies' for 'conduct problems' (not further defined) were trained in behavioural analysis and modification to alter the behaviour of their children. Careful pre- and post-measurements indicated that after eight weeks of parental intervention and a one-year follow-up, two-thirds of the problem children were behaving as well as a comparison group of children previously assessed as not displaying conduct problems. The optimism generated by the Hall and Patterson reports is not supported by a study carried out by Weathers and Liberman (1975). Twenty-eight adolescents on probation were referred for parent-based behavioural intervention. Only six completed the training period, a rate of drop-out which indicates one of the key difficulties of treatment in the natural environment. Treatment was carried out by a psychologist in the home setting and involved training parents and children in contingency management, behavioural contracting (see below) and social communication skills. The target behaviours included verbal abusiveness, staying out late at night and avoiding chores. A follow-up indicated no difference in target behaviour, except for verbal abusiveness, between these adolescents and 16 others who had dropped out after one school visit. More important, there was no difference between the groups on 'antisocial incidents' recorded by the probation department. It is important to note that parents are not the only sources of social control for the behaviour of adolescents. The peer group is likely to be at least as important, if not more so. Any natural environment programme, to be successful, must involve peers in addition to parents. Moreover, the Weathers and Liberman study did not include as specific target behaviours the antisocial acts which had led to contact with the probation service—hoping instead for generalization from other behviours.

Aversion Therapy

This has been used widely in the treatment of the addictions, principally alcoholism (Rachman and Teasdale, 1969), and of sexual variations, particularly homosexual behaviour, in which its efficacy has been quite marked (Feldman and MacCulloch, 1971). However, aversion therapy as a formal method of changing behaviour has been used only rarely in the control of offending by psychological methods of treatment, as opposed to the central role of such negative reinforcers as fines or imprisonment, usually inefficiently applied (see Chapter 9). Aversion therapy proper is to be distinguished from the time-out procedure, in which positive reinforcement is withdrawn, in that it involves the direct association of an aversive stimulus (typically mild electric shock or drug-induced nausea, in the treatment of sexual deviations and alcoholism, respectively) with the undesired response. A variation, termed anticipatory avoidance learning (Feldman and MacCulloch, 1971), allows the individual in treatment to avoid the aversive stimulus providing that he refrains from making the undesired response or terminates his performance of it (for example watching a slide of an attractive male). This method is particularly flexible in that it also enables the individual to perform instead an alternative response, such as watching a slide of an attractive female. A small number of paedophilic males (persons whose preferred sexual partner is a pre-adolescent boy, see Chapter 7) were among the two large groups of patients treated by Feldman and MacCulloch (1971). The criteria which predicted a well-maintained change of sexual preference were the same as those found for the larger group of male homosexuals whose preferred partners were other adult males, namely, a prior history of heterosexual arousal and the absence of certain types of a marked disorder or personality. This finding has been confirmed by Mellor (1970). However, it should be noted that the majority of the paedophiles who figured in the above two reports were self-referred, not court-referred. The number of the latter was too small for firm conclusions, but it is reasonable to assume they would be less likely on average to seek change than those who were self-referred, with a resulting poorer outcome. There are three reports of the successful behavioural treatment of exhibitionist behaviour (i.e. indecent exposure), two of which (Evans, 1968; McCulloch et al., 1971) used anticipatory avoidance learning. The third (Reitz and Keel, 1971) described a method which required the exhibitionist to expose himself to a group of unresponsive nurses (the exhibitionist's positive reinforcement appears to be the expression of horror, fear, etc., on the face of the victim, see Chapter 7), the result being a reduction in the behaviour. In this method the aversive consequence is inattention by the 'victim'. All three of the above reports concerned individuals who were referred for treatment, officially or unofficially, by legal agencies. In addition to training in avoidance, several reports have urged the importance of positive training in heterosexual social skills. A few reports of the systematic application to non-sexual offenders of aversive stimuli have been given. Levinson et al. (1968) used group therapy as an aversive stimulus to control rule-breaking in a correctional institution for adolescent boys. The boys could avoid group therapy by completing three successive months without misbehaviour. The result was a 43 per cent reduction in misconduct reports. What the staff think of as beneficial and hence to be sought after (in this case, group therapy) may be perceived very differently by the inmates. A particularly severe aversive stimulus, the injection of succinyl choline, which temporarily paralyses the recipient except for one arm, was described by Middleton (1964). The subject imagines himself avoiding temptation, signals when his image is clear and then receives oxygen which relieves his asphyxia. The probability of a subject not signalling seems rather low. No details as to outcome were supplied by Middleton. Even if this method was significantly more effective and efficient than any available alternative, it would need to be evaluated with particular care against the third criterion mentioned earlier, that of social acceptance. Finally, a report by Kellam (1969) is the closest in this area to the most typical example of offending, namely theft. The offender concerned, a 48-year-old housewife, had 10 previous convictions for stealing. A film was made of her stealing from a shop and this was inserted into a further film of a sequence of disapproving faces. The film was shown to the offender and she received electric shocks to coincide with the disapproving faces (thus it was hoped the shock-generated anxiety might become conditioned to the aversive social stimulus of a disapproving face). The offender reported a generalization of anxiety to shops that this persisted three months later, being particularly marked when she felt the urge to steal. At this point she would recall the film and the urge disappeared. No further reports of this particular offender have appeared. As a general principle, it would be desirable to train an alternative behaviour to the disapproved act, the most obvious one being making a selection from the shop and paying for it.

A method related to aversion therapy, namely *covert sensitization* (Cautela, 1967), has been applied to a variety of problem behaviours, although quantitative reports are sparse. Cautela (1967) has described the application of the method to a variety of patient groups seeking to avoid attractive but self-damaging behaviours (for example excess alcohol drinking). Following training in relaxation, the patient is asked to imagine successively approaching the attractive object, being sick while doing so and feeling relieved on turning away. Cautela gives a brief report of the application of covert sensitization to stealing from unoccupied cars, the sequence of imagined events being walking down the street, reaching for the car handle, feeling sick, running away and feeling better. Beyond the statement that 'juvenile offenders cooperate well', Cautela has given no information as to the numbers treated by this method or the results of treatment.

Observational Learning

Prentice (1972) divided into three groups 36 teenage boys convicted of theft. One group observed a model choosing aloud between pairs of statements, each of which contrasted a morally more desirable with a morally less desirable action. The model always chose the former. A second group observed the experimenter making the same consistent choice, and a third made their own choices, receiving no feedback from the experimenter. A later test on a parallel set of paired statements indicated that the first two groups chose the more desirable statements more frequently than the third group, indicating the effectiveness of both 'live' and 'symbolic' modelling. However, there were no differences between the groups in official arrest records nine months after training. This is hardly surprising, since there was only one trivial intervention, and that was confined to verbal statements and not extended to actual behaviour.

An interesting analogue study has been reported by Heisler (1974). On the basis of self-reported offending, he divided introductory psychology students at Southern Illinois University into groups of 'law violators' and 'law abiders'. All participants took an ability test which was marked while they were called out on a pretext, following which the participants had to report their own marks. Several experimental conditions were used, in all of which 'violators' cheated significantly more than 'abiders'. The lowest level of cheating for both groups was associated with exposure to severe threat of the consequences of cheating and a (posed) model caught for cheating. However, the maximum cheating by the violators was in the severe threat, *no model* condition, suggesting that a warning alone, without an actual example of the consequences of disobedience, might be counterproductive for those with a significant record of offending.

It has been suggested that training offenders to increase the period of time for which they are able to delay the receipt of positive reinforcement might reduce offending (see Mischel, 1968, for research into delay of gratification). Stumphauzer (1970) has described a technique which he based on Bandura and Mischel's (1965) report of the effectiveness of modelling in sharply reversing delay preferences. In a later paper (Stumphauzer, 1972), he applied the technique to 40 white inmates, aged 18–20, of a Florida correctional institution who had opted for an immediate but smaller reward on 70 per cent of a previously administered test series. The models were older and more prestigious boys (in terms of their work assignments). One list of choices was used as a base-line measure of the subjects' pretraining choice, one for the models' choices (observed by the subject) and one as a test for generalization after training. Exposure to a high-delay model significantly increased delay choices by the subjects. No change followed exposure to a low-delay model. The newly acquired high-delay behaviour generalized to responses to a list of methods for saving money. The experiment was not concerned with the control of offending behaviour as such.

The value of observational learning is well established in the treatment of phobic behaviours (Bandura, 1969) and deserves a much more adequate test in the context of criminal behaviour than is provided by the above reports. In general, it would be predicted that the behaviours of adolescent offenders would be particularly susceptible to the models provided by those of high status in areas of behaviour highly valued by the adolescents, an expectation supported, though somewhat indirectly, by reports by Harari (1971) and Ostrom *et al.* (1971).

Adjuncts to Behavioural Approaches

A number of specific adjuncts to broader approaches to the treatment of offenders are worth mentioning.

1. *Reinforcing initial attendance and other 'pretreatment' behaviours.* Schwitzgebel and his colleagues have used payments of money to ensure good initial attendance at interviews by young offenders. Schwitzgebel and Kolb (1964) gradually shaped up the interview-attending behaviour of an experimental group (not randomly constructed) and noted three years later that the members of the group had a better arrest record than a control group not systematically shaped. Regular attendance at interviews is argued by Schwitzgebel to prepare for regular job attendance; in turn, the latter may reduce the probability of further offending. In a related study, Schwitzgebel and Covey (1967) recruited

adolescent male offenders, randomly assigned them to several matched groups, and found that systematically giving positive reinforcement for positive statements during interview both increased the production of such statements and the regularity and promptness of attendance. The authors concluded that both the 'unpunctuality' and 'impulsivity' of young offenders were to do with their previous reinforcement history (punctual and non-impulsive behaviour had not received systematic positive reinforcement) rather than with any permanent 'traits' of personality.

2. *Behavioural contracting.* Stuart (1971) defines a behavioural contract as 'that which schedules the exchange of positive reinforcements between persons'. It thus specifies the positive reinforcements people deliver to each other in return for emitting, or suppressing, particular responses. (In simple terms, 'if you do X for me, I'll do Y, stop doing Z, etc., for you'.) Reports have appeared on the application of behavioural contracting to a number of problems, but Stuart's single case-report (1971) of an adolescent female offender seems to be one of the few in the criminal field. Another is provided by Jessness and De Risi (1973). The behavioural contracting approach is very appealing on commonsense grounds ('people like to know what to expect and where they stand') as well as being based on sound psychological principles, and it is well worth further study in the criminal field. It is related to the token economy and contingency management approaches in its emphasis on the contingencies which are associated with particular behaviours. Social psychologists have long emphasized that a specific public commitment markedly increases the probability of a person carrying out the behaviour concerned. The behaviour contracting approach goes further by spelling out what happens both if the contract is kept and if it is not kept.

3. *Time-out (t.o.) from positive reinforcement. Tyler and his colleagues have* given a number of reports of the effectiveness of completely removing positive reinforcement for undesired behaviours or removing the individual from the site in which positive reinforcement for such behaviours was received (for example by isolation) in markedly reducing the frequency of the undesired behaviour. Burchard and Tyler (1965) found that brief periods of social t.o. (unaccompanied by either threats or exhortations) reduced aggressive behaviour. This was restored when negative sanctions were removed and diminished once more when they were reinstated. Tyler and Brown (1967) sought to eliminate 'undesirable behaviour round the pool-room table'. Misbehaviour was followed by either 15 minutes in an isolation room or a verbal reprimand, the latter being more effective. However, no base-line measures (prior to the use of t.o. or reprimand) were taken, nor were the contingencies clearly spelled out in advance. The authors noted that many boys went to the t.o. room of their own accord, so that t.o. was not seen as a source of social disgrace; indeed, it may have evoked sympathy and hence support from other boys. They argue that mild punishment may thus be more effective than more severe punishment because it minimizes martyrdom and hence the search for revenge. Clearly, one problem is to find the level of punishment which is maximally effective in changing

behaviour without such undesired and counterproductive side-effects as increased resistance to attempts at control. Brown and Tyler (1968) used t.o. in an attempt to gain control over the behaviour of the leader of a group of adolescent offenders in an institution by imposing a period of isolation whenever he or his associates forced subservience from weaker members. Moreover, he was held accountable for any trouble caused by the others. He ceased both behaving disruptively and encouraging such behaviour by his peers. However, it is quite possible that in such a situation another leader may 'emerge'—the situation is a familiar one in politics whenever the leader of a group 'sells out'. It is necessary to ensure both that the leader receives positive reinforcement from authority for keeping his followers 'in line' and that the positive reinforcements he provides for them are more desirable than those offered by any would-be substitute leader.

4. *Reparation.* The recently established British Community Service Orders (Pease *et al.*, 1975) represent an attempt to apply the principle of reparation to the control of crime. Offenders are 'sentenced' to a fixed number of hours of work on such worthy projects as working with the handicapped, repairing churches and clearing canals. But the reparation is to the community at large and not to the particular victim. A study of direct reparation, or rather 'over-reparation', to the victim himself has been carried out by Azrin and Wesolowski (1974). They applied to a group of profoundly retarded inmates of an institution Azrin's 'over-correction' principle, already shown to be effective with aggressive acts, toilet-training and enuresis. Briefly, the principle asserts that disruptive activity is discouraged if the offender both corrects and over-corrects, and that the restored situation is better than the original one. The extension of the principle to the control of thefts was tested with the mentally retarded because thefts, typically of food items during mealtimes, were easily detected; it followed that theft prevention measures could be evaluated accurately. A group of 34 retarded patients who stole were required to 'correct'—to return what was stolen—for five days, and to 'over-correct'—to return the stolen item plus an additional item—for the next 20 days. During the correction phase there were 20 episodes of theft per day, and as many on the last as on the first day. There was an immediate sharp fall in the over-correction period, with no further thefts past the third day. The authors argue that over-correction has a number of crucial features, all of which would be expected to be relevant by a behaviourist approach. Withdrawal of the stolen item both terminates the positive reinforcement of theft and is itself a negative reinforcement— because greater effort is then required to obtain a replacement and doing so interrupts other pleasurable activities. Moreover, it provides a positive education in cooperative and helpful behaviour, because the thief practises the positive action of giving his own food item to his victim and is rewarded by the victim's pleasure. However, a sceptic might expect a person of more average intelligence to respond to the application of an over-correction approach in his institution by actually encouraging others to steal from him!

5. *Personality and method.* A final point concerns the possibility of matching

control methods to individuals, rather than applying the method regardless of individual differences. There are two main approaches: the first, which stems from the specificity model of behaviour—which asserts in essence that individual differences are 'situation-bound'—is that training methods have always to be matched to behaviour in the particular situation concerned; the second, which stems from the consistency view, is that such differences are 'person-bound'. It is the first view which has influenced the behaviour therapy methods of control which are reviewed in this chapter. There have been almost no attempts to compare the effects of the same method when applied to groups labelled as differing in some generalized aspect of personality. (In contrast, the psychotherapeutic methods have included many such studies.) This is the tactic proposed by Eysenck (1964). For example, it would be expected that the acquisition of desirable behaviours by an extraverted group of offenders would be slower than that of an introverted group, and would be improved by the concurrent use of a stimulant drug, such as amphetamine, considered to raise arousal level and thus to have an 'introverting' effect by increasing the rate of acquisition of learning. Eysenck (1964) cites a number of studies which can be interpreted as supporting this approach. Whether it will indeed be necessary to match training methods to personality questionnaire scores will depend on the outcome of the specificity–consistency controversy. If the compromise suggested in Chapter 6 proves correct, than it would follow that the extreme-scoring minority might indeed be more responsive to a specially adapted approach than to approaches appropriate to the majority.

The Achievement Place Studies

A long-term programme of research is being carried out by Phillips and his associates at the University of Kansas. Phillips (1968) describes Achievement Place as 'an example of a home-style, community based, treatment-facility' (p. 213). The first group to take up residence (Phillips, 1968) consisted of three boys who lived for six months 'as in a family', with a pair of experienced 'house-parents'. The boys were aged between 12 and 14 and had been described by the County Court as 'dependent and neglected'. They were from low-income families and had committed minor offences. A t.e. system was set up to modify specific target behaviours, such as aggressive statements, bedroom-cleaning and punctuality, all of which were brought under reinforcement control. The next report (Bailey et al., 1970) described the successful application of a t.e. programme to the unruly classroom behaviour of five boys, who were similar to the earlier group of three and were again housed in Achievement Place. The same report described two single case-studies, one concerning the application of the t.e. approach to the disruptive classroom behaviour of a boy still in the public school system. This was again successfully managed, as was that of a further boy for whom control over his newly satisfactory behaviour was gradually transferred from the token economy to the contingencies operating in the natural environment, a crucial point, as indicated earlier.

Phillips *et al.* (1971), studying a group of six Achievement Place boys, showed that losing points for lateness improved both punctuality and saving pocket money, confirming the finding of Phillips (1968) that (so-called) 'predelinquent behaviours' were amenable to operant control. Bailey *et al.* (1971) supported their argument that the youths themselves are an 'untapped resource' for training their peers by two studies, both of which showed that errors of verbal articulation could be successfully modified by a number of procedures, including modelling by peers and social approval by peers, as well as by contingent reinforcement by the receipt of points. Their notion is of a 'chain' of trainers, with each 'generation' of offenders in training modifying the behaviour of the next one. This is a most important point, as noted earlier, but there is a considerable distance from the reduction of articulation errors to the control of criminal behaviour.

Two reports by this group of workers are related to the study by Phillips *et al.* (1971) discussed above, in that they concern the source of the system of rewards for good behaviour. Phillips *et al.* (1973) found that the most effective system of rewards was one in which the boys elected one of their number as leader. The latter then assigned tasks to the others and rewarded or penalized them (on a points system) according to their performance. In his turn, the leader was controlled by his own loss or gain of points according to how well those under him worked. This is hardly a remarkable finding; the importance of working through a group's own informal social system of leadership, as opposed to the formal, externally imposed structure, was demonstrated by occupational psychologists many years ago (for example Homans, 1952). In line with this general conclusion, Phillips *et al.* (1973) found that a system of self-government was preferred by the boys to externally imposed rules. Of some interest, in view of Skinner's frequently reiterated assertion that negative reinforcement need never be used, was the finding that the boys preferred a combination of positive and negative sanctions to positive reinforcements alone.

Next, Fixsen *et al.* (1973) reported two experiments in which Achievement Place boys learned a system of rules and then maintained the observance of them by their peers. The rules were changeable only by 'family conferences'. In their first experiment it was found that more boys took part in discussions of the consequences for rule violations when they had responsibility for setting those consequences than when teachers or house parents did so. Under the former condition they also reported more violations of rules than in the latter, and did so both in an outside school and in Achievement Place, as well as in the wider community. Although the authors did not themselves make such a link, both findings are interpretable within the framework of dissonance theory, which would predict that a course of action embarked on under conditions in which the subject believed that he was free to choose another response would be more strongly adhered to than if the course of action was manifestly determined by some outside agency. However, the results of the second experiment contradict to some extent expectations derived from dissonance theory. It was found that the boys arranged fewer 'trials' (to determine the question of guilt for an alleged violation of a rule) when they were responsible for doing so than did the house-parents when they had the responsibility. If points were earned by the boy for calling trials, then more were called, but the increase was largely contributed by the more trivial infringements, suggesting a conflict with previous learned norms of 'not squealing'.

This reminds us of one of the central differences between the behaviours typical of those who seek help for problems from which they themselves suffer and those whose behaviour attracts the attention of social agencies because of the suffering of others. The former tend to cooperate with helping agents, for example by discussing their problems more or less freely, the latter have previously learned, both by modelling and direct reinforcement, the behaviours traditionally expected of offenders, one of which is not to assist social control agents to discover the offending of others. This fundamental *divergence of interests*, as perceived by offenders, is part and parcel of the fact that most offenders *benefit* from their behaviours, and most will only cease from them when the costs consistently outweigh the rewards. The A.P. studies, carefully designed and rigorously carried out though they are, exemplify one of the major conclusions which will be set out later concerning psychological research into the control of criminal behaviour: no *direct* attempt is made to change the illegal behaviours themselves. Instead, it is hoped that by changing behaviours which, though not in themselves illegal, are unacceptable in Achievement Place, such changes will generalize to the illegal behaviours. The test of this hope would be the future conviction rates of the A.P. treated boys as against those handled by other methods or completely untreated. Any such comparison would need to take into account not only the results obtained, but the economic costs of achieving them compared to those of other methods, including the costs of failure to socialize the boys concerned—these include the economic and psychological costs to the future victims and the economic costs to the community of future law enforcement and attempts at reformation or punishment. The first such outcome study of A.P. boys was reported at the 1972 Annual Convention of the American Psychological Association (Fixsen *et al.*, 1972). A comparison was made between 16 A.P. boys, 15 boys committed to an institution (Kansas Boys School) and 13 placed on probation, in terms of a number of pre- and post-treatment indices. The A.P. and institution boys were similar for pre-treatment police and court records, those of the probation boys being somewhat less serious. Two years after release, 19 per cent (three) of the A.P. boys, 53 per cent (eight) of the institution boys and 54 per cent (seven) of the probation boys had been reconvicted. Data on post-treatment school attendance and performance were similar for all three groups pre-treatment, but after treatment showed a marked superiority for the A.P. group over the other two groups.

In discussing their study the authors point out that: 'the boys were *not* randomly assigned to each group. Rather, they were committed to each treatment by the local juvenile court for the reasons *that we cannot specify*' (my italics)... 'the differences among the groups may be due to a "population effect" or to a "treatment effect".' In other words, the lower recidivism rate and improved educational performance of the A.P. boys might have been achieved by the successful members of the total A.P. group in either or both of the other two settings. The A.P. research team is now carrying out a study whereby A.P. youths are randomly selected, and the follow-up data will be of great interested.

Table 10.1. Comparative costs of Achievement Place and other settings

	Probation	Achievement place	Institution
Capital investment per youth	No data	$6000	$20,000 to $30,000
Yearly operating cost per youth	$500	$4100	$6000 to $12,000
Youths 'treated'	13	16	15
Youths 'successful'	7	13	8
Cost per 'successful' youth	$930	$5000	$16,900

Adapted from Fixsen *et al.* (1972).

In addition to studying the efficacy of their Achievement Place programme Fixen *et al.* (1972) also looked at efficiency, as shown in Table 10.1, which indicates that the operating costs per bed at A.P. were less than half those at the Kansas Boys School, and the capital costs of building about one-quarter. The authors argue that not only are group homes (for example A.P.) less costly, but also more humane, although they do not discuss whether considerations of humanity would outweigh those of economics if the relative costs were reversed. Nor do they discuss the relationship between the costs of *probation* and those of A.P. It is clear from Table 10.1 that the operating costs of probation are very considerably lower than those of A.P. The capital costs, not shown in Table 10.1, are also likely to be lower—office accommodation for the probation officers is likely to cost less than the living quarters, etc., for the A.P. boys and staff. If we combine the relative operating costs with the number of boys not reconvicted (seven out of the 13 probation boys and 13 out of the 16 of the A.P. group), then we arrive at a total yearly cost per successful boy of $930 for the probation method and $5000 for the A.P. method. (The costs are as at June 1969. Obviously, all those quoted will have risen considerably since then.)

The University of Hawaii Studies

A number of studies relevant to the control of criminal and precriminal behaviour are being carried out, within a behavioural framework, by O'Donnell and his colleagues at the University of Hawaii. Some of the studies are still in progress. O'Donnell and De Leon (1974) set up a contingency programme related to school performance (points were received which could be exchanged for privileges or goods) in an adolescent correctional institution and noted gains of from 0·5 to 1·5 of a school grade (year) during a four-month period. The gains were not related to the time spent in the school and the authors suggested that at least a proportion of them were due to relearning—reexposure to previously well-learned but partially forgotten material improved the level of performance—rather than involving genuine new learning. This is an important point, which relates to the general distinction between learning and performance and should always be taken into account when evaluating reports of improvements said to indicate new learning. Fo and O'Donnell (1974) set up a 'buddy system' whereby youngsters, aged 11–17, received the friendship of an adult resident in their own community. The buddies sought to increase the performance of pro-social behaviours by the boys by making both their approval and the receipt of material reinforcers contingent on the performance of approved behaviour (i.e. friendship was given following approved and withheld following disapproved behaviours). The buddies had been trained previously for their roles as behaviour modifiers. It was found that school attendance improved and problem behaviours decreased in a group of 42 youngsters referred to the buddy system (it was not stated how many of these were officially offenders) but only in relation to *contingent* reinforcement. The problem of securing generalization therefore arises once more, and the authors emphasize the crucial role of the buddy in transferring ultimately his control to persons who figure in the natural environment of the boys. (Perhaps this could be achieved by drawing buddies *from* the natural environment of the boys; their effectiveness might be even greater if they were ex-offenders.)

In a further report of the buddy system, Fo and O'Donnell (1975) compared convicted offences by 264 boys randomly allocated to a buddy with 178 boys randomly allocated to serve as controls. The results were somewhat mixed. Whereas those with a previous record of offences improved through participation in the buddy system as compared with the controls, those with *no* previous record actually did worse. The authors suggest that their participation in the study may have led to social contacts between offenders and previous non-offenders, so that the latter learned criminal behaviours to which they were previously not exposed. This indicates that non-offenders participating in programmes designed to prevent the acquisition of criminal behaviours should be segregated as far as possible from existing offenders. Nevertheless, the success of the buddy system in reducing reoffending by previous offenders is encouraging.

O'Donnell et al. (1973) set up an athletic programme for which any youngster from an economically poor community was eligible. The opportunity to play football and other games was offered as a reward for academic work. During the four years of the project *not a single one* of the 200 youngsters who participated in the project had an official arrest record. Although no comparison group was set up which did not have access to football, the complete absence of arrests is obviously much better than could have been expected in almost any group of disadvantaged youths. However, it is possible that the fact that parents of the boys had themselves to apply for their sons' participattion may have resulted in a group from concerned homes which provided a good degree of social control which supplemented that provided by the project. Moreover, there are no data on the pretreatment arrest record of the youths. Nevertheless, it is obvious that the opportunity to play games and be coached by experts is a very potent reinforcer for approved behaviours for young people, and the converse—the prospect of losing the opportunity to do so—is likely to be an effective cue to avoid forbidden behaviour. In general, it is important to match reinforcers to their order of preference in the group under study.

In another study by O'Donnell and Stanley (1973), students who had dropped out of high school were enabled to earn money contingent on their academic performance. The results were extremely impressive for the seven (out of 11) who completed the programme; the average gain of school grades ranged from 6·0 to 8·3 years, and five of the seven were accepted into community colleges. If improving academic performance is relevant to the control of criminal behaviour, then it is clear that powerful reinforcers are readily available for rapidly improving the performance of those functioning at poor levels or who have dropped out of the educational system altogether for reasons other than organically based intellectual retardation.

The Social Setting of Behavioural Treatments

The best-designed programmes may founder on the lack of cooperation by those in daily contact with the offender.

Countercontrol by the Peer Group. Buehler *et al.* (1966) have shown how an institutional group of female adolescent offenders positively reinforced antisocial behaviour (i.e. those behaviours disapproved by the staff) such as rulebreaking, criticism of adults and aggression, and punished behaviour approved by the staff. They also found that the staff were less consistent in their use of positive and negative reinforcers than were the girls and applied them less frequently. In other words, the girls not only had a contrary set of goals to the staff, they also pursued them more effectively. Detailed observations of small units for male offenders were made by Polsky (1962), who showed that the peer subculture developed social hierarchies based on status, the highest esteem going to the boys who most exemplified the very opposite of the values and behaviours approved by the staff. Newcomers to the unit were shaped into the behaviours valued by the boys. Because the staff were outnumbered by the boys, they needed the cooperation of high-status boys to maintain order. Thus they confirmed the status of such boys and hence that of the behaviours they exemplified, so that pursuing the short-term goal of maintaining order made more difficult the long-term goal of changing undesirable behaviour. Finally, Polsky points out, many of the boys would spend further periods in other institutions to which they would transfer the value systems acquired in their first institution. The problems raised above apply also to attempts at control in the outside world, although perhaps less severely—offenders treated in their natural environment are potentially exposed to influences other than those exclusively favourable to offending. The question is worth investigating because the problem of counteracting on-going influences favourable to criminal behaviour is crucial to the success of any programme of control.

Non-cooperation by existing staff. Laws (1974) has described some of the difficulties he found in establishing and operating a token economy in a maximum security hospital. He comments that the system failed because 'it was never intended to succeed. From its inception to its demise, it was truly a "token" programme' (p. 34). Non-cooperation was made more possible by the retention by existing staff of overall administrative control, patient selection and staff selection.

The change agents currently employed in the correctional system, whether in institutions or in the community, tend to have a vested interest in continuing to use the methods with which they are familiar, ineffective though they are. Hence it is necessary to develop alternative training facilities for such agents, an example being Achievement Place. In addition, it is easier to recruit and train new change agents than to try to teach new behaviours to existing ones. In the latter case, the training must be very carefully graded and systematic so as gradually to change old and well-established but ineffective behaviours. Exactly the same requirements are necessary for changing ineffective into more effective change agents as for changing offenders—the analysis of the maintaining conditions for behaviour, and the designation, modelling and planned reinforcement of alternative behaviours.

The Behavioural Treatment of Offenders: Conclusions and Speculations

Compared with the record of solid achievement of the behaviour therapies in the treatment of psychological problems met clinically, the results of the treatment of offenders are much less impressive. There is no very clear-cut evidence of success in reducing reoffending by juveniles, let alone by adult offenders—rarely treated by behavioural methods. However, there are some indications that behavioural approaches are likely to be more successful than the psychotherapies in addition to the fact that they are based on well-established principles of behaviour: observational learning and contingency management principles appear promising, as does treatment in the natural environment, particularly when the reinforcers used are those of clear relevance to the offenders concerned. In the specific case of sex offenders, some success has been attained by a combination of aversive therapy and social retraining.

In considering the relative lack of success to date of behavioural approaches to offenders, two comments apply to the goals selected by virtually all behaviour therapists whose work we have reviewed.

First, they imply the same (usually unspoken) assumption as does the psychodynamic approach, namely, that criminal behaviour relates to some personal deficit in the offender, the typical area of emphasis being on a lack of educational skill. The implication is that if only he was fluent at reading, arithmetic or had a command of some job skill, he would not 'need' to offend. Hence, the behaviour being modified by behaviour therapists working with offenders tends to be reading or some other educational skill. Alternatively, attention is paid to deficits in the behaviour of the offender *within* an institutional setting, the emphasis being on improving his day-to-day conduct. What rarely has happened is a direct attempt to change the behaviour, outside the institution, which led to a conviction, whether this was theft, or violence, or some other criminal behaviour. This indirect approach is in very sharp contrast to the behavioural approach in the clinical field, in which the emphasis has been on the problem behaviour itself, rather than on some correlate or supposed 'cause'. For example, a person who is afraid of heights might be trained to feel relaxed and calm in high places and thus not to avoid them.

The second comment, which is related to the first, is that behaviour therapy treatments of offenders rather rarely use as outcome measures such conventional indices as reconviction (let alone self-reported or observed offending). Instead, they have been more concerned with demonstrating progress— frequently spectacular—in the non-criminal areas of behaviour which have been the focus of the behavioural intervention, such as reading skills or unsatisfactory conduct within the institution. Again, this is in sharp contrast with the situation in the clinical field, in which an improvement in the problem as defined by the patient has been the typical measure of outcome. As will be argued later, in more detail, in the criminological field the intervention agent is *inevitably* the agent of an offended-against society—which defines what constitutes the goal of treatment. Hence, outcome measures must be in terms of reoffending, an argument implicitly recognized by the typical use of the reconviction measure by students of the efficacy of penal systems. Psychotherapists have avoided such a bald version of their true function by casting the offender in the role of patient; he offends because he is suffering, hence treat him by relieving his underlying tensions. If this lowers recidivism, so much the better, but the major test of outcome for the psychotherapist is a reduction of the offender/patient's psychic distress. Not sharing the psychodynamicist's belief in 'underlying' causes, the behaviour therapist substitutes the notion of 'behavioural deficit', improvements in which constitute a successful outcome. Like the psychotherapist, the behaviour therapist is then able to maintain his traditional role as an 'agent of the patient', rather than that of an agent of society. This is of fundamental importance in understanding why behaviour therapists typically have not behaved in the criminal field as they do in the clinic, in which they deal directly with the problem of which the *patient* complains. If they were to do so in the case of offenders, their services would rarely be sought. It is possible that some offenders would like their offending behaviour altered; it is more likely that the majority would not, but would prefer to retain the responses associated with their criminal behaviours. This is not to say that offenders do not welcome the opportunity to improve their skills in reading, arithmetic or in some occupational area. It is probably preferable to be a literate than an illiterate offender. We return to this overriding problem of the social purpose of the treatment of offenders in the next chapter.

Assuming that behaviour therapists will seek to change criminal behaviours rather than to remedy educational deficits or improve behaviours within the institution, it seems important *both* to inhibit offending behaviours and to enhance alternative behaviours. Principles relevant to the effective use of negative reinforcement, drawn from reviews by Azrin and Holz (1966) and Johnston (1972), are set out below.

1. Negative reinforcements should be accurately described and measured and made variable over a wide range of values.

2. The approaching end of negative reinforcement should be clearly signalled. This argues against the use of indeterminate sentences unless constant feedback is given to the offender of his progress. Similarly, the effectiveness of t.o. is enhanced by providing ways to end t.o. such as alternative responses which are appropriately reinforced. The termination of t.o. should follow closely after the desired response is performed.

3. A very general negative reinforcement such as prison will reduce the performance of many positive and socially desirable specific behaviours as well as that of socially undesirable ones.

4. The impact of the negative reinforcement on the subject should be such as to allow no unauthorized means of attaining the positive reinforcers concerned.

5. It is necessary to distinguish between suppressing a developing mode of response and one which is well established, the latter being more difficult. Other things being equal, a given level of negative reinforcement will be more effective if applied to a first offender than to a recidivist. As noted in Chapter 9, it is usual to match a sentence to the previous history of offending, new offenders receiving mild 'punishments' to which they readily adapt. It follows that the initial severity of the negative reinforcement should be as great as is necessary to secure suppression of the undesired behaviour.

6. An increase in the rate of an undesired response following the cessation of negative reinforcement, analogous to spontaneous recovery, has been widely reported. An example would be returning to crime immediately after leaving prison. The increase in rate may be avoided if the negatively reinforced response is replaced by alternative socially acceptable responses, and by the generalization of reinforcement across a variety of situations, both of which will be

assisted by a systematic training in the internalization of social rules.

7. If no alternative response is available, the subject should have the opportunity to respond in a different situation in which the same response earns positive reinforcement rather than punishment. An example in the field of crime would be demonstrating to a skilled forger that he might earn an equally good income as a commercial artist. (This may sound easier in theory than it is in practice.)

Bandura (1973) has set out an excellent listing of principles relevant to the acquisition of *alternative* behaviours.

1. The conditions maintaining the undesired behaviour must be carefully analysed.

2. Change agents must be taught what are the changes required for successful outcome to produce a change of behaviour. (We might add that it is essential that change agents, whether in the natural environment or in a special one, are fully in agreement with the aims and methods of a behavioural programme.)

3. Alternative desirable behaviours must be demonstrated (modelled).

4. Trainers then oversee guided practice in the alternative behaviours.

5. The range of skills relevant to alternative behaviours is widened.

6. Successful outcomes of the alternative behaviours are deliberately arranged.

7. The individual concerned is given constant feedback of his performance (arranged to be successful—see 6 above) by several means, including videotape.

8. The alternative behaviours should be arranged and presented in increasing order of difficulty, increasing the likelihood that successful outcomes will indeed occur.

9. The newly trained alternative behaviours must be systematically elicited and positively reinforced in as many different contexts as possible, so as to elicit generalization across situations and time.

It is important that newly acquired behaviours not only generalize across situations and time, but become, as far as possible, independent of external control. The transition from external to internal control is best achieved by gradual steps, each step being systematically and positively reinforced. In addition, the nature of the reinforcer should also change gradually—for example, from material reward to social approval, the latter being much easier both to give and to withhold. Finally, control should be transferred from social approval to selfapproval.

At each stage, transfer from one stage to the next is made more likely if the individual verbalizes the contingencies and the behaviours involved (as described in the section in Chapter 2 dealing with Aronfreed's work). In addition, transfer is further improved by change agents demonstrating appropriate standards for the self-evaluation of the performance of alternative behaviours as well as setting out an explicit set of conduct guides, each associated with a specific reward for achieving the standard concerned. Next, the evaluation of his behaviour is transferred from the change agents to the offender himself, so that he gives positive reinforcers to himself or withholds them for unsatisfactory performance. The transfer of control from change agent to offender is assisted by role-playing (practising the alternative behaviours, avoiding previously tempting situations, etc.) and by making a public commitment to carry out alternative behaviours. Transfer is likely to be assisted also by training in covert rehearsal (see Chapter 2). Finally, it is hoped that after the offender has acquired and used new goals and standards by which to evaluate himself in his performance he will seek out new social groups with which to associate, groups whose preferred behaviours are likely to be similar to and hence support his own newly acquired ones. This will be assisted if he is trained systematically in the social skills to enter and succeed in these new social settings.

The above set of principles is perhaps easier to apply to aggressive than to other forms of criminal behaviour without the concurrent use of negative reinforcement. Whereas a non-aggressive response may well achieve the same goal at least as effectively, or even more effectively, than an aggressive one, it is much less easy to envisage alternative behaviours to theft which are as capable of yielding the same potential income. It is for this reason that a training programme which completely eschews the use of negative consequences may be less effective than one which combines carefully planned negative reinforcements for continued undesired behaviours and positive reinforcers for newly acquired desired behaviours.

Earlier, we reviewed psychotherapeutic attempts to prevent the development of offending in those predicted to be 'at risk'. Behaviour therapists have not yet made such attempts. If they were to do so they would be likely to concentrate on people in general rather than specific persons, and on designing social contexts as opposed to treatment for individuals. Such social management might include the following: ensuring that the communications media provide frequent examples of high-status social models carrying out positively reinforced pro-social behaviours, the converse being true for antisocial behaviours; considerably less publicity for successful than unsuccessful crimes; reducing the opportunities for crime by systematically training householders and business managements in crime prevention; and tightening up antifraud and anticorruption procedures in business and the public service. The above concentrates on the factors which directly instigate offending behaviours. In addition, social management programmes might seek to emphasize behaviours designed to assist actual or potential victims, drawing on the material discussed in Chapter 4 under the heading of helping behaviour. Finally, such programmes should begin in early childhood and continue throughout the adult years. This means providing opportunities for parents and teachers to learn effective social training methods and encouraging them to carry them out and, in the case of teachers, to evaluate the effectiveness of such programmes.

The behavioural training programmes discussed earlier in this chapter represent much of our current knowledge concerning how to change the criminal behaviours of those who have already offended and have been convicted, and how to maintain any changes which have occurred. Such knowledge has come largely from the application of experimental psychology to the behaviour therapy of a wide range of problem behaviours, from phobias to fetishisms. But the common factors in most such problems are that the sufferers lose much, benefit little and do not receive social support and approval for performing the problem behaviours. Most important of all, the sufferer has sought help, and is pleased when his problem behaviours cease. For the most part, criminal behaviours are damaging to their performers only if they are caught. 'Help' is not sought otherwise. Indeed, the offender may well resent and avoid attempts to change his behaviour; the more so, the more successful the offender has been.

How then are we to improve the outcome of behavioural treatments of offenders? There are three requirements. First, ensure that the technical features of the treatment programme are as satisfactory as possible. Second, accept that the target behaviour to be changed is that which led the offender into court and then into treatment—an offence against property or person. Third, as an inevitable corollary of the second, the adoption of reoffending, however indexed, as the key outcome criterion. The price of effective prevention and/or control might be a severe reduction of current personal freedoms. Thus we have now arrived at the social and ethical implications of attempts to control criminal behaviour. In the next chapter we take up some of these implications.

Chapter 11

The Social Context of Control

Legal and Determinist Views of Human Behaviour

The development of experimental psychology, which represents essentially the application of scientific method to human behaviour, has taken place only in the last 100 years, and the great bulk of that development has occurred in the last 30 years. Together with the rest of the sciences, experimental psychology is grounded on the notion that events are *determined*. In the case of human behaviour, the determining events for particular behaviours are either biological (predisposing or continuing), or environmental, or both. Certainly, humans reflect on their experiences, but the content of thought is traceable to experience; it does not arise *de novo*. Although there is disagreement as to the weight to be attached to the cognitive transformations of experience, it is reasonably safe to assert that most experimental psychologists take a broadly determinist view of man and that behaviour therapists are even more likely to do so.

In contrast, the legal view of human beings (McDonald, 1955), which is also the 'man in the street's' view, is that they have self-control and can 'choose' when to act and when not to. The implication is that an observer could not predict the behaviour of any given person, either from a knowledge of the current situation and of his previous behaviour, or of his position on a dimension, or dimensions, of personality. Thus the legal view is grounded in the notion of *free will*. However, there is an exception, namely, the mentally abnormal, who have been accorded a special, though changing, status by lawyers for many hundreds of years (see Chapter 7). According to the legal view, self-control and free will are impaired in abnormals, and self-control is linearly related to responsibility. Control is conscious in normals and unconscious in abnormals, implying the operation of different psychological principles in disease and in health.

The above is the view held by lawyers; it underpins and shapes the systems of trial and disposal of offenders. It is sharp distinction to that held by psychology, the scientific discipline which is specially concerned with behaviour. Although the law's notion of behaviour is an empirically unsupported relic, outdated by the development of the scientific study of behaviour, nevertheless it prevails, because the law is administered by those who hold that notion.

A clash of paradigms appears inevitable, indeed is already under way, as we shall see. A free-will, rather than a determinist, explanation of behaviour, except in instances of 'abnormality', is taken as a base-line by the law; the problem is then to set up rules under which 'abnormality' may be accepted as an explanation of law-breaking, or at least to ensure that a finding of guilt leads to 'treatment' rather than simple confinement. Thus a determinist approach is taken in instances which can be deemed 'abnormal'; in all other cases it is rejected. But why should determinism be restricted to *some* offenders? Casting the situation into a political framework, it is as if the law is prepared to grant primacy in certain (and relatively few) defined instances to medicine, but seeks to retain the preeminence of its own explanatory approach to behaviour in all others. However, an examination of the typical course of events concerning young persons charged with offences suggests that the lower courts frequently request a 'social report', in effect a listing of circumstances—typically, home background—which could 'explain' the offence committed. It seems that the notion of 'strain', whether residing in a social setting or in the individual himself, influences strongly the explanatory view of behaviour held by the lower courts for some offenders. The next step would be to admit that all effects have causes, that these causes may be biological predisposition, specific learning experiences and situations, or both, and that the consequences of his acts for the offender are important in maintaining criminal behaviour, as they are for all behaviours. Properly understood, a determinist view merely asserts that behaviours have causes; it does not necessarily attribute causation to any *particular* source. Thus, Skinner's emphasis on the environmental sources of behaviour is only one variety of determinism; Eysenck's view, equally determinist, asserts the importance of biological sources. (However, Skinner's behaviourism has come to be regarded as *the* psychological version of determinism.)

At present, the law is prepared to accept that criminal behaviour is determined when it can be associated with (no longer directly caused by) psychopathology. Yet the great majority of offenders do not fit the formal labels of 'psychotic', 'neurotic' or even 'psychopath'. Thus for the law to accept a determinist view of behaviour would be to result in an extension of the determinist principle to a population of offenders very many times greater than that affected by the M'Naghten test and even by the 1959 Mental Health Act. The opposition of the law to a determinist view of behaviour is powerful and almost unanimous. It is also somewhat ill-informed (for the most part; a number of American lawyers have written recent papers which indicate a considerable awareness of contemporary psychology, for example Wexler, 1973, see below). The following (Kuipers, 1974) represents a distillation of legal writings on determinism, together with the necessary corrections.

1. The abandonment of the responsibility principle might encourage a general indifference to the consequences of our actions (Jacobs, 1971). In fact, a central principle of determinism is that observed outcomes exert a major control over our future behaviour. The *attribution* of causation to

external or internal events is a subjective gloss on the *fact* of control.

2. The determinist view implies that offenders should be excused for their acts (Leiser, 1973). However, the determinist view is not 'to understand (i.e. explain) is to pardon', but 'to explain is to open up the possibilities of control'. The decision as to what consequence for the offender should follow a guilty verdict (i.e. whether control should be exerted, and if so in what form) is a socio-legal one. The psychologist's role is then to apply the expertise of his discipline to show how control might best be achieved. (Assuming both that the relevant specific knowledge exists and that he is prepared to act as an agent of social control—see later.)

3. If no-one should be punished for a bad deed, no-one should be rewarded for a good one (Leiser, 1973). As in the case of 2 above, the decision to attach consequences, punishing or otherwise, to a convicted act is a socio-legal one. The psychologist's contribution is to assert that providing this is done systematically, the probability is increased that the act will not be repeated; the exact probability will depend on the exact conditions of any positive reinforcement received for the forbidden act and the many variables relevant to the effects of punishment, as well as to the conditions under which alternative behaviours are trained. The psychologist does not make assertions about 'should' or 'should not', he simply points out that positive consequences strengthen behaviour, negative ones weaken it.

Perhaps the central point of a determinist rebuttal of the above misconceptions is that it has been empirically demonstrated that 'responsibility' (i.e. control) rests with the reinforcing stimuli (a biological determinist will add 'and/or biological variables'). It is an obvious logical fallacy to assert that if external stimuli are responsible for offending, then such behaviour is beyond the control of the legal authorities. On the contrary, determinism asserts that if the relationship between stimuli (whether internal or external) and responses is laid bare, then the behaviours concerned may be enhanced or inhibited readily as the legal or other authorities intend—given that the controlling stimuli are available for planned manipulation. That is, manipulation is technically possible; achieving it may require an extension of official control over individuals beyond that currently thought tolerable in our society. What the determinist view does imply is the removal of the concept of 'blame' as surplus. As Glueck (1962) puts it he (looks forward to the) 'twilight of futile blameworthiness and the businesslike search for likely causes (or crime) and for effective therapies' (p. 147). The determinist approach to the role of the court is well expressed by the memorandum to the Butler Committee of the British Psychological Society (Black *et al.*, 1973). It asserts that the function of the court is '(a) to assess if the accused committed the offence; (b) whether the public needs protection from him and (c) if so, what steps could be taken to reduce the likelihood of a recurrence of the offence' (p. 340).

The determinist/behaviourist approach to the control of criminal behaviour raises for its proponents three major problems. The first, which will be discussed in more detail shortly, arises when treatment programmes designed on broadly behaviourist lines conflict with separately decided civil rights. If civil rights considerations lead to the rejection of a behaviourist approach this does not, however, mean that the prisoner's behaviour is now 'free'—it is still controlled, but by an *unplanned* set of contingencies. Behaviour therapists, as do others working with 'patients' or 'clients', often obtain written consent from those seeking help. The consent system has been extended to prisoners. However, a self-consistent behaviourist approach should not take refuge in the doctrine of 'informed consent'—'consent' is itself a behavioural response determined by antecedent events and anticipated consequences. Hence it is *manipulable* both by attitude change methods and by giving the prisoner access to re-inforcers which remind him of the benefits of non-criminal behaviour—such as contacts with family and friends. (Parenthetically, it should be noted that there is an important difference between environmental manipulation and certain biological manipulations. For example, psychosurgery which has been used with the intent of controlling criminal behaviour, and has been powerfully attacked on ethical grounds, is inevitably *irreversible* because excised brain tissue cannot be replaced. In contrast, environmental control is completely reversible, indeed reversibility is one of the classical ways of demonstrating control by environmental manipulation.)

The second problem is essentially opposite in nature. Civil rights problems arise most severely when a behavioural control method is *effective*. If it is ineffective its use is likely to be temporary at the most. In contrast, what is the consequence for the determinist if *no* method of manipulation is shown to be effective? The determinist view is that treatment is only relevant if it effectively changes behaviour. But should offenders beyond change, and likely to reoffend, be released? The determinist, as citizen, would have to say no (but see the discussion in Chapter 9 based on Clarke, 1974, which cast doubt on the link between incarceration and a reduction in crime). The legal view is that imprisonment for 'incorrigibles' should be lengthy enough to protect society for a considerable period of time, but in most cases this falls short of a sentence for the whole of the individual's life. Indeterminate sentences are also disliked by civil rights protagonists.

A third problem for the behaviourist arises from the distinction between control after an offence and deterrence (prevention) in advance. Even if a particular behavioural method is effective with convicted offenders, does it exert a deterrent effect on those who have not yet offended? It is likely to do so only if it is both unpleasant *and* the probability of detection and conviction are both high. Yet 'unpleasantness' has no value as an end in itself in the context of changing the behaviour of convicted offenders. The most effective method may also be 'pleasant'—for example, the acquisition of useful alternative behaviours with a high probability of positive reinforcement for their performance. As we noted in Chapter 10, a psychological contribution to the deterrence of potential offenders (i.e. in addition to any increase in the efficacy and efficiency of control procedures applied to corrected offenders) will reside largely in the training procedures psychologists can offer to parents and teachers and to the system of rules which organizations of adults exert on their members.

Treatments are not either entirely effective or ineffective, but at some intermediate level of efficacy. What degree of difference in efficacy will persuade the penal authorities to replace conventional penal methods by a behavioural approach? (Because efficacy is likely to vary according to particular attributes of offenders, a predictive exercise will be necessary; further methods will need to be derived for those found not to respond to a particular behavioural approach.) The evaluation of comparative efficacy must also take it into account, as mentioned above, that a behavioural approach to the control of convicted offenders, which does not involve punishment, may well have a lesser deterrent effect on potential offenders than a conventional penal method which does, despite being more effective than the conventional method in reducing reoffending.

It is essential that behavioural approaches are used only if they are significantly *more* effective than conventional methods. Unless this requirement is met, behaviourally treated offenders may find themselves in the same unsatisfactory situation as those currently defined as 'abnormal' and 'treated' in non-prison settings—their treatments are largely ineffective, their length of stay frequently indefinite and their settings often as restrictive and depriving as prisons. Indeed, it may be that the deprivations suffered by 'patients' are actually more severe than are those experienced by 'prisoners'.

Psychological Approaches to Control: Civil Rights Criticisms

A major emphasis by psychologists and psychiatrists interested in criminal behaviour has been to regard such behaviour as indicating psychological disturbance. This has led to attempts to prevent the onset of criminal behaviour by 'treating' the individual in advance of the occurrence of the criminal behaviour. In Chapter 10 we reviewed a number of such attempts, which usually employed psychotherapy, and concluded that they had been rather unsuccessful. Can we conclude that attempts at prevention should, therefore, be abandoned, on grounds of inefficacy? Before doing so it is as well to consider the ethical arguments in favour of the preventive approach. If they are found cogent, the outcome may be a continued search for more effective methods, for example of a behavioural nature, rather than giving up the attempt. As summarized by Silber (1974), the arguments in favour of detecting the 'delinquency-prone' in advance are as follows: (1) it enables informal, civil, non-adversary proceedings to replace the formal adversary nature of a criminal trial; (2) it substitutes an indefinite sentence, during which treatment is given, for a definite sentence without treatment; (3) treatment would emphasize forming positive and supportive human relationships and thus provide a valuable social training as well as avoiding future damage to the potential offender. In rebuttal, Silber lists a number of equally persuasive arguments: (1) informal civil proceedings jeopardize a person's legal rights to counsel, to time to prepare a defence, to a specified indictment, and so on; (2) civil committment for an indefinite period is a judgment against the person, not against the act, and is a step towards a totalitarian society; (3) once a person is committed for 'treatment' normal civil liberties tend to be lost.

From the point of view of behaviourist psychology there is a very powerful objection to the preventive approach being applied to *specific*, *designated* individuals. This is that *all persons* are likely to offend, or not to offend, depending on the total set of experiences to which they are exposed. Thus the acquisition of criminal behaviour may be prevented as follows. First, ensure for people in general appropriate positive and negative learning experiences concerning generally agreed pro- and antisocial behaviours. Second, arrange social settings so that, for example, in situations in which offending behaviour might occur, the level of visible temptation is as low as possible, the chance of perceived detection is as high as possible and pro-social behaviours are positively reinforced. It may be (see Chapter 6) that, other things being equal, certain individuals are predisposed to be more socially influenceable than others, so that if the prevailing influences favour criminal behaviour, such individuals have a higher probability than others of acquiring criminal behaviours. But the most effective method with relatively predisposed persons, as with others, is to ensure that the social influences to which *all* members of a society are exposed are unfavourable to criminal behaviour.

Of course, once criminal behaviour has occurred and has been rewarded, the probability of *that* individual offending again is increased, as compared with a person who has not yet offended at all. At that point, treatment by behaviour control, if felt desirable in general, is applied to that particular individual and to his fellow offenders, to prevent reoccurrence. Such an approach both is consistent with well-established behavioural principles and does not disturb the general requirement that a person is judged innocent until he has been found guilty (i.e. he has actually carried out an offence).

However, the argument concerning the loss of civil rights by persons in treatment is still not disposed of. Even if we confine change programmes to those who have offended and have been found guilty, their civil rights are also placed in jeopardy. The problem has been very well discussed by Wexler (1973), a lawyer but very much at home with behaviourist concepts, in the context of token economy programmes for institutionalized psychotic patients. It applies with equal force to the civil rights of confined offenders. The key feature of token economies is that they involve the receipt of positive reinforcers for designated approved behaviours.

However, the American case of *Wyatt v Stickney* has made it clear that American law will not tolerate the use of forced patient labour devoid of demonstrable therapeutic purpose. The decision in *Wyatt v Stickney*, widely used in America as a precedent, barred privileges or release from hospital being conditional on the performance of labour involving hospital maintenance. This means that the receipt of basic reinforcers cannot be made contingent on appropriate behaviours. The consequence from the viewpoint of behaviour modification ... 'is that the items and activities that are emerging as absolute rights are the very same items and activities that behavioural psychologists would employ as reinforcers—that is as "contingent rights"' (Wexler, 1973, pp. 11–12). The force of the above statement derives from the *Wyatt* definition of minimum rights in terms of specific physical and recreational facilities. Thus 'the major problem faced by the token economy is the current trend towards an *expansion* of the category of protected inmate interests' (Wexler, 1973, p. 17). According to Wexler, one possible answer to the problem is to seek individualized behaviour modification programmes which would utilize as reinforcers items and activities over and above those defined by *Wyatt* as minimum absolute rights. Such items and activities would be peculiar to individuals; examples include perusing mail-order catalogues, being served soft instead of hard-boiled eggs, and feeding kittens. However, Wexler misses the point of the real force of the *Wyatt* decision. *Any* reinforcer, however idiosyncratic, may be argued to be a basic right for that particular individual and thus debarred from use in a programme of behaviour modification. It seems preferable to use as reinforcers tokens exchangeable for monies which can then be used to purchase any desired reinforcer.

Wexler goes on to point out that token economy programmes, while effective in promoting socially desired behaviours within hospitals, have been less effective in transferring generalized coping behaviours to the outside world after discharge. Treatment programmes are desirable which not only stress positive training and involve no deprivation of basic rights but in addition successfully overcome the transfer problem. As an example of such a programme Wexler cites work by Fairweather *et al.* (1969), which was based on the reasonable assumption that on discharge long-stay psychotic patients would benefit if they could exercise problem-solving and decision-making skills. To achieve this, prior to discharge, small cohesive groups of patients were established, which effectively controlled the activities of their members. A step-wise progression in the achievement of relevant skills was rewarded by money and pass privileges for individuals; the group as a whole was also rewarded or demoted for general progress. The results, which were very good as indicated by post-discharge employment and community adjustment, were achieved without the deprivation of basic reinforcers. We might note also that Fairweather *et al.* sought to identify the relevant broad classes of behaviours which patients would require and then systematically trained them in their acquisition.

Above, we discussed criticisms of behavioural methods which made the receipt of basic positive reinforcers contingent on certain behaviours, rather than regarding them as rights. Severe criticism has also been expressed of the explicit use of aversive stimuli in the application of punishment paradigms to modification procedures. *Time* (1974) gave a graphic description. 'The convicted child molester in Connecticut state prison at Somers reclines on a treatment table with an electrode wired to his upper thigh. Whenever pictures of naked children are flashed on a screen, he gets stinging shocks in his groin.' As a further example of the use of aversive stimuli, *Time* stated 'At the Iowa Security Medical Faculty, inmates who commit infractions like lying or swearing are given a shot of apomorphine, which brings on violent vomiting for 15 minutes or more' (p. 42). Here attention is focused on *means* rather than *ends*. It reminds us that ethical debates include both components.

There is no mistaking the considerable public unease evoked by the programmed control of prisoners, both in Britain and the USA. Such programmes, though publicly associated with behavioural methods, are sometimes very poorly conceived and even contrary to the actual findings of experimental psychology. For example, public attention in Britain was drawn, during October 1974, to the existence in Wakefield Prison of 'control units' for particularly troublesome prisoners. As described by the *Sunday Times* (1974), prisoners are confined alone for 90 days, are required to work effectively and to behave well. Misbehaviours, including stopping work, breaking objects and shouting at prison officers, are punished by beginning again the 90-day period of solitary confinement. Successfully completing the period qualifies the prisoners for phase 2, a further 90 days which are less arduous. Nevertheless, misbehaviour during phase 2 results in beginning phase 1 all over again. From the legal rights point of view the system is unsatisfactory—allocation to it cannot be appealed against and there is no access to the prisoner by boards of visitors who normally adjudicate on most serious prison offences. 'It is possible therefore for a prisoner to remain in phase 1 for a more or less indefinite period and without access to an independent authority' (*Sunday Times*, 1974, p. 1). Psychologists, as well as expressing concern at the diminution of legal rights, would criticize the system as bad psychology. During phase 1 'good' behaviours go unrewarded until the 90 days have elapsed; there are no intermediate rewards to maintain and strengthen a desired behaviour. Moreover, the whole context of phase 1 militates against 'good' behaviour and increases the probability of 'bad' behaviour. Phase 1 is not dissimilar to the partial sensory deprivation situation, in which there is a reduction both of the level of stimulation and of the variability of stimulation. A typical finding of sensory deprivation research is that subjects behave so as to increase whatever source of stimulation they are allowed access to, even when this is as minimal as a lever which may be pressed (Schultze, 1965). In phase 1, about the only way to vary the stimulation is to behave 'badly', resulting in a visit from the prison officer and a return to day 1. This is analogous to the situation in a ward for the severely retarded. The attention of nurses is given only when bizarre behaviours such as head-banging occur, thus reinforcing head-banging behaviour. Non-bizarre behaviour does not attract attention and so is not reinforced.

Several American prisons have instituted behaviour modification programmes under the general heading of START (Special Treatment and Rehabilitative Training), 'a standard step movement program with three levels or privileges. A higher level could only be reached after a prisoner's minutely monitored behaviour at the previous level passed muster' (*Time*, 1974, p. 43).

The account in *Time* also described how prisoners participating in a number of such programmes had filed suit against further participation with the help of the American Civil Liberties Union Foundation. According to *Time*, an official of the ACLU estimated that some form of behaviour modification is in use in 20 states. *Time* concluded with a reference to the Colorado Closed Adolescent Treatment Center (CAT) for 'incorrigible adolescents', who 'run their own behaviour modification programme, with adult guidance', which has worked so well that the participants are loth to leave. This raises two important points. The first is of relevance to the general problem of changing behaviour in an environment other than the natural environment of the person concerned. The institutional environment may become seen as so pleasant (in behavioural language, the source of many highly valued reinforcers) that a return to the outside world is perceived as aversive. The great importance of generalization is once more emphasized. The second point goes to the heart of the ethical dilemma of the change agent. *Time* wrote approvingly of the CAT project because the *inmates* as well as the authorities of the institution and the general public are all perceived to benefit. The issue of *cui bono* (to whom good?) is likely to become the central one in the debate over the ethics of change. It seems that the liberal section of Western society is agreed that 'manipulation' is permissible only if the manipulated persons, as well as society in general, benefit.

An attack of a somewhat different kind has been made by Kimbles (1973), who asserts that for blacks antisocial behaviour represents the only available social protest against 'the oppressive reality of their lives in the ghetto'. Control and manipulation by behaviour modification runs counter to the black's life-style and does much harm because it encourages him to continue avoiding responsibility for his own actions. It also confirms the belief of the black that he is worthless and without power. Behaviour modification is unlikely to give the black what he needs—'the experience of self worth and value in the presence of caring others'. Finally, it alienates the black from his environment— a context in which antisocial behaviour is adaptive. Kimble's first point represents a misunderstanding. Behaviour modification procedures are simply methods for the acquisition or change of behaviours, which can include coping strategies and skills of all kinds, thus increasing the individual's subjective sense of control over his environment. His second point is well taken. A general political and economic programme to better the lives of all dwellers in the inner areas of cities is required. Behaviour modification methods might be an important part of such a general plan of action, and may even be crucial to its success. For example, American Head Start and British Educational Priority Area programmes stand or fall not only by the amount of money invested in them, but by the care with which target behaviours are identified and systematic approaches to achieve them put into effect.

In Britain, Holden (1965) has sharply criticized the use of aversion therapy for the treatment of offenders, addressing his remarks particularly to physicians whose function he argued is to relieve the suffering of those who 'want help'.

Doctors, he asserts, should not be the moral arbiters or agents of society. In doing so he echoes Wootton (1963): 'The doctor ... who undertakes the psychiatric treatment of offenders is not quite like a doctor, even a psychiatrist ... he has in effect become an agent of the State—part of the machinery of law enforcement'. She continues: 'If the profession is to assume what are essentially corrective rather than therapeutic functions, it is surely important that this should be done openly, and not by any specious pretence that the two categories are indistinguishable' (p. 200).

The argument applies with particular force to the increasing Russian practice of giving psychiatric diagnoses, such as 'paranoid schizophrenia', to distinguished political dissidents, instead of their earlier practice of imprisonment or excution. The diagnoses are assigned to the dissident concerned by qualified psychiatrists who are thus acting as 'agents of the state'. (It is not necessary to argue at length the view that reasoned political disagreement hardly qualifies for the label 'paranoid schizophrenia'. If that were the case, large numbers of the population of the Western countries would receive the label at an election in which their side was defeated, unless they were prepared to reverse their stand, losing it once again as their own party returned to power.) The suppression of rationally expressed political opposition is unsatisfactory enough; even more so is its apparent legitimization by psychiatrists. Thus runs the classical liberal view, which would, in addition, draw a clear distinction between the right of the state to suppress political dissent and to control conventional criminal behaviour. However, radical sociologists are beginning to argue that the confinement of offenders is also in the nature of a political act. They see it as likely that prisoners will begin to define their situation in political terms (Cohen and Taylor, 1972).

Whose side are we on: The Goals of Research and Control

Thus far we have been concerned with the ethics of applying methods to the control of criminal behaviour which are derived from research findings concerning the explanation of behaviour in general. A more basic ethical problem is raised by a paper by Becker (1967), entitled 'Whose side are we on?'. Becker argues that sociological research is inevitably contaminated by sympathy for one side or the other. Traditionally, research workers have been implicitly 'on the side of' the official power structure, but increasingly the causes of such 'deviant' groups as drug-takers and homosexuals are being taken up by sociologists. Certain prisoners are also attracting active sympathy. Cohen and Taylor (1972), taking up Becker's point, argue that criminological research which is not sympathetic to the deviant group must be sympathetic to the official side. They continue, 'a principal function of official research into crime and punishment is to reassure the public that the problem is being scientifically tackled' (p. 25), and assert that the most desirable attribute of officially sponsored research is its high WDP (window-dressing potential). A high WDP is achieved by research aims which are comprehensible to most politicians and administrators and are presented in a simple and direct way, but whose results are ambiguous and generate statements of the type 'more research is needed'. Cohen and Taylor (1972) characterized their own research stance as follows, 'we haven't simply played the role of detached seekers after information'. Moreover, they 'abandoned the idea of correction and instead (sought to) empathize and comprehend'.

It is true that criminological research is inevitably action research in the sense that its results may influence practical social policy. It is also true that the sympathies of criminological researchers will be engaged. But it is not necessarily an either/or situation, with the choice of 'sympathy' one between offenders and officialdom. There is a third party, namely, the victims of offences. Moreover, the word is not divisible into *permanent* offenders and *permanent* victims. It is possible that the same research worker may at one and the same time feel a sympathy for the offender confined in an unpleasant setting and for the suffering of what offender's victims. In addition, it is possible for the research worker to perceive the current offender as someone who may previously have been a victim and may be one again. Similarly, the current victim may have offended and may do so again. The researcher himself is likely to have been both offender and victim. The third choice open to him is to support the view that, other things being equal, actions which reduce offending *behaviour* are more desirable than actions which increase it or leave it unchanged. ('Other things being equal' include agreeing with the designation of a particular behaviour as being illegal—i.e. socially undesirable—as well as that it is not the more or less inevitable consequence of an intolerable social setting.)

Provided that the researcher has acquired a strong attachment to the desirability of research which both asks important questions and tackles them in methodologically satisfactory ways, criminological research, though much more difficult than research on (for example) perceptual illusions carried out in a laboratory, may produce results which are as reliable and as valid. The point is that criminological research is more difficult; therefore, it requires *more* rigour, not less, as Cohen and Taylor seem to assert. This is as true of research into the causes and control of crime as of research into the causes and treatment of psychological problems from which the individual himself suffers. Psychological distress is distressing to the onlooker; his desire to help is strong. Apparently effective treatment must be questioned with great care—otherwise distress will be all the greater when an initial promise proves fruitless. The social and personal distress caused by offending behaviour is also great. Many researchers will feel moved by the victims of theft and fraud. But once again, methods of control must be developed and evaluated with great care. The radical sociologist might be able to agree with this argument to some extent, but at this point he will ask the researcher to relate the control of crime to the causes of crime. What if those causes arise from living in a social setting in which crime is the only possible alternative to a miserable and distressing existence? As mentioned above, the point is well taken. Such social conditions undoubtedly exist, but theories of social distress do not account for the fact that crime has increased while the average real income has increased.

How helpful is the assertion (see Chapter 8) that the latent function of deviance is political in deciding the desirability of professional involvement in criminal research and control? When the deviance concerned is in fact political, in the usual sense of the term, or is 'victimless', then the assertion may be a helpful guide to action. However, it seems much less useful when the deviance concerns crimes against persons or property. It is very difficult to envisage any political change in Western society which would shift such crimes from a deviant to a non-deviant status. The problem for psychologists, psychiatrists and others is thus laid bare. It is whether or not to apply their professional skills to control criminal behaviours of a basically non-political nature in which there is undeniably a victim or victims, however remote. It has to be admitted that no hard- and-fast guides to action can be derived from either the findings of experimental psychology which, like the rest of science, are concerned with methods, not objectives, or from the existing professional practices of clinical psychologists. These may be summarized as follows: we work, usually, with persons who have sought help for distress which they themselves suffer; the objectives of therapy are set by the client, and the expertise of the psychologist is relevant both in assisting clients to work out the objectives they seek and in devising the means to achieve them. The consequence of a successful outcome of therapy (and 'success' is defined by the client) is that the *client* benefits. As argued earlier, the 'strain' theories, whether of the individual or of society, do not fit more than a small minority of offenders; the majority is accountable for by the same principles of behaviour as fit socially acceptable behviour. In brief, crime is under the control of its consequences. Thus, instead of reforming society or helping the distressed offender, the task of the psychologist, if taken on, is to assist the offended against *society* to achieve *its* ends of reducing future criminal behaviour by convicted offenders; perhaps even to devise and apply social training systems which will reduce the probability of offending by those who have not yet done so.

The problem of whether psychologists should involve themselves in these purposes, and if so to what extent and in respect of what offences, has been discussed at length by Robinson (1974). He has tried to set out principles to guide treatment aimed at *non-consenting* persons or those not able to give informed consent. (It was pointed out earlier that to the behaviourist 'consent' is itself a potentially manipulable behaviour.) In doing so he assumes that some form of coercion is inescapable in a free society and argues forcibly that it is only in cases involving the principle of 'private harm' (Feinberg, 1973) that coercive intervention is justified. Robinson gives attempted suicide as an example of private harm. He specifically excludes intervention under the principle of 'public harm', as an example of which he mentions the disclosure of state secrets. (However, it can be assumed that public harm would also include theft and assault.) 'Behavioural and medical scientists have no role in arbitrating the competing claims between individuals and society in general. Our charge is to inform, not to transform, our fellow citizens, unless they seek such help with the full knowledge of the consequences attending those receiving it—...

Practitioners must exercise informed restraint . . . this . . . should begin with the refusal to administer compulsory therapy in all cases not embraced by the principle of *private harm*. Even in these cases there are limits to involuntary therapeutic intervention. These . . . are best established by balancing the potential harm of treatment against the real damages contained in the courts' sentence' (Robinson, 1974, p. 238). He is arguing for an extension of the traditional role of the therapist only to those individuals who damage themselves but seem to be unware of doing so. Robinson thus specifically excludes an involvement in the control of crimes against property and persons. Yet psychologists already are concerned in such work, as witness the many reports cited in Chapter 10. It has been argued that the way in which they are involved, typically training skills judged beneficial to the offender, implies that they still perceive their role as the agent of the patient, not of society, yet society evaluates their work in terms of reconvictions, i.e. of benefit to society.

It is difficult to escape the conclusion that if psychologists involved in work with offenders do indeed benefit those offenders, such benefit is going to be judged by society as a secondary contribution to the major goal of intervention —the benefit of future potential victims. It is true that *both* offenders and potential victims may benefit, so that the demands of the traditional role of therapists and of society's requirements are satisfied equally. But what if the most effective means to secure society's ends involve no gain to the offender? Indeed, if he is deprived, through treatment, of those responses in his total repertoire which are relevant solely or largely to criminal ends, he may actually lose. In the long run, all those concerned in correctional work with offenders will have to face the question of *cui bono*—to whom good? If both offenders and society gain, then the ethical struggle is easier than if only society gains. This ethical dilemma is of major importance. How it is resolved will determine the questions asked and the ways in which they are answered in a major area of applied psychology, namely, the explanation and control of criminal behaviour.

Perhaps the most haunting implication of continued research into the control of criminal behaviour is this. Even granted that it is socially desirable to help those who may be assaulted or robbed by controlling such behaviours, what do we feel about the possibility of applying techniques developed for that purpose to persons whose only offence is to question the established political system and who cast their questions solely in non-violent forms? Some psychologists might feel comfortable about applying behavioural methods to those convicted of theft or assault. But most, if not all, would be very opposed to applying them to a British or American equivalent of Solzhenitsyn. Such opposition might be so great as to sharply restrict the application to offenders of behavioural methods of control and of research into such methods. Another key question concerns the right of the convicted person to refuse treatment but instead to opt for a penal sentence, perhaps imprisonment for a defined period of time, with clear safeguards such as access to a visiting tribunal. For those prisoners who agree to treatment, what should be their rights in respect of selection of goals and methods as compared to the rights of the general public to be protected by effective methods and goals relevant to the proscribed behaviours? I have argued elsewhere (Feldman, 1976b) that in general clients seeking help for their own problems should have the overriding choice as to methods and goals (minors and the severely handicapped raise special difficulties). Should we apply this rubric to those whose behaviour is, in most instances, at least as damaging to others as it is to themselves? In the case of offenders the person seeking the services of the psychologist is often not the person who will receive treatment, but a magistrate or judge acting on behalf of potential victims. In short, in the case of psychological problems, client and sufferer are usually one and the same person; in the case of criminal behaviours, they will often be different people.

It is not only psychologists and psychiatrists who must ask themselves such questions; the debate must involve all the professions involved in the legal process, the elected representatives of the public and the public themselves, all of whom are potential offenders as well as potential victims.

Chapter 12

Concluding Statement

As well as reviewing progress to date, this book has attempted to provide a framework for further studies into the description, explanation and control of criminal behaviour. The framework has three aspects: learning, individual predisposition and social reaction (labelling). All three components of the framework are relevant both to offences against the person and against property. The first component is the most important influence for the majority of instances of offending behaviour, but for some persons, at the extreme of the major dimensions of personality, or suffering from particular psychological problems, predisposition is of considerable importance. In addition, for some persons who exemplify the prevailing stereotype of the 'offender', social labelling is a considerable influence. But whereas learning variables exert their effects at all stages—the acquisition, performance and maintenance of criminal behaviour—predisposition has more effect on acquisition and labelling on maintenance than on the other stages.

The learning component of the framework has two broad subsections: learning not to offend—due to training in socially acceptable behaviours, maintained by negative consequences for infractions and positive ones for rule-keeping; learning to offend, maintained by positive consequences for offending, even when these are interspersed with negative ones, because of the powerful maintaining effects of intermittent reinforcement. Laboratory-derived analogies provide useful information and refine variables which should now influence the design of field studies. Of particular interest will be the reward–cost approach to the performance of crime, particularly when this takes into account the interactions with previous outcomes. It is emphasized throughout as a central concept that behaviour is maintained or inhibited by its consequences. This aspect should also inform reward–cost studies.

We have also suggested that cognitive processes are relevant to the maintenance or change of behaviour. This is likely to be important both in the offence-related and the victim-related aspects of criminal behaviour. The mechanisms of cognitive dissonance reduction help to reduce self-perceived discrepancies between previous and present behaviours, as these concern both offences and victims, and we have particularly emphasized that distorting the extent of aversive consequences for victims assists in maintaining both criminal behaviour by offenders and failure to intervene by onlookers. Another important 'cognitive' process is that some people may have developed, following appropriately rewarded external behaviours, a self-reinforcement system which includes self-approval for attaining certain standards of performance of successful criminal acts, and thus helps to maintain such behaviours.

So much for environmental variations which relate to the acquisition, performance and maintenance of victim-related behaviour by offenders and onlookers. A complete account of criminal behaviour would have to include the possibility that certain broad social situations—for example, membership of a particular class or culture, or living in a particular geographical area— might effect the probabilities of acquiring and performing criminal behaviours, and of such behaviours being maintained or reduced. While this is correct, it remains the case that the processes and variables involved are the same, irrespective of the particular setting. However, certain settings may lead to a greater consistency of behaviour than others, so that the differences between settings become relevant to the next stage of a research enquiry into both offence-related and victim-related aspects of criminal behaviour. This will arise if certain individuals are indeed more consistent than others in the performance, or lack of performance, of criminal behaviours. The first explanatory candidate is the outcome of earlier experiences. The second candidate, which we discussed in the chapter on personality, is a predisposition to respond differently to learning experiences relevant to criminal behaviour, due to variations in the response either to experiences *unfavourable* to offending, or to experiences *favourable* to offending, or both. We pointed out that account must be taken of possible interactions between type of learning experience and 'personality' dimensions, so that a relative lack of success in avoidance training may be due to a less than optimal match between the technique used and the relevant attributes of the person to whom it is applied. However, we suggested that what appeared to be genetically based predispositions are likely to assist more in accounting for the behaviour of the relatively consistent minority than that of the relatively inconsistent majority. Moreover, genetic predisposition and environment will be found to interact in complex ways, so that relatively small initial differences may be enhanced greatly by differential social shaping. For example, current adult sex differences in behaviour may be much greater than if both males and females had received the same social training. Similarly, the labels 'outgoing' (extravert) and 'shy' (introvert) may lead to sharply different social responses, the performance of extraverted behaviours by the former being attended to and thereby enhanced, that by the latter being ignored and thus weakened. Of the three personality dimensions we discussed, it is the P dimension which appears most potentially relevant to the victim-related aspects of crime. It may be that individuals vary in their probability of acquiring responses which limit aversive consequences, either to their own victims or to those of others. Once again, of course, this is the last stage of any such enquiry; only when we have demonstrated consistency in victim-related behaviour and failed to account for it in terms of consistency of experience will we turn to an explanation involving genetically based individual predispositions.

The third component of the framework, labelling theory, helps to account for the apparent excess in the official statistics of certain groups as compared with the population at large. It points to the important role of the social reactions of those in positions of power within the law-enforcement and penal systems in maintaining, perhaps even enhancing, the criminal behaviour of over-represented groups. This is not to deny that there may be a genuine excess in the ranks of offenders, for example of young males, simply that the excess is exaggerated by social response. Conversely, other social groups are under-represented: the same process of social reaction, by labelling them in *advance* as law-abiding, may lead to an official response to a criminal act of inattention, rather than attention, thus reducing the probability of the offender concerned proceeding to the stage of imprisonment and criminalization.

Our conclusion concerning explanation is that learning, genetically based predispositions and social labelling all have a part to play; they are complementary, not mutually exclusive.

A discussion of current penal methods concluded, inevitably, that they are largely, or entirely, ineffective and may even increase, through exposure to the criminogenic settings of prison, the extent of criminal behaviour. Considerations both of efficacy and efficiency and of humanity must inform any control attempts, arguments which underlay a review of psychological approaches to control. Neither psychotherapeutic nor behavioural methods can claim great success to date, although the latter appear more promising, particularly if behaviour therapists direct their attention to criminal behaviours *per se*, rather than to educational deficits or unsatisfactory institutional behaviour—hence the potential importance, despite the difficulties, of retraining in the natural environment. This led to the key questions of ethical and social objectives and restraints in the control of criminal behaviour. No conclusions were reached, except that it is of major social importance both that the questions raised be discussed and that the discussion is joined by all interested parties, including the general public, and not merely by those professionally concerned.

References

Adams, J. S. 'Towards an understanding of inequity', *Journal of Abnormal and Social Psychology*, **67**, 422 (1963).

Adams, R., and Vetter, H. J. 'Probation case-load size and recidivism rate', *British Journal of Criminology*, **11**, 390 (1971).

Adams, S. 'The PICO Project', In N. Johnston, L. Savitz and M. E. Wolfgang (Eds.), *The Sociology of Punishment and Correction*, New York, Wiley, 1962, pp. 213–24.

Aderman, D., and Berkowitz, L. 'Observational set, empathy and helping', *Journal of Personality and Social Psychology*, **14**, 141 (1970).

Adorno, T. W., Frenkel-Brunswik, E., Levinson, D. J., and Sanford, R. N. *The Authoritarian Personality*, New York, Harper, 1950.

Alker, H. A. 'Is personality situationally specific or intra-psychically consistent?', *Journal of Personality*, **40**, 1 (1972).

Allsopp, J. F. 'Extraversion, neuroticism, sensation-seeking and anti-social behaviour in rewards and controls as measured by self-report', Unpublished undergraduate dissertation, Department of Psychology, University of Birmingham, 1968.

Allsopp, J. F., and Feldman, M. P. 'Extraversion, neuroticism and psychoticism and anti-social behaviour in school girls', *Social Behaviour and Personality*, **2**, 184 (1975).

Allsopp, J. F., and Feldman, M. P. 'Item analyses of questionnaire measures of personality and anti-social behaviour in school', *British Journal of Criminology* (In press).

Amir, M. *Patterns in Forcible Rape*, Chicago, University of Chicago Press, 1972.

Amsel, A. 'Drive properties of the anticipation of frustration', *Psychological Bulletin*, **55**, 102 (1968).

Amsel, A. 'Frustrative nonreward in partial reinforcement and discrimination learning. Some recent history and a theoretical extension', *Psychological Review*, **69**, 306 (1962).

Anthony, H. Sylvia. 'Association between psychotic behaviour and delinquency', *Nature*, **183**, 343 (1959).

Archer, J. 'Sex differences in emotional behaviour: a reply to Gray and Buffery', *Acta Psychologica*, **35**, 415 (1971).

Aronfreed, J. 'The nature, variety and social patterning of moral responses to transgression', *Journal of Abnormal and Social Psychology*, **63**, 223 (1961).

Aronfreed, J. 'The effects of experimental socialization paradigms upon the moral responses to transgression', *Journal of Abnormal and Social Psychology*, **66**, 437 (1963).

Aronfreed, J. 'The origin of self-criticism', *Psychological Review*, **71**, 193 (1964).

Aronfreed, J. 'The internalization of social control through punishment: Experimental studies of the role of conditioning and the second signal system in the development of conscience', *Proceedings of the Eighteenth International Congress of Psychology*, Moscow, 1966.

Aronfreed, J. *Conduct and Conscience*, New York, Academic Press, 1968.

Aronfreed, J., Cutick, R. A., and Fagan, S. A. 'Cognitive structure, punishment and nurturance in the experimental induction of self-criticism', *Child Development*, **34**, 281 (1963).

Aronfreed, J., and Reber, A. 'Internalised behavioural suppression and the timing of social punishment', *Journal of Personality and Social Psychology*, **1**, 3 (1965).

Aronson, E., and Mettee, D. R. 'Dishonest behaviour as a function of differential levels of induced self-esteem', *Journal of Personality and Social Psychology*, **9**, 121 (1968).

Ayllon, T., and Azrin, N. *The Token Economy*, New York, Appleton-Century, 1968.

Azrin, N. H. 'Some effects of the intermittent schedules of immediate and non-immediate punishment', *Journal of Psychology*, **42**, 3 (1956).

Azrin, N. H., and Holz, W. C. 'Punishment', In W. K. Honig (Ed.), *Operant Behaviour*, New York, Appleton-Century-Crofts, 1966.

Azrin, N. H., and Wesolowski, M. D. 'Theft reversal: an overcorrection procedure for eliminating stealing by retarded persons', *Journal of Applied Behaviour Analysis*, **17**, 577 (1974).

Bacon, Margaret K., Child, I. L., and Barry, L. H. 'A cross-cultural study of correlates of crime', *Journal of Abnormal and Social Psychology*, **66**, 291 (1963).

Baer, D. M., Wolf, M. M., and Risley, T. R. 'Some current dimensions of applied behaviour analysis', *Journal of Applied Behaviour Analysis*, **1**, 91 (1968).

Bailey, J. S., Timbers, G. D., Phillips, E. L., and Wolf, M. W. 'Modification of articulation errors of pre-delinquents by their peers', *Journal of Applied Behaviour Analysis*, **4**, 265 (1971).

Bailey, J. S., Wolf, M. W., and Philips, E. L. 'Home-based reinforcement and the modifications of pre-delinquent classroom behaviour', *Journal of Applied Beaviour Analysis*, **3**, 223 (1970).

Bandura, A. 'Relationship of family patterns to child behaviour disorders', Progress Report 1960, Stanford University, Project No. M-1734, United States Public Health Service (1960).

Bandura, A. 'Influence of model's reinforcement contingencies on the acquisition of imitative responses', *Journal of Personality and Social Psychology*, **1**, 589–595, (1965).

Bandura, A. *Principles of Behaviour Modification*, New York, Holt, Rhinehart & Winston, 1969.

Bandura, A. *Aggression: A Social Learning Analysis*, New York, Prentice-Hall, 1973.

Bandura, A., and Jeffery, R. W. 'Role of symbolic coding and rehearsal processes in observational learning', *Journal of Personality and Social Psychology*, **26**, 122 (1973).

Bandura, A., and McDonald, F. J. 'The influence of social reinforcement and the behaviour of models in shaping children's moral judgements', *Journal of Abnormal Psychology*, **67**, 274 (1963).

Bandura, A., and Mischel, W. 'Modification of self imposed delay of reward through exposure to live and symbolic models', *Journal of Personality and Social Psychology*, **2**, 698 (1965).

Bandura, A., and Rosenthal, T. L. 'Vicarious classical conditioning as a function of arousal level', *Journal of Personality and Social Psychology*, **3**, 54 (1966).

Bandura, A., Ross, D., and Ross, S. A. 'Vicarious reinforcement and imitative learning', *Journal of Abnormal and Social Psychology*, **67**, 601 (1963).

Bandura, A., and Walters, R. H. *Adolescent Aggression*, New York, Ronald Press, 1959.

Bandura, A., and Walters, R. H. *Social Learning and Personality Development*, New York, Holt, Rhinehart & Winston, 1963.

Bannister, P. A., Smith, F. V., Hessin, K. J., and Bolton, N. 'Psychological correlates of long-term imprisonment. I. Cognitive variables. II. Personality variables', *British Journal of Criminology*, **13**, 312 (1973).

Barnett, S. A. 'Attack and defense in animal societies', In C. D. Clements and D. N. Lindsley (Eds.), *Aggression and Defense*, Los Angeles, University of California Press, 1967, pp. 35–56.

Baron, R. A. 'Magnitude of model's apparent pain and ability to aid the model as determinants of observer reaction time', *Psychonomic Science*, **21**, 196 (1970).

Baron, R. A. 'Exposure to an aggressive model and apparent probability of retaliation from the victim as determinants of adult aggressive behaviour', *Journal of Experimental Social Psychology*, **7**, 343 (1971a).

Baron, R. A. 'Aggression as a function of magnitude of victim's pain cues, level of prior anger arousal, and aggressor–victim similarity, *Journal of Personality and Social Psychology*, **18**, 48 (1971b).

Baron, R. A., and Bell, P. A. 'Aggression and heat: mediating effects of prior provocation and exposure to an aggressive model', *Journal of Personality and Social Psychology*, **31**, 825 (1975).

Baron, R. A., and Kepner, C. R. 'Model's behaviour and attraction toward the model as determinants of adult aggressive behaviour', *Journal of Personality and Social Psychology*, **14**, 335 (1970).

Barry, H. III., Bacon, Margaret, and Child, L. L. 'A cross-cultural survey of some sex differences in socialisation', *Journal of Abnormal and Social Psychology*, **55**, 327 (1957).

Bartholomew, A. A. 'Extraversion–introversion and neuroticism in first offenders and recidivists', *British Journal of Delinquency*, **10**, 120 (1959).

Bartholomew, A. A. 'Some comparative Australian data for the Maudsley Personality Inventory', *Australian Journal of Psychology*, **15**, 46 (1963).

Bartlett, F. C. *Remembering*, Cambridge, Cambridge University Press, 1932.

Becker, H. S. 'Whose side are we on?', *Social Problems*, **14**, 239 (1967).

Beker, J., and Heyman, Doris, S. 'A critical appraisal of the California Differential Treatment Typology of adolescent offenders', *Criminology*, **10**, 3 (1972).

Bell, R. Q. 'A reinterpretation of the direction of effects in studies of socialisation', *Psychological Review*, **75**, 81 (1968).

Belson, W. *Juvenile Theft: The Causal Factors*, New York, Hamper and Row, 1975.

Benson, G. 'Prediction method and young prisoners', *British Journal of Delinquency*, **9**, 192 (1959).

Berg, K. S., and Vidmar, N. 'Authoritarianism and recall of evidence about criminal behavior', *Journal of Research in Personality*, **9**, 147 (1975).

Berger, S. M., and Johansson, S. L. 'Effect of a model's expressed emotions on an observer's resistance to extinction', *Journal of Personality and Social Psychology*, **10**, 53 (1968).

Bergin, A. E. 'The effect of dissonant persuasive communications upon changes in a self-referring attitude', *Journal of Personality*, **30**, 423 (1962).

Bergin, A. E. 'The evaluation of therapeutic outcomes', In A. E. Bergin and S. L. Garfield (Eds.), *Psychotherapy and Behaviour Change: An empirical analysis*, New York, Wiley, 1971, pp. 217–70.

Bergin, A. E., and Garfield, S. L. (Eds.), *Handbook of Psychotherapy and Behaviour Change*, New York, Wiley, 1971.

Berkowitz, L. 'Some aspects of observed aggression', *Journal of Personality and Social Psychology*, **2**, 359 (1965).

Berkowitz, L. 'Responsibility, reciprocity, and social distance in help-giving: an experimental investigation of English social class differences', *Journal of Experimental Social Psychology*, **4**, 46 (1968).

Berkowitz, L. 'Social motivation', In G. Lindzey and E. Aronson (Eds.), *The Handbook of Social Psychology* (2nd Edn), Vol. 3, Reading, Mass., Addison-Wesley, 1969, pp. 50–135.

Berkowitz, L. 'Words and symbols as stimuli to aggressive responses', In J. F. Knutson (Ed.), *Control of Aggression: Implications from Basic Research*, Chicago, Aldine-Atherton, 1972, pp. 113–43.

Berkowitz, L. 'Reactance and the unwillingness to help others', *Psychological Bulletin*, **79**, 310 (1973).

Berkowitz, L. 'Some determinants of compulsive aggression: role of mediated associations with reinforcements for aggression', *Psychological Review*, **81**, 165–76 (1974).

Berkowitz, L., and Connor, W. H. 'Success, failure and social responsibility'. *Journal of*

Personality and Social Psychology, **4**, 664–669 (1966).

Bernard, J. L., and Eisenman, R. 'Verbal conditioning in sociopaths with social and monetary reinforcement', *Journal of Personality and Social Psychology*, **6**, 203 (1967).

Berscheid, Ellen, Boye, D., and Walster, Elaine. 'Retaliation as a means of restoring equity', *Journal of Personality and Social Psychology*, **10**, 370 (1969).

Berscheid, Ellen, and Walster, Elaine. *Interpersonal Attraction*, Reading, Mass., Addison-Wesley, 1969.

Black, D. A., Blackburn, R., Blackler, C. D., and Haward, L. R. C. 'Memorandum of evidence to the Butler Committee on the law relating to the mentally abnormal offender', *Bulletin of the British Psychological Society*, **26**, 331 (1973).

Black, D. J., and Reiss, A. J. 'Police control of juveniles', *American Sociological Review*, **35**, 63 (1970).

Blackburn, R. 'Dimensions of hostility and aggression in abnormal offenders', *Journal of Consulting and Clinical Psychology*, **38**, 20 (1972).

Blake, R. R. 'The other person in the situation', In R. Tagiuri and L. Petrullo (Eds.), *Person Perception and Interpersonal Behaviour*, Stanford, Stanford University Press, 1958, pp. 229–42.

Blumenthal, M. D., Kahn, R. L., and Andrews, F. M. 'Attitudes towards violence', Proceedings of the 79th Annual Convention of the American Psychological Association, Washington, D.C., 1971.

Boehm, L., and Nass, M. L. 'Social class differences in conscience development', *Child Development*, **33**, 565 (1962).

Bondesen, Ulla. 'Argot knowledge as an indicator of criminal socialisation', *Scandinavian Studies in Criminology*, **2**, 73 (1969).

Bowlby, J. *Forty-Four Juvenile Thieves*, London, Baillière, Tindall and Cox, 1946.

Bowlby, J. In *Why Delinquency?*, Report of the Conference on the Scientific Study of Juvenile Delinquency, London, National Association for Mental Health, 1949.

Bowlby, J., Ainsworth, M., Boston, M., and Rosenbluth, D. 'The effects of mother–child separation: A follow-up study', *British Journal of Medical Psychology*, **29**, 211 (1956).

Bowlby, J., and Salter-Ainsworth, M. D. *Child Care and the Growth of Love*, London, Penguin, 1965 (2nd Edn. abridged and edited by Margery Fry).

Box, S. *Deviance, Reality and Society*, London, Holt, Rhinehart & Winston, 1971.

Brackbill Y. 'The impairment of learning under immediate reinforcement', *Journal of Experimental Child Psychology*, **1**, 199–207, (1964).

Brehm, J. W. *A Theory of Psychological Reactance*, New York, Academic Press, 1966.

Brehm, J., and Cohen, A. R. *Explorations in Cognitive Dissonance*, New York, Wiley, 1962.

Brigham, J. C., Ricketts, J. L., and Johnson, R. C. 'Reported maternal and paternal behaviours of solitary and social delinquents', *Journal of Counselling Psychology*, **31**, 420 (1967).

Brock, T. C., and Buss, A. N. 'Effects of justification for aggression and communication with the victim on postaggression dissonance', *Journal of Abnormal and Social Psychology*, **68**, 403 (1964).

Bronfenbrenner, V. *Two Worlds of Childhood: U.S. and U.S.S.R.*, New York, Russell Sage, 1970.

Brown, G. D., and Tyler, V. O. 'Time-out from reinforcement: a technique for dethroning the "duke" of an institutionalised delinquent group', *Journal of Child Psychology and Psychiatry*, **9**, 203 (1968).

Bryan, J. H., and Kapche, R. 'Psychopathy and verbal conditioning', *Journal of Abnormal Psychology*, **72**, 71 (1967).

Buehler, R. E. 'Social reinforcement experimentation in open social systems', Paper presented to Annual Meeting of Western Psychological Association, San Francisco, U.S.A., May 4, 1967. Reprinted in Stumphauzer, J. E. (Ed.), *Behaviour Therapy with Delinquents*, Springfield, Thomas, 1973, pp. 250–63.

Buehler, R. E., Patterson, C. R., and Furniss, J. M. 'The reinforcement of behaviour in institutional settings', *Behaviour Research and Therapy*, **4**, 157 (1966).

Burchard, J. D. 'Systematic socialisation: A programmed environment for the habilitation of anti-social retardates', *Psychological Record*, **17**, 461 (1967).

Burchard, J. D., and Tyler, V. 'The modification of delinquent behaviour through operant conditioning', *Behaviour Research and Therapy*, **2**, 245 (1965).

Burgess, R. C., and Akers, R. L. 'A differential association-reinforcement theory of criminal behaviour', *Social Problems*, **14**, 128 (1966).

Burt, C. *The Young Delinquent*, London, University of London Press, 1923.

Burton, R. V. 'Generality of honesty reconsidered, *Psychological Review*, **70**, 481 (1963).

Burton, R. V., Maccoby, Eleanor, E., and Allinsmith, W. 'Antecedents of resistance to temptation in four-year-old children', *Child Development*, **32**, 689 (1961).

Buss, A. H. *The Psychology of Aggression*, New York, Wiley, 1961.

Buss, A. H. *Psychopathology*, New York, Wiley, 1966.

Butler (Lord). *Report of the Committee on the Mentally Abnormal Offender*, London, HMSO, 1975.

Burgess, P. K., 'Eysenck's theory of criminality: a new approach', *British Journal of Criminology*, **12**, 74–82 (1972).

Byrne, D. 'Repression–sensitization as a dimension of personality', In B. A. Maher (Ed.), *Progress in Experimental Personality Research*, Vol. 1, New York, Academic Press, 1964, pp. 115–68.

Byrne, D., and Lamberth, J. 'The effect of erotic stimuli on sex arousal, evaluative responses, and subsequent behaviour', Tech. Rep. of the Commission on Obscenity and Pornography, Vol. 8, Washington, D.C., United States Government Printing Office, 1971.

Bytheway, B. 'The statistical associations between social class and self reported delinquency', *International Journal of Criminology and Penology*, **3**, 229 (1975).

Calhoun, J. B. 'Population density and social psychology', *Scientific American*, **206**, 139 (1962).

Cameron, Mary O. *The Booster and the Snitch*, New York, Free Press, 1964.

Cautela, J. R. 'Covert sensitization', *Psychological Reports*, **20**, 459 (1967).

Chadwick, E. 'Preventive police', *London Review*, **1**, 301 (1829).

Chaiken, J. M. 'The impact of police activity on crime: robberies on the New York City Subway System', RAND Institute, 1974.

Chambliss, W. J. *Crime and the Legal Process*, New York, McGraw-Hill, 1969.

Chapanis, N. P., and Chapanis, A. 'Cognitive dissonance: Five years later', *Psychological Bulletin*, **61**, 1 (1964).

Chilton, R. J., and Markle, G. E. 'Family disruption, delinquent conduct and the effect of sub-classification', *American Sociological Review*, **37**, 93 (1972).

Christiansen, K. O. 'Threshold of tolerance in various population groups illustrated by results from Danish criminological twin study', In A. V. S. de Rueck and Ruth Porter (Eds.), *The Mentally Abnormal Offender*, Boston, Little, Brown, 1968, pp. 107–20.

Christiansen, K. O. 'Recidivism among collaborators', In M. E. Wolfgang (Ed.), *Crime and Culture: Essays in Honour of Thorsten Sellin*, New York, Wiley, 1969, pp. 254–83.

Christie, N. 'A study of self-reported crime', *Scandinavian Studies in Criminology*, **1**, 66 (1965).

Christie, R., and Geis, Florence. *Studies in Machiavellianism*, New York, Academic Press, 1970.

Christy, P. R., Gelfand, D. M., and Hartman, D. P. 'Effects of competition induced frustration on two classes of modelled behaviour', *Developmental Psychology*, **5**, 104 (1971).

Clark, J. P., and Tifft, L. L. 'Polygraph and interview validation of self-reported deviant behaviour', *American Sociological Review*, **31**, 516 (1966).

Clark, R. D. III, and Word, L. E. 'Why don't bystanders help? Because of ambiguity?', *Journal of Personality and Social Psychology*, **24**, 392 (1972).

Clark, R. D. III, and Word, L. E. 'Where is the apathetic bystander? Situational characteristics of the emergency', *Journal of Personality and Social Psychology*, **29**, 279 (1973).

Clarke, S. H. 'Getting' em out of circulation: does incarceration of juvenile offenders reduce crime', *Journal of Criminal Law and Criminology*, **65**, 528 (1974).

Cleckley, H. *The Mask of Sanity*, 4th Ed., St. Louis, Mosby, 1964.

Clemmer, D. *The Prison Community*, Boston, Christopher 1940.

Clinard, M. B. *The Black Market*, New York, Holt, Rhinehart & Winston, 1952.

Clinard, M. B. *Sociology of Deviant Behaviour*, 3rd Edn., New York, Holt, Rhinehart & Winston, 1968.

Clinard, M. B., and Quinney, R. *Criminal Behaviour Systems: A Typology*, New York, Holt, Rhinehart & Winston, 1967.

Clonninger, C. R., Reich, T., and Guze, S. B. 'The multi-factorial model of disease transmission. II. Sex differences in the familial transmission of sociopathy (anti-social personality)', *British Journal of Psychiatry*, **127**, 11 (1975).

Cloward, R. A., and Ohlin, L. E. *Delinquency and Opportunity*, New York, Free Press, 1960.

Coates, S. 'Homosexuality and the Rorschach test', *British Journal of Medical Psychology*, **35**, 177 (1962).

Cochrane, R. 'The structure of value systems in male and female prisoners', *British Journal of Criminology*, **11**, 73 (1971).

Cohen, A. K. *Delinquent Boys: The Culture of the Gang*, Glenine, Ill., Free Press, 1955.

Cohen, H. L., and Filipczak, J. *A New Learning Environment*, San Francisco, Josey-Bass, 1971.

Cohen, S., and Taylor, L. *Psychological Survival*, London, Penguin, 1972.

Collins, B. E., and Raven, B. H. 'Group structure: attraction, coalitions, communications and power', In G. Lindzey and E. Aronson (Eds.), *Handbook of Social Psychology*, Vol. 4, Reading, Mass., Addison-Wesley, 1969, pp. 102–204.

Corning, P. A., and Corning, C. H. 'Toward a general theory of violent aggression', *Social Science Information*, **11**, 7 (1972).

Cornish, D. B., and Clarke, R. G. *Residential Treatment and Its Effects on Delinquency*, London, HMSO, 1975.

Cowie, J., Cowie, Valerie, and Slater, E. *Delinquency in Girls*, New York, Humanities Press, 1968.

Craft, M. (Ed.). *Psychopathic Disorders and their Assessment*, Oxford, Pergamon, 1966.

Craft, M. J. 'English psychopaths and their treatment', *British Journal of Criminology*, **8**, 412 (1968a).

Craft, M. J. 'Psychopathic disorder: a 2nd trial of treatment', *British Journal of Psychiatry*, **114**, 813 (1968b).

Craske, S. 'A study of the relation between personality and accidents', *British Journal of Medical Psychology*, **41**, 399 (1968).

Cressey, D. R. 'Delinquent and criminal structures', In R. K. Merton and R. Nisbett (Eds.), *Contemporary Social Problems*, 3rd edn., New York, Harcourt Bruce Jovanovich, 1971, pp. 147–85.

Crowe, R. R. 'The adopted offspring of women criminal offenders: a study of their arrest records', *Archives of General Psychiatry*, **27**, 600 (1972).

Craig, M. M., and Furst, P. W., 'What happens after treatment', *Social Services Review*, **39**, 165–171, (1965).

Daniels, L. R., and Berkowitz, 'Liking and response to depending relationships', *Human Relations*, **16**, 141–148 (1963).

Darley, J. M., and Batson, C. D. '"From Jerusalem to Jericho": A study of situational and dispositional variables in helping behaviour', *Journal of Personality and Social Psychology*, **27**, 100 (1973).

Darwin, C. *The Expression of Emotions in Man and Animals*, London, John Murray, 1872.

Das, J. P., and Nanda, P. C. 'Mediated transfer of attitudes', *Journal of Abnormal and Social Psychology*, **66**, 12 (1963).

Davies, M., and Sinclair, I. 'Families, hostels and delinquents: an attempt to assess cause and effect', *British Journal of Criminology*, **11**, 213 (1971).

Davison, G. C., and Neale, J. M. *Abnormal Psychology*, New York, Wiley, 1974.

DeFleur, M. C., and Quinney, R. 'A reformulation of Sutherland's differential association theory and a strategy for empirical verification', *Journal of Research in Crime and Delinquency*, **3**, 1 (1966).

Delgado, J. M. R. 'Cerebral radio-stimulation in a monkey colony', *Science*, **141**, 161 (1963).

Delgado, J. H. R. 'Social rank and radio-stimulated aggressiveness in monkeys', *Journal of Nervous and Mental Diseases*, **144**, 383–90, (1967)

Dengerink, H. A., and Levendusky, P. G. 'Effects of massive retaliation and balance of power on aggression', *Journal of Experimental Research in Personality*, **6**, 230 (1972).

Denner, B. 'Did a crime occur? Should I inform anyone? A study of deception', *Journal of Personality*, **36**, 454 (1968).

Devlin, (Lord). *The Enforcement of Morals*, Proceedings of the British Academy, 1959, pp. 90–179. Cited by Kadish, S. H. 'Overcriminalization', In L. Radzinowicz and M. L. Wolfgang (Eds.), *Crime and Justice*, Vol. 1, *The Criminal in Society*, New York, Basic Books, pp. 56–71.

Dion, K. 'Physical attractiveness and evaluation of children's transgressions', *Journal of Personality and Social Psychology*, **24**, 207 (1972).

Dion, K., Berscheid, E., and Walster, E. 'What is beautiful is good', *Journal of Personality and Social Psychology*, **24**, 285 (1972).

Dollard, J., Doob, L. W., Miller, N. E., Mowrer, O. H., and Sears, R. R. *Frustration and Aggression*, New Haven, Conn., Yale University Press, 1939.

Dollard, J., and Miller, N. E. *Personality and Psychotherapy*, New York, McGraw-Hill, 1950.

Doshay, L. J. *The Boy Sex Offender and his Later Career*, New York, Grave and Stratton, 1943.

Douglas, J. M. B., and Bromfield, J. M. *Children Under Five*, London, Allen and Unwin, 1958.

Douglas, J. W. B. '"Premature" children at primary schools', *British Medical Journal*, **1**, 1008 (1960).

Douglas, J. W. B., and Ross, J. M. 'Characteristics of delinquent boys and their homes', In J. M. Thoday and A. S. Parkes (Eds.), *Genetic and Environmental Influences on Behaviour*, Edinburgh, Oliver and Boyd, 1968, pp. 114–27.

Dubanoski, R. P. 'Imitation as a function of role appropriateness of behaviour and response consequences to the model', Unpublished manuscript, University of Iowa, 1967.

Durkheim, E. *Suicide*, London, Routledge and Kegan Paul, 1970. First published in French, in 1897.

Eaton, J. W., and Weil, R. J. '*Cultural and Mental Disorders*, New York, Free Press, 1955.

Eaves, L., and Eysenck, H. J. 'The nature of extraversion: a genetical analysis', *Journal of Personality and Social Psychology*, **32**, 102–112 (1975).

Edwards, A. L. *Edwards Personal Preference Schedule*, New York, Psychological Corporation, 1959.

Efran, M. G. 'The effect of physical appearance on the judgement of guilt, interpersonal attraction, and severity of recommended punishment in a simulated jury task', *Journal of Research in Personality*, **8**, 45 (1974).

Elmhorn, K. 'Study in self-reported delinquency among school-children in Stockholm', *Scandinavian Studies in Criminology*, **1**, 117 (1965).

Elms, A. C., and Milgram, S. 'Personality characteristics associated with obedience and defiance towards authoritative command', *Journal of Experimental Research in Personality*, **1**, 282 (1965).

Empey, L. T., and Erickson, M. L. 'Hidden delinquency and social status', *Social Forces*, **44**, 546 (1966).

Empey, L. T., Erickson, M. L., and Scott, M. C. 'The Provo experiment: evaluation of a community program', In *Correction in the Community*, State Board of Correction, Sacramento, California, 1964, pp. 29–38.

England, R. W. 'A study of post-probation recidivism among five hundred federal offenders', *Federal Probation*, **19**, 10 (1955).

Ennis, P. H. *Criminal Victimization in the United States: A Report of a National Survey*, Washington, D.C., US Government Printing Office, 1967.

Epps, P., and Parnell, R. W. 'Physique and temperament of women delinquents compared with women undergraduates', *British Journal of Medical Psychology*, **25**, 249 (1952).

Epstein, R. 'Aggression towards outgroups as a function of authoritarianism and imitation of aggressive models', *Journal of Personality and Social Psychology*, **3**, 574 (1966).

Epstein, S., and Taylor, S. P. 'Instigation to aggression as a function of degree of defeat and perceived aggressive intent of the opponent', *Journal of Personality*, **35**, 265 (1967).

Erickson, K. T. 'Notes on the sociology of deviance', In H. S. Beiber (Ed.), *The Other Side: Perspectives on Deviance*, New York, Free Press, 1964, pp. 9–21.

Erickson, M. L. 'The group context of delinquent behaviour', *Social Problems*, **19**, 114 (1971).

Erickson, M. L. 'The changing relationship between official and self-reported measures of delinquency: an exploratory–predictive study', *Journal of Criminal Law. Criminology and Police Science*, **63**, 388 (1972).

Erickson, R. V. 'A comparison of two groups of institutionalized delinquents on Porteus Maze test performance', *Journal of Consulting Psychology*, **30**, 567 (1966).

Eron, L. D., Huesmann, L. R., Lefkowitz, M. M., and Walder, L. O. 'Does television violence cause aggression?', *American Psychologist*, **27**, 253 (1972).

Evans, D. R. 'Masturbating fantasy and sexual deviation', *Behaviour Research and Therapy*, **6**, 17 (1968).

Evans, D. R. 'Exhibitionism', In C. G. Costello (Ed.), *Symptoms of Psychopathology*, New York, Wiley, 1970, pp. 560–73.

Eysenck, H. J. *Manual of the Maudsley Personality Inventory*, London, University of London Press, 1958.

Eysenck, H. J. 'The effects of psychotherapy', In H. J. Eysenck (Ed.), *Handbook of Abnormal Psychology*, 1st edn., London, Pitman Medical, 1960, pp. 697–725.

Eysenck, H. J. *Crime and Personality*, London, Routledge, 1964.

Eysenck, H. J. *The Biological Basis of Personality*, Springfield, Ill., Thomas, 1967.

Eysenck, H. J. *Crime and Personality*, 2nd edn., London, Cranada Press, 1970.

Eysenck, H. J. 'Crime and personality reconsidered', *Bulletin of the British Psychological Society*, **27**, 23 (1974).

Eysenck, H. J. 'Genetic factors in personality development', In A. R. Kaplan (Ed.), *Human Behaviour Genetics*, Springfield, Ill., Thomas (In press.)

Eysenck, H. J., and Eysenck, S. B. G. 'On the dual nature of extraversion', *British Journal of Social Clinical Psychology*, **2**, 46 (1963).

Eysenck, H. J., and Eysenck, S. B. G. *Manual of the Eysenck Personality Inventory*, London, University of London Press, 1964.

Eysenck, H. J., and Eysenck, S. B. G. 'A factorial study of psychoticism as a dimension of personality', *Multivariate Behavioural Research* (special issue), 15 (1968).

Eysenck, H. J., and Eysenck, S. B. G. *Personality Structure and Measurement*, San Diego, Knapp, 1969.

Eysenck, H. J., and Eysenck, S. B. G. 'Crime and personality: an empirical study of the three-factor theory', *British Journal of Criminology*, **10**, 225 (1970).

294

Eysenck, S. B. G. *Manual of the Junior Eysenck Personality Inventory*, London, University of London Press, 1965.
Eysenck, S. B. G., and Eysenck, H. J. 'Crime and personality: item analysis of questionnaire responses', *British Journal of Criminology*, **11**, 49 (1971a).
Eysenck, S. B. G., and Eysenck, H. J. 'A comparative study of criminals and matched controls on three dimensions of personality', *British Journal of Social and Clinical Psychology*, **10**, 362 (1971b).
Eysenck, S. B. G., and Eysenck, H. J. 'The personality of female prisoners', *British Journal of Psychology*, **123**, 693 (1973).
Fagan, J. F. III, and Witryol, S. L. 'The effects of instructional set and delay of reward on children's learning in a simultaneous discrimination task', *Child Development*, **37**, 433 (1966).
Fairweather, G. W., Sanders, D. H., Maynard, H., and Cressler, D. L. *Community Life for the Mentally Ill: An Alternative to Institutional Care*, Chicago, Aldine, 1969.
Farley, F., and Farley, Sonja V. 'Extraversion and stimulus-seeking motivation', *Journal of Consulting Psychology*, **31**, 215 (1967).
Farley, F. H., and Farley, Sonja V. 'Stimulus seeking motivation and delinquent behaviour among institutionalized delinquent girls', *Journal of Consulting and Clinical Psychology*, **39**, 94 (1972).
Farrington, D. P., and West, D. J. 'A comparison between early delinquents and young aggressives', *British Journal of Criminology*, **11**, 341 (1971).
Feinberg, J. *Social Philosophy*, New York, Prentice-Hall, 1973.
Feldman, M. P. 'Pursuit motor performance and reminiscence as a function of drive level', In H. J. Eysenck (Ed.), *Experiments in Motivation*, Oxford, Pergamon, 1964, pp. 32–59.
Feldman, M. P. 'Decision taking in a hypothetical criminal situation by approved school and secondary modern school boys', Unpublished manuscript, University of Birmingham, 1966.
Feldman, M. P. 'Attitudes to criminal behaviours of approved school and secondary modern school boys', Unpublished manuscript, University of Birmingham, 1967.
Feldman, M. P. 'Co-operative avoidance: a paradigm for the study of helping', Unpublished manuscript, University of Birmingham, 1970.
Feldman, M. P. 'Abnormal sexual behaviour in males', In H. J. Eysenck (Ed.), *Handbook of Abnormal Psychology*, 2nd edn., London, Pitman Medical, 1973, pp. 131–70.
Feldman, M. P. 'Social psychology and behaviour therapy', In M. P. Feldman and Anne Broadhurst (Eds.), *The Experimental Bases of the Behaviour Therapies*, London, Wiley, 1976a.
Feldman, M. P. 'Behaviour therapy and society', In M. P. Feldman and Anne Broadhurst (Eds.), *The Experimental Bases of the Behaviour Therapies*, London, Wiley, 1976b.
Feldman, M. P., and Broadhurst, Anne (Eds.). *The Experimental Bases of the Behaviour Therapies*, London, Wiley, 1976.
Feldman, M. P., and Callister, Jennifer. 'Interpersonal helping behaviour: cognitive and situational aspects', Research Report: Social Science Research Council of Great Britain, Grant HR. 536/1, December 1971.
Feldman, M. P., and McCulloch, M. J. *Homosexual Behaviour: Therapy and Assessment*, Oxford, Pergamon, 1971.
Feldman, R. E. 'Honesty toward compatriot and foreigner: field experiments in Paris, Athens and Boston', *Proceedings, 76th Annual Convention, American Psychological Association*, 1968a, p. 375.
Feldman, R. E. 'Response to compatriot and foreigner who seeks assistance', *Journal of Personality and Social Psychology*, **10**, 202 (1968b).
Fenz, W. D. 'Heart rate responses to a stressor: a comparison between primary and secondary psychopaths and normal controls', *Journal of Experimental Research in Personality*, **5**, 7 (1971).

Ferguson, T., and Pettigrew, Mary, G. 'A study of 718 slum families rehoused for upwards of ten years', *Glasgow Medical Journal*, August (1954).

Feshbach, S. 'Aggression', In P. H. Mussen (Ed.), *Carmichael's Manual of Child Psychology*, Vol. II, New York, Wiley, 1970, pp. 159–259.

Feshbach, S., and Singer, R. D. *Television and Aggression: An Experimental Field Study*, San Francisco, Jossey-Bass, 1971.

Festinger, L. 'A theory of social comparison processes', *Human Relations*, 7, 117 (1954).

Festinger, L. *A Theory of Cognitive Dissonance*, Stanford, California, Stanford University Press, 1957.

Fine, B. J. 'Introversion–extraversion and motor vehicle driver behaviour', *Perceptual and Motor Skills*, 12, 95 (1963).

Fischer, W. F. 'Sharing in pre-school children as a function of amount and type of reinforcement', *Genetic Psychological Monographs*, 68, 215 (1963).

Fishbein, M. (Ed.), *Readings in Attitude Theory and Measurement*, New York, Wiley, 1967.

Fisher, G., and Howell, Leisla M. 'Psychological needs of homosexual paedophiles', *Diseases of the Nervous System*, 31, 623 (1973).

Fitch, J. H. 'Two personality variables and their distribution in a criminal population: an empirical study', *British Journal of Social and Clinical Psychology*, 1, 161 (1962).

Fixsen, D. L., Phillips, E. L., Harper, Deena S., Mesigh, J. Carol., Timbers, G. D., and Wolf, M. M. 'The teaching–family model of group home treatment', Presented at the American Psychological Association Annual Convention, Honolulu, Hawaii, September, 1972.

Fixsen, D. L., Phillips, E. L., and Wolfe, M. M. 'Achievement Place: experiments in self-government with pre-delinquents', *Journal of Applied Behaviour Analysis*, 6, 31 (1973).

Fo, W. S. O., and O'Donnell, C. R. 'The buddy system: relationship and contingency conditions in a community intervention program for youth with non-professionals as behaviour change agents', *Journal of Consulting and Clinical Psychology*, 42, 163 (1974).

Fo, W. S. O., and O'Donnell, C. R. 'The buddy system: effect of community intervention on delinquent offences', *Behaviour Therapy*, 6, 522 (1975).

Fodor, E. M. 'Delinquency and susceptibility to social influence among adolescents as a function of level of moral development', *Journal of Social Psychology*, 86, 253 (1972).

Ford, C. S., and Beach, F. A. *Patterns of Sexual Behaviour*, New York, Harper, 1952.

Fordham, Peta. *The Robber's Tale*, London, Penguin, 1968.

Freedman, J. L. 'Long term behavioral effects of cognitive dissonance', *Journal of Experimental Social Psychology*, 1, 145 (1965).

Freedman, J. L., and Doob, A. N. *Deviancy: The Psychology of Being Different*, New York, Academic Press, 1968.

Freedman, J. L., Wallington, Sue Ann, and Bless, Evelyn. 'Compliance without pressure: the effect of guilt', *Journal of Personality and Social Psychology*, 7, 117 (1967).

Friedlander, K. *The Psycho-analytical Approach to Juvenile Delinquency*, London, Routledge, 1947.

Fry, M. 'Justice for victims', *Journal of Public Law*, 8, 155 (1956).

Fulker, D. W., and Eaves, L. J. 'The interactions of genotype and environment in two personality traits', Unpublished manuscript, University of Birmingham, 1973.

Furneaux, W. D., and Gibson, H. B. *Manual of the New Junior Maudsley Personality Inventory*, London, University of London Press, 1966.

Gaertner, S. L. 'Helping behavior and racial discrimination among liberals and conservatives', *Journal of Personality and Social Psychology*, 25, 335 (1973).

Gaertner, S. L., and Bickman, L. 'Effects of race on the elicitation of helping behaviour: the wrong number technique', *Journal of Personality and Social Psychology*, 20, 218 (1971).

296

Gallup Poll Social Surveys Ltd. *Television and Religion*, London, London University Press, 1964.

Garabedian, P. G. 'Social rules and the processes of socialization in the prison', *Social Problems*, **11**, 139 (1963).

Garfinkel, H. 'Research note in inter- and intra-racial homicides', *Social Forces*, **27**, 370 (1949).

Gebhard, P. H., Gagnon, W. H., Pomeroy, W. B., and Christenson, Cornelia, V. *Sex Offenders: An Analysis of Types*, New York, Harper and Row, 1965.

Geen, R. G., and O'Neal, E. C. 'Activation of cue-elicited aggression by general arousal', *Journal of Personality and Social Psychology*, **11**, 289 (1969).

Geen, R. G., Stonner, D., and Shope, G. L. 'The facilitation of aggression by aggression: evidence against the catharsis hypothesis', *Journal of Personality and Social Psychology*, **31**, 721 (1975).

Gelfand, Donna M., Hartmann, D. P., Walder, Patrice, and Page, B. 'Who reports shoplifters? A field-experimental study', *Journal of Personality and Social Psychology*, **25**, 276 (1973).

Gerard, R. 'Institutional innovations in juvenile corrections', *Federal Probation*, **34**, 37 (1970).

Gibbens, T. C. N. 'The sexual behaviour of young criminals', *Journal of Mental Science*, **103**, 527 (1957).

Gibbens, T. C. N. *Psychiatric Studies of Borstal Lads*, Oxford, Oxford University Press, 1963.

Gibbens, T. C., Palmer, Clare, and Prince, Joyce. 'Mental health aspects of shoplifting', *British Medical Journal*, **3**, 612 (1971).

Gibbens, T. C. N., Pond, D., and Stafford-Clarke, D. 'A follow-up study of criminal psychopaths', *Journal of Mental Science*, **105**, 108 (1959).

Gibbons, D. *Changing the Lawbreaker*, Englewood Cliffs, New Jersey, Prentice-Hall, 1965.

Gibbons, D. C. 'Offender typologies—two decades later', *British Journal of Criminology*, **15**, 140 (1975).

Gibson, H. B. 'The spiral maze: a psychomotor test with implications for the study of delinquency', *British Journal of Psychology*, **54**, 219 (1964).

Gibson, H. B. 'Self-reported delinquency among schoolboys and their attitudes to the police', *British Journal of Social and Clinical Psychology*, **6**, 168 (1967a).

Gibson, H. B. 'Teachers' ratings of schoolboys' behaviour related to patterns of scores on the new Junior Maudsley Inventory', *British Journal of Educational Psychology*, **37**, 347 (1967b).

Glaser, D., and Rice, K. 'Crime, age and employment', *The American Sociological Review*, **24**, 679 (1959).

Glass, D. C., and Wood, J. D. Changes in liking as a means of reducing cognitive discrepancies between self-esteem and aggression', *Journal of Personality*, **32**, 531 (1964).

Glueck, Eleanor, T. 'Identification of potential delinquents at 2–3 years of age', *International Journal of Social Psychiatry*, **12**, 5 (1964).

Glueck, S. *Law and Psychiatry*, Baltimore, Johns Hopkins Press, 1962.

Glueck, S., and Glueck, E. *Unravelling Juvenile Delinquency*, Cambridge, Mass., Harvard University Press, 1950.

Glueck, S., and Glueck, Eleanor, T. *Physique and Delinquency*, New York, Harper, 1956.

Glueck, S., and Glueck, Eleanor, T. 'Potential juvenile delinquents can be identified: what next?', *The British Journal of Criminology*, **4**, 215 (1964).

Goffman, E. *Asylums*, London, Penguin, 1968.

Goffman, E. *The Presentation of Self in Everyday Life*, London, Allen Lane, 1969.

Gold, M. 'Suicide, homicide and the socialization of aggression', *American Journal of Sociology*, **63**, 651 (1958).

Gold, M. 'Undetected delinquent behaviour', *Journal of Research in Crime and Delinquency*, **3**, 27 (1966).

Gold, M. *Delinquency in an American city*, California, Brooks Cole, 1970.

Goldman, H., Lindner, L., Dinitz, S., and Allen, H. 'The simple sociopath: Physiologic and sociologic characteristics', *Biological Psychiatry*, **3**, 77 (1971).

Goldsteim, A., Heller, K., and Sechrest, L. *Psychotherapy and the Psychology of Behaviour Change*, New York, Wiley, 1966.

Goodstadt, M. S. 'Helping and refusal to help: a test of balance and reaction theories', Dept. of Psychology, University of Western Ontario, London, Canada, Research Bulletin No. 173, Feb. 1971.

Gordon, R., Short, J., Cartwright, D., and Strotbeck, F. 'Values and group delinquency: a study of street corner groups', *American Journal of Sociology*, **69**, 109 (1963).

Gottfredson, D. M., and Kelley, B. B. 'Interpersonal maturity measurement by California Psychological Inventory', Institute for the Study of Crime and Delinquency, California, Report No. 1, 1963.

Gough, H. G. *California Psychological Inventory*, Palo Alto, Consulting Psychologists Press, 1957.

Gouldner, A. 'The norm of reciprocity: a preliminary statement', *American Sociological Review*, **25**, 161 (1960).

Grant, J. D., and Grant, M. A. 'A group dynamics approach to the treatment of non-conformists in the navy', *Annals of the American Academy of Political and Social Science*, **322**, 126 (1959).

Gray, J. A. 'Sex differences in emotional behaviour in mammals including man: endocrine basis', *Acta Psychologica*, **35**, 29 (1971).

Gray, J. A., and Buffery, A. W. H. 'Sex differences in emotional behaviour in mammals including man: adaptive and neural bases', *Acta Psychologica*, **35**, 89 (1971).

Green, E. *Judical Attitudes in Sentencing*, London, Macmillan, 1961.

Greenwald, A. G. 'An amended learning model of persuasion', Paper read at Annual Convention, American Psychological Association, Washington, D.C., 1967.

Greenwell, J., and Dengerink, H. A. 'The role of perceived *versus* actual attack in human, physical, aggression', *Journal of Personality and Social Psychology*, **26**, 66 (1973).

Griffiths, A. W., Richards, B. W., Zaremba, J., Abramowicz, T., and Stewart, A. 'Psychological and sociological investigation of XYY prisoners', *Nature*, **227**, 290 (1970).

Grinder, R. 'New techniques for research in children's temptation behaviour', *Child Development*, **32**, 679 (1961).

Grinder, R. E., and McMichael, R. E. 'Cultural influence in conscience development: resistance to temptation and guilt among Samoans and American Caucasians', *Journal of Abnormal and Social Psychology*, **66**, 503 (1963).

Grünhut, M. *Juvenile Offenders Before the Courts*, Oxford, Clarendon, 1956.

Grünhut, M. *Probation and Mental Treatment*, London, Tavistock, 1960.

Grygier, T., Nease, Barbara, and Anderson, C. S. 'An exploratory study of halfway houses', *Crime and Delinquency*, **16**, 280 (1970).

Guardian. 'Where the prisoners do time-and-a-half', August 30th, 1973, p. 5.

Guardian. 'Penal reform', November 13th, 1974, p. 13.

Guardian. 'Surrender—with a huge ransom', Saturday, September 30th, 1975, p. 3.

Gunn, J. 'A rehabilitation workshop for offenders', *British Journal of Criminology*, **12**, 158 (1972).

Gunn, J., and Bonn, J. 'Criminality and violence in epileptic prisoners', *British Journal of Psychiatry*, **118**, 337 (1971).

Hall, R. V., Axelrod, S., Tyler, Lucillia, Grief, Ellen, Jones, F. C., and Robertson, Roberta. 'Modification of behaviour problems in the home with a parent as observer and experimenter', *Journal of Applied Behaviour Analysis*, **5**, 53 (1972).

Hamilton, D. W. 'Selection of selfish and altruistic behavior in some extreme models', In J. F. Eisenberg and W. S. Dillon (Eds.), *Man and Beast: Comparative and Social Behaviour*, Washington, D.C., Smithsonian Institute Press, 1971.

Haney, C., Banks, C., and Zimbardo, P. B. 'Interpersonal dynamics in a simulated prison', *International Journal of Criminology and Penology*, **1**, 1 (1973).

Harari, H. 'Interpersonal models in psychotherapy and counselling: a socio-psychological analysis of a clinical problem', *Journal of Abnormal Psychology*, **78**, 127 (1971).

Hare, D. R. *Psychopathy: Theory and Research*, New York, Wiley, 1970.

Hare, R. D. 'Psychopathy and preference for immediate over delayed punishment', *Journal of Abnormal Psychology*, **71**, 25 (1966).

Hare, R. D. 'Discrimination of conditioned electrodermal and cardiovascular responses in psychopaths', Paper read to Workshop on Psychopathy, Society for Psychophysiological Research, Boston, November 9–12, 1972a.

Hare, R. D. 'Psychopathy and physiological responses to adrenaline', *Journal of Abnormal Psychology*, **79**, 138 (1972b).

Hare, R. D., and Craigen, D. 'Psychopathy and physiological correlates of direct and vicarious stress in a mixed motive game situation', *Psychophysiology*, **11**, 197 (1974).

Hare, R. D., and Quinn, M. 'Psychopathy and autonomic conditioning', *Journal of Abnormal Psychology*, **77**, 223 (1971).

Hargreaves, D. H. *Social Relations in a Secondary School*, London, Routledge and Kegan Paul, 1967.

Harlow, H. F. 'Sexual behaviour in the rhesus monkey', In Beach, F. A. (Ed.), *Sex and Behaviour*, New York, Wiley, 1965.

Hartig, Monika, and Kanfer, F. H. 'The role of verbal self-instructions in children's resistance to temptation', *Journal of Personality and Social Psychology*, **25**, 254 (1973).

Hartmann, D. P. 'Influence of symbolically modelled instrumental aggression and pain cues on aggressive behaviour', *Journal of Personality and Social Psychology*, **11**, 280 (1969).

Hartshorne, H., and May, M. A. *Studies in Deceit*, New York, Macmillan, 1928.

Hartup, W. W., and Coates, B. 'Imitation of peers as a reinforcement from the peer group and rewardingness of the model', *Child Development*, **38**, 1003 (1967).

Hathaway, S. R. *Minnesota Multiphasic Personality Inventory: Manual*, New York, Psychological Corporation, 1951.

Hathaway, S. R., and Monachesi, E. D. 'The M.M.P.I. in the study of juvenile delinquents', In Rose, A.M., (Ed.), *Mental Health and Mental Disorder*, Routledge, 1956.

Hausner, G. *Justice in Jerusalem*, London, Nelson, 1967.

Hebb, D. O. 'Drives and the C.N.S. (Conceptual nervous system)', *Psychological Review*, **62**, 243 (1955).

Heisler, G. 'Ways to deter law violations: effects of levels of threat and vicarious punishment on cheating', *Journal of Consulting and Clinical Psychology*, **42**, 577 (1974).

Hessin, K. J., Bolton, N., Smith, F. V., and Bannister, P. A. 'Psychological correlates of long term imprisonment', *British Journal of Criminology*, **14**, 150 (1974).

Hetherington, E. Mavis, and Frankie, G. 'Effects of parental dominance, warmth, and conflict on imitation in children', *Journal of Personality and Social Psychology*, **6**, 119 (1967).

Hicks, D. J. 'Imitation and retention of film-mediated aggressive peer and adult models', *Journal of Personality and Social Psychology*, **2**, 97 (1965).

Hill, D., and Pond, D. A. 'Reflections on 100 capital cases submitted to electroencephalography', *Journal of Mental Science*, **98**, 23 (1952).

Hindelang, M. 'The relationship of self-reported delinquency to scales of the C.P.I. and the M.M.P.I.', *Journal of Criminal Law, Criminology and Police Science*, **63**, 75 (1972).

Hindelang, M. J. 'Variations in personality and attributes of social and solitary self-reported delinquents', *Journal of Consulting and Clinical Psychology*, **40**, 452 (1973).

Hindelang, M., and Weis, J. G. 'Personality and self-reported delinquency: an application of cluster analysis', *Criminology*, **10**, 268 (1972).

Hirschi, T. *Causes of Delinquency*, California, University of California Press, 1970.

Hodges, E. F., and Tait, C. A. 'A follow-up study of potential delinquents', *American Journal of Psychiatry*, **120**, 449 (1965).

Hoebel, E. A. *The Law of Primitive Man*, Cambridge, Mass., Harvard University Press, 1954.

Hoelle, C. 'The effects of modelling and reinforcement on aggressive behavior in elementary school boys', *Dissertation Abstracts*, **29B**, 3483 (1969).

Hoffman, M. L. 'Power assertion by the parent and its impact on the child', *Child Development*, **31**, 129 (1960).

Hoffman, M. L. 'Altruistic behaviour and the present-child relationship', *Journal of Personality and Social Psychology*, **31**, 937–943 (1975).

Hoffman, M. L., and Saltzstein, H. D. 'Parent discipline and the child's moral development', *Journal of Personality and Social Psychology*, **5**, 45 (1967).

Hogan, R. 'Moral conduct and moral character: a psychological perspective', *Psychological Bulletin*, **79**, 217 (1973).

Hogarth, J. *Sentencing as a Human Process*, Toronto, Toronto University Press, 1971.

Hoghughi, M. S., and Forrest, A. R. 'Eysenck's theory of criminality. An examination with approved school boys', *British Journal of Criminology*, **10**, 240 (1970).

Holden, H. M. 'Should aversion and behaviour therapy be used in the treatment of delinquency', *British Journal of Criminology*, **5**, 377 (1965).

Homans, G. C. 'Group factors in worker productivity', In Swanson, G. E., Newcomb, T. M., and Hartley, E. L. (Eds.), *Readings in Social Psychology*, New York, Holt, 1952, pp. 637–49.

Homans, G. C. *Social Behaviour: Its Elementary Forms*, New York, Harcourt Brace and World, 1961.

Hood, R. *Sentencing in Magistrates' Courts*, London, Stevens, 1962.

Hood, R., and Sparks, R. *Key Issues in Criminology*, London, Weidenfeld and Nicholson, 1970.

Hope, K., Philip, A. E., and Loughran, J. M. 'Psychological characteristics associated with XYY sex-chromosome complement in a state mental hospital', *British Journal of Psychiatry*, **113**, 495 (1967).

Hutchings, B., and Mednick, S. 'Registered criminality in the adoptive and biological parents of registered male adoptees', In R. Fieve, H. Brill and R. Rosenthal (Eds.), *Genetics*, Baltimore, Johns Hopkins University Press, In press, cited by Rosenthal (1975).

Hutchinson, R. R., Azrin, N. H., and Hunt, G. M. 'Attack produced by intermittent reinforcement of a concurrent operant response', *Journal of the Experimental Analysis of Behavior*, **11**, 489 (1968).

Insko, C. A., and Oakes, W. F. 'Awareness and the "conditioning" of attitudes', *Journal of Personality and Social Psychology*, **4**, 487 (1966).

Isen, A. M. 'Success, failure, attention and reaction to others: the warm glow of success', *Journal of Personality and Social Psychology*, **15**, 294 (1970).

Jacobs, F. G. *Criminal Responsibility*, London, Weidenfeld & Nicholson, 1971.

Jamieson, R. B. 'Can conditioning principles be applied to probation?', *Trial Judges Journal*, **4**, 7 (1965).

Jensen, G. T. 'Crime doesn't pay: correlates of shared misunderstanding', *Social Problems*, **17**, 189 (1969).

Jessness, C. F. *The Fricot Ranch Study*, Research Report No. 47, California Youth Authority, Sacramento, California, 1965.

Jessness, C. F., and Derisi, W. J. 'Some variations in techniques of contingency management in a school for delinquents', In J. S. Stumphauzer (Ed.), *Behaviour Therapy with Delinquents*, Springfield, Ill., Thomas, 1973, pp. 196–238.

Jinks, J. L., and Fulker, D. W. 'Comparison of the biometrical genetical, MAVA, and classical approaches to the analysis of human behaviour', *Psychological Bulletin*, **73**, 311 (1970).

Joffe, J. M. *Prenatal Determinants of Behaviour*, Oxford, Pergamon, 1969.

Johnston, J. M. 'Punishment of human behaviour', *American Psychologist*, **27**, 1033 (1972).

Jones, R. A. 'Volunteering to help: the effects of choice, dependence and anticipated dependence', *Journal of Personality and Social Psychology*, **14**, 121 (1970).

Kadish, S. I. 'The crisis of overcriminalization', *The Annals of the American Academy of Political and Social Science*, **374**, 158 (1967).

Kalven, H., and Zeisel, H. *The American Jury*, New York, Little, Brown, 1966.

Kanfer, F. H., and Duerfeldt, P. H. 'Age, class standing, and commitment as determinants of cheating in children', *Child Development*, **39**, 544 (1968).

Karacki, L., and Levinson, R. B. 'A token economy in a correctional institution for youthful offenders', *The Howard Journal of Penology and Crime Prevention*, **13**, 20 (1970).

Kaufmann, H. 'The unconcerned bystander', Proceedings of the 76th Annual Convention of the American Psychological Association, **3**, 387 (1968).

Keasey, C. B. 'Experimentally induced changes in moral opinions and reasoning', *Journal of Personality and Social Psychology*, **26**, 30 (1973).

Kellam, A. M. 'Shoplifting treated by aversion to a film, *Behaviour Research and Therapy*, **7**, 125 (1969).

Kelley, H. H. 'The process of causal attribution', *American Psychologist*, **28**, 107 (1973).

Kelly, F. J., and Veldman, D. J. 'Delinquency and school dropout behavior as a function of impulsivity and non-dominant values', *Journal of Abnormal and Social Psychology*, **69**, 190 (1964).

Kelman, H. C. 'Human use of human subjects: the problem of deception in social psycholological experiments', *Psychological Bulletin*, **67**, 1 (1967).

Kelman, H. C. 'The rights of the subject in social research: an analysis in terms of relative power and legitimacy', *American Psychologist*, **27**, 989 (1972).

Kendler, Tracy, S. 'Development of mediating responses in children, In J. C. Wright and J. Kagan (Eds.), *Basic Cognitive Processes in Children*, Monographs of the Society for Research in Child Development, **28**, No. 2 (Serial No. 86), 33 (1968).

Kiesler, C. A., Kiesler, Sara B., and Pallak, M. S. 'The effects of commitment to future interaction on reactions to norm violations', *Journal of Personality*, **35**, 585 (1967).

Kimbles, S. L. *Behaviour Therapy with Delinquents*, Springfield, Ill., Thomas, 1973, pp. 49–53.

Klein, M. W., and Crawford, L. Y. 'Groups, gangs and cohesiveness', *Journal of Research in Crime and Delinquents*, **4**, 63 (1967).

Klinger, E., Albaum, A., and Hetherington, M. 'Factors influencing severity of moral judgements', *Journal of Social Psychology*, **63**, 319 (1964).

Kloek, J. 'Schizophrenia and delinquency', In Rueck and Porter (Eds.), *The Mentally Abnormal Offender*, Boston, Little, Brown, 1968, pp. 19–35.

Knight, B. J., and West, D. J. 'Temporary and continuing delinquency', *British Journal of Criminology*, **15**, 43 (1975).

Kohlberg, L. 'The development of moral character', In Hoffman, M. L., *et al.* (Eds.), *Child Development*, Vol. 1, New York, Russell Sage Foundation, 1964.

Kohlberg, L. 'State and sequence: the cognitive developmental approach to socialization', In Gosler, D. A. (Ed.), *Handbook of Socialization Theory and Research*, New York, Rand McNally, 1969, pp. 347–480.

Koller, K. M. 'Parental deprivation, family background and female delinquency', *British Journal of Psychiatry*, **118**, 319 (1971).

Kranz, H. *Lebenschicksale krimineller Zwillinge*, Berlin, Springer-Verlag, 1936.

Krasner, L. 'Studies of the conditioning of verbal behaviour', *Psychological Bulletin*, **55**, 148 (1965).

Krasner, L., and Ullman, L. P. *Behaviour Influence and Personality: the Social Matrix of Human Action*, New York, Holt, Rhinehart & Winston, 1973.

Krauss, H. H., Robinson, I., Janzen, W., and Cauthen, N. 'Predictions of ethical risk taking by psychopathic and non-psychopathic criminals', *Psychological Reports*, **30**, 83 (1972).

Krebs, D. L. 'Altruism—an examination of the concept and a review of the literature', *Psychological Bulletin*, **73**, 258 (1970).

Kugelmass, S., and Breznitz, S. 'The development of intentionality in moral judgement in city and kibbutz adolescents', *Journal of Genetic Psychology*, **111**, 103 (1967).

Kuipers, E. 'Legal views of determinism', Unpublished manuscript, University of Birmingham, 1974.

Kulik, J. A., Stein, K. B., and Sarbin, T. R. 'Disclosure of delinquent behaviour under conditions of anonymity and non-anonymity', *Journal of Consulting and Clinical Psychology*, **32**, 506 (1968).

Kuo, Z. Y. 'The genesis of the cat's response to the rat', *Journal of Comparative Psychology*, **11**, 1 (1930).

Landy, D., and Aronson, E. 'The influence of the character of the criminal and victim on the decisions of simulated jurors', *Journal of Experimental Social Psychology*, **5**, 141 (1969).

Lang, A. R., Goechner, D. J., Adesso, V. J., and Marlatt, A. G. 'Effects of alcohol on aggression in male social drinkers', *Journal of Abnormal Psychology*, **84**, 508 (1975).

Lange, J. *Verbrechen als Sochicksal*, Leipzig, Georg Thieme Verlag, 1929.

Latané, B. 'The urge to help', Paper presented at the Meeting of the American Psychological Association, Washington, D. C., September, 1967.

Latané, B., and Darley, J. *The Unresponsive Bystander: Why Doesn't He Help?*, New York Appleton-Century-Crofts, 1970.

Laws, D. R. 'The failure of a token economy', *Federal Probation*, **38**, No. 3, 3 (1974).

Lawson, R. B., Greene, R. T., Richardson, J. S., McClure, G., and Padina, R. J. 'Token economy program in a maximum security correctional hospital', *Journal of Nervous and Mental Diseases*, **152**, 199 (1971).

Leftcourt, H. M., Barnes, K., Parker, R. D., and Schwartz, F. 'Anticipated social censure and aggression–conflict as mediators of response to aggression induction', *Journal of Social Psychology*, **70**, 251 (1966).

Lefurgy, W. G., and Waloshin, G. W. 'Immediate and long-term effects of experimentally induced social influence in the modification of adolescents' moral judgements', *Journal of Personality and Social Psychology*, **12**, 104 (1969).

Lehrman, D. S. 'A critique of Konrad Lorenz's theory of instinctive behaviour', *Quarterly Review of Biology*, **28**, 337 (1953).

Leiser, B. M. *Liberty, Justice and Morals*, New York, Macmillan, 1973.

Lemert, E. M. *Social Pathology*, New York, McGraw-Hill, 1951.

Lemert, E. *Human Deviance: Social Problems and Social Control*, 2nd edn., Englewood Cliffs, Prentice-Hall, 1972.

Lerner, M. J., and Mathews, Gail. 'Reactions to suffering of others under conditions of indirect responsibility', *Journal of Personality and Social Psychology*, **5**, 319 (1967).

Lesser, G. S., and Abelson, R. P. 'Personality correlates of persuasibility in children', In C. I. Hovland and I. L. Janis (Eds.), *Personality and Persuasibility*, New Haven, Yale University Press, 1959, pp. 187–206.

Levinson, R. B., Ingram, G. L., and Azcarate, E. 'Aversive group therapy. Sometimes good medicine tastes bad', *Crime and Delinquency*, **14**, 336 (1968).

Leyens, J. P., Camino, L., Parke, R. D., and Berkowitz, L. 'Effects of movie violence in aggression in a field setting as a function of group dominance and cohesion', *Journal of Personality and Social Psychology*, **32**, 346 (1975).

Liebert, R. M. 'Television and Social learning: Some relationships between Viewing Violence and behaving aggressively'. In J. P. Murrary, E. A. Rubeinstein, and G. A. Comstock (Eds.), *Television and Social Behaviour*, Vol. 2, *Television and Social learning Explorations*, Washington, D.C., Govt. Printing Office, pp. 1–42 (1972).

Lifton, R. J. *Thought Reform and the Psychology of Totalism*, New York, Norton, 1961.

Lindzey, G. 'Morphology and behaviour', In G. Lindzey and C. S. Hall (Eds.), *Theories of Personality: Primary Sources and Research*, New York, Wiley, 1965, pp. 344–54.

Lippit, R., Polansky, N., and Rosen, S. 'The dynamics of power', *Human Relations*, **5**, 37 (1952).

Litt, S. 'Perinatal complications and criminality', *Proceedings of the Annual Convention of the American Psychological Association*, **7**, 239 (1972).

Little, A. 'The increase in crime 1952–62: an empirical analysis of adolescent offenders', *British Journal of Criminology*, **5**, 77 (1965).

Logan, C. H. 'Evaluation research in crime and delinquency: a reappraisal', *Journal of Criminal Law, Criminology and Police Science*, **63**, 378 (1972).

Lombroso, C. *Crime, its Causes and Remedies*, Trans. Horton, Boston, Little, Brown, 1911.

London, P. 'The rescuers: motivational hypotheses about Christians who saved Jews from the Nazis', In J. Macaulay and L. Berkowitz (Eds.), *Altruism and Helping Behaviour*, New York, Academic Press, 1970, pp. 241–50.

Loomis, S. D. 'EEG abnormalities as a correlate of behaviour in adolescent male delinquents', *American Journal of Psychiatry*, **121**, 1003 (1965).

Loomis, S. D., Bohnert, P. J., and Huncke, Sheila. 'Predictions of EEG abnormalities in adolescent delinquents', *Archives of General Psychiatry*, **17**, 494 (1967).

Lorenz, K. *On Aggression*, New York, Harcourt Brace Jaranovich, 1966.

Lykken, D. T. 'A study of anxiety in the sociopathic personality', Doctoral dissertation, University of Minnesota, Ann Arbor, Mich., University Microfilms, No. 55, 944 (1955).

Macaulay, S., and Walster, E. 'Legal structures and restoring equity', *Journal of Social Issues*, **27**, 173 (1971).

Maccoby, Eleanor E. 'Dependency behaviour', In P. Mussen (Ed.), *Carmichael's Manual of Child Psychology*, 3rd edn., New York, Wiley, 1966.

Maccoby, E. *The Development of Sex Differences*, London, Tavistock, 1967.

McCandless, B. R., Persons, W. S. III., and Roberts, A. 'Perceived opportunity delinquency, race and body build among delinquent youth', *Journal of Consulting and Clinical Psychology*, **38**, 281 (1972).

McClintock, F. H., Avison, N. H., Savill, N. C., and Worthington, V. L. *Crimes of Violence*, London, Macmillan, 1963.

McClintock, F. H., and Gibson, E. *Robbery in London*, London, Methuen, 1961.

McCord, Joan, and Clemes, S. 'Conscience orientation and dimensions of personality', *Behavioural Science*, **9**, 19 (1964).

McCord, W., McCord, J., and Zola, I. K. *Origins of Crime: A New Evaluation of the Cambridge–Somerville Youth Study*, New York, Columbia University Press, 1959.

McCulloch, M. J., Williams, C. M., and Birtles, C. J. 'The successful application of aversion therapy to an adolescent exhibitionist', *Journal of Behaviour Therapy and Experimental Psychiatry*, **2**, 61 (1971).

MacDonald, J. E. 'The concept of responsibility', *Journal of Mental Science*, **107**, 705 (1955).

McFall, M., and Lillesand, Diane, B. 'Behaviour rehearsal with modelling and coaching in assertion training', *Journal of Abnormal Psychology*, **77**, 313 (1971).

McGrath, P. 'The English special hospital system', In M. J. Craft (Ed.), *Psychopathic Disorders*, Oxford, Pergamon, 1966, pp. 135–44.

McGuire, W. J. 'The nature of attitudes and attitude change', In G. Lindzey and E. Aronson (Eds.), *Handbook of Social Psychology*, Vol. 3, 2nd edn., Reading, Mass., Addison-Wesley, 1969, pp. 136–314.

McKee, J. M. 'Contingency management in a correctional institution', *Educational Technology*, **11**, 51 (1971).

McKerracher, D. W. 'G.S.R. activation and autonomic arousal during a conditioning procedure', *Alberta Psychologist*, **9**, 16 (1969).

McNeil, D., and Levison, N. 'Maturation rate and body build in women', *Child Development*, **34**, 25 (1963).

Maleska, H. E., and Muszynski, H. 'Children's attitudes to theft', In K. Danziger (Ed.), *Readings in Child Socialisation*, Oxford, Pergamon, 1970.

Mannheim, H., and Wilkins, L. T. *Prediction Methods in Relation to Borstal Training*, London, HMSO, 1955.

Martin, D. N., and Warde, Susan. 'The performance of approved school boys on the Gibson spiral maze', *British Journal of Psychology*, **62**, 551 (1971).

Martin, Irene. 'Somatic reactivity: 1. methodology and somatic reactivity. 2. interpretation', In H. J. Eysenck (Ed.), *Handbook of Abnormal Psychology*, 2nd edn., London, Pitman Medical, 1973, pp. 309–61.

Martin, J. P. *Offenders as Employees*, London, Macmillan, 1962.

Martin, M., Burkholder, R., Rosenthal, T. L., Tharp, R. G., and Thorne, G. L. 'Programming behaviour change and reintegration into school milieu of extreme adolescent deviates', *Behaviour Research and Therapy*, **6**, 371 (1968).

Matza, D. *Delinquency and Drift*, New York, Wiley, 1964.

Matza, D. *Becoming Deviant*, New Jersey, Prentice-Hall, 1969.

Mays, J. B. *Crime and the Social Structure*, London, Faber, 1963.

Mead, M. *Sex and Temperament in Three Savage Tribes*, New York, Morrow, 1935.

Medinnus, G. R. 'Age and sex differences in conscience development', *The Journal of Genetic Psychology*, **109**, 117 (1966).

Megargee, E. I. 'Undercontrolled and overcontrolled personality types in extreme antisocial aggression', *Psychological Monographs*, **80**, No. 3 (1966).

Meichenbaum, D. H., and Goodman, J. 'Training impulsive children to talk to themselves: a means of developing self-control', *Journal of Abnormal Psychology*, **77**, 115 (1971).

Mello, N. K. 'Behavioral studies of alcoholism', In B. Kissin and H. Bergliefer (Eds.), *The Biology of Alcoholism*, Vol. 2, New York, Plenum, 1972.

Mellor, Valerie. 'The treatment of paedophiles by anticipatory avoidance learning', Unpublished manuscript, Crumpsall Hospital, Manchester, 1970.

Merbaum, M., and Kazaoka, K. 'Reports of emotional experiences by sensitizers and repressors during an interview transaction', *Journal of Abnormal Psychology*, **72**, 101 (1967).

Merton, R. 'Social structure and anomie', In D. R. Cressey and D. A. Wood (Eds.), *Delinquency, Crime and Social Process*, New York, Harper and Row, 1969, pp. 254–84.

Messick, H. *Lansky*, New York, Berkley Publishing Corporation, 1971.

Metfessel, M., and Lovell, Constance. 'Recent literature on individual correlates of crime', *Psychological Bulletin*, **39**, 133 (1942).

Meyer, H. J., Bargatta, E. F., and Jones, W. C. *Girls at Vocational High*, New York, Russell Sage Foundation, 1965.

Michael, C. M., and Coltharp, F. C. 'Application of Glueck social prediction scale in the identification of potential juvenile delinquents', *American Journal of Psychiatry*, **32**, 264 (1962).

Middleton, P. M. 'Motor deprivations on paralyzed awareness in the treatment of delinquency', Paper read at the International Congress of Social Psychiatry, London, 1964.

Midlarsky, Elizabeth. 'Some antecedents of aiding under stress', *Proceedings of the Annual Convention of the American Psychological Association*, **3**, 385 (1968).

Midlarsky, Elizabeth, and Bryan, J. H. 'Training charity in children', *Journal of Personality and Social Psychology*, **5**, 408 (1967).

Milgram, S. 'Behavioural study of obedience', *Journal of Abnormal Social Psychology*, **67**, 371 (1963).

Milgram, S. 'Group pressure and action against a person', *Journal of Abnormal Psychology*, **69**, 137 (1964).

Milgram, S. 'Liberating effects of group pressure', *Journal of Personality and Social Psychology*, **1**, 127 (1965a).

Milgram, S. 'Some conditions of obedience and disobedience to authority', *Human Relations*, **18**, 57 (1965b).

Milgram, S. *Obedience to Authority*, London, Tavistock, 1974.

Milgram, S., and Toch, H. 'Collective behavior: crowds and social movements', In G. Lindzey and E. Aronson (Eds.), *Handbook of Social Psychology*, Vol. 4, 2nd edn., New York, Addison-Wesley, 1969, pp. 507–610.

Miller, L. C. 'Southfields: Evolution of a short-term inpatient treatment centre for delinquents', *Crime and Delinquency*, **16**, 305 (1970).

Miller, R. E. 'Experimental approaches to the physiological and behavioural concomitants of affective communication in rhesus monkeys', In S. A. Altmann (Ed.), *Social Communications Among Primates*, University of Chicago Press, 1967, pp. 125–34.

Miller, R. E., Banks, J. H. Jr., and Ogawa, N. 'Role of social expression in cooperative-avoidance conditioning in monkeys', *Journal of Abnormal and Social Psychology*, **67**, 24–30, (1963).

Miller, R. E., Cavl, W. F., and Mirsky, I. A. 'Communication of effect between feral and socially isolated monkeys', *Journal of Personality and Social Psychology*, **7**, 231 (1967).

Miller, R. E., Murphy, J. V., and Mirsky, I. A. 'The relevance of facial expression and posture as cues in the communication of effect between monkeys', *Archives of General Psychiatry*, **1**, 480 (1959).

Mischel, W. *Personality and Assessment*, New York, Wiley, 1968.

Mischel, W., and Liebert, R. M. 'Effects of discrepancies between observed and imposed reward criteria on their acquisition and transmission', *Journal of Personality and Social Psychology*, **3**, 45 (1966).

Mitchell, H. E., and Byrne, D. 'Minimizing the influence of irrelevant factors in the court-room: the defendant's character, judge's instructions, and authoritarianism', Unpublished manuscript, Purdue University, 1973a.

Mitchell, H. E., and Byrne, D. 'The defendant's dilemma: effects of jurors' attitudes and authoritarianism on judicial decisions', *Journal of Personality and Social Psychology*, **25**, 123 (1973b).

Mohr, J. W., Turner, R. E., and Jerry, M. B. *Paedophilia and Exhibitionism*, London, Oxford University Press, 1964.

Morgan, P. *Child Care: Sense and Fable*, London, Temple Smith, 1975.

Morris, N. *The Habitual Criminal*, London, Longmans Green, 1951.

Morris, T. *The Criminal Area*, London, Routledge & Kegan Paul, 1957.

Mosher, D. L. 'Verbal aggressive behavior in delinquent boys', *Journal of Abnormal Psychology*, **73**, 454 (1968).

Moss, M. K., and Page, R. A. 'Reinforcement for helping behaviour', *Journal of Applied Social Psychology*, **2**, 360 (1972).

Mowrer, O. H. *Learning Theory and Behaviour*, New York, Wiley, 1960.

Naess, S. 'Mother child separation and delinquency', *British Journal of Delinquency*, **10**, 22 (1959).

Nagel, S. S. 'The tipped scales of American justice', In A. S. Blumberg (Ed.), *The Scales of Justice*, Chicago, Aldine, 1970.

Nelson, A. E., Grinder, R. E., and Mutterer, M. L. 'Sources of variance in behavioural measures of honesty in temptation situations', *Developmental Psychology*, **1**, 265 (1969).

Nelson, J. D., Gelfand, D. M., and Hartmann, D. P. 'Children's aggression following competition and exposure to an aggressive model', *Child Development*, **40**, 1085 (1969).

Newman, D. J. 'Pleading guilty for considerations: A study of bargain justice', *Journal of Criminal Law, Criminology and Police Science*, **46**, 780 (1956).

New York Times. 'One of fifteen shoplifts, study discloses', December 2nd, 1970, C. 45.

Nye, F. I. *Family Relations and Delinquent Behavior*, New York, Wiley, 1958.

Oaks, D. H., and Lehman, W. 'Lawyers for the poor', In A. S. Blumberg (Ed.), *The Scales of Justice*, Chicago, Aldine, 1970.

O'Donnell, C., Chambers, E., and Ling, K. 'Athletics as reinforcement in a community program for academic achievement', Unpublished manuscript, University of Hawaii, 1973.

O'Donnell, C. R., and De Leon, Jean L. 'A contingency program for academic achievement in a correctional setting: gains and time in school', *Journal of Community Psychology*, **1**, 285 (1974).

O'Donnell, C. R., and Stanley, Kathleen, 'Paying students for academic performance', Unpublished manuscript, University of Hawaii, 1973.

Offenbach, S. I. 'Reinforcer acquisition in discrimination learning', *Psychological Reports*, **19**, 843–49 (1966).

Ogden, D. A. 'Use of surgical rehabilitation in young delinquents', *British Medical Journal*, **2**, 432 (1959).

O'Leary, K. O. 'The effects of self-instructions on immoral behaviour', *Journal of Experimental Child Psychology*, **6**, 297 (1968).

Olweus, D. 'Bullies and whipping boys', In J. de Wit and W. W. Hartup (Eds.), *Determinants and Origins of Aggressive Behaviour*, The Hague, Mouton, 1975.

Osborne, D. K., and Endsley, R. C. 'Emotional reactions of young children to TV violence', *Child Development*, **42**, 321 (1971).

Ostrom, S. M., Steele, C. M., Rosenblood, Lorna K., and Mirels, H. L. 'Modification of delinquent behaviour', *Journal of Applied Social Psychology*, **1**, 118 (1971).

Owen, D. R. 'The 47, XYY male: a review', *Psychological Bulletin*, **18**, 209 (1972).

Parke, R. D., Berkowitz, L., Leyens, J. P., and Sebastian, R. 'The effects of repeated exposure to movie violence on aggressive behaviour in juvenile delinquent boys', In L. Berkowitz (Ed.), *Advances in Experimental Social Psychology*, Vol. 8, New York, Academic Press (In press).

Parke, R. D., Wiederholt, C., and Slaby, R. G. 'The effect of exposure to a model's aggressive verbalizations on the observer's motor aggression', Unpublished manuscript, University of Wisconsin, 1972.

Parker, T. *The Frying Pan: A Prison and its Prisoners*, London, Gollancz, 1970.

Parlett, T. A. A., and Ayers, J. D. 'The modification of criminal personality through massed learning by programmed instruction', *Canadian Journal of Corrections and Criminology*, **13**, 155 (1971).

Pasewark, R. A., Bernard, J., and Watson, R. C. 'Associated personality differences in delinquents and non-delinquents', *Journal of Personality and Assessment*, **35**, 159 (1971).

Patchett, K. W., and McLean, J. D. 'Decision making in juvenile cases', *Criminal Law Review*, 53 (1956).

Patterson, G. R. 'Interventions for boys with conduct problems: multiple settings, treatments and criteria', *Journal of Consulting and Clinical Psychology*, **42**, 471 (1974).

Pease, K., Durkin, P., Earnshaw, I., Payne, D., and Thorpe, J. *Community Service Orders*, London, HMSO, 1975.

Penney, R. K. 'Effect of reward and punishment on children's orientation and discrimination learning', *Journal of Experimental Psychology*, 75, 140 (1967).

Persons, R. W. 'Relationship between psychotherapy with institutionalized boys and subsequent community adjustment', *Journal of Consulting Psychology*, **31**, 137 (1967).

Phillips, E. L. 'Achievement Place: Token reinforcement procedures in a home style rehabilitation setting for "pre-delinquent" boys', *Journal of Applied Behavior Analysis*, **1**, 213 (1968).

Phillips, E. L., Phillips, Elaine A., Fixsen, D. L., and Wolfe, M. M. 'Achievement Place: Modification of the behaviours of pre-delinquent boys within a token economy', *Journal of Applied Behavior Analysis*, **4**, 45 (1971).

Phillips, E. L., Phillips, Elaine A., Wolf, M. M., and Fixsen, D. L. 'Achievement Place: development of the elected manager system', *Journal of Applied Behaviour Analysis*, **6**, 541–561, (1973).

Piaget, J. *The Moral Judgement of the Child*, London, Kegan Paul, 1932.

Piliavin, I., and Briar, S. 'Police encounters with juveniles', *American Journal of Sociology*, **70**, 206 (1964).

Piliavin, I. M., Hardyck, A. J., and Vadum, A. C. 'Reactions to the victim in a just or non-just world', Paper presented at the meeting of the Society of Experimental Social Psychology, Bethesda, Maryland, August, 1967.

Piliavin, I. M., Hardyck, A. J., and Vadum, A. C. 'Constraining effects of personal costs on the transgressions of juveniles', *Journal of Personality and Social Psychology*, **10**, 227 (1969).

Piliavin, J. A., and Piliavin, I. M. 'Effect of blood on reactions to a victim', *Journal of Personality and Social Psychology*, **23**, 353 (1972).

Piliavin, I. M., Rodin, J., and Piliavin, J. A. 'Good Samaritanism: a underground phenomenon?', *Journal of Personality and Social Psychology*, **13**, 289 (1969).

Piliavin, I. M., Vadum, A. C., and Hardyck, A. J. 'Delinquency, personal costs and parental treatment: A test of a reward–cost model', *Journal of Criminal Law, Criminology and Police Science*, **60**, 165 (1969).

Pittel, S. M., and Mendelsohn, G. A. 'Measurement of moral values', *Psychological Bulletin*, **66**, No. 1, 22 (1966).

Pittman, D. J., and Handy, W. 'Patterns in criminal aggravated assault', *Journal of Criminal Law, Criminology and Political Science*, **55**, 462 (1964).

Polsky, H. W. *Cottage Six: The Social Systems of Delinquent Boys in Residential Treatment*, New York, Russell Sage Foundation, 1962.

Porro, C. R. 'Effects of the observation of a model's affective responses to her own transgression on resistance to temptation in children', *Dissertation Abstracts*, **28**, 3064 (1968).

Porterfield, A. L. *Youth in Trouble*, Fort Worth, Texas, Lee Potishman Foundation, 1946.

Porteus, B. D., and Johnson, R. C. 'Children's responses to two measures of conscience development and their relation to sociometric nomination', *Child Development*, **36**, 703 (1965).

Powell, D. A., and Creer, T. L. 'Interaction of developmental and environmental variables in shock-elicited aggression', *Journal of Comparative and Physiological Psychology*, **69**, 219 (1969).

Prentice, N. M. 'The influence of live and symbolic modelling in promoting moral judgement of adolescent delinquents', *Journal of Abnormal Psychology*, **80**, 157 (1972).

Prentice, N. M., and Kelly, F. J. 'Intelligence and delinquency: a reconsideration', *Journal of Social Psychology*, **60**, 327 (1963).

Price, W. H., and Whatmore, P. B. 'Behaviour disorders and pattern of crime among XYY males identified at a maximum security hospital', *British Medical Journal*, **1**, 533 (1967a).

Price, W. H., and Whatmore, P. B. 'Criminal behaviour and the XYY male', *Nature*, **213**, (1967b).

Quay, H. C. 'Personality and delinquency', In H. C. Quay (Ed.), *Juvenile Delinquency*, Princeton, N. J., Van Nostrand, 1965.

Quinney, R. *Critique of Legal Order: Crime Control in Capitalist Society*, Boston, Little, Brown, 1974.

Rachman, S. J. *The Effects of Psychotherapy*, Oxford, Pergamon, 1972.

Rachman, S. J., and Teasdale, J., *Aversion Therapy and the Behaviour Disorders*, London, Routledge and Kegan Paul, 1969.

Radzinowicz, L. *Sexual Offences*, London, Macmillan, 1957.

Radzinowicz, L. 'Preface', In F. H. McClintock and F. Gibson, London, Macmillan, 1961, pp. vii–xix.

Reckless, W. C. 'A non-causal explanation: Containment theory', *Excerpta Crimonologica*, **2**, 131 (1962).

Rees, L. 'Constitutional factors and abnormal behaviour', In H. J. Eysenck (Ed.), *Handbook of Abnormal Psychology*, 2nd edn., London, Pitman Medical, 1973, pp. 487–539.

Reitz, W., and Keil, W. 'Behavioural treatment of an exhibitionist', *Journal of Behaviour Therapy and Experimental Psychiatry*, **2**, 67 (1971).

307

Reitzes, D. C. 'The effect of social environment upon former felons', *Journal of Criminal Law, Criminology and Police Science*, **46**, 226 (1955).

Rest, J., Turiel, E., and Kohlberg, L. 'Level of moral development as a determinant of preference and comprehension of moral judgements made by others', *Journal of Personality*, **37**, 225 (1969).

Rettig, S. 'Ethical risk sensitivity in male prisoners', *British Journal of Criminology*, **4**, 582 (1964).

Rettig, S. 'Ethical risk taking in group and individual conditions', *Journal of Personality and Social Psychology*, **4**, 648 (1966).

Rettig, S., and Pasamanick, B. 'The differential judgement of ethical risk by cheaters and non-cheaters', *Journal of Abnormal and Social Psychology*, **69**, 110 (1964).

Rettig, S., and Rawson, H. E. 'The risk hypothesis in predictive judgements of unethical behaviour', *Journal of Abnormal and Social Psychology*, **66**, 243 (1963).

Rettig, S., and Singh, P. N. *Israel Annals of Psychiatry*, **1**, 225 (1963).

Rettig, S., and Sinha, J. B. 'Bad faith and ethical risk sensitivity', *Journal of Personality*, **34**, 275 (1966).

Rettig, S., and Turoff, S. J. 'Exposure to group discussion and predicted ethical risk taking', *Journal of Personality and Social Psychology*, **7**, 177 (1967).

Richmond, M. S. 'Measuring the cost of correctional services', *Crime and Delinquency*, **18**, 243 (1972).

Rickles, N. K. *Exhibitionism*, Philadelphia, Lippencott, 1950.

Robin, G. D. 'The corporate and judicial dispositions of employee thieves', In E. O. Smigel and H. L. Ross, *Crimes Against Bureaucracy*, New York, Van Nostrand Deinhold, 1970, pp. 124–46.

Robins, L. N. *Deviant Children Growth Up*, Baltimore, Williams and Wilkins, 1966.

Robinson, N. 'Harm, offence and nuisance', *American Psychologist*, **29**, 233 (1974).

Rokeach, M. *Beliefs, Attitudes and Values*, San Francisco, Josey-Bass, 1968.

Rosanoff, A. J., Handy, L. M., and Plesset, I. R. 'The etiology of child behaviour difficulties, juvenile delinquency and adult criminality with special reference to their occurrence in twins', *Psychiatric Monographs* (California), No. 1 Sacramento, Department of Institutions, 1941.

Rose, G. 'Early identification of delinquents', *British Journal of Criminology*, **7**, 6 (1967).

Rosen, I. 'Exhibitionism', In I. Rosen (Ed.), *The Psychology and Treatment of Sexual Deviation*, London, Oxford University Press, 1964.

Rosenhan, D. L. 'The natural socialization of altruistic autonomy, In J. Macaulay and L. Berkowitz (Eds.), *Altruism and Helping Behavior*, New York, Academic Press, 1970, pp. 251–68.

Rosenhan, D. L. 'On being sane in insane places', *Science*, **179**, 250 (1973).

Rosenkrans, M. A., and Hartup, W. W. 'Imitative influences of consistent and inconsistent response consequences to a model on aggressive behavior in children', *Journal of Personality and Social Psychology*, **7**, 429 (1967).

Rosenthal, A. M. 'Study of sickness called apathy', *New York Times*, Magazine Section, May 3rd, 1964, p. 24.

Rosenthal, D. *Genetics of Psychopathology*, New York, McGraw-Hill, 1971.

Rosenthal, D. 'Heredity in criminality', *Criminal Justice and Behaviour*, **2**, 3 (1975).

Rosenthal, R. *Experimenter Effects in Behavioural Research*, New York, Appleton-Century-Crofts, 1966.

Ross, M., Thibaut, J., and Evenbeck, S. 'Some determinants of the intensity of social protest', *Journal of Experimental Social Psychology*, **7**, 401 (1971).

Rosser, P. 'An analysis of the variables which influence the deterrent effects of punishment', Unpublished manuscript, Department of Psychology, University of Birmingham, 1975.

Roth, M. 'Cerebral disease and mental disorders of old age as causes of antisocial behaviour', In Rueck and Porter (Eds.), *The Mentally Abnormal Offender*, Boston, Little, Brown, 1968, pp. 35–8.

Rotter, J. B. 'Generalised expectancies for internal versus external control of reinforcement', *Psychological Monographs*, **80**, (Whole No. 609) (1966).

Rule, B. G., Dyck, R., McAra, M., and Nesdale, A. R. 'Judgements of aggression serving personal versus prosocial purposes', *Social Behavior and Personality*, **3**, 55 (1975).

Rutter, M. 'Parent–child separation: Psychological effects on the children, *Journal of Child Psychology and Psychiatry*, **12**, 233 (1971).

Rutter, M. *Maternal Deprivation Reassessed*, London, Pelican, 1972. *San Francisco Chronicle*. 'A badge for killing reds', June 11th, 1970, p. 23.

Sandler, J. 'Masochism: an empirical analysis', *Psychological Bulletin*, **62**, 179 (1964).

Saxby, P., Norris, A., and Feldman, M. P. 'Questionnaire studied self-reported antisocial behaviour and extraversion in adolescents', Unpublished manuscript, Department of Psychology, University of Birmingham, 1970.

Scarr, S. 'The inheritance of sociability', *American Psychologist*, **20**, 524 (Abstract) (1965).

Schachter, S. 'Criminal sociopathy, epinephrine and avoidance learning', In S. Schachter, *Emotion, Obesity and Crime*, New York, Academic Press, 1971, pp. 152–83.

Schachter, S. *The Psychology of Affiliation*, Stanford, Stanford Clairensety Press, 1959.

Schachter, S., and Latané, B. 'Crime, cognition and the autonomic nervous system', In M. R. Jones (Ed.), *Nebraska Symposium on Motivation*, Lincoln, University of Nebrasks, 1964, pp. 221–75.

Schalling, D., and Holmberg, M. 'Extraversion in criminals and the "dual nature" of extraversion: Comments based on the results obtained by inventories', *Report of Psychology Laboratories, University of Stockholm*, 1970, No. 306.

Schlesinger, A. M. Jr. *A Thousand Days: John F. Kennedy in the White House*, New York, Houghton Mifflin, 1965.

Schmidt, G., and Sigusch, V. 'Changes in social behaviour among young males and females between 1960–1970', *Archives of Sexual Behaviour*, **2**, 27 (1972).

Schneider, K. *Psychopathic Personalities*, 9th edn., London, Cassell, 1959.

Schofield, M. *The Sexual Behaviour of Young People*, London, Pelican, 1965a.

Schofield, M. *Sociological Aspects of Homosexuality*, London, Longmans, 1965b.

Schofield, M. *The Strange Case of Pot*, London, Pelican, 1971.

Schopler, J., and Bateson, N. 'The power of dependence', *Journal of Personality and Social Psychology*, **2**, 247 (1965).

Schrag, E. *Crime and Justice: American Style*, Washington, D.C. GPO, 1971.

Schuessler, K. F., and Cressey, D. R. 'Personality characteristics of criminals' *American Journal of Sociology*, **35**, 476 (1950).

Schulsinger, F. 'Psychopathy, heredity and environment', In L. Erlenmayer-Kimling (Ed.), *International Journal of Mental Health*, **1**, 190 (1972).

Schultze, J. *Sensory Restriction: Effects on Behaviour*, New York, Academic Press, 1965.

Schur, E. M. *Crimes without Victims: Deviant Behaviour and Public Policy: Abortion, Homosexuality, Drug Addiction*, Englewood Cliffs, New Jersey: Prentice-Hall, 1965.

Schwartz, R. D., and Skolnick, J. H. 'Two studies of legal stigma', In H. S. Becker (Ed.), *The Other Side*, New York, Free Press, 1964, pp. 103–18.

Schwitzgebel, R., and Covey, T. N. 'Short-term operant conditioning of adolescent offenders on socially relevant variables', *Journal of Abnormal Psychology*, **72**, 134 (1967).

Schwitzgebel, R., and Kolb, D. A. 'Inducing behaviour changes in adolescent delinquents', *Behaviour Research and Therapy*, **1**, 297 (1964).

Scura, W. C., and Eisenman, R. 'Punishment learning in psychopaths with social and nonsocial reinforcers', *Corrective Psychiatry and Journal of Social Therapy*, **17**, 58 (1971).

Sears, R. R., Maccoby, Eleanor, E., and Levin, H. *Patterns of Child Rearing*, Evansten, Peteron, 1957.

Seay, W., Alexander, B. K., and Harlow, H. F. 'Maternal behaviour of socially deprived rhesus monkeys', *Journal of Abnormal and Social Psychology*, **69**, 345 (1964).

Seligman, M. E. P. *Helplessness*, San Francisco, Freeman, 1975.

Sellin, T., and Wolfgang, M. E. *The Measurement of Delinquency*, New York, Wiley, 1964.

Shaver, K. G. 'Redress and conscientiousness in the attribution of responsibility for accidents', *Journal of Experimental Social Psychology*, **6**, 100 (1970a).

Shaver, K. G. 'Defensive attribution: effects of severity and relevance in the responsibility assigned for an accident', *Journal of Personality and Social Psychology*, **14**, 101 (1970b).

Sheldon, W. H. *The Varieties of Temperament: A Psychology of Constitutional Differences*, New York, Harper 1942.

Shields, J. *Monozygotic Twins brought up Apart and Together*, Oxford, Oxford University Press, 1962.

Shields, J. 'Heredity and psychological abnormality', In H. J. Eysenck, *Handbook of Abnormal Psychology*, 2nd edn., London, Pitman Medical, 1973, pp. 540–603.

Shoham, S., Ben-David, Sarah, and Smilansky, J. O. 'Rehabilitation treatment in institutions for juvenile delinquents in Israel', *Abstracts on Criminology and Penology*, **11**, 2 (1971).

Short, J. F., and Nye, F. I. 'Extent of unrecorded juvenile delinquency', *Journal of Criminal Law, Criminology, and Police Science*, **49**, 296 (1958).

Shortell, J., Epstein, S., and Taylor, S. P. 'Instigation to aggression as a function of degree of defect and the capacity for massive retaliations', *Journal of Personality*, **38**, 313 (1970).

Siegel, A. E. 'The influence of violence in the mass media upon children's role expectation', *Child Development*, **29**, 35 (1958).

Sigall, H., and Ostrove, Nancy. 'Beautiful but dangerous: effects of offender attractiveness and nature of the crime as juridic judgements', *Journal of Personality and Social Psychology*, **31**, 410 (1975).

Silber, D. E. 'Controversy concerning the criminal justice system and its implications for the role of mental health workers', *American Psychologist*, **29**, 234 (1974).

Silver, A. W. 'TAT and MMPI Psychopathic deviant scale differences between delinquent and non-delinquent adolescents', *Journal of Consulting Psychology*, **27**, 370 (1963).

Silverman, W. H. 'The effects of social contact, provocations, and sex of opponent upon instrumental aggression', *Journal of Experimental Research in Personality*, **5**, 310 (1971).

Singer, J. L. 'The influence of violence portrayed in television or motion pictures upon overt aggressive behaviour', In J. L. Singer (Ed.), *The Control of Aggression and Violence*, New York, Academic Press, 1971, pp. 19–60.

Sloane, H. C., and Ralph, J. L. 'A behaviour modification programme in Nevada', *International Journal of Offender Therapy and Criminology*, **17**, 290 (1973).

Smith, C. E. 'Recognizing and sentencing the exceptional and dangerous offender', *Federal Probation*, **4**, 3 (1971).

Smith, J., and Lanyon, L. I. 'Prediction of juvenile probation violators', *Journal of Consulting and Clinical Psychology*, **32**, 54 (1968).

Smith, R. E., Smyth, Lisa, and Lien, P. 'Inhibition of helping behaviour by a similar or dissimilar non-reactive fellow bystander', *Journal of Personality and Social Psychology*, **23**, 414 (1972).

Solomon, R., Turner, Lucille, and Lessac, M. S. 'Some effects of delay of punishment on resistance to temptation in dogs', *Journal of Personality and Social Psychology*, **8**, 233 (1968).

Spence, K. W. *Behaviour Therapy and Conditioning*, London, Oxford University Press, 1956.

Spergel, I. *Racketville, Slumtown, Haulberg: An Exploratory Study of Delinquent Subculture*, Chicago, University of Chicago Press, 1964.

Sperlinger, D. J. 'A repertory grid and questionnaire study of individuals receiving treatment for depression from general practitioners', Unpublished Ph.D. thesis, University of Birmingham, 1971.

Staats, A. W. 'An integrated-functional approach to complex human behaviour', In

B. Kleinmuntz (Ed.), *Problem Solving: Research, Method and Theory*, New York, Wiley, 1966.

Staats, A. W., and Staats, C. K. 'Attitudes established by classical conditioning', *Journal of Abnormal and Social Psychology*, **57**, 37 (1958).

Staub, E., and Feagans, L. 'Effects of age and number of witnesses in children's attempts to help another child in distress', Paper presented at the 40th annual meeting of the Eastern Psychological Association, Philadelphia, Pennsylvania, April 1969.

Steadman, H. J., and Cocozza, J. J., 'Stimulus/response: We can't predict who is dangerous', *Psychology Today*, **8**, 32 (1975).

Stefanowicz, J. P., and Hannum, T. E. 'Ethical risk-taking and sociopathy in incarcerated females', *Correctional Psychologist*, **4**, 138 (1971).

Stewart, D. J. 'Effects of social reinforcement on dependency and aggressive responses of psychopathic, neurotic, and subcultural delinquents', *Journal of Abnormal Psychology*, **29**, 76 (1972).

Stotland, E. 'Exploratory investigations of empathy', In L. Berkowitz (Ed.), *Advances in Experimental Social Psychology*, Vol. 4, New York, Academic Press, 1969.

Stuart, R. B. 'Behavioural contracting within the families of delinquents', *Journal of Behaviour Therapy and Experimental Psychiatry*, **2**, 1 (1971).

Stumpfl, F. *Die Ursprunge des Verbrechens om Lebenshauf Von Zwillingen*, Leipzig, Georg Thieme Verlag, 1936.

Stumphauzer, J. S. 'Modification of delay choices in institutionalised youthful offenders through social reinforcement', *Psychonomic Science*, **18**, 222 (1970).

Stumphauzer, J. S. 'Increased delay of gratification in young prison inmates through imitation of high delay peer models', *Journal of Personality and Social Psychology*, **21**, 10 (1972).

Stürup, G. K. 'Will this man be dangerous?', In A. V. S. de Rueck, and R. Porter (Eds.), *The Mentally Abnormal Offender*, London, Churchill, 1968.

Sunday Times. 'Cops are robbers', October 6th, 1974.

Sunday Times. 'Jail's grim secret', October 20th, 1974, p. 1.

Sunday Times. 'Model jail fails to reform prisoners', November 30th, 1975.

Sutherland, E. H. *The Professional Thief*, Chicago, University of Chicago Press, 1937.

Sutherland, E. H. 'Crime and business', *The Annals*, **217**, 113 (1941).

Sutherland, E. H., and Gressey, D. R. *Criminology*, 8th edn., New York, Lippincott, 1970.

Sutker, P. B. 'Vicarious conditioning and sociopathy', *Journal of Abnormal Psychology*, **76**, 380 (1970).

Sutker, Patricia B., Gil, Sandra H., and Sutker, L. B. 'Sociopathy and serial learning of CVC combinations with high and low social content ratings', *Journal of Personality and Social Psychology*, **17**, 158 (1971).

Sykes, G. M. *The Society of Captives*, Princeton, New Jersey, Princeton University Press, 1958.

Tannenbaum, P. H. 'Studies in film- and television-mediated arousal and aggression: A progress report', In G. A. Comstock, E. A. Rubinstein and J. P. Murray (Eds.), *Television and Social Behaviour*, Vol. 5, Television effects: Further explorations, Washington, D.C., Government Printing Office, 1972, pp. 309–50.

Taylor, S. P. 'Aggressive behaviour and physiological arousal as a function of provocation and the tendency to inhibit aggression', *Journal of Personality*, **35**, 297 (1967).

Taylor, S. P., and Epstein, S. 'Aggression as a function of the interaction of the sex of the aggressor and the sex of the victim', *Journal of Personality*, **35**, 474 (1967).

Taylor, S. P., and Gammon, C. B. 'Effects of type and dose of alcohol on human physical aggression', *Journal of Personality and Social Psychology*, **32**, 161 (1975).

Teresa, V. (with Renner, T.) *My Life in the Mafia*, New York, Doubleday, 1973.

Teuber, N., and Powers, E. 'Evaluating therapy in a delinquency prevention program', *Proceedings of the Association for Research in Nervous and Mental Diseases*, **3**, 138 (1953).

Tharp, R. G., and Wetzel, R. H. *Behaviour Modification in the Natural Environment*, New York, Academic Press, 1969.

Thibaut, J. W., and Kelly, H. H. *The Social Psychology of Groups*, New York, Wiley, 1959.

Thomas, D. S. *Social Aspects of the Business Cycle*, London, Routledge, 1925.

Thomas, C. W. 'Prisonization or resocialization? A study of external factors associated with the impact of imprisonment', *Journal of Research in Crime and Delinquency*, 13 (1973).

Thorne, G. L., Tharpe, R. G., and Wetzel, R. J. 'Behaviour modification techniques: New tools for probation officers', *Federal Probation*, **31**, 21 (1967).

Tilker, H. A. 'Socially responsible behaviour as a function of observer responsibility and victim feedback', *Journal of Personality and Social Psychology*, **14**, 95 (1970).

Time. 'Busting public servants', April 23rd, 1972, p. 26.

Time. '"Behaviour mod" behind the walls', March 11th, 1974, pp. 42–3.

Tinbergen, N. 'On war and peace in animals and man', *Science*, **160**, 1411 (1968).

Tittle, C. R., and Tittle, D. P. 'Social organisation of prisoners: an empirical test', *Social Forces*, **43**, 216 (1964).

Toch, H. *Violent Men*, Chicago, Aldine, 1969.

Tolsma, F. J. *De Betekemis van der Verleidung in Homofiele Ontirikkelingen*. Amsterdam, Psychiatrijudicial Society, 1957.

Trasler, G. 'Criminal Behaviour' In H. J. Eysenck (Ed.), *Handbook of Abnormal Psychology* (Second Edn.), London, Pitman Medical, pp. 67–96, 1973.

Turiel, E. 'An experimental test of the sequentiality of developmental stages in the child's moral judgements', *Journal of Personality and Social Psychology*, **3**, 611 (1966).

Turner, C. W., Layton, J. F., and Simon, L. S. 'Naturalistic studies of aggressive behaviour: aggressive stimuli, victim visibility and horn honking', *Journal of Personality and Social Psychology*, **31**, 1098 (1975).

Tuxford, J. 'Treatment as a circular process', Report to the King Edward Hospital Fund, unpublished, 1962.

Tyler, V. O., Jnr., and Brown, G. D. 'The use of swift brief isolation as a group control device for institutionalized delinquents', *Behaviour Research and Therapy*, **5**, 1 (1967).

Tyler, V. O., and Kelly, R. F. 'Predicting the behaviour of institutionalised delinquents with—and without—Cattell's HSPQ', *Educational and Psychological Measurement*, **31**, 1019 (1971).

Ullmann, L. P., and Krasner, L. *A Psychological Approach to Abnormal Behaviour*, New York, Prentice-Hall, 1969.

Ulrich, R. E., and Azrin, N. H. 'Reflexive fighting in response to aversive stimulation', *Journal of the Experimental Analysis of Behaviour*, **5**, 511 (1962).

Vandenberg, S. G. 'Contributions of twin research to psychology', *Psychological Bulletin*, **66**, 327 (1966).

Venables, P. E. 'Psychophysiological variables', In M. P. Feldman and Anne Broadhurst (Eds.), *The Experimental and Theoretical Bases of the Behaviour Therapies*, London, Wiley, 1976, pp. 43–72.

Vernon, P. E. *Personality and Assessment: A Critical Survey*, London, Methuen, 1964.

Vernon, W., and Ulrich, R. 'Classical conditioning of pain elicited aggression', *Science*, **152**, 668 (1966).

Voss, H. L. 'The predictive-efficiency of the Glueck Social Prediction Scales', *Journal of Criminal Law, Criminology*, and Police Science, **54**, 421 (1963).

Voss, H. L. 'Differential association and containment theory: A theoretical convergence', *Social Forces*, **47**, 381 (1969).

Waddington, C. H. *The Ethical Animal*, Chicago, University of Chicago Press, 1967.

Wadsworth, M. E. J. 'Delinquency in a national sample of children', *British Journal of Criminology*, **15**, 167 (1975).

Wagner, C., Manning, S., and Wheeler, L. 'Character structure and helping behaviour', *Journal of Experimental Research in Personality*, **5**, 37 (1971).

Waldman, D. M., and Baron, R. A. 'Aggression as a function of exposure and similarity to a non-aggressive model', *Psychonomic Science*, **23**, 381 (1971).

Walker, N. *Crime and Punishment in Great Britain*, Edinburgh, Edinburgh University Press, 1965.

Walker, N. *Crimes, Court and Figures. An Introduction to Criminal Statistics*, London, Pelican, 1971.

Wallace, J., and Sadalla, E. 'Behavioural consequences of transgression. 1. The effects of social recognition', *Journal of Experimental Research in Personality*, **1**, 187 (1966).

Wallerstein, J. S., and Wyle, C. J. 'Our law-abiding law-breakers', *Probation*, **25**, 107 (1947).

Walster, Elaine. 'Assignment of responsibility for an accident', *Journal of Personality and Social Psychology*, **3**, 73 (1966).

Walster, Elaine. '"Second-guessing" important events', *Human Relations*, **20**, 239 (1967).

Walster, Elaine, Berscheid, Ellen, and Walster, G. W. 'New directions in equity research', *Journal of Personality and Social Psychology*, **25**, 151 (1973).

Walters, R. H., and Brown, M. 'Studies of reinforcement of aggression: III Transfer of responses to an interpersonal situation', *Child Development*, **34**, 563 (1963).

Walters, R. H. 'Delay of reinforcement gradients in childrens learning', *Psychonomic Science*, **1**, 307–308, 1964.

Walters, R. H., Parke, R. D., and Cane, Valerie. 'Timing of punishment and the observation of consequence to others as determinants of response inhibitions', *Journal of of Experimental Child Psychology*, **2**, 10 (1965).

Wardle, C. J. 'Two generations of broken homes in the genesis of conduct and behaviour disorders in children', *British Medical Journal*, August 5th, 349 (1961).

Warren, Margaret Q., Palmer, T. B., Neto, V., and Turner, J. K. 'Community Treatment Project: Research Report No. 7', California Youth and Adult Correction Authority, Sacramento, California, 1966.

Washington Post. 'White House parties', December 15th, 1972.

Watson, J. B. *Psychology from the Standpoint of a Behaviourist*, Philadelphia, Lippincott, 1919.

Weathers, L., and Liberman, R. P. 'Contingency contracting with families of delinquent adolescents', *Behaviour Therapy*, **6**, 356 (1975).

Weeks, H. A. *The Highfield Project and its Success*, In N. Johnston, L. Savitz and M. E. Wolfgang (Eds.), *The Sociology of Punishment and Correction*, New York, Wiley, 1962, pp. 203–12.

Weiner, N. L. 'The effects of education on police attitudes', *Journal of Criminal Justice*, **2**, 317 (1974).

Weiss, R. F., Buchanan, W., Alstatt, Lynne, and Lombardo, J. P. 'Altruism is rewarding', *Science*, **171**, 1262 (1971).

Welford, C. 'Labelling theory and criminology: an assessment', *Special Problems*, **22**, 332 (1975).

Werner, J. S., Minkin, N., Minkin, Bonnie, L., Fixsen, D. C., Phillips, E. L., and Wolf, M. M. '"Intervention Package": an analysis to prepare juvenile delinquents for encounters with police officers', *Criminal Justice and Behaviour*, **2**, 22 (1975).

West, D. J. *The Habitual Prisoner*, London, Macmillan, 1963.

West, D. J. *Murder followed by Suicide*, London, Heinemann, 1966.

West, D. J. *The Young Offender*, London, Pelican, 1967.

West, D. J. *Present Conduct and Future Delinquency*, London, Heinemann, 1969.

Wexler, D. B. 'Token and taboo: behaviour modification, token economies and the law', *California Law Review*, **61**, 81 (1973).

Wheeler, S. 'Socialization in correctional communities', *American Sociological Review*, **26**, 697 (1961).

Wheeler, S. 'Sex offences: A sociological critique', In J. H. Gagnon and W. Simon (Eds.), *Sexual Deviance*, New York, Harper and Row, 1967, pp. 79–104.

White, G. M. 'Immediate and deferred effects of model observations and guided and unguided rehearsal on donating and stealing', *Journal of Personality and Social Psychology*, **21**, 139 (1972).

Wilkins, L. T. 'A small comparative study of the results of probation', *British Journal of Delinquency*, **8**, 201 (1958).

Willett, T. C. *Criminal on the Road*, London, Tavistock, 1964.

Williams, G. 'The definition of crime', In J. Smith and B. Hogan (Eds.), *Criminal Law*, 2nd edn., London, 1955, pp. 17–23.

Wilson, J. Q. 'If every criminal knew he would be punished if caught', *New York Times Magazine*, January 28th, **9**, 44, 52 (1973).

Winkler, R. C. 'The relevance of economic theory and technology to token reinforcement systems', *Behaviour, Research and Therapy*, **9**, 81 (1971).

Winnick, C. 'The psychology of juries', In H. Toch (Ed.), *Legal and Criminal Psychology*, New York, Holt, Rhinehart & Winston, 1961, pp. 96–120.

Winter, K., Broadhurst, Anne, and Glass, A. 'Neuroticism, extraversion and EEG amplitude', *Journal of Experimental Research in Personality*, **6**, 44 (1972).

Woalinder, J. 'Transvestism, definition and evidence in favour of occasional deviation from cerebral dysfunction', *International Journal of Neuropsychiatry*, **1**, 565 (1965).

Wolfenden (Committee). 'Our approach to the problem', *Report of the Committee on Homosexual Offenders and Prostitution*, London, HMSO, Cmnd, Cmnd. 246, 1957.

Wolfgang, M. E. *Patterns in Criminal Homicide*, Philadelphia, University of Philadelphia Press, 1958.

Wolfgang, M. E. 'Why criminal statistics?', In L. Radzinowicz and M. E. Wolfgang (Eds.), *Crime and Justice: Vol. 1. The Criminal in Society*, New York, Basic Books, pp. 130–131, 1971.

Wolfgang, M. E., Figlio, R. M., and Sellin, T. *Delinquency in a Birth Cohort*, Chicago, University of Chicago Press, 1972.

Woodside, Moya, 'Probation and psychiatric treatment in Edinburgh', *British Journal of Psychiatry*, **118**, 561 (1971).

Woodward, Mary. *Low Intelligence and Delinquency*, Institute for the Study and Treatment of Delinquency, 1955. Revised edition, 1963.

Woodward, Mary. The diagnosis and treatment of homosexual offenders', *British Journal of Delinquency*, **9**, 44 (1958).

Wootton, Barbara. *Social Science and Social Pathology*, London, Allen and Unwin, 1959.

Wootton, Barbara. 'The law, the deviant, and the doctor', *British Medical Journal*, **1**, 197 (1963).

Wright, D., and Cox, E. 'A study of the relationship between moral judgement and religious belief in a sample of English adolescents', *Journal of Social Psychology*, **72**, 135 (1967).

Wright, D., and Cox, E. 'Changes in moral belief among sixth-form boys and girls over a seven-year period in relation to religious belief, age and sex difference', *British Journal of Social and Clinical Psychology*, **10**, 332 (1971).

Wyatt v. Stickney, **34**, 4 F. Supp. 373 (M.D. Ala. 1972) (Bryce and Searcy Hospitals).

Yates, A. J. 'Abnormalities of psychomotor functions', In H. J. Eysenck (Ed.), *Handbook of Abnormal Psychology*, 2nd edn., London, Pitman Medical, 1973, pp. 261–83.

Zajonc, R. B. 'Attitudinal effects of mere exposure', *Journal of Personality and Social Psychology, Monograph Supplement*, **9**, Part 2, 1 (1968).

Zillman, D. 'Excitation transfer in communication-mediated aggressive behaviour', *Journal of Experimental Social Psychology*, **7**, 419 (1971).

Zimbardo, P. G. (Ed.) *The Cognitive Control of Motivation*, Glenview, Illinois, Scott Foreman, 1969.

Zuckerman, M., Kolin, E. A., Price, L., and Zoob, I. 'Development of a sensation-seeking scale', *Journal of Consulting Psychology*, **28**, 477 (1964).

Zuckerman, M., Persky, H., Link, K. E., and Basu, G. K. 'Experimental and subject factors determining responses to sensory deprivation, social isolation and confinement', *Journal of Abnormal Psychology*, **73**, 183 (1968).

Author Index

322

Subject Index